LEEDS UNITED:

A Wonderful Mishmash!

The Story Of Leeds United's 2020/2021 Season

Leeds United Mishmash

The History of Leeds United Football Club in one Image'.

My thanks to Alex Bennett and his fabulous website www.roundheadillustration.com for allowing me to use part of his wonderful Leeds United Mishmash art for the front cover of the book. Copies of the Leeds United Mishmash poster and all of his other team mishmash posters can be viewed and bought on the link above.

By the same author:

All books available from Amazon.co.uk

LEEDS UNITED, IN PURSUIT OF THE PREMIERSHIP
The 2010/2011 season
LEEDS UNITED, LIGHT AT THE END OF THE TUNNEL
The 2011/2012 season
LEEDS UNITED, Déjà vu
The 2012/2013 season
LEEDS UNITED,FIASCO
The 2013/2014 season
LEEDS UNITED, *The Kids Are Alright!*
The 2014/2015 season
LEEDSUNITED,MISSION:IMPOSSIBLE
The 2015/2016 season
LEEDS UNITED, When the Stars Almost Aligned
The 2016/2017 season
LEEDS UNITED, Give us Strength!
The 2017/2018 season
LEEDS UNITED, *Bins, A Bucket, But No Cigar*
The 2018/2019 season
LEEDS UNITED: Covid Interruptus!
The 2019/2020 season

Click link to view books on Amazon: Amazon.co.uk

For all those we have lost

#FreeBenWhite

There was no three-month break this year between the new and the old seasons; Covid-19 had messed up all the usual scheduling. The 2019/2020 Championship season ended for Leeds with that victory over Charlton on 22nd July but the play-off final between Brentford and Fulham wasn't until 4th August and yet the new English Premier League (EPL) season would kick-off on 12th September. Hence it was a hectic few weeks for the club to prepare itself, while Covid ensured that we supporters generally still had plenty of time on our hands.

Some Leeds players jetted off to Spain for a well-earned holiday in the sun as soon as the formalities of the Player of the Year Awards were complete, only for the government to re-impose a 14-day quarantine requirement for holidaymakers returning from various countries, including Spain and its islands, due to another surge in Covid cases throughout Europe. The club quickly sent out messages to the players to return home for fear they could otherwise miss the start of pre-season training.

The EPL composition for 2020/21 was complete when Fulham won that play-off final against the Bees 2 – 1 and hence the Cottagers joined Leeds and West Brom going up from the Championship while Norwich, Bournemouth, and Watford went out of the EPL. Aston Villa had been saved from the drop by that infamous failure of Hawk-Eye to spot that Villa keeper Orjan Nyland carried the ball over his own goal line in their game against Sheffield United. Had that 'goal' stood, the Villa and not Bournemouth would have gone down. Covid-19 was still accounting for the deaths of up to 100 people every day, and any return to normal life was only occurring in very tiny steps. Most shops and businesses were open again but the wearing of face masks was now mandatory in most indoor settings. The first pilot for the return of crowds to sporting events in England took place with a cricket friendly at The Oval, between Surrey and Middlesex, where 1,000 spectators were allowed in under social distancing rules. Proposed additional test events, including more cricket at Edgbaston, were then canned as Covid-19 cases began to rise again in the UK. There was talk that football might not see a return to full stadiums at all during the forthcoming season. Once again the gods had conspired to hit Leeds fans the hardest as we contemplated not seeing EPL football in the flesh for months to come having already waited 16 years for the opportunity.

The first big question to be answered for Leeds fans this summer was the same one asked ahead of the previous season; would Marcelo Bielsa accept the offer of another contract extension? The Argentine master had never stopped anywhere more than two seasons in his entire managerial career but no one believed he would be able to walk away from an opportunity to pit his wits in the greatest league in the world. The word was that he'd put forward several conditions to be met before he would commit to signing up for another year. It was believed a strengthening of the squad was a prime condition and it was rumoured Bielsa had specified five positions where he wanted to improve his options as well as wanting confirmation that none of his preferred existing players would be sold.

Money ought not to be a significant problem for Leeds any longer, as we'd now finally got our noses into the very deep and well-filled EPL trough. Andrea Radrizzani had come out shortly after our promotion was confirmed to tell reporters he now believed the club's value had trebled to around £300m compared to the £100m he'd invested so far. He believed that turnover should be comfortably between £180m and £200m for our first year back in the big league (it was £49m as reported in the accounts to the end of June 2019 and £54m for the year to July 2020) and he was saying he was determined to enjoy the ride for a few years more and had no intention yet of selling up and taking his profit. Indeed he stated his long-term aim was to run a group with two or three football clubs around Europe. He committed to continuing to build the club with investment on and off the pitch, telling the Italian paper Corriere della Sera: *"Leeds is a lively, electric, passionate city. The brand is famous worldwide... Potentially the value can reach one billion. But first we have to stay in the EPL for at least three years, then we can also fly to Europe, the goal is obviously to go to the Champions League. Dreaming big is a duty for those who do business."*

The first signing of the summer saw Leeds take up the option we had on Illan Meslier: he was signed on a three-year deal for a rumoured £5m from FC Lorient from whom the young keeper had been loaned last season.

It was awards time of course and, at the Player of the Year evening, Pablo Hernandez unsurprisingly won the main prize. The Players' Player of the Year choice was Stuart Dallas while the Young Player of the Year award went to Ben White who most Leeds fans were desperate to see signed on a permanent deal. It appeared that Brighton were playing hardball on that one though and an initial bid of £22m had apparently already been turned down. Immediately Twitter was awash with *"#FreeBenWhite"* tweets containing pictures of everything from sky banners to messages written in the sand on the beach. The awards evening was another behind closed doors event with only the players and staff present but it was screened live on LUTV to at least ensure some of the fans got to see it. The show, compèred by Emma Jones and Jermaine Beckford, was completed with a set by the Kaiser Chiefs who opened, appropriately enough, with their rendition of *"We Are The Champions!"*

The final knockings of the 2019/2020 season were played out behind closed doors too, including the FA Cup final in an empty Wembley Stadium; Arsenal beat *Fat Frank's Chelsea*, 2 – 1, with more dire refereeing from Anthony Taylor and with VAR refusing to overturn his questionable decisions. Chelsea also got hammered in the Champions League, going out 7 – 1 on aggregate to Bayern Munich in the round of 16. Back at Wembley, we saw Wycombe Wanderers win the League One play-off final to join Coventry and Rotherham in the Championship next season, while Northampton

Town, who only finished 7th in League Two, won through the play-offs beating Cheltenham Town who finished 4th. In the non-league play-off final it was Harrogate Town who won through, beating Notts County 3 – 1 to join automatically promoted Barrow in the Football League. At least Harrogate's CNG Stadium was a ground I'd already been to a couple of times, with Leeds in a pre-season game and with Worcester City in the National League, so I didn't need to put it on my '92' to-do list. I *did* need to add Barrow though, and the new Brentford ground they'd be using this coming season. I still hadn't done the new Spurs ground either but, hopefully, and Covid permitting, I'd get there to watch Leeds in the coming months. A new Wimbledon ground was also not far from completion and would go on my list as and when.

The new Scottish season was soon underway with the Premiership teams playing their opening fixtures of the 2020/21 campaign on 1st August. It was as predictable as ever though as Celtic won their opening game against Hamilton Academical 5 – 1 to go straight to the top of the first table as they looked to win a tenth title on the trot, although Rangers would have something to say about that in due course. Another Hamilton was more successful this weekend; Lewis won the British Grand Prix on three wheels, so far ahead was he when he picked up a puncture on the last lap. Formula One continued to vie with the Scottish Premiership for the title of *'Most Predictable Sport in the World'*. We did at least now have one reason to keep an eye on the Premiership though; Leeds sent young striker Ryan Edmondson out on loan to Aberdeen. Ryan was a 65th-minute substitute for the Dons in their opening game, a 0-1 defeat to Rangers, but then had to wait as the next Dons game was postponed; eight players broke lockdown rules to go drinking in the centre of Aberdeen and two went down with Covid. Within days it was then announced that Ryan Edmondson was back at Leeds; he'd injured an ankle and was out for a few weeks.

I was still finding it difficult to shift my focus from the Championship to the EPL; until the new fixtures came out I really had nothing to plan for so, inevitably, I drifted back to the Championship where there was still plenty happening. There was uproar for example when the EFL announced they'd finally concluded their deliberations over the alleged financial irregularities in the books of Sheffield Wednesday. The Owls were handed a penalty of 12 points but it was not to be effective until the 20/21 season, thus saving them from certain relegation this summer. Apparently, they were saved from a heavier points deduction because the action of including in their 17/18 accounts the sale of their ground which took place in June 2019 was not considered *"dishonest"*. Well, I was hard-pressed to think of another term to describe it and that was without even considering how the hell Hillsborough could possibly be given a value of £60m. Crikey, West Ham's London Stadium was only valued at £40m! Charlton Athletic were pretty naffed-off too; they couldn't understand why the penalty was not applied to the season just ended. If it had, then Wednesday and not Lee Bowyer's Charlton would have gone down. Incredibly, the 12-point penalty was then halved prior to the start of the new season.

We assumed Marcelo was going to sign on the dotted line imminently when we saw via Phil Hay's Twitter account that Leeds were *"having very positive talks with Marcelo daily."* I assumed that meant the club were putting into place everything Marcelo was requesting. Meanwhile, other signatures *were* finding their way onto contracts as Leeds sent out young striker Kun Temenuzhkov to Spanish Segunda Division B side Real Union for a season-long loan. That was two young strikers already shipped out, suggesting Marcelo wanted experience not youth up front if Patrick Bamford was to be challenged.

Presumably, it was down to Victor Orta to continue the dialogue with Marcelo as Radrizzani was said to be talking with the San Francisco 49ers about increasing their investment in Leeds. The New York Times reported that the 49ers were enjoying the ride with Leeds, especially since promotion had probably tripled the £10 million investment they'd already made. Regarding further investment, Paraag Marathe, the 49ers' representative on the Leeds board, told the American paper: *"It's something that we are absolutely hoping to do."*[1] American team owners already had a presence in several EPL boardrooms including: Man United where the Glazer family had been involved since 2005; Arsenal where LA

---

[1]   https://www.nytimes.com/2020/07/31/sports/soccer/leeds-united-san-francisco-49ers.html

Rams owner E. Stanley Kroenke held sway; and Fulham, with Shahid Khan who also owned the Jacksonville Jaguars. In fact, if rumours were to be believed, Sig. Radrizzani was a busy man at the moment as he was then said to be part of a group of Italian businessmen trying to buy Italian Serie A club Genoa C.F.C. which had been up for sale for many years. 'Genoa Cricket and Football Club', to give it its full name, is the fourth oldest club in Italy, with a history stretching back 125 years. This news of course tied in with Radrizzani's comments about wishing to own two or three separate clubs.

Internally the club continued with its contract negotiations and soon the deals to sign Helder Costa permanently and Jack Harrison on another season-long loan were completed. Harrison was pictured, pen in hand, wearing a natty new dark blue Leeds training top with Adidas branding and the Clipper Logistics and SBOTOP logos. Big Leeds fan Steve Parkin's Clipper organisation had been announced as the new training kit sponsor while SBOTOP, a new betting brand, was to be the club's principal sponsor whose logo would appear on the new Adidas first-team shirt that everyone was eager to see. The five-year deal with SBOTOP, part of the e-gaming group Celton Manx based in the Isle of Man, was said to be the largest commercial deal in the history of the club and was the result of many months of discussion between the two parties. Celton Manx had history in the EPL with West Ham in the recent past.[1]

The wait went on to hear if Marcelo had yet signed but there were regular sightings of him in the Wetherby area suggesting he hadn't gone very far. The campaign to set Ben White free was also still in full swing as Leeds fans voted in their thousands to ensure he won the Championship Goal of the Month Award for July. His volley in the 14th minute against Charlton secured a massive 81% of the public vote.

The 4th signing of the summer came on August 10th; Joe Gelhardt, an 18-year-old striker from Wigan Athletic, signed on a four-year deal. Gelhardt made 17 appearances for the Latics last season including two first-team starts and scored his debut senior goal last

---

[1] https://www.manxradio.com/news/isle-of-man-news/celton-manx-sbotop-to-sponsor-leeds-united/

September against Hull. It looked like one for the future, not the EPL... And another followed quickly as 16-year-old Charlie Allen, an attacking midfielder, was signed on a three-year deal from Northern Ireland side Linfield. The Leeds connection there was current Linfield manager, former Leeds striker David Healy. Then we landed 18-year-old full-back Cody Drameh from Fulham. It was hard to resist the temptation to see all this as long-term planning. Either that, or we were going to have a real tilt at winning promotion from Premier League 2 Div. 2 with our Under-23s or even the EFL Trophy now that our newly awarded 'Category One' status for the academy meant we were eligible to field an Under-21 side in that competition. Jamie Shackleton was another youngster secured as he landed a new four-year deal. The 20-year-old had already been with Leeds for 13 years and had 48 senior appearances and two league goals to his name. Mateusz Bogusz was also handed a new contract, keeping him at Elland Road until the summer of 2023. It was a surprise to me to read that Bogusz was still only 18, having been really impressed with his performances in Oz on that pre-season tour more than a year earlier.

The two signings we were desperate to hear about were Marcelo Bielsa and Ben White but, as mid-August arrived, neither was yet done. In fact, the BBC was reporting that Brighton had decided White was not for sale, even at the rumoured £30m Leeds were prepared to pay. It would be a blow if we didn't get White but I felt £30 million was way too much anyway for a 22-year-old with no EPL experience... Still, the campaign went on to *#FreeBenWhite* and a banner even appeared hanging from a bridge across the M1!

The final rounds of the Champions League were shoe-horned into a rapid-fire 11 days from 12th August to the 23rd with the quarter and semi-finals now being one-leg affairs. Whether it was that change or just coincidence, the competition suddenly came alive. In the first quarter-final, RB Leipzig scored an 88th-minute winner to defeat Atlético Madrid 2 – 1. The following night Paris Saint-Germain scored two goals in added time to beat Atalanta 2 – 1 and then, on a steamy Friday night in the middle of a thundery heatwave, we watched our TVs in amazement as Bayern Munich annihilated Barcelona 8 – 2. In the last of the quarter-finals, Lyon beat Manchester City 3 – 1. PSG and Bayern would go on to meet in the final having beaten RB Leipzig and Lyon respectively.

Certainly not half-Koch!

The draw for the initial group stages of the EFL Trophy pitched the Leeds United U21s into a group with Accrington Stanley, Blackpool, and Barrow, with all three games to be played away from Elland Road. My eyes lit up when I saw the name Barrow and I immediately wondered if there would be any chance of attending the game and getting their stadium ticked off my '92 to do' list. The FA had at least now announced that non-league games below National League level need no longer be played behind closed doors if sufficient Covid safety precautions were in place. Having heard that news only this week, I was also hoping to get to see my other team Worcester City in the near future but they were said to be struggling to work out how to make their new ground Covid safe.

Leeds continued merrily signing up youngsters; the latest being 17-year-old Dani van den Heuvel, a goalkeeper brought in from Eredivisie side Ajax; I guess we could expect some *clean* handling from him…

The votes of Leeds United fans ensured Luke Ayling won the PFA Championship Player of the Season Award this week, beating off competition from the likes of Eberechi Eze, Matheus Pereira, Aleksandar Mitrovic, and Brentford duo Ollie Watkins and Said Benrahma. As the only defender on the list, it was extra satisfying to see our 'Bill' take the award.

Thursday 20th August was the day we were all waiting for; no, not Marcelo or Ben signing, but the day the EPL fixtures were released. Our first game was a mouth-watering prospect at Anfield; The Champions of the EPL against the Champions of the Championship! A fabulous way to start our next journey but just tinged with the sadness of knowing we'd not actually be there to see it live. There was still hope that by October *some* fans would be allowed inside EPL grounds but, thus far, that was only a vague plan being worked on by the authorities. The new kit we'd be wearing at Anfield went on sale this same day and CEO Angus Kinnear told reporters that the club had sold more of the new white home shirts in the first hour on sale this year than we did in the whole of the first day last season; suffice to say Twitter was full of fans complaining the Leeds website had collapsed under the pressure! The kit itself was generally a hit with the fans; an all-white shirt with three royal blue Adidas stripes on each shoulder, the Adidas logo and the slightly remodelled Leeds badge on the front alongside the SBOTOP branding. Over 300,000 of these shirts would be sold in the first month of being on sale; a new club record.

The news regarding Ben White was not quite so positive; another bid had supposedly been rejected and this time it seemed to be the £30m that had been muted for a while. Angus Kinnear was fairly sanguine about it though as he told the press: *"If we don't get Ben White we have other targets that are at an advanced stage"*. He was a bit more evasive about getting the Bielsa signature though, saying only that it was proving difficult to get the great man to find a slot in his work schedule to sit down and put pen to paper... I know he's a complex character but that just sounded unprofessional.

Hardly a day went by this summer without Leeds being linked with a new potential signing. This week the name of Ryan Kent cropped up again, just as it did in the close season in 2019. Kent was now a £10 million-rated winger with Rangers and Steven Gerrard was still saying he was not for sale. He tweeted *"We want the player to stay here as do the board"*.[1] As that one seemed to cool another one immediately began to heat up: we were said to be interested in Rodrigo Moreno from Valencia. He was another in a similar midfielder-come-striker mould. Meanwhile, a former Leeds player of that ilk got his goal scoring with Rangers off to a good start as Kemar Roofe notched one on his first full start for the Gers. It's a moment that will crop up for years to come in a *"What was strange about Roofe's first goal for Rangers?"* way. The name on the back of his shirt read: 'ROFFE'. No doubt someone at the club was picking up his or her P45 come Monday morning!

Someone still in a job, for the next four years at least, was young Alfie McCalmont who was given a new four-year deal at Leeds as the focus on the youngsters continued while we still awaited any

---

[1] *https://onefootball.com/en/news/steven-gerrard-says-rangers-star-ryan-kent-wont-be-sold-to-leeds-30781180*

additions to the 1st XI over what we worked with last season. Meslier, Costa and Harrison were sorted of course but if Ben White was a non-starter then we looked a bit light at centre-back and I was desperate to see us invest in a quality goal-scorer; someone to put some pressure on Paddy Bamford who was, at best, unproven at EPL level.

There were now just three weeks to go before that Anfield return but, while there was clearly concern among the ranks of the fan base, the club officials didn't appear to be too worried about the lack of transfer activity, as witness Kinnear's comment about alternatives to Ben White being *"...at an advanced stage."* In fact, Kinnear was as interested in discussing off-field matters as he was player targets when he was interviewed for 'The Square Ball' podcast. *"Redeveloping the West Stand can take the capacity up to 50,000"* he told them and, to highlight why it was needed he reported that some 20,000 fans had recently taken up the offer of a place on the season-ticket waiting list, an option that cost each of them £10! Not that there was any short-term prospect of them *getting* a season-ticket; the expansion of Elland Road was said to be an 'aspiration' that would not become a commitment until Leeds' EPL status had been cemented for at least three years.

The final act of the elongated 2019/2020 football season was the Champions League Final, held in Lisbon on Sunday 23rd August. Bayern Munich came out on top, beating PSG 1 – 0 in a tight-fought game. It was the first time any side had won the Champions League by winning every game played in the competition and it was Bayern's 21st consecutive victory in all competitions. They'd scored an incredible 159 goals in 52 games, losing only five; the best team in Germany was rightly crowned the best team in Europe.

Leeds' return to the EPL was probably one reason for the inclusion of Kalvin Phillips in the latest England squad as Gareth Southgate prepared for Nations League games against Iceland and Denmark. Phillips' teammates Liam Cooper (Scotland), Stuart Dallas (NI), Tyler Roberts (Wales), Ezgjan Alioski (North Macedonia) and Matty Klich (Poland) also got the call, although Tyler Roberts was then withdrawn with an apparent injury and returned to Leeds. It was yet one more injury in a whole string of them since joining Leeds and there was even talk he might be leaving the club, so little had he played; 54 appearances and seven goals in two seasons and most from the bench.

One man not going to feature for England was Manchester United's Harry Maguire who was removed from the squad after being caught up in a holiday fracas in Mykonos. He was found guilty of aggravated assault, resisting arrest and attempted bribery and was sentenced to 21 months and ten days, suspended due to his previous good record. He returned to England and stated he would be appealing all the charges. Maguire, his brother and a friend were forced to endure two nights in police cells following a brawl, which is said to have erupted after rival fans publicly taunted the footballer on a day of heavy drinking in a beach bar on the famous party island and after Maguire's sister, Daisy, was allegedly targeted. Maguire reportedly ran up a £63,000 bar bill!

Back on planet Leeds and young forward Rafa Mujica was sent out on loan to Spanish Segunda Division side Real Oviedo having also been on loan in Spain the previous season at both Extremadura UD and Villarreal. He was probably passed on the other side of the revolving door by Sam Greenwood, a young Arsenal striker who Leeds snapped up on a three-year contract much to the annoyance of many Arsenal fans. Greenwood played in the Arsenal U23 EPL 2 (Div. 1) side last season. Then finally, on Saturday 29th August, Leeds announced the two big signings that had been rumoured for several days. Rodrigo Moreno Machado, a 29-year-old Spanish international striker, was signed from Valencia for what was said to be a new Leeds United record fee of around £27m. Signed on a four-year deal, Rodrigo was no stranger to the EPL having played for Bolton Wanderers back in 2010/2011 making 17 (that number will not go away) appearances for the Trotters. He would be well known to Kiko Casilla as a teammate in the Spanish squad and also Helder Costa who would have been with him during his time at Benfica. That was the striker we all wanted and soon the centre-back we needed was announced as well. Robin Koch, a 24-year-old German international, was signed from SC Freiburg in the Bundesliga on another four-year deal. With Brighton announcing that they had no intention of selling Ben White any time soon to any of their EPL rivals, this centre-back signing seemed pretty much, err, Koch-on.

I have to admit, every time I hear the name 'Koch' I can't help but think about the naughty old Anglo-Saxon riddle my Dad used to retell: *"I grow very erect, tall in a bed, and bring tears to a maiden's eye. What am I?"* Answer at the end of the chapter! There were some concerns over the injury record of Rodrigo but Koch joined us on the back of 87 games in three seasons, scoring five goals and winning his first two senior caps for Germany last autumn.

For me, those two huge signings were the ones to put my mind at rest that we were now well-placed to give the EPL a real go; the squad still wasn't huge but that was the way Bielsa liked to operate. There were however strong rumours doing the rounds that Leeds had not finished their transfer business yet. There was talk of another bid going in for Ryan Kent, despite Rangers' statements that he was going nowhere, while another 'Rodrigo' was also said to be on our radar. This one was Rodrigo de Paul, a midfielder currently on the books of Udinese Calcio, the Italian Serie A outfit. There was also a suggestion that Bielsa had now been persuaded that another dedicated centre-back would be a good idea rather than relying on moving the likes of Luke Ayling and Leif Davis if need be. The man thought to be lined up was Josko Gvardiol, an 18-year-old Croatian defender who last season broke into the GNK Dinamo Zagreb side. Quite where the money would come from if they all joined us, I had no idea, but no one could say we were going into this new EPL era half-Koch...

Answer to the riddle: I'm an Onion!

Pre-Season

L eeds were not making much noise about pre-season, no noise at all in fact, with no schedule of pre-season games and no mention on the website of the first friendly which was played at the Bet365 Stadium on 1st September; we'd get to see if our lads could do it on a warm Tuesday night in Stoke!

It was a confusing time for all the major teams as they tried to get back up to speed after the shortest of short close seasons and with many of their players away with the international sides preparing for the first round of Nations League games next week; just a few days before the opening games of the new English season. Leeds were struggling as much as most, with numerous players missing, so it was a pretty makeshift side that was named by the Leeds United official Twitter account for the trip to the Potteries:

Casilla
Davis Ayling (Capt) Casey Douglas
Struijk
Costa Shackleton Hernandez Harrison
Bamford

Subs: Caprile, Poveda, Roberts, Gotts.

The defence looked nothing like I expected to see turn out at Anfield in ten days' time so I wasn't expecting us to be watertight... but it was still something of a surprise as the Stoke goals steadily filtered through on Twitter during the afternoon. One other surprise, adding to my already confused state of mind, was the inclusion on the bench of Tyler Roberts, just days after he was withdrawn from the Welsh Nations League squad when he was said to be injured. Maybe it was more a lack of fitness than any specific injury but I made a mental note to 'watch this space'.

Stoke had pretty much a full-strength side, including the likes of Jack Butland, Tom Ince, Ryan Shawcross, Nathan Collins, and Lee Gregory and they were just too strong for us. Watching the highlights on a Stoke City YouTube video later that night was a bit like watching that Carabao Cup game at Elland Road last season when a similarly under-strength Leeds defence was found out by Stoke in the first half before we brought on three subs and made a game of it after that. The frailties shown by Leeds this time around were very familiar; the first came from a corner-kick but it was a tad unfortunate. Luke Ayling threw himself into the path of a rocket from Tom Ince that was thus deflected away for a corner but Ayling was still getting treatment on the touchline when Stoke touched the corner short. They then lofted a high ball over to the back post, just as Ayling got the referee's permission to race back on. Kiko Casilla then did what we've seen Kiko do on far too many occasions as he leapt and flapped at the ball, swiping it back into the danger zone near the penalty spot. Liam Lindsay had already replaced an injured Ryan Shawcross for the Potters and now Lindsay swung a boot at the loose ball striking it against the leg of Ayling who'd got back into the middle. The ball rebounded perfectly to the left boot of Nathan Collins and he walloped it past Casilla. I shrugged and took another sip of malt; it was late, we had friends staying and everyone else had gone to bed leaving me to the laptop and the whisky. The goal came in the 24th minute of the game and the Stoke celebrations sounded as hollow as ever as they echoed around the empty stadium.

Stoke were playing in their new all-black away strip, with Leeds in their new white home ensemble but it was mainly the black shirts marching forward in the first half; a half of just 40 minutes for some reason as would be the second period. The second half began with another reminder of one of the few irritating features of our otherwise sensational and successful 19/20 season; in the very first minute of the new half we saw that Patrick Bamford was still not exactly Harry Hotshot!

Douglas and Harrison combined well on the left wing with Harrison eventually outwitting Nathan Collins to get the ball back to Douglas and he, much as Stoke did for their goal, launched the ball first time towards the back post. Lindsay rose to head it away but only found substitute Robbie Gotts, 15 yards out and wide of the right post. Gotts took one touch and then tried a shot on the half volley that squirted off to the left but perfectly to Patrick Bamford, in space between two defenders and no more than seven yards out with only the keeper, Jack Butland between him and glory. I've watched this bit of video at least a dozen times and I still don't know what Bamford was trying to do. It looked like he was maybe trying to cushion the ball on his right thigh but instead he only managed to knee it a couple of feet wide of the right-hand post.

Minutes later and it was 2 – 0 and this particular game was just about done; it was a Stoke goal but it could easily have come from the Bielsaball training manual. Stoke moved the ball steadily down their right wing with that man Nathan Collins again before Robbie Gotts intercepted outside the Leeds box. The ball broke to Lee Gregory who immediately found Tom Ince on the left, with Jamie Shackleton giving him far too much space. Ince was able to look up, pick his spot and send in a perfect left foot cross that just beat the jump of Luke Ayling but neatly found the head of Lee Gregory behind him. Gregory's header was straight out of the textbook; hard down into the turf and then up into the 'postage stamp' in the top right corner.

Stoke added a third just after the hour mark when Tom Ince easily rounded Shackleton in the Leeds area before firing past Casilla and that was after Liam Lindsay really ought to have buried a header direct from a right wing corner; he put that one wide when it looked easier to score. 3 – 0 to Stoke and the impression I got from the highlights was that Leeds were lucky to get nil! It was a lethargic looking, strangely subdued performance from Leeds but it was only half the side I expected to see come out at Liverpool and it was, as far as we knew, only the first full game we'd played since beating Charlton five weeks earlier. Nothing to worry us, but nothing to get excited about either.

Stoke City 3 **Leeds United 0** (Collins 24, Gregory 52, Ince 62)

The Nations League international games began on Thursday, 3rd September and the main interest for Leeds fans was the Group 'A4' game between Germany and Spain that, on paper, (don't forget to look out for the odd pun!) was a real clash of the Titans. In the starting XI for Spain was new Leeds striker Rodrigo Moreno while on the bench for Germany was 'Koch Robin' as he'd already been dubbed by various Leeds Twitter wags. Rodrigo's first major contribution to the game was an early chance when a German tanked a back-pass that went horribly wrong, putting in Rodrigo outside the box with the German keeper, Kevin Trapp unable to live up to his name. Sadly, our new man dillied and dallied and the chance was gone. In fact, on commentary we were then informed that our £27 million signing was not actually a prolific scorer of goals at all and that his main forte was in providing assists for others. Apparently, in the season just ended, only Messi and Suarez had contributed more assists in Spanish league football. That was disappointing for me; I still felt what we really needed was a goal poacher. Under Bielsa, creating chances had never really been a problem... scoring them sometimes had!

The Germans took a 51st-minute lead but it wasn't until the second minute of added time at the end of the game that we saw £13 million Robin Koch come on as a late substitute, presumably to bolster the German defences and see the game out. I cringed as I noticed Koch was wearing '17', with all the connotations that number has had for Leeds since Massimo Cellino first pointed out its association with bad luck several years ago. There was a certain irony that, with almost the last act of the game, Rodrigo rose to head the ball down to Jose Gaya who smacked the equaliser into the net; another assist for Rodrigo. And who was launching himself at Rodrigo to try to prevent him getting to the ball? You guessed it, Koch Robin himself; *All the birds of the air fell a-sighing and a-sobbing, when they heard the bell toll for poor Cock Robin.*

Leeds had so many players away on international duty that it was no surprise to see another make-shift side line up for the second and final pre-season game, played at Thorp Arch on the Saturday just ahead of England's first Nations League game, in Iceland. Hence, with the Leeds game available on the Leeds TV channel LUTV and the England game following on Sky, it was a day in front of the TV for me. Little did I know then how this was to become the norm for so many weekends to come.

Leeds were missing Rodrigo and Koch but also Meslier (French U21s), Kalvin Phillips (called up by England), Klich (Poland), Alioski (North Macedonia), Stuart Dallas (NI) and Liam Cooper (Scotland) who might all be reasonably expected to feature in the squad for the opening EPL game at Anfield in a week's time. Hence I had no great expectations that Leeds would pip (I hope you are all up to speed with your Dickens' novels...) a half-decent Portuguese Primeira Liga side, F.C. Paços de Ferreira, but it would be good to watch a full Leeds game again for the first time since that Charlton celebration fest back in July.

Casilla
Ayling (Capt) Davis Casey Douglas

Struijk
Hernandez (Gotts 73) Shackleton Roberts Harrison
(Poveda 70)
Bamford (Cresswell 88)

Subs: Caprile, Poveda, Costa, Gotts, Jenkins, Cresswell.

Hence it was pretty much the team we saw Leeds put out at Stoke but with Tyler Roberts starting in place of Helder Costa and with Luke Ayling in his more familiar right-back berth, which made more sense as that's where he'd mostly play in the regular side this season, or so you would think. We could see two players who'd obviously caught Bielsa's eye in pre-season as they were promoted to the 1st XI bench; 18-year-old defender Charlie Cresswell and midfielder Jack Jenkins.

Leeds opened the game brightly and most of the early chances came our way. Patrick Bamford had a good long-range effort saved and then Ollie Casey put a header from a Douglas corner just wide. Tyler Roberts hit a decent shot from the edge of the area too but again that was well saved by the busier of the two keepers. It was an interesting watch but all the time I was thinking how irrelevant it was watching only half of what I expected the side to be that would run out at Anfield. Yes, it was good to see the form of the few players we *would* see in Liverpool, Luke Ayling for example was prominent and looked just as good as he had at the back end of last season, while Harrison and Bamford looked sharp and purposeful too. Pablo Hernandez was very quiet I thought and we saw little of his magic which perhaps he was saving for the bigger stages to come. Other than that though it was merely encouraging to see that we had some decent youngsters coming through the ranks. Pascal Struijk looked an excellent prospect and he was clearly carrying on from his superb exploits at the end of the Championship campaign. For me, he was an obvious understudy for Kalvin Phillips in that defensive midfield role and, whisper it quietly, I reckoned he'd eventually be a better player even than Kalvin and definitely more positive in his play. Leif Davis and Jamie Shackleton were also impressive.

It was still a long way from an EPL atmosphere of course. The TV backdrop of a row of smart brick-built houses with bedrooms overlooking the pitch and a few individuals leaning on the perimeter fence gave it a Sunday league feeling, but the one thing that would be similar in these Covid-dictated times was the eerie echo of a few shouted instructions against the background of an otherwise silent football ground. Football fans everywhere were now resigned to not seeing a live professional game until at least the beginning of October. I was still pretty disappointed mind when on 36 minutes Leeds conceded another poor goal, just as we did at Stoke only days earlier.

The Portuguese side easily intercepted a Leeds throw-in with a well-timed header near the halfway line and then moved the ball through the centre with Joao Amaral going through unchallenged and then taking Leif Davis out of the game with a quick one-two. The number '77' was then one-on-one with Kiko Casilla at his near post. No one was marking Lucas Silva at the back post and he stabbed the ball home as it came through Kiko's bandy legs and across the face of goal. It was a piece of dire defending but I was confident an almost totally different defence would be in place come the following Saturday, with probably only Luke Ayling surviving.

Leeds hit right-back with an equaliser straight from the restart as Tyler Roberts was brought down on the right corner of the Pacos box. Douglas whipped a lovely ball into the near post and Pascal Struijk nipped in to beat the Pacos keeper to head home. In the second half it was all Leeds and after one sighter that Pablo Hernandez launched into the farmer's field behind the goal, in the 54th minute he then latched on to a low cross from Bamford on the right to smash a terrific right foot shot into the top right corner. He'd been quiet all game, but the magic was still there. Leeds wrapped up the game in the 77th minute with another Bamford assist – it was almost as if Paddy was aware of the reputation of Rodrigo – this time flicking the ball over the defence into the path of Helder Costa in the inside left slot and Costa buried an accurate left-footer inside the far post. It was a good run-out for the players available, but how useful it was in giving any clue to the names on that next team-sheet or the form they'd be in, I wasn't sure.

Leeds United 3 Pacos Ferreira 1 (Silva 36, **Struijk 38, Hernandez 54, Costa 77**).

Good News – Bad News!

Engand had a fortunate 0 – 1 win against Iceland, the team that hustled us out of Euro 2016 in the round of 16. Kyle Walker, the man who allegedly sampled the delights of a couple of call-girls during the Covid lockdown, got himself sent off in the 70th minute but England hung on and then, in the 89th minute, were awarded a penalty for a handball that also saw Sverrir Ingason sent off. Raheem Sterling dinked in the penalty but then, in the final moments, a rash Joe Gomez foul offered the hosts a reprieve. Birkir Bjarnason clipped his penalty over the angle of post and bar.

Manchester City's Phil Foden was given a full debut and Manchester United's teenage striker Mason Greenwood came on late in the game for his debut but both then disgraced themselves. The two youngsters became the centre of a media storm with tales that they'd broken the squad's Covid protocols by meeting two women in an area outside the team's Covid secure bubble, albeit still within the same hotel. The pair were fined 250,000 Icelandic krona (£1,360) by local police and were immediately dropped from the squad and would travel home rather than continue with the team to their next game in Denmark. I could only assume they'd been shown the ropes by Kyle Walker! Covid was still in the news every day and after a midsummer lull it appeared that cases in most countries were now increasing again. In years gone by the appearance of a bloke in a mask entering a shop generally meant trouble but these days it was the appearance of anyone *not* in a mask that was considered sinister! The increase in cases in the UK was a worrying development that threatened to end what little hope we had of watching Leeds in the flesh in the foreseeable future.

EFL Cup 1st Round games were already taking place in an underwhelming sort of a way, the games being treated like pre-season friendlies in most cases and, along with the very early qualifying rounds of the FA Cup, were the only games yet taking place in England. Non-league clubs were allowed to accept crowds of up to 300 and I'd nabbed one of the 300 tickets for Worcester City's first home league game that was coming up on September 9th. Never had I been quite so excited to grab a ticket for a non-league football match! Leeds, now being an EPL side, would join the EFL Cup in round 2 and we were drawn at home to Hull City, a game that would take place on the Wednesday after our Anfield game. If we could beat the Tigers then we'd face a trip to either West Ham or Charlton in the 3rd Round which had already been drawn. It was difficult to keep up with the sequence of fixtures, so complicated was the scheduling for the new season.

On Monday 7th September, while Gareth Southgate's England were preparing for their game in Denmark with a reduced squad that, Leeds fans calculated, gave Kalvin Phillips a better chance of making his debut, I had to decide whether to watch Stuart Dallas play for Northern Ireland (NI) against Norway or Liam Cooper for Scotland in the Czech Republic. Both games were on different Sky channels at the same time. On the strength of the fact that 'Norn Ireland' also had former Leeds keeper Bailey Peacock-Farrell in goal and young Alfie McCalmont on their bench and that Norway had Alf-Inge Rasdal Haaland's son Erling up front, I plumped for NI. It was probably the right choice as there were three goals in the opening seven minutes, including a stunning strike from the Leeds born Haaland. Norway romped to a 1 – 5 win with Haaland bagging another fine goal in what was NI's first home game under new manager Ian Baraclough. At the end of the match, Haaland and Dallas swapped shirts and had a quick man-hug that the cameras picked out; Erling clearly having a few words with Stuart. It was no doubt something to do with his dad being a Leeds legend and maybe young Erling asked Stuart for his shirt as a surprise gift for his old man; Dallas confirmed later that Erling was merely wishing him and Leeds well in the EPL. Who knows, one day we may yet see another Haaland in a Leeds shirt.

The Scotland game was a more sedate affair with Liam Cooper playing the full 90 minutes and the Scots beating a makeshift Czech side that had a completely different squad from the one that beat Slovakia the previous week. Two of their players in that squad came into contact with a backroom staff member who'd tested positive for Covid-19 and thus the whole original squad had to be stood down. It highlighted just how naïve and reckless Greenwood and Foden had been in Iceland trying 'to score' *after* the game; the ramifications of not following the Covid rules were potentially huge and Covid was still a threat to live football continuing, even behind closed doors.

It was a good news - bad news week for Leeds as we counted down to the last few days before the Liverpool game. The bad news was that the FA came through with a £20,000 fine for the club for our players' overzealous celebrations at Derby as we basked in the glory of winning the Championship. Once again Leeds fans were up in arms as we'd all seen similar pictures on social media of West Brom and Liverpool players doing the same – letting off various pyrotechnics – on their big days inside The Hawthorns and Anfield respectively without any censure from the FA at all! Leeds' case was decided by the FA's Independent Regulatory Commission (IRC) and they were at least persuaded of the mitigation that:

"a. No one was threatened or endangered by the conduct.

"b. No one was injured and

"c. Immediate admission and apology by the Clubs (sic)"

As a result of the mitigating circumstances they kindly reduced the fine from £30,000 to £20,000. The IRC also wrote in its written reasons: *"We are surprised the Club could not identify from a small number of candidates who brought the devices to the ground and gave them to the players."* [1] The club was keeping shtum about that but the smart money said Alioski was probably involved!

The second bit of bad news was that the U21s got hammered in their first EFL Trophy game at Accrington. For some reason Leeds opted to play a very young side comprising mainly U18 players and, not surprisingly they got thumped, 7 – 0. The game was shown on the Accrington Stanley YouTube channel if you were happy to give them £10; I opted instead to watch the Denmark v England game, after all it was one of the good news bits of the week.

This good news was that Kalvin Phillips made his England debut. He was possibly helped by the fact that the squad was two men down now that Greenwood and Foden were on their bikes back home having also allegedly had rides in Iceland too whilst breaking Covid-19 protocols. It wasn't much of a match to watch sadly, a bit of a nil-nil bore-fest, but Kalvin acquitted himself well despite England playing a very conservative three at the back with two defensive midfielders in Phillips and Declan Rice; it was a

---

[1] *The FA v Leeds United AFC – 7 Sept 2020 Written Reasons, FA Website.*

formation that might have been necessary against a better side than the Danes but in this one it merely stifled ambition.

The good news – bad news theme for me continued on the Wednesday ahead of our opening game; just three days remained until the new journey commenced. It was the bad news first as Prime Minister Boris Johnson appeared in a 4 pm Government briefing for the first time in several weeks as reported cases of Covid-19 continued to rise exponentially. As yet the hospital admissions and deaths had not followed the same trend but the analysis portrayed in the briefing showed it was mainly the young – 21 to 29 – age range that was spreading and catching the disease and the fear was that they would pass it on to their parents and grandparents eventually. That was when panic stations would really set in again. So, the PM announced that from the following Monday, 14th September, the Covid rules would be tightened again. The 'Rule of Six' would come into play and gatherings inside and outside would be limited to six people or the number in your particular household if that was already more than six. He mentioned the pilot sports events that were being trialled and, although he didn't exactly say they'd be suspended completely, he did come up with the word "abridged" suggesting the return of fans into football grounds, previously targeted for October 1st, might be further delayed. The Scots came out at the same time and pushed back their start date from September 14th to 5th October "at the earliest" although the two test events scheduled for the coming weekend - Aberdeen v Kilmarnock and Ross County v Celtic - would go ahead. Meanwhile, the day before the new restrictions were announced, and presumably with that original 1st October date in mind, Leeds asked their fans to send in details of any "groups" we wished to form so that in the event of ticket ballots at least we could attend and sit together with our mates. The groups were limited to just ten people but our little group that meets in the Old White Hart immediately put in our request so that at least we could all meet up as we did in the past. The new 'Rule of Six' seemed to cast doubt on that even being legal though!

I was making the most of the current rules as I headed down the M6 and M5 for my first taste of a live, in the flesh game since our home match with Huddersfield back on 7th March; wow, did that seem a long time ago now? I'd snaffled a ticket, one of just 300, for

Worcester City's first home Midland Football League, Premier Division game of the season; their first game at their new ground in Claines Lane in Worcester. The City had been playing in exile for the previous seven years, first at Kidderminster and then Bromsgrove. It was a strange and slightly nervy occasion but really well organised with plenty of parking at the nearby Royal Grammar School Grange sports complex, a ten-minute walk to the new ground, a temperature check at the entrance and a check to ensure everyone had registered their details in case there was a Covid incident and track and trace needed to come into play. It was great to be back watching football live though and I thoroughly enjoyed the evening despite the City putting in a very Leeds United-like performance; total domination of the game yet losing it to one of the few chances Tividale got when their striker suddenly morphed into Ronaldo for a few seconds as he whipped the ball into the top corner. At the other end, City had chance after chance but we were more Bam Bam than Christiano and every chance went begging. If I wasn't going to be seeing much of Leeds this season then at least it looked like there would be some decent non-league football to watch.

I still felt there was every likelihood that the EPL would find a way to persuade the Government that they could put games on safely and, for me, the persuading factor was going to be, as it always is with the EPL, money. EPL chief, Richard Masters came out immediately before the PMs appearance on TV to say it was *"absolutely critical"* fans were allowed back into stadiums as soon as possible and that failure to do so would cost the EPL clubs some £700 million this season. Presumably, the TV deal was being amended upwards as it was announced that every EPL game in September would be shown live on TV on one platform or another. This coming weekend alone I would be hoping to watch all eight EPL games scheduled from Saturday through to Monday evening; the two games involving the Manchester clubs had been postponed due to their late involvement in the previous season's European competitions or else there would have been two more. I'd have square eyes by the end of that lot!

It's only Anfield if it's full

O n Thursday it was EPL press conference day as all the managers were required to do their bit to hype up an already pretty hyped-up season start. For Leeds it was Marcelo Bielsa of course and the first bit of news everyone wanted confirmed was that he'd actually signed his new contract. Perhaps they'd been saving the news for today, which just happened to be Andrea Radrizzani's 46th birthday. Asked about his future, Bielsa, via his new and as yet un-named interpreter, insisted: *"I will be working the next season at Leeds United. Everything has been sorted and it's definite I will be here next season."*[1]

On the two new signings Bielsa, for once, gave nothing away about whether they'd be starting on Saturday or not, but he did confirm that both *"are in very good physical condition."* On his team's tactics in the EPL he confirmed: *"To begin with we will try to play*

---

[1] https://www.bbc.co.uk/sport/live/football/54098651/page/2

the same way." Bielsa suggested that playing Liverpool behind closed doors would be a very different proposition to playing in front of the usual crowd of in excess of 50,000. *"We are going to play at Anfield, but it is only Anfield if it is full,"* he said. And that was that; the next time we'd see him would be on TV as he took his seat in the dugout after shaking hands, or more likely these Covid-sanitised days, elbow bumping Jurgen Klopp.

With every EPL game in September being televised live while there remained no chance of fans being allowed in the grounds, I was ready for a mammoth session in front of the box. It all started on Friday night really, when the first Championship game of the new season was carried live on Sky; Watford beat Neil Warnock's Middlesbrough 1 – 0 with an 11th-minute goal by defender Craig Cathcart. I watched with mild interest but, almost overnight, my focus had switched pretty much exclusively to the EPL. That started with a 12:30 pm kick-off at Craven Cottage where Arsenal were the visitors. Fulham toiled unsuccessfully and looked to me a worse team than the one we walloped only a few weeks earlier on our march to the Championship title. Arsenal scored three but could have doubled that with a bit more luck in front of goal. I'd increased my interest in all the teams in the EPL this season by entering a team in the Fantasy EPL and so was well chuffed that Pierre-Emerick Aubameyang grabbed the last of the three Arsenal goals to boost my opening day points tally.

No one knew where the rumour started, but it was being widely touted that Liam Cooper was likely to miss the Liverpool game with an ankle knock picked up playing for Scotland. Even our little Leeds United WhatsApp group, the folk I used to meet up with in the Old White Hart before home games, had picked up on the rumour but we'd have to wait until 4:30 pm, an hour before we kicked off, to get confirmation.

Whilst watching the Fulham game, I was also putting the finishing touches to a giant spreadsheet I'd created listing all 20 EPL sides, with all of their first-team squads and shirt numbers together with columns for appearances and goals. It was my way of getting to know the division having pretty much ignored it for the previous 16 years while all my attention was focussed on Leeds and the Championship, or League One when we plumbed that particular depth! I'd already learned a lot about the various players in each squad just by entering their names in the spreadsheet; did you know for example that Fulham had a goalkeeper called Alphonse Areola? Well there you go then; it was a great way to keep abreast of all the details...

The second game of the day was a 3 pm kick-off at Selhurst Park where Crystal Palace were playing Southampton. The interest this time for me was Wilf Zaha, another key member of my Fantasy League Team. Hey presto, in the 13th minute Andros Townsend crossed and Zaha, unmarked at the back post, placed a side-foot volley inside the post. It was mildly annoying that VAR ruled out another Zaha strike later in the game and he also missed another sitter, but Palace were good value for a 1 − 0 victory.

The Palace game was into the last twenty minutes when my phone beeped again and this time one of the WhatsApp group had helpfully posted a picture of a screenshot showing the Liverpool team; no one bothered to post the Leeds team until I asked. When it eventually popped up, there was no Liam Cooper.

Meslier
Ayling (Capt) Koch Struijk Dallas
Phillips
Costa Klich (Shackleton 81) Hernandez (Roberts 62) Harrison
Bamford (Rodrigo 62)

Subs: Casilla, Casey, Shackleton, Poveda, Rodrigo, Alioski, Roberts.

Liverpool: Alisson, Alexander-Arnold (Matip 89), Gomez, van Dijk, Robertson, Keita (Fabinho 59), Henderson (Jones 66), Wijnaldum, Salah, Firmino, Mané. Subs not used: Adrian, Milner, Minamino, Origi. Referee: Michael Oliver.

Cooper had failed a late fitness test. Hence the call went out to young Pascal Struijk to fill in alongside debutant Robin Koch; we'd never now know if Koch would have started anyway had Coops been fit or whether he'd have been sat alongside our other new boy, Rodrigo Moreno, on the bench. It was certainly not ideal to be starting a game against the best team in England, the current Champions, with a brand new centre-back partnership that had never played together before. What would Salah, Firmino and Mané make of it? James Milner, who 17 years earlier had been in the Leeds line-up when we made our last visit to Anfield in the EPL, was on the Liverpool bench for this one.

It would be said of this game that it was probably the most exciting game the EPL had ever seen on opening day and the action was pretty much non-stop from the 1st to the 90th minute. I've written before many times about how Leeds have had a history of building up the hype before a game only to then let us down with a bump within seconds of the start, usually due to a catastrophic error or maybe a dire refereeing decision going against us. Well, as early as the 3rd minute of this one, it was all happening again...

I was still settling in, beer in hand, just thinking how I'd grown used to watching these behind closed door games on TV; the piped crowd noise actually sounding pretty realistic to me. I didn't think about it unless I noticed the background shots of the vast Anfield arena showing giant banners covering the acres of empty seats. For three and a half minutes Liverpool dominated the possession and Leeds, with only rare touches, got no more than a couple of yards into the Liverpool half before the red tide swept back towards the Anfield Road end that Leeds were defending. Suddenly, Mané had the ball in the Leeds left-back area being marshalled by Luke Ayling while Stuart Dallas covered off a pass to Firmino on the corner of the area. Mané shifted the ball to Salah who turned full circle away from the attentions of Pascal Struijk to fire at goal. The ball struck the arm of Robin Koch and instantly Michael Oliver was pointing at the penalty spot. Oh boy did that moment feel *"Leedsy"*! How many times had this happened to us before; hopes sky high before the start and then our dreams squashed underfoot within seconds. It was a very familiar feeling. This was unjust though. Yes, the ball had struck Koch on his outstretched right arm, but it only did so after a wicked deflection off his right knee. No way could Koch have avoided the ball then cannoning onto his arm. The EPL website covers such a situation:

"Deflections;

*"EPL players will be allowed extra leeway when it comes to ricocheted handballs. It is often impossible to avoid contact with the ball if it has deflected off the body of an opponent, team-mate, or even another part of the own player. So a handball **will not** be awarded if the ball touches a player's hand/arm directly from their*

own head/body/foot or the head/body/foot of another player who is close/nearby. "[1]

That was clear then, Oliver had obviously not spotted the ricochet but, since this was the EPL, we had VAR to protect us! Well, no, not exactly. If VAR reviewed the incident it did it bloody quickly and, if it did, it either didn't pick up the deflection or the idiot doing the review didn't know the rule. The spot-kick was allowed to be taken and Mo Salah smashed it down the middle while Illan Meslier dived away to his left. I felt sick to my stomach; it was the worst possible start to our EPL journey and, not for the first time in our long history, the game had wronged us. I could only assume that Robin Koch himself didn't know the rule either or surely he'd have demanded that referee Oliver went to look at the pitch-side monitor, something the football authorities were now recommending referees did if there was any doubt in their minds. Four minutes gone and Leeds were a goal down.

It took Leeds a few minutes to acclimatise to the sheer pace Liverpool were playing at but, slowly we did, and we even had the ball in the Liverpool net in the 8th minute. A little dinked cross from the right by Hernandez caused confusion in the area and Liverpool only cleared as far as Klich. He headed the ball back towards the penalty spot where Harrison scrapped for it and pushed it forward to Costa who slotted it inside the post. Sadly, Costa was marginally offside. We then saw Harrison just fail to get the ball across to Bamford as Leeds grew and grew into the game as we approached the 11-minute mark with the ball back with Meslier.

Illan side-footed the ball out to Kalvin Phillips, back to goal and midway in the Leeds half on the left but, for once, with no red shirt at his back. He was able to turn, look up and spot a darting run from Harrison down the left wing; he launched the ball towards him. Harrison had the close attention of Trent Alexander-Arnold but Jack was nimble and Jack was quick and skipped inside and then got the run of the ball to avoid a challenge from Joe Gomez before lashing a right foot shot low into the left corner of the net. We had a game on and, sat on his blue bucket, we saw a rare glimpse of

---

emotion from Marcelo Bielsa as a punch of the air saw him lose half the cup of coffee he was holding! We got to the 20th minute without further drama, another eight minutes during which Leeds gave as good as they got in an end-to-end game played at breath-taking speed. Then Pablo Hernandez inadvertently conceded a corner-kick under pressure from Andy Robertson. I have to confess, for a few seconds I'd forgotten we were rubbish at defending corners. Robertson himself placed the ball down, stood back with both arms raised in a signal to his teammates and then launched the ball into the middle. In a flash it was in the back of our net.

It was the head of Virgil van Dijk that did the damage as he managed to get himself free from Robin Koch who just stumbled as he tried to stay with the Dutch defender. It seemed that all the familiar ailments we'd seen Leeds suffer from for years and years in the Championship had followed us into the EPL; we still had chronic bad luck and we were still a soft touch at corners. 20 minutes gone and we were a goal down again. It had not been a great start to his Leeds career for Robin Koch and I could almost hear the Twitter keyboard warriors rehearsing their Koch-up puns. I was trying to avoid them, although with Klich, Klopp and Koch all involved in the game it was tempting to try to weave something in about a three-legged horse on a cobbled street...

Leeds could have got straight back on level terms inside two minutes as next we saw another familiar sight; Patrick Bamford was sent through one-on-one with the Liverpool keeper Alisson but, as he did so many times last season, he fluffed his lines and took too long getting his feet in the right order and the chance was gone. This time though, within another ten minutes he'd made amends.

In the meantime, Meslier was called upon twice; once to safely clutch a 25-yard drive by Jordan Henderson and then to acrobatically tip over an inadvertent shot at his own goal that flew off the boot of Pascal Struijk. Then, the next Leeds move started from the left foot of Illan Meslier again. He tapped the ball out to Phillips and Leeds played the ball to and fro a few times before returning it to Meslier to try again. This time he clipped it out towards Stuart Dallas on the Leeds left; Dallas cushioned the ball neatly on his right thigh inside to Klich who instantly flicked it back to Dallas in an exaggerated one-two. Dallas allowed the ball to bounce a couple of times and then half-volleyed it towards the edge of the Liverpool penalty area. Patrick Bamford was watching with interest as it fell behind van Dijk who stuck out a boot. He got it all wrong though and the ball merely dropped for Bamford who took one touch and then clipped it past the onrushing goalkeeper. It took a bobble off Alisson's outstretched leg but still bounced nicely inside the far corner of the net. It was Bamford's second ever EPL goal, having once scored for Middlesbrough in their final game of the 2016-17 season when they were relegated. It was now 2 – 2 in this amazing encounter but, once again, Leeds were only level for a couple of minutes as the goals continued to rain in.

We were into the 32nd minute and Bamford's shot had trickled over the Liverpool goal line just two minutes earlier. Now Luke Ayling and then Pablo Hernandez gave away free-kicks as first one then the other stumbled into Mané, midway in the Leeds half. Pablo, who usually starts the season so well, looked to be struggling with the pace of the game and I was already wondering if maybe this would prove to be a season too far for the little magician, although surely the pace of this one wasn't going to be replicated every week, even in the best league in the world? Andy Robertson stood over the free-kick and then clipped a curling left-footer over the top of the Leeds defensive line. Pascal Struijk stretched every sinew to get his head to it but he was facing his own goal and could only back-head it out to the edge of the area. He had to go for it as that dick van Dijk was right there as well but his header dropped perfectly for the one man you wouldn't want it to; Mo Salah, perhaps the deadliest striker in the EPL. Every Leeds man was focused on the ball and now Salah was unmarked with all the time in the world to stun the ball with his right foot and then put his left boot through it to send it spearing into the top right corner. It was an unstoppable shot. 3 – 2 to Liverpool and we were still only just over half an hour into the game. It seemed whatever Leeds could do, Liverpool could do just that little bit better. Bielsa was now on his feet, prowling about like a wounded tiger as he shouted instructions while his coaches ran round in circles trying to translate them into messages the players might understand. Then the great man would settle back down on his haunches, an improbable position for a slightly overweight 65-year-old; I should know! Had I actually been in the stands, I'd probably have been watching Bielsa as much as events on the pitch, so animated was he.

Incredibly, despite the regular setbacks, Leeds' enthusiasm never seemed to dim and for the rest of the half we once again matched the men in red move for move. Sure, Liverpool always looked the more assured, the more precise on the ball, but hell, you'd expect that, this was like the 6th form boys playing the new intake! There was one more incident before the halftime break as Helder Costa took a tumble under a challenge from Mo Salah. Replays showed there was the slightest tap on Costa's ankle by the Liverpool man who got nowhere near the ball. It was tempting to think if it had been the other way round Oliver may well have been pointing at the spot again but, maybe I'm getting paranoid... doesn't mean I'm wrong though of course!

Halftime was a chance to catch our breath and get another beer before settling back in front of the TV. I wondered how the Shropshire Whites were getting on; they'd organised a supposedly Covid secure session at Shifnal Town FC's social club. That was a step too far for me I'm afraid as I wasn't convinced there would be much social distancing going on, especially since Shifnal were playing a local derby FA Cup preliminary round game against Bridgnorth Town, so it was sure to be busy even with restricted numbers. Shifnal went on to win that one 4 – 1, so at least the locals would be happy. My other team, Worcester City were also in FA Cup action and they too won through to the next round with a 2 – 1 victory over Walsall Wood.

Back to Anfield and the second half began with Leeds now defending the Kop, an end where I'd stood many a time in the late 70s when just rocking up to pay on the gate when Leeds were in town. It was a huge terrace then of course, an amazing place to watch football from, squeezed in shoulder to shoulder with thousands of Scousers, many peeing on the steps as it was so much hassle to get to the bogs! Incidentally, just in case you don't know why they are called Scousers the traditional explanation is that scouse is a contraction of 'lobscouse', which was a type of stew (Norwegian in origin), once popular amongst sailors and still eaten in Liverpool today.

Back to the game and the second half was certainly played at a reduced pace and Leeds kept themselves in with a chance right until the final seconds. In fact the second period was more of a chess match than anything, both sides cancelling each other out really. Liverpool did have one good early chance when Wijnaldum struck from close range but, not for the first time, Meslier was equal to it and palmed it away. The young French keeper had been perhaps the stand-out Leeds player so far. Leeds had the ball in the Liverpool net again at one point as Robin Koch lifted a pass over the home defence for Jack Harrison to run on to. Jack chipped Alisson and then Alexander-Arnold headed the bouncing ball into his own net. Only then did the flag go up for offside, as is the case now with VAR. Harrison was a yard offside. Bielsa made his first changes after 61minutes; Rodrigo replacing Bamford and Tyler Roberts replacing a subdued Pablo Hernandez. Whether it was a result of this new impetus or whether we'd have scored anyway, we'll never know but, in the 66th minute, Leeds levelled for the third time.

There was a short delay as we moved into the 65th minute while Liverpool made their second change of the day as Henderson was replaced by Curtis Jones; they'd introduced Fabinho for Keita six minutes earlier. Liverpool were waiting to throw the ball in, deep inside their own right-back quarter. When the throw eventually came it was intercepted on the first bounce by the head of Koch who knocked it forward towards Phillips. Matty Klich then took it off Phillips' toes and pushed it out to the right to Helder Costa. Klich then made a dash into the Liverpool area into a decent space and pointed to Costa to play the ball back in front of him. The pass was superbly weighted and cut through five Liverpool players before arriving on the Pole's right foot. One touch stopped the ball and then a second, a right foot volley, crashed it inside the left post. It was a sumptuous Bielsaball move and a superbly calm finish from our number '43'. Incredibly, after 66 minutes, Leeds were holding the Champions in their own back yard to a 3 – 3 draw.

The minutes ticked by agonisingly slowly as we moved into the final stages of the game. I'm sure every Leeds fan watching around the country, like me, was willing the clock to go faster. If the game ended now it would be an almost perfect start to our EPL journey and, knowing how we'd been wronged by the incorrect award of that early penalty, the draw was actually the least we deserved. As

I've said more times than I care to remember though, the word *"deserved"* is not in the football dictionary. I knew full well that the quality and guile this Liverpool side possessed was quite capable of fashioning a winner somehow or other and it would be so 'Leeds United' to shoot ourselves in the foot right at the death. Curtis Jones tried to con referee Oliver in the 75th minute as he collapsed when Stuart Dallas nicked the ball off his toes in the Leeds area but that one was turned down and VAR didn't seem to check it. Kalvin Phillips then did his best to reprise his Blackburn free-kick goal as he whipped a 35-yarder just past the left post. We were into the final quarter of an hour.

Leeds showed their fragile nature again at another Liverpool right wing corner as Virgil van Dijk came through unchallenged to smash the ball into the net but this time we were rescued by the referee who saw a bit of a push off the ball by Curtis Jones on Koch. Young Koch was going to have to learn quickly to stand firm back there. We were now into the last ten minutes and Leeds made their final change as Jamie Shackleton replaced a very tired-looking Mateusz Klich. Leeds were sitting back a little too deep for my liking and we were now finding it hard to get the ball up to Rodrigo who, from memory, had hardly touched the ball despite constantly racing around trying to close down Liverpool players. We were losing possession too easily on the rare occasions we crossed the halfway line; hardly surprising if our players were as nervous as I was. Bielsa looked nervous too, as he was one minute down on his haunches and then up on his feet the next while barking out instructions all the time. Firmino should probably have put us out of our misery in the 86th minute as he suddenly popped up six yards out with the ball at his feet but somehow scuffed his shot and it was blocked away for another Liverpool corner; they'd now won nine against none for Leeds. There were just three and a half minutes of normal time left as the left wing corner came across. Once again Leeds looked uncertain as to who was doing what and this time Kalvin Phillips was challenging with van Dijk at the near post. Neither got much on it and it dropped at their feet before Phillips, falling backwards, just hooked it up in the air where it came down near the penalty spot. Fabinho, a white '3' on his red shirt got his foot to the falling ball just as Rodrigo dangled a leg out as well. The Liverpool man was way too clever though and, feeling the

Spaniards boot against his leg he threw himself to the turf and Michael Oliver had that gleeful look on his face again as he pointed to the spot. I suppose VAR checked it, but it didn't take long and this one was hard to argue with. We would see dozens of penalties won like this in the EPL this season, players are looking for that slight touch all the time and if you miss the ball you are asking for trouble. I had that 'Leeds United' feeling again, so very close, so valiant and yet, to be honest, so careless at the death. Mo Salah slammed home the spot-kick, this time in the left corner, for his hat-trick. I didn't expect we'd come back a 4th time and I was still shaking my head as the final whistle blew.

All the pundits were full of praise for Leeds but there was just something a little patronising about it all; you know: *"The brave newcomers did well but Liverpool always just had too much for them"*. That sort of thing. I knew full well that we'd been done by an incorrect decision on that first penalty - the rules were clear and yet so few people seemed to be aware of them – while our own inability to deal with corner-kicks was a long-standing issue that we really needed to sort out. Maybe Robin Koch would help in that respect once he got his feet firmly under our table.

In his post-match press interview, Bielsa was more concerned with ensuring his new interpreter was heard than many of the answers he gave, as he twice told him to *"speak up"* and to direct his answers to the reporters not to him! Perhaps, like our players, this EPL lark would come more naturally to him after a few more games.

There was still one more game to come after our match ended and I watched that too, my fourth game of the day, as Newcastle won 0 – 2 at a very poor-looking West Ham. Then, on Sunday I managed two more TV games as West Brom crashed 0 – 3 at home to Leicester City with Jamie Vardy bagging two penalties, and then a dire Spurs lost 0 - 1 at home to a dogged looking Everton. Two more games, the final two of this first weekend would take place on Monday evening as Sheffield United hosted Wolves and then Brighton faced high spending Chelsea. The EPL season was underway.

Liverpool 4 **Leeds United 3** (Salah 4 pen, 33, 88 pen, **Harrison 12**, van Dijk 20, **Bamford 30**, **Klich 66**)

Behind Closed Doors. **Round 1 League Pos: 13th** (4 teams not playing).

A Bit of Déjà Vu

In those final two games of round 1 of the new EPL season, Sheffield United lost to Wolves 0 – 2 with two goals in the first six minutes and then Chelsea won at Brighton 1 – 3. I watched both those games too and was fascinated to see how Ben White got on in the Brighton defence. He did OK to be fair, nothing outstanding but certainly OK against a fancied Chelsea attack; he limped off late in the game though.

It was another annoying week for me; the Leeds United U23s were opening their PL2 account at Stoke City on Monday night, a game played at their Clayton Wood training ground, literally 20 minutes up the road from me. Of course it was another behind closed doors affair so I wouldn't be there, just as I couldn't attend the pre-season friendly at the Bet365 the other day; flipping frustrating being so close. Mind you, when I saw the team we were putting out I was less bothered. It was a tricky week for Marcelo Bielsa, not only did we have this game but we also had an EFL Cup tie at Elland Road on Wednesday night and then the next EPL game, against Fulham on Saturday. My guess was that any U23 players not involved with the first-team squad *would* be involved against Hull, as I was convinced none of the players who started at Anfield would feature again until the Fulham match. I was right and the U23 team Bielsa fielded at Clayton Wood was a very inexperienced side indeed. Only Robbie Gotts had a realistic chance of first-team involvement this season and he *did* start alongside Caprile, Huggins, Drameh, Hosannah, McCalmont, Jenkins, Stevens, McKinstry (Galloway 80), Greenwood and Gelhardt. The other subs; Van Den Heuvel, Mullen, McMillan and young Charlie Allen didn't get on the pitch. Stoke included the veteran Ryan Shawcross in their ranks as he completed his latest injury comeback. Leeds were behind in the first 60 seconds, conceding a goal similar to many we've seen the big boys succumb to; a left wing corner, no one taking control and former Dortmund striker Gabriel Kyeremateng hooking the ball over his shoulder into the net. The 21-year-old would go on to score three more, including a penalty, as Stoke romped to a 4 – 0 win.

The rumours were flying around again this week about Leeds' interest in Rodrigo de Paul, an attacking midfielder currently with Udinese in Italy, a player said to be valued at £35m. Leeds fans went into meltdown as the player apparently commented on a Twitter thread between two Leeds fans that he was keen to join the club but then quickly deleted the tweet, although not before it was spotted by the Leeds Twitter watch-guard. There was also still talk that the Whites harboured hopes of landing Josko Gvardiol, the Dinamo Zagreb defender. Dinamo were knocked out of the Champions League qualifiers this week and that was said to improve our chances. Meanwhile the battle over who owned big Jean-Kevin Augustin still raged between Leeds and RB Leipzig, neither club apparently wanting him! Leeds were arguing that since they sent Big Kev back at the end of his loan on 30th June they could not then be held to the contract clause committing us to take up the option to buy if we were promoted with him at the club since we were not promoted until July! There was plenty of mileage left in that one, unlike in Big Kev's legs. Another big striker, Jay-Roy Grot, was also still haunting the corridors of Thorp Arch. Grot was now likely to be on Leeds' books at least until the January transfer window as he'd picked up a serious knee injury whilst on loan with Dutch side Vitesse Arnhem, back in March. Then he suffered with a bacterial infection resulting from the operation and was now back in Leeds recuperating.

Covid was still dominating the news throughout Europe as reported cases continued to rise exponentially in most countries, including the UK. The Rule of Six started on Monday this week and numerous local areas imposed even tougher restrictions. The Government was however still allowing organised sport to continue to trial events with spectators present. Nine EFL games were chosen for the next round of league games to each be played in front of no more than one thousand fans. Notionally, we were all still hoping the October 1st date could be met for a return to all grounds in limited numbers but no one was confident it would happen unless the current rise in case numbers could be reversed.

Covid was weighing heavily on football finances of course and another well-known club bit the dust this week as Macclesfield Town were wound up owing more than £500,000, including a sizeable chunk to the taxman. The club had been in trouble for years and racked up numerous points deductions last season for failure to pay wages on time and for failure to fulfil some of its fixtures. That meant they were relegated from the Football League once all the deductions were applied, saving Stevenage who would otherwise have finished below them. Focus then shifted to my old mate the Shrimper's team; Southend United. They too were in court this week but their winding-up petition was postponed for a fourth time with the club saying their recent ground sale would free up funds in the near future; they too owed in the region of half a million quid.

Another signing was announced for the U23s, another attacker, 18-year-old Crysencio Summerville from Feyenoord for an undisclosed fee. He was clearly another one earmarked for the future, not this season, if indeed he would ever break into the first-team.

I was feeling slightly odd on Wednesday; I was driving down to Worcester again to watch the City and, whisper it quietly, not attempting to watch the Leeds game against Hull that was available at £10 a throw via the Carabao Cup website. It wasn't the £10, honestly, I'm not that tight! It was the temptation of seeing live, in the flesh football. I'd enjoyed my trip the previous week, despite the 130-mile round trip and the fact that the City got beat! I was enjoying a half-pound cheeseburger and then a Mars Bar whilst watching the Worcester City and Romulus players going through their warm-up routines when the Leeds team sheet was posted on our White Hart WhatsApp group:

Casilla (Capt)
Shackleton Cresswell Davis Douglas
Casey (Struijk 45)
Poveda Roberts Bogusz (Gotts 78) Alioski
Rodrigo

Subs: Meslier, Struijk, Phillips, Gotts, Harrison, McCalmont, Bamford.

Hull City: Ingram, Coyle, Jones, McLoughlin, Elder, Docherty, Batty, Scott, Honeyman (Jones 81), Lewis-Potter (Mayer 45), Wilks (Chadwick72). Subs not used: Emmanuel, Samuelsen, Greaves, Cartwright. Referee: David Webb

It was pretty much what I expected, certainly in terms of none of the Anfield starters being in the XI. Many fans thought it likely that Robin Koch would play, just to get more game time, but I thought that was way too risky until Liam Cooper was fit or another centre-back appeared through the door. In fact, the only thing that got some fans riled was the inclusion of Kiko Casilla as captain; some of our fans were not prepared to forgive him for his indiscretion at Charlton last season for which he got that eight game ban. It was not an issue for me at all; if he did what he was alleged to have done then he'd already been punished enough and deserved to be left alone now and if Bielsa was to be believed then it was the players who'd chosen him as their skipper for the night. The only interest in the Hull City line-up was the inclusion of Mallik Wilks up front and young Lewie Coyle at full-back; both former Leeds men of course.

I've now had chance to watch the re-run of the game and I have to say the reports I was getting from my little WhatsApp group were pretty much spot on; Leeds had plenty of ball but created very little with it whilst, at the back, the defence never looked really settled or in control. It didn't help that, for the second game running, we conceded inside the first five minutes and it was a poor, poor goal to give away. To make matters worse, it was Mallik Wilks who got it. Jamie Shackleton chased back to tidy up a long through ball by sliding it neatly back to Casilla with Keane Lewis-Potter looking every bit like the sound of his first name. Casilla lazily stroked the ball out to the left touchline where Leif Davis took one out of Casilla's book, being far too slow to get there before Wilks did! Mallik then came inside, played a short ball to Honeyman who, in turn, touched it to James Scott who immediately gave it back to Wilks who shot. The ball took a deflection off Davis and that was enough to beat Casilla; a goal down before you could say Rodrigo Moreno Machado who'd hardly had a touch yet. At halftime it was 0 – 0 at Worcester and it was 0 – 1 up at Elland Road and the only difference seemed to be that we'd had not a sniff of a chance where I was but Hull could have run up a cricket score in Leeds.

Watching the replay of the Leeds game just now, I have to say the second half wasn't much different, although Marcelo had clearly decided Oliver Casey was struggling in the 'Kalvin' role in front of the back four. At halftime he swapped Casey for Pascal Struijk who'd shown us before he is a natural for that position. Not that it really changed anything; it was still Kiko who was by far the busier keeper doing some decent work between the sticks while Hull missed chances too.

My game finished 0 – 0, with City doing another passing impression of Leeds; bossing possession but failing to create too many chances and then missing those that they did. I checked the WhatsApp group and couldn't tell what the score was at Leeds although the comments being posted were not exactly encouraging. *"Get Alioski off and Harrison on, Gjanni is making my blood boil"* wrote Richard, while Cambridge Rob noted: *"Our experienced players haven't done the kids any favours."* My usual travel buddy, Kentley the Stokie was still being optimistic… or sarcastic, I couldn't quite work out which as he posted: *"I think we'll win on pens and captain Kiko will be the hero!"* Guitar John countered that though with *"Can't see it at the moment…this is awful!"* I guessed we were still a goal down but then up popped another post from John that suggested we'd equalised at the death: *"Lucky, lucky Leeds!"* he posted. Never in my fifty-odd years of supporting the club had I heard that said before! I checked the BBC Sport website on my phone and, sure enough, it was reporting that Alioski had scored in the 3rd minute of added time!

Watching the goal back as I write this report, it was doubly amazing; Leeds had only gone and scored from a corner! Barry

Douglas floated the ball into the middle from the left wing in front of the empty Revie Stand, now completely denuded of all those crowdies that used to wobble about in there during the 'ghost games'; I never did get to spot where mine was! The ball came down near the back post and a combination of Robbie Gotts' right boot and that of a defender managed to volley the ball straight back to Douglas on the byline. This time Douglas lifted the ball in towards the near post where it flicked off a head towards the back post again. Young Cresswell nodded it back in again and this time it just evaded a stretching Rodrigo before arriving perfectly on the left foot of Gjanni Alioski about 12 yards out. The little man from North Macedonia expertly lifted the ball into the roof of the net.

I was now sat in the car at the Royal Grammar School sports centre, waiting for news of the penalties and I couldn't help thinking back to last season when we'd faced an almost identical situation. Back then Leeds put out a very inexperienced side at Elland Road against Stoke City in the FL Cup 2nd round, just days after the full side walloped them 0 – 3 in the league. Stoke went two goals to the good with two strikes at the end of the first half in that game but three halftime changes by Bielsa got Leeds going and we pulled the deficit back and should arguably have won it before the penalties. Sadly, this was more like last season than I wanted it to be as, once again, we went out of the competition on penalty kicks. I waited and waited for some news and all I could see was *"penalties in progress"* on the BBC website. Eventually, Kev W, aka Barlow Boy, sent one final WhatsApp message that read: *"Dave... Rodrigo scored, Alioski missed, Roberts scored, Kiko saved, Poveda scored, Douglas scored, Struijk scored, Davis scored, Gotts scored, Casilla scored, Shackleton missed. Out on pens 9-8"* and that was the Carabao EFL Cup journey over for another year. The prize would have been a trip to the London Stadium to play West Ham which would have been a great day out had we been allowed to go but, as things stood, we wouldn't, so it was no real hardship. I started the car and set off on the 65 mile journey back up the M5 and M6 thinking what a real pain this Covid pandemic had become.

Leeds United 1 Hull City 1 (Wilks 5, **Alioski 90+3**)
BCD Hull City win 8 – 9 on penalties.

Seventh Heaven...Just!

In his press conference ahead of the Fulham game, on Thursday afternoon, Marcelo Bielsa was mainly questioned about the decision to award the captaincy to Kiko Casilla against Hull. Question after question pursued this, to me, ridiculous and pointless line with Bielsa merely reiterating that Kiko was respected by all the players and also had his backing. The journos maintained that the decision had upset many fans but I have to say I could count on the fingers of one hand the number I'd seen or heard complaining. For me, Kiko had served his time and he deserved now to be allowed to continue his career. Whether he was good enough to keep goal for us was another matter altogether!

Other questions tried to push Bielsa to say when Rodrigo would start an EPL game, pointing at the energy he'd shown on Wednesday in the Cup game with Hull. Bielsa told the reporters, all still taking part in the presser remotely due to Covid restrictions, that Rodrigo was ready now... but he still wouldn't start on Saturday. Bamford again it would be then, in fact everything pointed to the starting XI being exactly the same as at Anfield, give or take the fitness of Liam Cooper.

Fulham began their campaign with that 0 – 3 defeat to Arsenal, but they had come through a midweek EFL Cup game successfully against Ipswich, with Aleksandar Mitrovic scoring the only goal of the game. That suggested that 'Mitro' might start against Leeds whereas he'd only been on the bench against the Gunners. Two things stuck in my mind from the game against the Cottagers in June; that awful challenge Mitrovic put in on Ben White in the first few minutes that should have seen him sent off; and the way Fulham bossed the first half before Pablo Hernandez took to the field. This was no easy game, but it was one I felt we really could do with winning to lay down a bit of a marker and to confirm that the strong performance at Anfield was not just beginner's luck.

The U23s played again on the Friday ahead of our Fulham match and, at the second attempt, they got off the mark with a 2 – 2 draw with Wolves at Thorp Arch, having lost that first match at Stoke. It probably should have been three points as Leeds held a 2 – 0 lead at halftime with goals from Joe Gelhardt and Sam Greenwood. The full team was: Van Den Huevel, Drameh, Casey (Cresswell 45), Hosannah, Huggins, McCalmont, Jenkins, Stevens, McKinstry (Gotts 45), Gelhardt, and Greenwood. Subs not used were Caprile, Galloway, and McMillan.

It was a TV weekend for me again; all ten games of week 2 of the EPL season were being shown live, on BT Sport, Sky and even the BBC had a game. Each match was scheduled with a different start time so it was possible, if you had the stamina, to watch them all; I was trying to do as many as possible. I was sure my fascination with the EPL would fade at some point but, for now, I was hooked. The first one, Everton v West Brom, clashed with a pre-match Skype get-together our Leeds United WhatsApp group had organised so I missed the majority of that one, although we did get regular updates as Cambridge Rob and Guitar John kept one eye on it. Everton came out on top 5 – 2 but that flattered a very sticky toffees' performance helped by the sending off of Albion's Kieren Gibbs for a push in the face of James Rodriguez which, obviously, the Everton man made the most of with an exaggerated 'collapse'. Albion manager, Slaven Bilic was then also 'sent off' at halftime as he remonstrated with referee Mike 'Deadly' Dean. Most of our little sample of Leeds fans were confident Leeds would see off Fulham, apart from Rob and me; Cambridge Rob had a gut feeling we'd lose, while I went for a 1 – 1 draw. I wasn't yet confident enough in our defence, not knowing if Liam Cooper would be fit and, in any case, knowing that Robin Koch was still finding his feet. The likelihood that Mitrovic would start also concerned me, as well as the fact that Anthony Taylor was down to referee. There was some good news though; Taylor was stuck on the M62 in a traffic jam and Kevin Friend was on standby to fill in.

I spotted the line-ups on a couple of tweets from the Fulham official Twitter feed; the good news was that Liam Cooper was fit again so, on the Twitter post I saw, it was the same line-up that started at Anfield but with Coops replacing Pascal Struijk who dropped to the bench. Aleksandar Mitrovic started for Fulham. I was settled in front of the TV with a full glass in good time for the 3 pm kick-off but then nearly spilled my beer as the team listed on the BT Sport screen showed Rodrigo in our starting XI. They soon explained that Pablo Hernandez had felt a problem in his groin during the warm-up. That was a blow; it had only been the arrival of Pablo on the pitch at halftime in that game in June that really tamed Fulham that day. We were also missing Kiko Casilla who was absent from the Leeds bench, said to have picked up an injury against Hull, although some folk unkindly suggested he probably just missed the bus since he generally fails to catch anything. More bad news was that Anthony Taylor had arrived in time!

Meslier
Ayling Koch Cooper (Capt) Dallas
Phillips
Costa Klich Rodrigo (Roberts 45) Harrison
Bamford (Alioski 70)
Subs: Caprile, Struijk, Shackleton, Poveda, Alioski, Bogusz, Roberts.
Fulham: Areola, Tete, Hector, Odoi, Bryan, Zambo Anguissa, Reed (Lemina 70), Kamara (Kebano 58), Onomah (De Cordova-Reid 58), Cavaleiro, Mitrovic. Subs not used: Rodak, Cairney. Ream, Knockaert.
Referee: Anthony Taylor.
Fulham had my favourite pun-inspiring goalkeeper in their starting XI; Areola. I hoped he wouldn't stand out too much today…

- 43 -

Elland Road looked magnificent in the TV pictures; an aerial shot showing the turf looking lush and green and huge Leeds banners covered most of the seats in the lower tiers of each stand. All the crowdies had gone, stored away somewhere for later collection, no doubt removed in the hope that the go-ahead would be given soon for at least a few real fans to take their places if those pilot games going on this weekend were without drama. This was the first EPL game at Elland Road since a 3 – 3 draw with Charlton, our final game before relegation in 2004. Everything was set but I had no idea I was about witness a game every bit as nerve-shredding as that Anfield cracker.

A goal had been scored inside the first five minutes of both of Leeds' games so far this season; one by Liverpool and one by Hull; now it was our turn. The game started with a Fulham kick-off but not before both sides took a knee in support of the campaign to end racism. A few teams – notably Coventry City and Queens Park Rangers in their Friday night Championship game – had now decided to end that practice and I have to say I thought it was time to move on. It had been a useful statement, a public reminder of the issue, but for it to become a pre-match ritual seemed to reduce its impact to me. Nevertheless it would continue for months to come in the EPL. Fulham had an early free-kick that speared just past the right-hand post but then Leeds got their first attack going, only ended as Fulham full-back Joe Bryan slid in to deny Luke Ayling by putting the ball behind for a Leeds corner. Kalvin Phillips delivered it from the right wing.

Leeds have been poor with our own corners for a few seasons now and of course we've been equally poor at defending them, but we were about to see that Fulham were just as bad. As the ball came across it just took a touch off a Fulham head but then carried on towards Helder Costa who was free as a bird about 12 yards beyond that back post and level with the edge of the six-yard box. Costa took the ball on his left foot, allowed it to bounce once and then volleyed high into the net off the underside of the bar. It was a remarkable strike and maybe another sign of the increasing confidence of a player who was finally starting to show his best form after a difficult first season. Leeds were ahead after only four minutes and twenty-three seconds and we should have known we were about to set off on yet another rollercoaster ride.

Leeds had a couple more early corners and Robin Koch was unlucky to see a fine header tipped over the bar from the third, another one delivered by Kalvin Phillips from that right wing. Two more quickly followed and Leeds were camped in the Fulham half, we were comfortable. Then we had another one of those unfathomable defensive brain fade moments we've seen far too often over the years; we were into the 33rd minute. Joe Bryan went chasing after a nothing sort of a ball that was heading away from goal and towards the byline on the left side of the Leeds area with Robin Koch looking happy to marshal him away. Then, for whatever reason, Koch slid in and then pulled out at the last minute, something I've heard before somewhere, but Joe Bryan was far too aware of the opportunity, dragged his back foot and down he went. Anthony Taylor was soon pointing at the spot. Having watched countless replays I'm still not even convinced there was any contact but it was a daft and needless attempt at a challenge and, for the second week running we had a Koch cock-up to deal with. Predictably, VAR didn't see there had been any 'clear and obvious' issue with the ref's call and, unless the technology one day goes a step further and we introduce the equivalent of cricket's 'Snicko' or 'Ultra-Edge' to detect these finest of contacts, we are stuck with players cheating. Mitrovic was soon whacking the ball under the diving Meslier for the equaliser. It was another lesson for Koch and once again a comfortable-looking Leeds lead was squandered. Not for long though; this rollercoaster was now reaching full speed and, less than five minutes later, we were ahead again and this time it was a Fulham defender committing Hara Kari.

Leeds had a throw-in on their right wing near the halfway line which Luke Ayling eventually threw long into the centre of the pitch to Matty Klich. Klich turned nearly full circle to allow him to pass it out to the Leeds left where Jack Harrison collected. He looked up, saw the run into the box from Patrick Bamford and clipped the ball over towards the Leeds striker. For me, there was no way Bamford was reaching the ball which was just too far ahead and above him, but Joe Bryan was the wrong side of his man and he obviously thought Bamford might get the header in. To make absolutely sure he didn't, Bryan put his right hand out and gave Bamford a little push. Once again, it was probably not enough of a push to send our man to the floor, but Bamford went down heavily as is now obligatory and was soon appealing. Once again Taylor pointed to the spot and once again a quick VAR check saw nothing wrong with Taylor's assessment. Matty Klich took the kick and casually waited to see Areola dive to the left as he placed the ball pretty much down the middle. I'm tempted to say Klich made a right t*t out of areola… but that's a pun too far even for me! It was all a bit too casual for my liking by Klich but it did the trick; 2 - 1 to Leeds and that was the halftime score.

Five minutes of the second half passed with little of note to report and then, suddenly, the game burst into life again. We were into the 50th minute as a long Fulham clearance was taken down on his chest by Liam Cooper. He prodded the ball forward to Mateusz Klich who did that 360 degree turn again as he waited to spot an opening or a run. It was Patrick Bamford who obliged again, dashing through the red-shirted Fulham defence and Klich's pass was perfect. Paddy took the ball on his left foot in the inside left channel and then stroked it neatly past Areola from 15 yards with his right. It was a sumptuous finish from a player who was really starting to look the part; maybe the lack of a crowd was helping a man who always seemed lacking in confidence in front of goal or maybe it was the arrival of real competition for his place in the shape of Spanish international Rodrigo Moreno. Whatever it was, I was starting to appreciate this new Paddy Bamford. I was appreciating him even more just seven minutes later as Leeds raced into a seemingly unassailable 4 – 1 lead.

Meslier clipped another inch-perfect clearance out to the Leeds left wing where Jack Harrison somehow got up to skim a header on to Bamford who was a few yards further up that touchline and midway in the Fulham half. Bamford performed a quick step over and then knocked the ball ahead and effectively started a twenty-yard sprint race with Denis Odoi. Incredibly, Paddy won, and was soon just six yards from the byline and outside the left edge of the area with Odoi blowing through his backside and two yards behind. Paddy had a quick look across the box, spotted the late run from Costa, and Helder met it perfectly on his favoured left foot to crash it into the top left corner from 12 yards. Wow! I could hardly believe it; Patrick Bamford racing down the wing and providing an assist for Costa; who wrote this script? Well, I suppose I should at that point have just reminded myself that 'we are Leeds' and we don't do comfortable...

The goals were now coming every five minutes or so and, in fact, this was a bit of a thing in the EPL so far this season; defences seemed to still be on their hols while the attacking players were all on fire! We were still only in the 62nd minute as Liam Cooper cleared his lines from deep in his own left-back area. The ball just flicked off the boot of Patrick Bamford and instead fell at the feet . of Fulham's Michael Hector who prodded it forward to the dangerous-looking and long-named André-Frank Zambo Anguissa, the Cameroon international midfielder. He looked well marked by Kalvin Phillips but somehow wriggled free and Phillips decided, wrongly as it happens, not to do the old fashioned professional foul, not to take one for the team. Anguissa was thus free and able to slide the ball through into the path of Bobby Cordova-Reid who'd got goal-side of Stuart Dallas. The whole move had been a catalogue of errors of judgement and positional mistakes by Leeds and Reid took full advantage by driving a low right foot shot across Meslier and into the far corner. 4 – 2 suddenly looked a lot less secure than 4 – 1 but it soon became even worse; another five minutes passed and then we saw the seventh goal of the game.

Leeds had started to get caught in possession or give the ball away cheaply far too often, almost uncharacteristically really and I wondered if that was down to not having the easy option of a pass to Pablo Hernandez available. When he's on the pitch he seems always to find space but today we'd often struggled to do that. Rodrigo had tried to play the role first half and was then substituted at the break by Tyler Roberts but, truth be told, neither is a Pablo. Now it was Helder Costa out on the Leeds right wing getting robbed of the ball and a quick Fulham ball forward saw a shot from Mitrovic well blocked by a combination of Koch and Dallas. The ball ricocheted away to the Fulham right wing and came out to Kenny Tete who used his head and whipped the ball in first time. Mitrovic was then head and shoulders above a flaky Liam Cooper to thump a towering header past Meslier and the lead was down to one. It was another dire goal to concede and letting in a header inside the box is another age-old problem we'd suffered with for years. To be fair, until that moment we'd dealt with Mitrovic pretty well, usually with Robin Koch taking care of him; he was just too clever and powerful for Coops though.

The inevitable thought going through my head was that, once again, good as we'd been throughout the game, you don't get anything in this league for looking pretty. Had Leeds conceded again and dropped a point or, God forbid, conceded twice more and dropped all three, it would have surely knocked our confidence for six. All the positivity built up at Anfield would have disappeared quicker than our crowdies and probably just as permanently. There were more moments of danger for Leeds in the final twenty minutes and Kebano, a second-half sub for the Londoners, even smacked a low shot against the post, but this time Leeds survived and, for the second week running, we finished 4 − 3 but this time on the right end of the score-line.

Bielsa made a strange Alioski for Bamford substitution in the 70th minute to help protect the now slender lead and afterwards he was clearly concerned about some aspects of our play. In his post-match interview for Match Of The Day, again conducted through new interpreter Andres Clavijo, he hit upon the main feature we'd seen both at Anfield and in this one at Elland Road. In the past under Bielsa we'd usually created many chances but not put enough of them away, but now it was the complete opposite; our finishing had been absolutely clinical. Bielsa recognised this but warned: *"This won't be a constant all year. It is very difficult to maintain the efficiency [in front of goal] we have had in these first two games. The characteristic of our game is to create goal-scoring opportunities. In these two games we have created very little but we have scored all our chances."* Regarding the defensive lapses, Bielsa also admitted: *"We are worried"* which was akin to Queen Victoria telling us she was: *"not amused!"*

The main thing though was we were up and running with three points on the board and, most of the time, we'd shown, as we did the previous week, that we were not out of our depth at the new level. Indeed, if we could get the defence operating more as it did last season, then the immediate future looked very bright.

The final two games this September Saturday saw Man United lose 1 − 3 at home to Crystal Palace and Arsenal win their second game, 2 - 1 against West Ham who'd now lost twice. Palace were inspired by Wilf Zaha who boosted my Fantasy League points with another couple of goals but West Ham could count themselves unlucky not to get a point.

On Sunday the games continued, starting with another strange one at St Mary's where Southampton dominated against Spurs, took the lead, and then collapsed in the second half to lose 2 – 5 with four goals from Son Heung-Min; all four following Harry Kane assists. With Kane getting the 5th Spurs goal as well, he also boosted my Fantasy League standings. The goals continued to rain in as Brighton then walloped Newcastle 0 – 3 at St James'. I didn't really watch either of those games as I was writing up this chapter but I did then settle down to enjoy Chelsea v Liverpool; the first clash this season of two of the so-called big six. It was a tight game until just before halftime when Chelsea had Andreas Christensen sent off. Playing Liverpool with 11 is hard enough, with ten it's nigh on impossible and Liverpool went on to win 0 – 2, although Chelsea's luck was clearly out as they also had a penalty saved. The final Sunday game saw an injury ravaged Burnley lose 4 – 2 to Leicester. Monday evening brought the final two games of week 2; Villa played Sheffield United in a repeat of their controversial 'Hawk-Eye' game and Wolves hosted Manchester City. Villa scraped past the ten men of the Blades after centre-back John Egan was sent off rather harshly in the 12th minute. It was a bad day all round for the sorry Blades who also had a penalty saved and lost 1 – 0. City were cruising 0 – 2 until Wolves grabbed a late life-line but then City scored again at the end to win it 1 – 3. Leeds ended the week 10th in the table, exactly halfway up, or halfway down, depending on whether you're a glass half full or half empty sort of a person. All things considered, it was a case of so far so good. That John Egan red card was a help too; our next game was a trip to Bramall Lane.

Perhaps the funniest football story of the weekend occurred in Wakefield during the semi-pro game between Carlton Athletic and Ilkley Town in the West Yorkshire League. The game was halted for 20 minutes when an Alpaca escaped from a nearby farm and invaded the pitch. One spectator said he was used to seeing the odd donkey turn out for Carlton but never before had he seen an alpaca!

Leeds United 4 Fulham 3 (**Costa 5, 57,** Mitrovic 34 pen, 67, **Klich 41 pen, Bamford 50,** De Cordova-Reid 62)
BCD. Round 2 League Pos: 10th.

Bamford Blunts Blades!

L eeds continued to dabble in the market this week with one outgoing and one incoming player. Out went Jordan Stevens; he joined League One Swindon Town on loan. Then the news broke, courtesy of a tweet from Spanish club Real Sociedad, that a deal had been agreed *"in principle"* for their central defender Diego Llorente to join Leeds. The 27-year-old made his international debut for Spain in 2016 and had five caps to his name, while last season he clocked up 30 appearances for Real who finished 6th in La Liga. It would take another few days to be announced formally but, by Thursday 24th September, Llorente was a Leeds player with a four-year deal agreed and the number '14' shirt with his name on it.

Another name mentioned as a target was Michael Cuisance, a midfielder with Bayern Munich. It was seen as the one area of the pitch where Leeds were still light, particularly as Pablo was struggling to stay fit. This rumour had been doing the rounds for a while but it seemed to die this week with reports that Bayern had now decided he was not for sale. The respected German magazine *Sport Bild* reported that with Thiago Alcantara having gone to Liverpool and Javi Martinez pondering a move as well, they didn't want to further dilute their midfield resources.[1]

The chances of seeing Leeds live any time soon evaporated this week as Boris Johnson announced new measures to try to stem the surge in Covid cases that was now seeing more than 5,000 positive tests recorded every day; almost back to the level we saw in the first wave. The 'Rule of Six' limited virtually all social gatherings to just half a dozen people inside or outdoors, while pubs, clubs, restaurants and casinos would soon be closing every night at 10 pm. Just weeks after a government campaign to get folk back to work, the plea was now once more for as many as possible to work from home. The likelihood of a return to normal this side of Christmas was seen to be about as likely as an appearance by Adam Forshaw. All the test events to trial how crowds could return safely were paused again and the hoped for October 1st return was binned.

I was still getting my regular fix of live football though and this week Worcester City entertained Stafford Rangers in an FA Cup tie. It was the same MO as before; A maximum of 300 tickets sold online, a temperature check at the gate and social distance as best you could around the perimeter fence. It proved to be a bad night all round; I was reminded of the creature comforts we're used to at the big grounds… like a roof over your head. It poured with rain for much of the game and there was no cover whatsoever. Add to that the fact that City lost 2 – 3, albeit to a side a couple of leagues higher up the football pyramid, and my night was complete. The only good thing was I bumped into Gary M, another lad blessed with the good fortune of supporting both Worcester and Leeds. We consoled each other that at least we were getting to see some live footy and, despite the result, it was a cracking game that was in the balance until the final whistle. As I drove back up the M5 I wondered if I'd be seeing any more FA Cup games live this season; would we be back inside Elland Road by January when the 3rd round rolled up? We could but hope.

---

[1]   https://www.bavarianfootballworks.com/2020/9/24/21454309/bayern-munich-michael-cuisance-leeds-united-olympique-marseille-thiago-alcantara-javi-martinez

We lost another former player this week; Peter Hampton died suddenly aged just 66. Peter had the misfortune to be at Leeds as a left-back in the early 70s when we also had Terry Cooper, Trevor Cherry and Frank Gray, so his opportunities were limited. He did have a run of games in the 76/77 season though, so I saw quite a bit of him as I was at most of our home games that season, travelling across from my digs in Manchester by train every other week. It was the season I managed to collect enough programme tokens to get tickets for the FA Cup run, including the quarter-final at Wolves and the semi at Hillsborough against them from over the hills. Hampton played in all five of the FA Cup ties and even scored in the 3rd round game against Norwich which we won 5 – 2. It was one of only three goals he scored for Leeds in over 80 appearances spanning eight seasons.

We were back in the routine now; press conference every Thursday or Friday and then a game at the weekend. This week it was a Sunday noon kick-off for Leeds at Bramall Lane. Bielsa reported that we wouldn't be seeing Pablo Hernandez for another couple of weeks but other than that everyone was fit… apart from Adam Forshaw obviously; his recuperation had been stalled following yet another *"setback"*. Bielsa confirmed that either Tyler Roberts or Rodrigo Moreno would play in place of Pablo. We also learned that Alfie McCalmont had been shipped out on a season-long loan to Oldham Athletic as the club continued to try to get the players on the fringes of the first-team squad some much needed competitive game time. That one gave Leeds fans a bit of mental anguish; Harry Kewell was the manager at Boundary Park and most still wanted him to fail miserably as punishment for accepting a transfer to Galatasaray in Turkey after his spell at Anfield, but everyone wanted young McCalmont to do well.

Before Leeds would play there was a now regular schedule of four games on Saturday; each timed to kick-off one after the other so that fans could, in theory, watch them all. For the first time this season I wasn't going to see any of these as I was building a shed and laying turf at my son's place but we were getting regular score updates throughout the day. There was plenty of controversy too, starting with a 2 – 3 Manchester United win at Brighton that was achieved through a penalty scored in the 10th minute of added time at the end of the game. The final whistle had been blown, but VAR was still studying a possible handball which was eventually given as a Man United penalty which Bruno Fernandes converted. The game had another penalty and Brighton, incredibly, hit the woodwork five times which was apparently a new EPL record. The handball was one of many controversial penalties given as players and officials all started to adjust to the new handball guidance. Effectively the rule had been changed so that now, if the ball hit the arm outside of the natural silhouette of the player and below the armpit, then a penalty would be awarded regardless of intent. This rule had been in place throughout Europe last season and had almost doubled the number of handball penalties awarded. This was also now evident in the EPL with 20 awarded in the first 26 games. We had a pandemic going on in the world and a *'pendemic'* going on in the game! The new handball rule was causing many big names to complain, including Roy Hodgson who declared on Match Of The Day: *"It's killing the game"*. It was also interesting that only two penalties had been saved; largely due to VAR ensuring the keepers' feet remained on the goal line until the ball was struck. That seemed way too much of an advantage to the penalty taker to me, especially when many of the penalties were awarded for players blatantly simulating fouls in the first place!

In the other games on Saturday, Hodgson's Palace lost at home to Everton 1 – 2, with another of the controversial handball penalties, while Chelsea came back from three down to draw 3 – 3 at the Hawthorns, a game conspicuous by the lack of a penalty. However, this time Slaven Bilic was adamant there *was* a handball in the lead up to the 93rd minute Chelsea equaliser. For me, there were two issues; yes the handball rule was a farce but, equally, far too many penalties were being won by attacking players diving to the turf at the slightest of touches. Yes, I was still sore over the Koch and Rodrigo penalties at Anfield. The final game, on Saturday night, was a 0 – 1 victory for Southampton at Burnley.

Perhaps the strangest football story of the day though concerned the visit of Oxford United to Accrington Stanley. Jeff Stelling reported on Sky that an alcohol-based disinfectant had been used to cleanse the Oxford team coach as part of their Covid precautions. Unfortunately, the spray got into the breathalyser system used by the driver and that closed down the coach systems as soon as he blew into it as part of his routine checks! If triggered, the system automatically shuts down for six hours during which the coach can't be started. This meant the team and staff were stranded at their hotel, still half an hour from Accrington. Eventually they managed to ferry everyone to the ground in a fleet of cars and taxis and, when the results came through later, it didn't appear to have done Oxford any harm: they still won the game 1 – 4.

The game against the Blades was being shown on BT Sport which is always a pain for me because I don't subscribe to BT. I do though have a couple of logins courtesy of Cambridge Rob and my son Adam that I can use to watch games on the laptop. I'd noticed that the picture was a lot more stable just using the laptop rather than hooking it up to the TV via the HDMI lead, so that was the MO for today. These Covid enforced TV marathons had made us all a lot more tech-savvy!

Meslier

Ayling Koch Cooper (Capt)

Phillips Dallas

Costa (Poveda 66) Roberts (Rodrigo45, Alioski 90+1) Klich

Harrison

Bamford

Subs: Caprile, Struijk, Davis, Shackleton, Poveda, Rodrigo, Alioski.

Sheffield United: Ramsdale, Basham, Ampadu, Robinson, Baldock, Lundstram (Norwood 64), Berge, Osborn, Stevens, McGoldrick (McBurnie 74), Burk (Sharp 74). Subs not used: Foderingham, Fleck, Lowe, Jagielka.

Referee: Paul Tierney.

I was in place on the sofa just in time to see the line-ups and the Leeds formation was not shown as I've just posted it here. BT had it down as a normal 4 – 1 – 4 – 1 which is what everyone assumed it would be but we'd all forgotten that Sheffield United play with two strikers; McGoldrick and Burke in this case. Everyone knows that when the opposition play two up top, Bielsa plays a central three at the back with wingbacks doing the wide defensive duties. Almost as soon as the Blades kicked off, it was clear this was the case but unusually, this time, Stuart Dallas had been allocated a sort of roving midfield role; he was absolutely everywhere!

This would prove to be a good contest and for a long time it looked like my nil-nil prediction would prove correct. It wasn't that either team lacked any attacking intent, it was just that both goalkeepers were in the form of their lives. The first half was a story of near misses and fine saves. Leeds' first sight of goal came courtesy of a wicked shot from Luke Ayling that Aaron Ramsdale pushed round the post. Next, a Kalvin Phillips free-kick found the head of Patrick Bamford but that one went over the top. It would be a feature of the game that Bamford was unusually successful in the air all day long and after the game he confessed it was a tactic for him to try to get between the inexperienced centre-back trio the Blades had been forced to employ following the suspension of John Egan and an injury to Jack O'Connell. Back came the Blades though and just before the half-hour mark Luke Ayling gave the ball away on halfway, having slalomed his way there from deep in his own half. In a flash it was taken down the Sheffield left wing and was then driven low across the Leeds box and, as McGoldrick stepped over it, I'm sure Leeds fans all over the country said a little prayer. There was John Lundstram, arriving perfectly, a yard to the right of the penalty spot with only Meslier to beat. Lundstram caught it perfectly on his right instep and directed it, textbook fashion, towards the inside of the left post. Then, incredibly, we saw the ball tipped around that post for a corner. Replays showed Meslier starting to move to his left and then throwing himself full length to his right to get a big strong right hand on it. Remember that Gordon Banks save against Pele all those years ago? Well, this was as good, possibly better as the ball was travelling so quickly. That was one big save each.

A couple of minutes later and Bamford was there in the middle again with another header, this time from a Jack Harrison left-wing cross; again the header went a foot too high but Bamford was clearly in the mood and, dare I say it, looking most un-Bamford like! As the first half began to ebb away it was mainly Leeds making the chances and next it was the Irish Rover, Stuart Dallas in the ever so slightly Irish-looking blue and green away strip who weaved his way into the box to toe-poke a shot that was heading for the top left corner. Ramsdale pulled out another top drawer save to tip that one around the post. Not to be outdone, Meslier was straight back in the action as George Baldock got away far too easily from Harrison. This time the young Leeds stopper had to acrobatically turn away a pile-driver from Baldock that was otherwise destined for our top right corner. Halftime, nil-nil, but not your average nil-nil sort of a game.

The one Leeds player not really 'on it' was Tyler Roberts. We know he's no Pablo but we really did need him to get more involved than he was. It was no surprise to see that Bielsa pulled him off at the break (no, I'm not doing that joke again!) and we had another chance to see how Rodrigo was developing under Bielsa. It didn't immediately change the MO of the game mind you. Straight from the restart Leeds won a left wing corner and when McGoldrick headed it clear it looped out onto the left boot of Helder Costa. He caught it perfectly on the full but, would you believe it, that man Ramsdale was diving away to his left to turn that one round the post yet again. Both keepers looked unbeatable and I wondered again if that nil-nil prediction would be on the money. Patrick Bamford was doing all he could to try to prevent that and next he drove into the box before letting fly from the right corner of the six-yard area; again Ramsdale was in the way. Our shooting accuracy was pretty good and a high percentage of our attempts were at least finding the target; something Bielsa warned might not be the case all the time, as we saw last season. Just around the hour mark we saw what he meant.

Luke Ayling played a speculative long ball down the inside right channel and two Blades defenders got it all wrong as they tried to intercept it. The first swung a boot and missed and then, as the ball ran on towards the area, the Irish Rover was there again on the blind side of the second defender. He nipped in to claim the ball between the keeper and defender and then even rounded Ramsdale. Sadly it then went all Pete Tong as Stuey badly scuffed his shot towards the unprotected net which allowed the retreating Chris Basham to hook it away. Dallas should have put that one away and it would go down as a big chance missed.

On the 66 minute mark Bielsa twisted again, this time giving an EPL debut to Ian Poveda who replaced Helder Costa who had just started to fade. Within minutes Poveda was showing his enthusiasm as he sprinted the length of the pitch along with the imposter that was wearing Patrick Bamford's number '9' shirt. Both men travelled at speeds hitherto unseen from either with Bamford pulling defenders with him to the right as Poveda cut-in onto his left foot to strike at goal where, predictably, Ramsdale was there leaping to the rescue again. I have to admit I was pretty nervous as the game moved into the final ten minutes; mentally I'd settled for that nil-nil draw and I knew it would be a devastating blow of typically Leeds United proportions if we were to concede a goal now, having probably just about deserved to win. It didn't really cross my mind that maybe we'd snatch a goal of our own this late on; it's not what Leeds do is it? Well, perhaps that's true of Leeds United BB – Before Bielsa – but not anymore. It was only just under two years earlier of course when we snatched a late winner at Bramall Lane on our previous visit, then a crucial Championship game. That came from a late cock-up from the then Blades on-loan keeper, Dean Henderson, chasing a mishit John Egan back pass and then giving it straight to Jack Clarke, remember him? Clarke clipped the ball inside and Pablo finished with aplomb. No, I didn't even consider we might win this...

The team clearly did though and, with only two minutes of normal time left, we were pushing forward as if it was the first minute; no thought here of defending the point. Suddenly Klich won a tussle on the left wing before moving inside. A sharp pass forward found Rodrigo looking all Pabloesque on the edge of the Blades' area and eager to make an impact. He fought for the ball and then pushed it back out to the left wing to Jackie Harrison. Harrison knew instinctively what to do, Bamford would tell us after the game that he'd told Jack to keep firing the ball in towards those centre-backs and he'd try to get in between them. So, no need to even look up for Jack, he stopped the ball with one touch and curled it over into the middle with a second. There was Patrick Bamford, the new, super-efficient, fast-as-lightning Patrick Bamford, rising between two defenders. He admitted later that the ball struck him on the nose not the forehead but it was directed perfectly back across the keeper and nestled delightfully inside the left post. As Max Boyce once said in a slightly different context; *"It landed like linen"* softly caressing the net and then the turf in the corner. If Paddy continues to score as regularly as this and if he continues to bang them in with his nose we'll have to rename him 'Sniffer'... The cameras cut to show the Leeds bench and there was an animated Marcelo Bielsa, both fists clenched in a rare show of jubilation. It was a good moment and I'm sure all Leeds fans, like me, started to think... I wonder, I wonder what we are really capable of this season?

That's the way it ended and, as the cameras panned around the pitch at the final whistle, players of both sides collapsed onto their backsides on the turf; they'd all given their everything in a close game that was dominated by the keepers, although the stats showed that Leeds bossed the possession to the tune of 64%. We also outshot the home side by 17 (my favourite number) to 14 but with Leeds getting an impressive nine on target, albeit most palmed away by Ramsdale. Sheffield hit the target just four times, bringing out the best in my Man of the Match, Illan Meslier. For a fiercely fought Yorkshire derby it was also amazing that Leeds conceded only four free-kicks for foul play during the whole game compared with 18 by the Blades. It was a disciplined, efficient performance from Leeds and defensively we looked, for the first time this season, a solid, well-balanced unit. The three at the back worked well and the freedom it allowed the Irish Rover meant he ran Meslier a close second for my Man of the Match title.

In the remaining three games played this Sunday, Spurs had to settle for a 1 – 1 draw with Newcastle, Man City surprisingly lost 2 – 5 at home to Leicester, and West Ham finally got points on the board with a 4 – 0 walloping of Wolves. The Newcastle equaliser was another controversial penalty, in the 97th minute; Andy Carroll heading the ball against the upraised arm of Eric Dier from point-blank range. In the Man City game we had no less than three penalties, all for Leicester and all resulting from Leicester players getting behind their City markers and then falling to ground when they felt the slightest of touches. Anywhere else on the pitch and I don't think any of them would have even been given as fouls but Michael Oliver gave them all and VAR backed him every time. City actually bossed the game with 72% of the possession and more than twice the number of goal attempts and, while many Leeds fans only saw the result and immediately announced City were there for the taking when they arrived at Elland Road in a week's time, I was less convinced. I couldn't see Mike 'Deadly' Dean awarding Leeds one dubious penalty, let alone three!

Sheffield United 0 **Leeds United 1 (Bamford 88)**
BCD. **Round 3 League Pos: 7th**.

Citeh

The final two EPL games of week 3 saw Villa thrash Fulham at Craven Cottage (0 - 3) and Liverpool ease past Arsenal (3 - 1) to join Everton and Leicester at the top of the table as the three sides still with a 100% record after three games. Thankfully there was no more controversy and no more penalties, although the pundits and statisticians had already predicted that we were on for an all-time record number of penalties this season.

On Planet Leeds, the Under 23s were in action again and, at the third time of asking, they recorded their first win in PL2 (Div. 2) with an impressive looking 1 – 3 rout of Sunderland. All three goals came from recent signing Sam Greenwood, including one spectacular free-kick; something he would soon be making a habit of. Arsenal fans seeing this immediately took to Twitter to vent their anger at the fact the Gunners had let go of a young player they all felt had a bright future. One tweeted: *"Still blows me away that we thought it was a good idea to let him go".*

Saturday had been a pretty good day for three Leeds players who'd all been loaned out recently. Jordan Stevens scored just seven minutes into his debut for Swindon Town, only days after moving to the Robins and his effort, one of four Swindon goals in a 4 – 2 win over Burton in League One, was immediately entered into the Town poll for goal of the month. Once Leeds fans spotted the Twitter poll online there was no doubt who was going to win it! Alfie McCalmont also got straight into action for his new side, playing the full 90 minutes for Oldham against Crawley Town in League Two but he was on the losing side as the Latics went down 2 – 3. Finally, Ryan Edmondson was back fit and had returned to Aberdeen, having somehow been fixed up by the Leeds medics in double-quick time. He saw action as a late substitute for the Dons as they won 0 – 3 at Ross County. We'd now be on the lookout for news of the latest Leeds man to go out on loan; Bryce Hosannah had joined League Two Bradford City.

There was only one more round of EPL games before the next international break and, for Leeds, it was the visit of Manchester City, a 5:30 pm kick-off on Saturday, 3rd October. We would then have two weeks off before we hosted Wolves. The first call-ups were already being announced for a busy period of international games and the first Leeds man involved was Liam Cooper. He was included in the Scotland squad ahead of three games they were due to play, against Israel, Slovakia, and the Czech Republic. Kalvin Phillips was named in the England squad again and our two new Spaniards, Llorente and Rodrigo were both named in the Spanish squad. Indeed, there were very few Leeds first-teamers not going on international duty at one level or another.

All international players were going to start to feel the pressure as the domestic games were still coming thick and fast; this week saw the Carabao Cup in action again as they got back into synch with the normal timescale despite having started a month later than usual. The last sixteen teams were all whittled down to the quarter-finalists this week with Spurs, Brentford, Newcastle, Man City, Man United, Everton, Stoke City and Arsenal all winning through. That was the EFL Cup done with now until three days before Christmas.

In the Bielsa press conference this week the great man confirmed that Jack Harrison was not permitted to play against his parent club

Man City, on Saturday; Gjanni Alioski was set to fill in, he told the once again remotely based journalists. Pablo Hernandez would also continue to be missing through injury. Bielsa wouldn't comment on the supposedly imminent arrival of Michael Cuisance who'd allegedly flown to Leeds for a medical earlier in the week. The big turnaround from that suggestion in *Sport Bild* that Bayern wouldn't part with their prized midfielder seemed to have come out of the blue and it had since been widely reported that Leeds had beaten off interest from both Newcastle and Marseilles to agree an £18m deal with a buy-back clause to allow the German club to repurchase Cuisance at some point in the future. Bielsa would only comment: *"I would prefer to talk about him when he is officially our player, I don't want to repeat the episode with Dan James."*

Just hours later those words seemed more than prophetic as BBC Radio broadcaster Adam Pope tweeted: *"The Cuisance deal is not happening. The search for another midfielder continues. #lufc"*. It did indeed have all the hallmarks of the infamous collapse of the Dan James deal last year. Incidentally, there had been rumours that Leeds had enquired about James' availability again this Summer but, although Man U were not averse to letting him go, James had decided he wanted to stay put and fight for his place with the Reds. It did suggest though that Leeds were still trying to recruit both a midfielder and a winger before the current window closed next week. The official word was that a problem occurred with the results of the medical Cuisance undertook but, not wanting a few facts to spoil a good line, I'll leave the final word on the Cuisance fiasco to my mate Kev of the @LeedsUnited_Mad website. He tweeted: *"Just like 1975. Bayern absolutely taking the 'Michael' yet again! #lufc"* It couldn't have been an immediate problem for the young midfielder though as, within hours, it was announced he *had* been snapped up by Marseille after all, on a one-year loan deal.

It wasn't only the senior Leeds players now getting international call-ups; when the England U19 squad was announced this week there were no less than three Leeds players named. Charlie Cresswell, Joe Gelhardt, and Sam Greenwood were all included in the squad for the upcoming double-header against Scotland. Greenwood celebrated his inclusion by scoring the winner in the next PL2 game; a 1 – 0 victory over Middlesbrough that saw Jack

Harrison get a rare U23 run-out due to him not being eligible to face Citeh.

The EPL games for round 4 were all shoehorned into two days to clear the way for the internationals; on Saturday there were four, including the Leeds v Man City match and then the remaining six were scheduled throughout Sunday afternoon and evening. As was now my regular weekend MO, I was sat on the sofa in our front room, laptop primed and TV on standby, ready for the first game, a 12:30 pm kick-off between Chelsea and Crystal Palace being shown on BT Sport. Chelsea blitzed the Palace 4 – 0 with four second-half goals, including two more penalties which, though soft, were the sort now regularly given in the EPL. Before the start and before the teams took the knee as was still occurring at almost all TV games, there was also a minute's silence in honour of Sgt Matiu Ratana, 54, a Police Officer from Goring, near Worthing who died after being shot in the chest at Croydon Custody Centre in the early hours of Friday, September 25th.

The second game of the day was also on BT and so I watched on the laptop again as another goal-fest unfolded, this time a 4 – 2 win for Everton against Brighton. Surprisingly, not a penalty was to be seen in this one and Everton, with Dominic Calvert-Lewin grabbing his 6th league goal of the season already, went top of the table with a 100%, 12-point record. Finally it was our turn, a 5:30 pm kick-off live on Sky against the 'Cityzens'.

The build-up to this game was all about Bielsa and Guardiola; master craftsman and apprentice, messiah and disciple. The two had long been part of a mutual appreciation society, with Pep often saying Bielsa was the best coach in world football and Bielsa once saying *"You can't copy the beauty of Guardiola's teams."*[1] They'd come up against each other three times in the past, all when Bielsa was with Athletic Club Bilbao and Pep was manager at Barcelona in the 2011/12 La Liga season. The score so far was 2 – 0 to Pep with one game drawn. Pep came out on top when the two teams met in the Copa del Rey final and in the La Liga game at the Camp Nou but, in their first-ever meeting, in the La Liga game at the old

---

[1]   *https://totalfootballanalysis.com/article/bielsa-vs-guardiola-athletic-club-vs-barcelona-from-201112*

San Mamés Stadium in Bilbao, they drew 2 – 2 in a thrilling game played out in appalling heavy rain with a certain Lionel Messi grabbing the equaliser for Barca in the last minute. The forecast for our game this weekend was also for heavy rain as the first big named storm of the 20/21 winter, storm Alex, was expected to drop a month's worth of rain on parts of France and the north of England in just a few days.

After the usual interminable pre-match studio discussions analysing every possible angle of the game during which the general consensus amongst the pundits – Jamie Redknapp and Micah Richards – was that a high scoring draw was the most likely outcome finally, host Kelly Cates, formally Kelly Dalglish, daughter of Sir Kenny, handed over to the commentators Martin Tyler and Gary Neville.

Meslier
Ayling Koch Cooper (Capt) Dallas
Phillips
Costa Roberts (Rodrigo 56) Klich (Davis 77) Alioski
(Poveda 45)
Bamford

Subs: Caprile, Davis, Llorente, Struijk, Shackleton, Poveda, Rodrigo.

Manchester City: Ederson, Walker, Rúben Dias, Laporte, Mendy (Aké 71), De Bruyne, Rodri, Foden, Torres (Bernardo Silva 65), Mahrez (Fernandinho 77), Sterling. Subs not used: Steffen, Stones, Delap, Palmer.

Referee: Mike Dean.

There had been a scare ahead of kick-off that Liam Cooper had failed a fitness test, a rumour that spread across Twitter like wildfire apparently because 'Coops' was spotted during the warm-up still wearing a heavy coat! Twitter can be a dangerous place once a rumour starts because there are too many folk eager to pounce on it and proclaim it as a fact that they had uncovered; trying to persuade us they are 'ITK' – In The Know. They aren't of course, they're just trying to grab followers. In the event, a lot of them had egg on their keyboards and there was a mad scramble to delete tweets before the ITK brigade were called out! Coops was fit and the Leeds team was exactly as we all guessed it would be: unchanged from Bramall Lane apart from the ineligible Jackie

Harrison being replaced by Alioski, just as Bielsa had suggested would be the case. Sky gambled on the formation being the same as at Bramall Lane and had us set up in a 3 - 2 - 4 - 1 formation on the screen, but it soon became apparent we were actually back to Bielsa's usual 4 – 1 – 4 – 1 set up and City lined up in 4 – 3 – 3 manner, so it was exactly as those three previous Bielsa-Guardiola encounters had played out. City had their new signing straight in at centre-back; Rúben Dias alone had cost City a rumoured £65m whereas Leeds had so far brought in around ten first-team and U23 players for around £84m.

One thing we did learn from Martin Tyler though was that referees had now been instructed to modify their interpretation of the handball guidance yet again. There had been such an outpouring of complaints from senior figures in the game that the FA had now told the referees not to give handball where it was considered a defender had no way to avoid the ball hitting the arm or hand as with some of the point-blank examples we'd seen so far. Some sense at last prevailing with that call although we wouldn't get our point back stolen from us at Anfield over the Koch 'handball'.

The rain lashed down as the game started but out on the pitch it was a whirlwind that Leeds were struggling against as City tore into us seemingly determined that their 2 – 5 defeat to Leicester a week earlier would not be repeated. There were only three minutes on the clock as Kevin De Bruyne lined up a free-kick about 30 yards from goal after Raheem Sterling had performed a pretty good 'Ayling Flop' under the slightest of pressure from Ayling himself. In hindsight it was obvious what De Bruyne was thinking as he moved further and further to his left while watching Illan Meslier move slightly towards the right post as the City man waited to take the kick. Sure enough the City '17' swept the ball towards the now gaping hole we could see to the left of Meslier and Leeds were only saved by the thickness of that post as the ball cannoned against it and away to safety. It was a sign of how Leeds would have to be mentally aware as well as physically adept if we were to get something from this game and a good early lesson for Meslier.

Leeds hardly had a sniff of the ball for the first ten minutes as City racked up four corners as well as that free-kick, but a header from the fourth of those corners that went wide and a couple of blocked shots were the only other dangerous moments. Patrick Bamford then blotted his otherwise immaculate early-season copybook as he stupidly flailed an arm in the face of Laporte on a rare visit into City territory. Laporte went down like the proverbial sack of spuds as is the modern way and Mike Dean was soon scribbling the moniker of Lord Bamford on his yellow card.

It was 13 minutes before Leeds had a first sight of goal and that came when a first time Luke Ayling cross was met firmly by the head of little Alioski but the ball flew a yard over the bar. I settled back in my seat a little more comfortably at that point and had another sip of Red Stripe as I thought we'd weathered the early storm. Not so; I should have been aware that we were approaching the 17th minute...

Raheem Sterling was enjoying his battles with Luke Ayling and had already seen the Leeds man on his backside a few times before he popped up again in that 17th minute. Meslier had cleared the ball down the middle but only to Mendy who immediately ran with it before trying to slot it through the centre of the Leeds defence. Liam Cooper blocked it but didn't get it very far and Phil Foden collected and knocked it wide to Sterling on the left. He easily came inside the stumbling Ayling, then Cooper, and then fired the ball low inside the right post past an ungainly effort by Phillips who'd turned his back on the ball. It was City's 8th attempt at goal and their second on target. Little did we know at the time that they wouldn't hit the target again all evening!

Sure they had more chances – a header from a corner flashed wide and another Sterling shot skidded past a post – but nothing that troubled Meslier, while Leeds, slowly but surely grew into the game. All the while Bielsa marched back and forth in the technical area, almost in time with the Vitality sausage dog we could see running along the electronic perimeter advertising boards presumably looking for Jessica Ennis-Hill. Then he'd crouch on his haunches (Bielsa that is, not the dog) and you could almost hear his brain whirring as he contemplated his next move. Leeds were slowly balancing up the possession stats now and even the bookings were levelled when Mendy tripped Costa needlessly but perhaps in another sign of growing frustration as it was Pep Guardiola who was now the more animated coach on the side-lines. I was enjoying a second Red Stripe by now and sank further into the sofa before I sat up expectantly as Leeds burst into the City area. We'd played seven consecutive passes as we sought an outlet before Liam Cooper clipped his favourite diagonal ball to Matty Klich who soon escaped the clutches of Sterling to head for the edge of the City area. He then touched the ball to Bamford who quickly moved it further left to Roberts and then onto Dallas who was now behind the City back line. It was only a strong arm from Kyle Walker that shoved Dallas off the ball just as he aimed his shot, making the save easier for Ederson who pushed it away for a corner. It was Bielsaball at its finest, but had Dallas chosen to throw himself to the floor I'm pretty sure Deadly Dean would have had to give a penalty. It was no less soft than the three pens City gave away the previous week when Leicester were perhaps more cute than Dallas was here. Now the game came alive as City broke away at the other end and Phil Foden rasped another shot at the Leeds goal, again missing the target. The game looked more like that Liverpool epic now but without the accuracy of shooting we saw in that one and the task facing Leeds no longer seemed quite as onerous as it did at the start. A wide-angled shot of the empty stadium showed the many flags still adorning the South Stand, the Norman Hunter South Stand as it was now of course. There in the middle, slightly wonkily hung, was the Shropshire Whites' banner reminding me of many great trips to Leeds in the past. The rain was still pouring down and suddenly Luke Ayling was one-on-one with Ederson as Mendy failed to deal with a long ball. Ayling skipped round a desperate lunge from Laporte but his left foot shot was palmed away by the keeper. That was the last action of the first half.

For the second half, all that thinking Bielsa had been doing resulted in the arrival on the pitch of Ian Poveda; replacing Alioski who'd not really been much of a threat going forward. Now Poveda would try on the right wing with Helder Costa switching to the left. From the very start of the new half Poveda made an impression and, with only 39 seconds on the clock, he zipped past three defenders to hammer across a low ball that Dias just took off the toes of Patrick Bamford for a corner. Predictably nothing came of the corner and the cameras cut to the crouching figure of Bielsa again, deep in thought and seemingly studying the turf in the technical area as the rain continued to fall.

Leeds dominated the possession at the start of the new half and looked very comfortable without creating any significant chances, while City seemed happy to sit back and wait for any Leeds mistakes. As the half wore on the pace started to pick up, despite the pitch inevitably getting heavier with the constant watering it was getting from the heavens. Leeds made a second change in the 56th minute as Rodrigo replaced Roberts and his impact would prove both crucial and immediate. There was now a Rodrigo on the pitch for both sides of course.

A Leeds clearance was headed away by City midway in their own half, falling to Helder Costa in the inside left spot about ten yards inside the City half. Costa cleverly back-heeled it to Matty Klich who set off towards the City area before knocking it left again to Rodrigo, near the left corner of the box. The Spaniard looked to see what was on but, seeing nothing obvious in the middle, went on his own and, as Dias backed off and backed off, Rodrigo let fly with his left boot. The ball was destined for the top left corner before a combination of Ederson's big right hand and the angle of post and bar saw the shot deflect into the Kop for another Leeds corner. Kalvin Phillips swung the ball into the middle, Ederson flapped at it and it fell at the feet of Rodrigo who turned and scooped it into the net. Imagine the scenes had we all been there in the Kop; my seat is about fifteen yards from where Rodrigo turned and scored.

The game was now end-to-end, a corner for City at one end and then a Kalvin Phillips shot that Ederson saved at the other. Then a De Bruyne right-footer slid past the right post. On commentary Gary Neville told us *"It's a right scuffle now!"* as first one side attacked and then the other, the slick pitch making the ball skid along with added pace. Mahrez hit one high into the South Stand almost hitting that Shropshire Whites flag.

A Liam Cooper header from a left wing Phillips free-kick slammed against the post but that one was offside but Neville was now talking about Leeds *"ruffing up"* City. He was trying to explain why he'd played Rodrigo on the right wing when he was manager at Valencia, just as we saw the Spanish player twist a header towards the top right corner. Yet again a big hand from Ederson reached up and turned it over the bar. This was superb now from Leeds who had City on the proverbial ropes. Mendy just couldn't cope with Poveda and soon City pulled Mendy off and replaced him with Nathan Ake. Back came City and Meslier had to be clever to steal the ball off Sterling's toes when the City man got the run on Robin Koch; all three men ending up in a tangle in the Leeds area as if playing a wild drunken game of Twister.

The final change for Leeds came with 15 minutes left and it looked like an attempt by Bielsa to hang on to what he had; a point. Leif Davis was on for his EPL debut to replace the tired legs of Mateusz Klich. It was perhaps an understanding by Bielsa that Leeds had just about given their all. Certainly in the final ten minutes I began to get more and more nervous as Leeds appeared to run out of fuel. The final minutes were mostly spent with the ball in and around the Leeds final third and several times City hammered the ball in towards the Leeds goal but still without the accuracy they needed. There were several handball shouts and appeals for penalties as Leeds players threw themselves in the way of the ball, but thankfully Mike Dean waved them all away and VAR didn't take issue with his calls. It would have been a travesty had Leeds conceded in these final few seconds but that didn't mean it wouldn't transpire; we saw it happen at Anfield of course. We had to endure three added minutes as well but we got there safely despite almost losing Stuart Dallas to a red card as he launched himself through the back of Bernardo Silva; presumably Mike Dean gave him the benefit of the doubt in the atrocious conditions and only yellow was raised. The final act was a desperate diving header from Bamford in his own box forcing a decent save from his own keeper before Dean finally brought this pearl of a game to an end.

Marcelo Bielsa remained crouched, head down staring at the turf for several seconds before rising to his feet to hug Pep Guardiola, a moment caught on camera that perhaps reminded both men of a similar result in similar conditions in Bilbao all those years ago. This was lauded as an incredible game by all who saw it. Temporarily, Leeds were up to 5th in the table, but there were still seven more games to be played before this 4th round of games was complete.

In the final game this Saturday, Newcastle beat Burnley 3 – 1, including another penalty, although Burnley keeper Pope would have needed some mighty prayers answered to get away with his foul on Ryan Fraser.

On Sunday there were six more games, and, in the final two, some incredible scorelines. In the two lunchtime kick-offs, West Ham ruined Leicester's 100% record as they 'hammered' the Foxes 0 – 3, while at St Mary's the Saints bagged two goals to beat the Baggies. Then Arsenal just shaded their home game with Sheffield United 2 – 1 and Wolves beat Fulham 1 – 0. That meant Burnley, Sheffield United and Fulham all remained rooted to the bottom of the early table with 'nil points' said in a French accent. At the top, Everton were leading the way with their 100% record still intact and 12 points in the bag, but Liverpool would join them with the same record if they could win at Aston Villa which most pundits expected them to do. Villa had played a game less but were also sitting on a 100% record, albeit only the two games. Before that match though we had the clash between Manchester United and Spurs at Old Trafford.

Man United had scraped past Brighton in their previous game, on the South Coast, but had surprisingly lost their opening game at Old Trafford 1 – 3 to Crystal Palace. No one was prepared for what was about to take place. The game began with a penalty awarded inside 30 seconds as Davinson Sanchez barged Anthony Martial to the ground with Bruno Fernandes putting away the spot-kick with his familiar hop, skip and a jump technique. But then, within another seven minutes, Spurs had taken a 1 – 2 lead. The goals continued to flow as the Reds' defence was pulled to shreds and at halftime the London side was 1 – 4 to the good and Martial was off the pitch; sent off in the 28th minute for gently slapping Erik Lamela's face after the Spurs man did pretty much the same to him. That was unlucky and probably unfair but the Reds defending could not be defended. In the second half things went from bad to worse for the Red Devils and Spurs added two more to win the game 1 – 6 including yet another penalty. Wow, I watched that game in its entirety on Sky and could hardly believe what I was seeing. I then settled down to watch the final game before the international break brought a temporary halt to the season; Aston Villa v Liverpool.

If we thought the Manchester United game was bizarre then it was soon eclipsed with the goings-on at Villa Park and we all started to wonder what on earth was happening in the EPL this season. Villa were ahead in the 4th minute; a mistake by stand-in Liverpool keeper Adrian who misplaced a short pass straight to Jack Grealish.

Grealish poked the ball across the area and Ollie Watkins stabbed it into the empty net. All was then calm for twenty minutes or so and then Watkins burst down the left, cut inside and speared the ball into the top corner. We thought order was being restored when Mo Salah blasted home a loose ball for 2 – 1 but within six minutes John McGinn had restored the two goal lead and four minutes later Watkins grabbed his hat-trick with a header to put Villa 4 – 1 up at halftime. It was so similar to the previous game where Spurs had gone in 1 – 4 up at Old Trafford and these Reds were about as shocking in defence as the other ones!

The goals continued to flow after the break, with Ross Barkley scoring on his debut following his loan move from Chelsea; Mo Salah pulled one back (doing my Fantasy League team no harm at all) and then Villa added two more from Jack Grealish to end the game with a record-breaking 7 – 2 victory! Astonishing! It was almost as if the strange circumstances of this strangest of seasons was finally affecting the teams. Maybe the short pre-season due to the late finish to last season or the untimely international break or maybe playing in empty stadiums was finally all taking its toll. Who knows?

What we did know was that, as many players disappeared off to their respective nations' team hotels, it was Everton sat at the top of the table with four wins from four. Next came Villa with three from three and an incredible plus nine goal difference thanks to Liverpool's generous defence. Leicester, Arsenal and Liverpool also had nine points, albeit from four games, and then came four sides with seven points from four games including Leeds of course. It had been a fascinating first few weeks of the season and I couldn't wait for it to get started again in two weeks' time, once the international interlude was over. Oh, and the final word on the weird and wonderful events of this Sunday in the EPL goes to the wag who posted on Twitter: *"Well, at least Manchester United kept to the Covid-19 rules: they only let in six…"*

Leeds United 1 Manchester City 1 (Sterling 17, **Rodrigo 59**)
BCD. Round 4 League Pos: 8th.

Break

The 'Rule of Six' was still very much in play as there was no sign of the Covid-19 pandemic relenting any time soon. Huge swathes of the North of England were suffering tougher local restrictions, while nationally the number of cases continued to rise to levels not seen even during the worst of the first wave of the disease. It still seemed unfair though that the UK Government was refusing to allow spectators into the bigger sports grounds over here when in Germany, for example, they'd now started to allow significant numbers into Bundesliga games. I was particularly annoyed that I couldn't go up to Barrow for the next Leeds game in the EFL Trophy; the U21s were there on Monday night, 5th October, and I needed that ground for my '92' portfolio. Maybe I was better off not going though, as the Leeds U21s could only draw 2 – 2 despite having been two goals up inside 38 minutes, both scored by the highly rated Max Dean. With EFL Trophy rules awarding an extra point to the winners of the penalty shoot-out in the event of a draw, it was then disappointing to hear that we missed out on that by losing the shoot-out 4 – 3. Leeds therefore sat bottom of Group G with just 1 point from their first two games and looked favourites to be eliminated after the group stages.

It was also transfer deadline day this Monday and I have to say I couldn't resist watching most of the Sky show during the evening and enjoyed the banter between Harry and Jamie Redknapp who were the main studio pundits. All of the Leeds interest was in whether we could land the signature of the young Brazilian, 23-year-old left winger Raphinha who was said to be nearly a done deal from French club Rennes. The Michael Cuisance saga was brought to an end as it was confirmed he'd now signed for Marseille on a one-season loan, with no mention of any medical issues. Perhaps the one-year deal with an option to buy was the way Marseille were protecting themselves just in case whatever the Leeds medicos found did ever crop up in future.

We waited and waited for confirmation of the Raphinha deal but it did look as if it was done as Leeds went into comedy mode tweeting a picture of a plate of fish and chips next to a contract with the comment: *"Don't go to bed just yet… there is still work to be done #lufc"* This came at 10:30 pm, an hour after a relaxed looking Angus Kinnear was interviewed live at Elland Road on the Sky show. As well as suggesting that *"hopefully"* a deal would be announced shortly, he was also asked about Victor Orta. Apparently there had been rumours (later confirmed to be true) that Roma had put together a detailed offer seeking to persuade him to join them. Kinnear responded in typically mischievous manner, telling the Sky reporter: *"Well, Victor has been a massive part of our success both in the Championship and the squad he's building in the EPL so there is interest from other clubs in Victor and it doesn't surprise us. But we're not letting him go anywhere, and, if they saw his behaviour in the directors' box they wouldn't want him either!"*

The reason it took so long to announce the signing of Raphinha became clear just after 10:30 pm when a natty video of him arriving in Leeds, signing the contract, and picking out his number '18' shirt was posted on the club's Twitter account; the video must have taken a couple of hours at least to produce! The Brazilian was the 13th signing of the Summer and brought our total spending to something approaching £100m. Only Chelsea, Man City and Villa had spent more this window. Those that looked destined to play an immediate part in the EPL were Costa, Harrison (loan), and Meslier – all previous loanees of course – Rodrigo, Koch, Llorente, and now, we assumed, Raphinha. The rest, Joe Gelhardt, Charlie Allen, Cody Drameh, Dani van den Heuvel, Sam Greenwood, and Crysencio Summerville all looked less likely to feature with the big boys. If they were all up to scratch though it looked like a successful window. There could still be further additions of course, as transfers from the EFL could be made for another 11 days, although the only position Leeds didn't appear to have covered was that usually occupied by Pablo Hernandez; I didn't consider any of the new boys were tailor-made for that role.

One more piece of business that didn't seem quite sorted was that argument Leeds were having with RB Leipzig over Jean-Kevin Augustin and who exactly owned his contract. The fact he joined Nantes this week sort of suggested Leeds were off the hook but we awaited official confirmation of that.

Gareth Southgate's problems never seemed to diminish much as he continued to stumble across youngsters in his squad not behaving. Following the recent cases of Foden and Greenwood straying from the fold and, before that, Harry Maguire's Greek Odyssey, news broke now that three more youngsters were in trouble and already declared to be out of contention for this week's friendly with Wales. Tammy Abraham, Ben Chilwell, and Jadon Sancho all attended a surprise birthday party for Abraham, organised by his friends and family. Twenty or more people were in attendance thus breaking the Rule of Six. The breach cost the three players their places against Wales but the Met Police decided against prosecuting; the party organisers could have been fined up to £10,000 under Covid rules for their error of judgement.

The first big sacking of the season occurred this week at hapless Nottingham Forest. As the trees began losing their leaves so Forest, who'd lost all five games this season, scoring just one goal, lost their manager. Sabri Lamouchi was out and, within minutes, Chris Hughton was in. I've tried and tried to come up with a better tree pun for this story but I'm stumped...

The first international action involving a Leeds player came at St. Georges where England's U19s raced into a 3 – 1 lead over Scotland with young Charlie Cresswell scoring on his debut. Sadly, the goal was then struck from the record books as the game was abandoned, with Covid once again providing a *stark* warning that it could pop up anywhere at any time. This time it was Billy Stark, the U19s head coach testing positive during the game (in preparation for the return match) that caused the abandonment.

With no immediate likelihood of watching Leeds in the flesh, we had to be content this week with an announcement that the live screening of all EPL games would be extended through to the end of November at least. There was a catch though; each round of games would now see five of the ten matches screened on either BT Sport or Sky but the remaining five would be available only on a Pay Per View (PPV) basis. The problem was the PPV price was a staggering £14.95 per game. For me, personally, I had no problem in forking out 15 quid for a Leeds game – after all, I'd pay much more than that for a 'normal' match-day – but it would test my resolve in trying to watch *every* EPL game! It was as predictable as an Adam Forshaw injury update that the very first game announced for the new PPV schedule was Leeds' trip to Villa Park, a game now brought forward 24 hours to Friday 23rd October.

The first Leeds player in senior international action this break was Stuart Dallas. He was named Man of the Match as NI drew one apiece with Bosnia-Herzegovina in the vital European Championship play-off game in Sarajevo. NI won the penalty shoot-out 3 – 4 to go through to face Slovakia in the play-off final in November after Slovakia beat the Republic of Ireland (RoI), also on penalties. In fact, the penalty theme of this strange season seemed inescapable as another Leeds man, Liam Cooper was part of the Scotland side that scraped through on penalties against Israel to also win a play-off showdown. They'd face Serbia in November for a place at the Euro finals. There was less drama for Ezgjan Alioski, he played a full 90 minutes and picked up a yellow card as North Macedonia beat Kosovo 2 – 1 and they'd now travel to Georgia for their play-off final to see if they could win a place in the Euro 2021 finals; Euro 2020 as it was still badged. England and Wales had already qualified of course but Kalvin Phillips and Tyler Roberts both got another 90 minutes for England and Wales respectively in a 3 – 0 England friendly win at Wembley. Most pundits agreed that Kalvin had a decent game.

With my appetite for TV football still whetted, on Friday night this week Sky showed the League One encounter in which Fleetwood Town walloped Hull City 4 - 1. There was plenty of ex-Leeds interest with former Whites' keeper Alex Cairns on the bench for Fleetwood and Lewie Coyle on the visitors' bench while Mallik Wilks played up front for the Tigers. At one time I think we all thought those three would have more of a future at Elland Road than proved to be the case. The result was a strange one in that Hull had won all four of their League games up 'til now while Fleetwood had lost three of theirs; maybe it was the torrential rain that made the game a bit of a lottery. In fact the conditions, heavy rain and wind, were similar to when Leeds were last at Fleetwood, in August 2016 in the League Cup when Coyle was in the Leeds team and Cairns was again on the Fleetwood bench; we all needed our Fleetwood Macs that night too…

Next it was the turn of some of our new boys; Nations League games began again during this break and first up were Spain who beat Switzerland 1 – 0 and then Germany who won 1 – 2 in

Ukraine. Both Rodrigo and Diego Llorente were unused subs for Spain as was Robin Koch for Germany. Mateusz Klich played 70 minutes for Poland as they drew 0 – 0 with Italy. Alioski played the full 90 as North Macedonia drew 3 – 3 in Estonia, Kalvin Phillips was a 66th-minute sub as England beat Belgium, Stuart Dallas again starred for NI despite the Green Army going down 0 – 1 to Austria, and Tyler Roberts was an unused sub as Wales drew with RoI. The games were coming thick and fast and many international sides were then into their third game of the week as the end of this break was finally in sight. Thankfully, Robin Koch was only an unused sub again as Germany and Switzerland drew 3 - 3. I say thankfully because the news of our other centre-backs was not great. Both Liam Cooper (Scotland) and Diego Llorente (Spain) had been sent home early having picked up groin strains. Had Koch picked up one as well that would really have been a kick in the crotch... Our other Spanish international, Rodrigo Moreno, played 58 minutes as Spain surprisingly went down 1 - 0 in Ukraine. The final few games were played on Wednesday 14th October; Matty Klich got 64 minutes as Poland eased by Bosnia-Herzegovina 3 – 0, Alioski scored an added-time penalty for North Macedonia to rescue a point against Georgia and, finally, Kalvin Phillips played the full game as England came unstuck losing 0 – 1 to Denmark. That game was marred by some dreadful refereeing that saw Harry Maguire's season go from bad to worse with two yellow cards and a consequent 31st-minute dismissal; an appalling penalty decision against Kyle Walker that gave the Danes the game; and a red card after the final whistle for Reece James who finally lost his rag with the aptly named referee *Jesus* Gil Manzano!

Covid was still the main topic on every news broadcast and the situation throughout Europe continued to worsen. New measures were now in force with every region in England being placed in one of three tiers; Medium, High, and Very High. To begin with, just the Liverpool area went into what was effectively a diluted lock-down as the first 'Tier One' region but it was quickly followed by Greater Manchester. The mothballed Nightingale hospitals were being readied again in Sunderland, Manchester, and Harrogate as hospital admissions inevitably followed the increase in cases that were now regularly topping 17,000 each day. It was against this background that a petition was started to get fans back into professional football grounds; the petition quickly reached the 100,000 signatures needed for Parliament to have to debate the issue and within days that number had doubled again.

I saw another example this week as to how 'safe' football could be with limited crowds; I'd been successful in getting one of 600 tickets made available for the FA Cup tie between Stafford Rangers and Hereford FC. I'd been to Worcester City every Wednesday for five weeks, including the FA Cup defeat *to* Stafford Rangers, and saw no issues with their 300 capacity limit and it was just as safe at the bigger Marston Road home of Stafford. After beating Worcester in the 1st qualifying round, Stafford then went through the next round on penalties at Buxton before being drawn against Hereford. There was once again plenty of room to keep a decent distance between the fans, although the home fans behind the one goal didn't seem to worry too much about social distancing when Rangers scored two late goals to go through to the next round 3 – 1. It was a damn good game too; Rangers coming back from a goal down and it was in the balance until that third goal went in during added time at the end. There was something pleasurable about seeing a team called Hereford knocked out of the FA Cup too... Hereford's predecessors, Hereford United, knocked Leeds out in a 1st round replay in November 2007, while we were more focussed on eliminating that 15 point penalty in our first season in League One with Dennis Wise and his wobbly eyes. Hereford are also arch enemies of my beloved Worcester City, there being just 29 miles between them and with United often playing in the same division as City in the old Southern League.

The fact that the Government was still not letting the professional game admit spectators was continuing to place almost terminal pressure on the finances of all clubs below the TV revenue-awash EPL, to the extent that the EFL clubs were looking to the EPL to bail them out of the crisis. Ever looking for an opportunity to strengthen their grip on the English game, a new blueprint for the sport was released this week – Project Big Picture - following discussions between the owners of Liverpool and Manchester United and EFL Chairman; former Liverpool CEO Rick Parry. In short they were offering a further £250m for the EFL in return for removing the one-club-one-vote stewardship of the EPL. They also wanted a reduction in the number of EPL Clubs to 18 and a new format for relegation and promotion from the Championship to include an end-of-season mini-tournament. It would mean the 3rd, 4th and 5th sides in the Championship and the side finishing 16th (in the new 18 club format) in the EPL fighting it out over the final spot with the top two still going up automatically. The League Cup and Community Shield would be scrapped, Championship parachute payments would be ended and the voting rights would be held by the nine clubs with the longest history of EPL membership; the so-called 'big six' plus Everton, Southampton and West Ham. Parry had apparently got the vast majority of the EFL clubs aligned behind him but when it came to the EPL clubs, the plan bombed. At a full meeting of all EPL clubs, the proposal was unanimously rejected, although it was acknowledged that a new way forward would have to be found and they would continue to work on creating a new strategic plan. In the meantime, a £50m rescue package was agreed for League One and League Two although no agreement was reached on what to do about the Championship. Somewhat predictably, it was only hours before the EFL clubs collectively came out and declared £50m wasn't enough and any deal had to look after all 72 EFL clubs. Hours after that declaration, a group consisting of former England defender Gary Neville, retired Olympian Denise Lewis, and ex-FA Chairman David Bernstein combined to call for the independent regulation of English football to solve its *"crisis"*. Funnily enough it was something I felt the game needed, there was just too much self-interest involved at the top of the game and had been for years; the game had shown itself incapable of sensible self-reform. The trio were part of a group that issued a manifesto for change called 'Saving Our Beautiful Game'. The other members of this little band of aspiring football saviours were Andy Burnham (Mayor of Greater Manchester), David Davies (Former FA executive director), Conservative MP Helen Grant, Lord Mervyn King (former Bank of England governor) and ex-Aston Villa director and lawyer Greg Scott. It remained to be seen if they could become the catalyst for real change in the game but it was hard to see how those running the sport, those with the real clout, could be persuaded to let go of it. We didn't know at the time, but the greed of the big clubs would rear its ugly head again later in the season.

Wolves

It was appropriate as we prepared to face Wolves that one Wolves old boy was in the spotlight at Leeds. Barry Douglas had been the subject of various rumours throughout the recent transfer window but now details emerged that he was joining Blackburn on a season-long loan as the extended domestic transfer window deadline approached. With his contract due to expire at the end of the season it was effectively goodbye to the popular Scot. Another Leeds player, one at the opposite end of his career, also had a move to the EFL. Robbie Gotts was clearly well thought of at Leeds but he wasn't getting regular game time so it was a no-brainer really for the impish Leeds man to accept a loan move to the Imps, Lincoln City; a club flying high in League One after only recently winning promotion in 2018/19.

The piece of contract news most widely appreciated this week though concerned Gaetano Berardi. He was given a deal running to the end of the 2020/2021 season, despite the fact that his ACL injury and rehab would probably keep him out of action for the majority of the new contract period. It was one more sign of the positive way the club was run these days and the fan goodwill such actions generate is hard to overestimate. The quote of the week on this came, unsurprisingly, from the Leeds United wordsmith himself, Angus Kinnear. In his programme notes for the Wolves game Kinnear wrote: *"While we knew Gaetano would have happily performed the operation himself (making the incisions with a rusty stud key and stitching the wound with a discarded boot lace) the club had him treated at a state-of-the-art facility in Barcelona with the intention of extending his contract for another year."*

The U23s played their 5th game of the PL2 season on the eve of the next round of EPL games and, unfortunately, they lost again, this time 3 – 2 at Reading. It was another very young Leeds side though, even by U23 standards. Rising star Sam Greenwood was missing with an ankle injury picked up whilst with the England U19s and Leeds had several lads who were only 16. Max Dean and Josh Galloway got the goals for Leeds.

In the Marcelo Bielsa press conference ahead of the Wolves game, we learned that the Liam Cooper injury was slightly less severe than that of Diego Llorente and that Liam had a chance of making the game. Pablo Hernandez was also said to be fit again while Marcelo confirmed that, other things being equal, Raphinha would also be in the squad.

On Saturday, the first two of four EPL games played ended in draws; Everton's 100% record ended as they drew 2 – 2 with Merseyside rivals Liverpool and Chelsea threw away a 2 – 0 lead to draw 3 – 3 with Southampton. In the evening games, Manchester City beat Arsenal 1 – 0 while Manchester United won 1 – 4 at Newcastle with three goals coming in the final ten minutes. On Sunday there were three more draws; Sheffield United v Fulham, Palace v Brighton and Spurs v West Ham all ending level. There were loads more goals too, including six in that game at Spurs where the home side raced into a 3 – 0 lead in the first 15 minutes and then the Hammers grabbed three of their own in the last 15 as this crazy EPL season continued to entertain at every turn. The final game on Sunday saw Aston Villa remain the only side with a 100% record as they beat Leicester City 0 – 1. Next up for the Villa of course was our visit to Villa Park on Friday. The two remaining games this week would see West Brom host Burnley and then, finally, Leeds host Wolves in a live on Sky TV game. The word was that Sky and BT didn't get many folk shelling out £14.95 to watch the PPV games and, in fact, Newcastle fans led the way by boycotting their game with Man United and giving the cash instead to a food bank charity. During breaks from gardening I found all of the PPV games being streamed live on the internet so, if you looked hard enough, there was no need to pay anyway. I watched most of the West Brom v Burnley game on a free internet stream and, by the end, I was glad I hadn't bothered to pay the £14.95 as it was destined to end nil-nil; the first goalless result in this, the 47th EPL game played so far. Both teams remained in the bottom four of the table along with Fulham and Sheffield United.

On the dot of 7 pm the @LUFC Twitter account posted *"Your #LUFC starting XI..."* with a graphic listing the selected team. Contrary to many rumours flying around social media, Liam Cooper was listed to play, alongside Robin Koch in the centre of defence. Hence the only changes to the side that started against Manchester City before the international break were the return of Jack Harrison, now eligible to play again, and Rodrigo who was favoured instead of Tyler Roberts. Pablo Hernandez and Raphinha were both on the bench.

The trouble was though that by 7:45 pm, all of us Leeds fans sat in front of our TVs could now see 'Coops' limping away from the warm-up shaking his head and pointing to his leg. There was only one thing that could possibly have been worse than a limp Cooper and that was a limp Koch! Minutes later it was confirmed that Cooper was out and Pascal Struijk would step up to take his place. The focus would very much be on Koch to rise to the occasion.

Meslier
Ayling (Capt) Koch Struijk (Hernandez 75) Dallas
Phillips
Costa (Poveda 71) Rodrigo Klich Harrison (Raphinha 82)
Bamford

Subs: Casilla, Shackleton, Hernandez, Raphinha, Roberts, Alioski, Poveda.

Wolves: Patrício, Boly, Coady, Kilman, Semedo, Dendoncker, João Moutinho (Neves 82), Neto (Marçal de Oliveiraat 89), Saïss, Jiménez, Castelo Podence (Traoré 65). Subs not used: Ruddy, Hoever, Soares Silva, Otasowie. Referee: David Coote.

The first half was a pretty comfortable experience for Leeds fans; I watched with surprisingly little anxiety and I don't think it was the regular pints of Red Stripe I was getting through. Having shown in the first four games that we were more than capable of holding our own in the EPL, there was a strange calm about everything Leeds United, unlike the constant stress of previous years when we knew it was all about getting promoted. Now it was, at least for the time being, just a matter of not getting relegated and we'd looked far better than that so far. I was also now attuned to watching games on TV and hardly noticed there were no fans in the grounds; the tailored soundtracks sounded pretty realistic to me as I could hear the familiar strains of *"Marching On Together"* periodically throughout the game.

Leeds were on top for most of the first 45 minutes, bossing the possession and looking much quicker and fitter than a very Portuguese-looking Wolves in their maroon and green ensemble. Wolves' Portuguese manager, Nuno Espirito Santo had surrounded himself with Portuguese players; ten in all in his squad and that meant his team were all technically brilliant ball players but Leeds had them blowing out of their proverbial arses as they chased around trying to get the ball off us! I'd seen at first-hand how important technical skills were in Portuguese football when Mrs W and I went with my lad Mark on a summer tour with his junior team back in 2006; most junior teams over there have their own artificial pitches which demand good ball control.

Wolves had started the season in a similar manner and against mostly the same teams as Leeds; we'd both won at Bramall Lane and at home against Fulham and we'd both faced Manchester City, although Leeds got a point in that one whereas Wolves lost 1 – 3. It was the one game we'd played against different opponents though that suggested Leeds should have the edge; whereas we shipped four at Anfield including two penalties, we did at least get three ourselves, but Wolves got hammered at West Ham 4 – 0. This first half seemed to suggest the form book was right.

Leeds were camped in the Wolves half for much of the time and both Costa and Harrison regularly got crosses towards Patrick Bamford, albeit few actually hit the intended target. We fashioned nine attempts at goal but none could really be considered a 'big chance' and probably wouldn't feature as such in the Opta stats in post-match reports. Bamford did have the ball in the net at one point, nipping in to finish neatly with his head after a corner was headed on by Jack Harrison. That one was quickly ruled offside after a VAR check. Bamford had other attempts too but all difficult chances. The problem that was looming in my mind though was that Wolves were doing pretty much what Wolves always do; they were soaking up the pressure, defending stoutly and were frustrating the hell out of Leeds. I'd read in the match-day programme that Wolves had failed to score in the first half in 20 of their previous 26 EPL games but their second-half performances were always superb. In fact, had the EPL games the previous season ended at halftime, Wolves would have been relegated; only Bournemouth had a worse first half record. By contrast though, had the games only *started* at halftime, then Wolves would have been third behind only Manchester City and Liverpool; Wolves were unashamedly second half specialists.

I was convinced Bielsa would turn to Pablo Hernandez at halftime, for me it seemed the obvious choice to unlock a stubborn defence and Bielsa had used the same MO during those ghost games at the end of last season; rationing the use of Pablo's old legs. Knowing Wolves' second half specialty also surely demanded Leeds step things up themselves. But no, there were no changes from either coach and I still think we made an error there.

From the start of the second half it was clear that Wolves were living up to their billing as second half experts. They had the ball in our net within minutes of the restart as Romain Saiss latched onto a loose header by Robin Koch. Saiss teed the ball up and lashed it on the volley low into the right corner of the net but, as with Bamford's first-half header, VAR correctly flagged up an offside in the lead up to the goal. Moments later and Podence tested Meslier as our young keeper had to throw himself to his right to push the ball out for a corner. The writing was on the wall.

My next worry was the appearance of Adama Traore, a 65th-minute substitute for Wolves replacing Podence. I'm sure all Leeds fans that were at the Riverside that night remembered how he destroyed us on a cold snowy evening in March, 2018. That was the night Patrick Bamford got a hat-trick against us. Traore has phenomenal pace and I wondered if he would tip the balance of the game in their favour. As it happens, he didn't, but Lady Luck did.

A long diagonal ball, left to right and aimed at Jimenez, suddenly had Pascal Struijk slipping over and, though he recovered quickly, he was then always a yard or two behind the Wolves striker as he shimmied along the edge of the Leeds box right to left. He went past Stuart Dallas too and then checked back onto his right foot as Dallas bought the dummy. There appeared to be no power whatsoever in the shot though as Jimenez casually lifted the ball towards the right corner where Meslier had it easily covered and was ready to collect. In the way though was the head of Kalvin Phillips and his attempt to head the ball wide of the other post went horribly wrong as he merely deflected it *inside* that post with Meslier stranded. It was just 'one of those things', a bad rub of the green and it capped a pretty poor second half showing by Phillips who would later disclose that he'd injured a shoulder and would be missing for a few weeks.

It was classic Wolves, an MO that had seen them consolidate their position as a top-seven side in the EPL, finishing 7th in both seasons since their promotion. There was a lesson to be learned here for Leeds; chances made was not the critical metric, it was taking them that was all-important. Finally Bielsa turned to his bench and, by the end, he had Poveda, Hernandez, and Raphinha on and Costa, Struijk, and Harrison on the sidelines. Pablo was superb as always and it only annoyed me more that we hadn't got him on earlier, but even Pablo couldn't engineer an opening good enough for a goal. He almost did, as a trademark side-foot shot was deflected inches over the bar.

A 0 – 1 defeat it was, our first home defeat in the EPL this time around. Marcelo Bielsa summed it up pretty adroitly as he told the BBC after the game: *"In the first half we should have established a difference. In the second half it was more even."*

Leeds would thus end round 5 in a solid mid-table position on seven points, along with West Ham, Man City, Southampton, Palace, and Newcastle; good company but I knew it should really have been 3rd place, ahead of Liverpool on goal difference and only behind Everton and Aston Villa who'd played a game less and still had that 100% record. Our next game was less than 96 hours away; Villa Park beckoned.

Leeds United 0 Wolverhampton Wanderers 1 (Jimenez 70)
BCD. Round 5 League Pos: 10th.

Villa Vanquished

As we waited for the Villa game there was plenty of football around to keep us occupied. In Scotland it was a good week for Ryan Edmondson; he grabbed two goals, an assist, and the Man of the Match award as Aberdeen beat Hamilton Academical 4 – 2 in the Premiership to keep the Dons third behind runaway leaders Rangers and Celtic.

The Champions League games began this week with wins for Liverpool, Manchester City, and Manchester United, the latter an impressive 1 – 2 result at Paris Saint-Germain. Chelsea drew their home game with Sevilla. In the Europa League there were wins for Tottenham, Arsenal, Leicester, and Rangers, so the defeats for Celtic at home to A C Milan, and Dundalk at home to Molde were the week's only domestic club reverses. Kemar Roofe was in the news again, this time with his name correctly spelled on the back of his Rangers shirt. He scored an outrageous goal, launching the ball from halfway to beat the Standard Liege keeper in added time to give the Gers a 0 – 2 win. Former Leeds man Jack Clarke also got four minutes at the end of Spurs' home win against the Austrian side Lask, a game that also saw the full debut of returning superstar Gareth Bale. He'd joined Spurs on a season-long loan, with the Londoners said to be paying £220,000 a week of his £600,000-a-week Real Madrid salary!

The EPL clubs all announced their final 25-man first-team squads this week for the first half of the season and Leeds' was something of a surprise. The rules dictate that each team can only name a maximum of 17 (it would be wouldn't it?) players who are 'home-grown'. A 'Home-Grown Player' is a player who, irrespective of nationality or age, has been registered with any club affiliated to the FA or the FA of Wales for a period, continuous or not, of three entire seasons, or 36 months, before his 21st birthday (or the end of the season during which he turns 21). Players under the age of 21 don't need to be registered, hence why first-team squad regulars Illan Meslier, Pascal Struijk, and Ian Poveda were not included. Leeds listed just 18 players but the name that jumped off the page was that of Jay-Roy Grot. Bielsa had clearly decided JRG was not part of his plans and hence he'd spent most of the previous two seasons out on loan to Dutch sides VVV Venlo and Vitesse Arnhem. However, he suffered a serious knee injury in March requiring an operation and then picked up a bacterial infection requiring two further sessions under the knife. Hence although listed and eligible to play it was unlikely he'd be fit before the next transfer window when most pundits expected him to be sold anyway.

In the press conference ahead of the Villa trip, Bielsa was in combative mood as the journos tried to coax information from him. One began by asking how we would cope without Kalvin Phillips who the club had suggested could be out for around six weeks. *"Who said he'll be out for six weeks?"* Bielsa asked sharply via his interpreter of the journo who sheepishly replied *"Well, err, the club"*. Bielsa shrugged and muttered something to the effect that it could be more or less than six weeks and implied that no one could possibly know how long it would be! He was more forthcoming on his plan to replace Kalvin and stated firmly that Pascal Struijk would play that role. Another journalist then asked if Bielsa was happy with his *"small squad"* to which the great man replied *"The squad is not small, we have two players for every position"* and he started to list them. *"Bamford and Tyler, Pablo and Rodrigo..."* I got the impression that something had irked our coach but had no idea what it could be but it was interesting to me that he clearly saw Rodrigo as the cover for Pablo Hernandez, although he did also comment that most of the players could also play other positions.

I think all Leeds fans probably thought the Villa game would be as tough as any we'd yet faced. They'd completely turned themselves around this season having only just avoided the drop by an accident of fate weeks earlier when Hawk-Eye had a day off. Now they'd become one of the fancied teams, having posted a 100% record from four games and having battered Liverpool 7-2 before the international break. I wasn't as convinced as some that they were actually as good as their results suggested, but their confidence would certainly be high.

There was a confident air about Leeds too though, despite the setback suffered against Wolves the previous week. Most observers, including me, felt we'd played well in that game and only lost it through a moment of bad luck when that ball bounced off Kalvin's bonce. Ahead of the game there was news to breed even more confidence amongst the Leeds fan base.

It was a generally held belief that Marcelo Bielsa would leave us at the end of this season; the logic being that he'd never stopped anywhere more than two seasons in the past, let alone three, and I suppose most of us were also factoring in his age. He was already at retirement age and he was working a long way from home. He had also always insisted on one-year contracts or one-year extensions such as he currently had. However, speaking at the press conference he hinted that the possibility of staying at Leeds after his current contract expired was not beyond the bounds of possibility. *"I'm very comfortable living and managing in England,"* he said. *"Annual contracts does not mean I am not open to staying here longer."* As the YEP put it when reporting this revelation, *"... those 21 words will be good news for Whites fans who don't like to think about a post-Bielsa world at Leeds United."*[1]

---

[1]   *https://www.yorkshireeveningpost.co.uk/sport/football/leeds-united/comfortable-leeds-united-boss-marcelo-bielsa-open-staying-beyond-current-contract-3012441*

There was doubt about the involvement of Liam Cooper in this game throughout the week and so it came as no real surprise when I spotted the team pop up on the Leeds United Twitter feed that his name was missing.

Meslier
Dallas Ayling (Capt) Koch Alioski
Struijk (Shackleton 21)
Costa (Raphinha 83) Rodrigo (Hernandez 79) Klich Harrison
Bamford

Subs: Casilla, Davis, Shackleton, Hernandez, Raphinha, Roberts, Poveda.

Aston Villa: Martínez, Cash, Konsa, Mings, Targett, McGinn, Douglas Luiz, Trézéguet (Traoré 66), Barkley, Grealish, Watkins. Subs not used: Steer, Hourihane, Nakamba, Engels, El Mohamady, Davis. Referee: Paul Tierney.

With Cooper out and Llorente also injured, and Barry Douglas now plying his trade at Blackburn, the side sort of picked itself. Luke Ayling moved to centre-back and took the Captain's armband, Stuart Dallas moved from left-back to right-back and Alioski took over on the left. We'd already been told that Struijk would fill in for Phillips. For Villa, the obvious players we had to keep an eye on were the crafty (some would say cheating) Grealish who was always likely to con a referee into giving a rash penalty or booking an opponent; Ollie Watkins, who'd already proved he could score goals at this level; and the Chelsea loanee Ross Barkley.

This was the first Leeds game to be screened under the new PPV schedule and I was a little nervous that I'd not get a decent stream to watch it on but, equally, I was adamant I wasn't paying another £14.95. It wasn't the money; that was neither here nor there and I'd have spent way more on the day out had I been allowed to go to Villa Park. It was the principle that, to me, it was just too much for the average football fan to fork out on top of the subscriptions already being paid for Sky and BT. I was still watching almost all of almost every EPL match and the new PPV rules would have meant I'd have to pay another £74.75 every week if I wanted to continue watching the five non-broadcast games as well as the five covered by the subscription. If you were to believe the fans posting on Twitter, then my view was pretty general and the majority seemed to be saying they would not pay the £14.95. In fact this seemed to be supported by the news that donations to Leeds-based food banks raised over £40,000 in the five days leading up to the game as the Leeds United Supporters Trust urged fans to boycott PPV, much as was seen in Newcastle the previous week when the Toon Army also boycotted their game with Manchester United. If you did the maths though, even £40,000 represented only about 2,700 fans making a stand in this way. Sure, there must also have been thousands like me who didn't pay the £14.95 *or* donate but it was a long way short of the estimated usual TV audience for a Leeds game of in excess of 500,000! I would love to know the actual numbers that subscribed!

As it happens, the illegal stream I found was perfect! It was in HD quality and there were only a few occasions when the laptop screen froze as it buffered. I did notice that it was about three minutes behind the BT Box Office broadcast though judging by the delay between some of the WhatsApp messages I was getting and me seeing what they were on about! But so what? I couldn't help wondering why on earth anyone would pay the £14.95. I was all set, laptop on lap, Red Stripe to hand and more chilling in the fridge, notebook ready!

The first half gave comfort and concern in equal measure, just as we saw against Wolves on Monday night. Part of the concern was that Pascal Struijk, good as he was playing, had been booked very early in the game when Jack Grealish did one of his dying swan impressions. Shortly after, Struijk gave away another free-kick and, despite the game being only 20 minutes old, Bielsa reacted. He was clearly concerned that Villa were now targeting Struijk and, so early in the game, it would have been footballing suicide had he picked up a second yellow card. Pascal was given the hook and Jamie Shackleton jogged on to take his place. It was a sign both of the Leeds domination and Shackleton's composure that we didn't have cause to even think about that change again for the remainder of the game.

Leeds were completely dominant in terms of possession and racked up plenty of attempts at goal, ten in all during the first half, and yet it was Villa who came closest to scoring. Half of the Leeds attempts came from Patrick Bamford, including a diving header that he really should have scored from, and a more difficult cross that he met on his right foot that he also put wide. The diving header would probably end up in the 'big chances missed' column, as would Rodrigo's effort when he scooped the ball at goal from a low Alioski cross. That one hit Konsa and flew behind for a corner. At the other end the one clear-cut chance Villa had saw Ollie Watkins capitalise on a mistake by Luke Ayling but, by the time the ball arrived with Grealish and he fired in a left foot shot, Ayling was back on the goal line to block the effort with inches to spare. No goals at halftime and the spectre of that Wolves game was just hovering there reminding us that possession is nothing without putting the ball in the net. I held that thought as I sipped on the huge gin and tonic Mrs W had just brought in; she clearly recognised there was tension in the air even though she couldn't see the laptop screen and I had the headphones plugged in!

The second half started with another warning and it was that annoying bloke Grealish who posted it again. This time he collected the ball only yards outside his own area and then darted between Robin Koch and Helder Costa and raced over the halfway line towards the Leeds box. Costa had given up the chase but Koch eventually caught Grealish but then bought a side-step from the Villa man that left him near the penalty spot. Still Grealish didn't pull the trigger though and neither did he spot Ollie Watkins just yards away unmarked. Grealish sold another dummy to Luke Ayling who slipped on his backside and, at the same time, skirted Alioski who had to ensure he didn't get close enough to allow another Grealish dive. Finally the shot came but Illan Meslier was in the way to block it with his legs and away for a corner. When the corner came across it all looked very 'Leedsy' again as Konsa got around Luke Ayling to volley in a shot that Meslier did brilliantly to tip over the bar with a strong left hand. And breathe...

The way things then panned out, that was the last worry in this game and the rest of it was pretty much plain sailing as, finally, we put some chances away; or at least Paddy Bam-Bam Bamford did. The first came after a quick Leeds break that started on the right but then swept down the left wing with Alioski finding Harrison who, in turn, rolled the ball into the path of Rodrigo. The Spaniard took the ball on into the area and shot left-footed but Martinez in the Villa goal got down to palm that one away but not far enough. Patrick Bamford was on it in a flash to whip it into the net just before a sliding challenge came in from Tyrone Mings. It was a real goal poacher's goal; think Lineker or maybe Jimmy Greaves if you are of my vintage. The goal came in the 55th minute and, as I said, we never looked in danger after that. 12 minutes later we were two to the good and cruising.

Ross Barkley pushed a tired-looking ball over the halfway line in the centre of the pitch straight to Stuart Dallas who quickly knocked it back along the turf into the path of Klich who neatly turned to his left when Barkley was banking on him going right. Barkley limply put an arm out as if to pull Klich back but then thought better of it, almost as if he couldn't quite be arsed. Klich was away now in acres of space and he was able to prod the ball through the legs of Douglas Luiz to Patrick Bamford who was stationed in the 'D' outside the Villa area. He had two Villa defenders in front and another two closing in on him from behind but he was so quick with his feet that in no time at all he'd trapped the ball, touched it to his left and then whipped it into the top right corner in one smooth action and all with his left foot! It was the sort of goal you might just nod sagely about if you saw Pablo Hernandez do that but at this moment I was up out of my chair punching the air. It was a sumptuous finish from a man who I had completely changed my view of in the last few months. Never did I think he had it in him to look so comfortable as a striker in the EPL; to be honest I seriously wondered if he'd been hypnotised or if it wasn't actually Patrick James Bamford in that number '9' shirt anymore; perhaps it was an imposter! As the cameras panned onto the Villa keeper Martinez he could clearly be seen mouthing the word *"Wow!"* with a completely gobsmacked look on his face. It was a breath-taking strike. Mind you, if we thought that was a good goal... there was better still to come!

We were into the 74th minute now, just seven minutes since the second goal, and Meslier pinged the ball out to Dallas in the right-back berth. Dallas prodded the ball forward and ·more central to Rodrigo who was now taking up those *"gimme the ball"* positions that Pablo so loves. Rodrigo took a couple of touches and then looked up to see Costa making a run down the right wing. The Spanish midfielder hit a gentle five iron half the length of the pitch and inside the Villa left-back, a little too wide really but Costa managed to collect it just inside the right touchline. Costa shuffled towards the right edge of the Villa box with a line of four claret and blue shirts stretched across the area. Leeds had Shackleton making a run towards Costa, Bamford further across, and Harrison and Alioski on the far side; it was effectively four v four. Costa played the ball to the feet of Shackleton and kept running past him to collect the one-two before playing the return first time to the feet of Patrick Bamford. Paddy was surrounded by the four Villa defenders now, you could literally have thrown the Shropshire Whites' flag over them all but somehow none of them went for the ball while Bamford took one, two and then with his third touch and stepping around the ball he scooped it into the top left corner of the net. I've often described Bamford's close footwork as akin to Bambi on ice in the past, now he was doing an impression of Vaslav Nijinsky.[1] Patrick Bamford thus had the second hat-trick of his career and Leeds fans will forever remember them both. His first was that treble he got at the Riverside against us on that snowy night one March and now his second was this magnificent trio of efforts at Villa Park. By a strange quirk of history, today also just happened to be the 75th anniversary of the founding of JCB, the Staffordshire-based digger manufacturer that took the initials of its founder, the late Joseph Cyril Bamford, a distant relative of our own 'Lord' Bamford. It was also the 75th birthday of the current real Lord Bamford, Anthony, JC's son. There were going to be a few decent Bamford parties tonight! I'd started to ponder just how good a player Bamford might have been had his secondary school, Nottingham High, played soccer when he was there; they didn't, it was a rugby union playing school and Bamford thus played full-back the whole time he was there which might explain why he often hits the ball over the crossbar!

The game wasn't quite over of course and Leeds sent on Raphinha and Hernandez for the final ten minutes in place of Costa and Rodrigo. Had this been the perfect, perfect night for Leeds they would have combined for a goal too. We saw the sort of passing the Brazilian is capable of as he dissected the Villa defence to put Jack Harrison in the clear and he cut the ball back perfectly to Hernandez, unmarked in the centre of the Villa box and no more

---

[1] *Vaslav Nijinsky was a Polish ballet dancer and choreographer cited as perhaps the greatest male dancer of all time.*

than 14 yards out. Sadly, Pablo seemed to stretch for the ball and ballooned it over the bar; it would have been the icing on a sumptuous cake.

The result temporarily put Leeds into the top three in the early table since we were first to play in this 6th round of games, a position we could only have dreamed about when we first saw the fixture list. We'd amassed ten points from our six games and we'd already played the two best teams in the division and a side that had a 100% record until we showed up. There was every reason to be confident now that this Leeds squad was capable of having a very comfortable season. For me, it actually felt very much like the Wilkinson era at the end of the 80s and early 90s. Then too Wilko came in with Leeds languishing in the second tier of English football and after doing nothing memorable for around 16 long years. It took Wilko two seasons to get Leeds promoted after having to drag the club kicking and screaming into a more modern era of the game, to make us a more professional outfit in every aspect of the sport just as Bielsa had now done. Bielsa had brought his unconventional methods to Leeds and, in particular, had refined the facilities at Thorp Arch that had remained largely undeveloped since Wilko set it all up. In our first season in the top-flight under Wilko, Leeds were immediately competitive and finished a strong 4th in the table and then, I hardly dare say this, we won the title the following year. It was impossible not to make the comparison with what was going on with this Bielsa regime but, equally, I knew there was a lot of water to flow along the River Aire before another title could be contemplated...

Leeds seemed to have settled perfectly into EPL life and, whereas we'd always created a load of chances under Bielsa, we'd not always been as clinical in putting them away and many fingers, including mine, had pointed in the direction of Patrick Bamford trying to explain why that was. Now Bamford appeared to be a new man, a real striker with a quick mind and quick feet. It was a bit like the transformation we saw in Chris Wood who also got a name for himself as a squanderer of chances before suddenly starting to hit the net on a more regular and consistent basis. Long may this continue for Patrick Bamford too. In fact, if he keeps delivering like this we'll have to rename him Postman Pat, never mind Sniffer! Was it anything to do with there being no fans in the stadiums at the moment? Some folk suggested it was, in that Bamford had always seemed to be acutely aware of his own shortcomings and had sometimes shown his annoyance when criticisms were voiced from the stands. I wasn't sure, but there was no doubt Paddy had now shown exactly what he is capable of so it was now up to the team to keep creating those chances and for Bamford to keep putting them away. Leeds had already scored 12 goals in just six games and Bamford had half of them. It was the most goals scored at this stage by a promoted side since Middlesbrough got 12 way back in the 92/93 season!

Villa boss Dean Smith was sanguine after the game as he noted that his side were second best for much of the night, although he did rue the missing of the few early chances Villa did create. Speaking to the BBC he said: *"Who knows what would have happened if we had scored? That is the first time we have been behind in a game and we didn't handle it very well."* In his comments to the Match Of The Day team, Bielsa echoed that saying: *"We scored first and were a little bit lucky they didn't score some of the chances they had."* No one who watched the game though could be in any doubt that this was a real statement from Leeds, a performance of real quality and dominance.

The remaining games were played out over the next three days and I confess I watched pretty much all of them. On Saturday the four games saw West Ham draw 1 – 1 with Manchester City, Palace win 1 – 2 at Fulham to leave the Cottagers at the bottom with still just a single point, Man U and Chelsea play out a goalless bore draw, and Liverpool start to get into their stride with a 2 – 1 win over Sheffield United who were locked with Fulham on that one-point mark. On Sunday, Southampton ended the last unbeaten run in the division beating Everton comfortably 2 – 0, Wolves drew with Newcastle, and Arsenal surprisingly lost 0 – 1 to Leicester City.

On Monday, the final two games saw Brighton and Wolves draw 1 – 1 and Spurs win 0 – 1 against Burnley, a result that left Burnley joint bottom along with Sheffield United and Fulham all on the one point; Burnley did at least still have a game in hand.

Aston Villa 0 **Leeds United 3 (Bamford 55, 67, 74)**
BCD. **Round 6 League Pos: 6th**.

Flaws Feed Foxes!

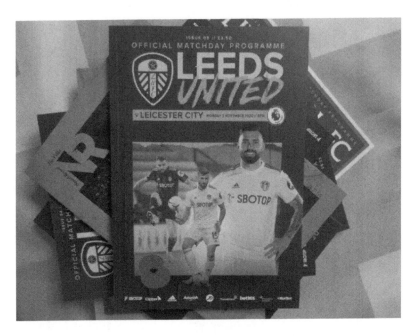

The U23s continued to go well in their inaugural PL2 Division 2 season as they beat top of the table Norwich City 2 – 0, although with the strength of team we put out it would have been disappointing had we lost. The goals came from Poveda and Raphinha but we also had Casilla, Struijk, Hernandez and Tyler Roberts in the side, all getting valuable match time as they awaited their chances with the first-team. Leeds were now 3rd in the table, level on 10 points with Middlesbrough and now just two points adrift of the Canaries.

Ajax cleaned up this weekend as they set a new Dutch Eredivisie record beating VVV-Venlo 13 - 0. That beat their own previous record - a 12-1 win over Vitesse in 1972. Where have you heard the two club names VVV-Venlo and Vitesse before? They are the two clubs where Jay-Roy Grot was out on loan over the last couple of seasons.

It was a dreadful time for adding to the departed this week, beginning with the death of Frank Bough. When I was growing up

Bough was the face of TV sport, along with David Coleman. For fifteen years between 1968 and 1983 he was a regular host for the BBC's flagship Saturday afternoon sports show, *Grandstand* and later he was a mainstay on the early evening *Nationwide* programme, a forerunner of the current *One Show*. Within days of Bough's departure we learned of the deaths of comedian Bobby Ball, the former Welsh rugby international JJ Williams, World Cup winner Nobby Stiles, and then former Bond-film star, Sean Connery. They were all huge names from the worlds of entertainment and sport during my teenage years and it really made me think about my own mortality! They were all in their 70s or 80s, or even 90s in the case of Connery, so I reckoned I might still have a few years left but then we learned of the death of Marius Zaliukas, the Lithuanian centre-back who signed for Leeds in 2013 under Brian McDermott and played alongside the likes of Tom Lees and Jason Pearce. Zaliukas was only 36-years-old and was yet another ball-player to be taken by MND; the dreadful disease Rob Burrow was diagnosed with the previous year and with which a very good friend of ours was currently battling. Sadly, my main memory of Zaliukas in a Leeds shirt will always be that 6 – 0 drubbing we received at Hillsborough in January 2014; no one who was there that day will ever forget it although many left shortly after halftime when the third goal went in. It was the day when Jimmy Kebe and Cameron Stewart both made their debuts for Leeds but they'd go on to make a combined total of just 20 appearances, although that was probably 20 too many!

In fact it was bad news wherever you looked this week; another spate of Islamist terror attacks hit France and then Austria while Covid was continuing its relentless comeback throughout Europe. In the UK the Prime Minister was forced to announce a second national lockdown following similar moves in Northern Ireland, Scotland, and Wales, while simultaneously raising the terrorist threat level in the UK. In fact the only good news was that Kimberly Clark, the maker of Andrex toilet rolls, announced it was fully prepared for the next round of panic buying with 100 million rolls said to be stockpiled in various UK warehouses! That was more than enough for a new round of bog-roll keepie-uppie videos to be made.

Back on planet Leeds and the next Bielsa press conference took place on Friday, 30th October, ahead of our next game, Leicester City, another one to feature in the scheduled Sky Monday Night Football slot. At least that meant I wouldn't need to scan the internet for another dodgy stream. The only significant news to come out of the conference was that Liam Cooper was now fit again but both Diego Llorente and Kalvin Phillips remained on the injury list. Bielsa wouldn't be drawn on whether it would be Pascal Struijk or Jamie Shackleton who'd deputise this time for Phillips. A name likely to feature on Monday night was Aiden; storm Aiden was the latest officially named storm heading our way and bringing loads more rain.

The EPL kicked off week 7 with a Friday night clash between Wolves and Crystal Palace which Wolves won comfortably 2 – 0 to move themselves into the top six. On Saturday, there were three more games all won by the fancied teams; Manchester City won 0 – 1 at Sheffield United, Chelsea won 0 – 3 at Burnley, and Liverpool edged past West Ham 2 – 1 at Anfield. The so-called 'big six' were finally getting their houses in order and, on Sunday, the remaining three of that particular club were all in action. Spurs beat Brighton 2 – 1 while Arsenal pulled off the result of the weekend winning 0 – 1 against Manchester United who thus became the only one of the big six not to win this weekend. Meanwhile, two of the early pace-setters, Aston Villa and Everton, both lost their second games on the bounce; Villa shipping four more goals to go down 3 – 4 at home to Southampton and Everton 2 – 1 at Newcastle. It all suggested that the cream of the EPL was finally rising to the top. It was going to be interesting to see how we got on against the Foxes to see which of us was going to keep pace with the early leaders and who might fall away. Before our game there was the battle at the bottom between Fulham and West Brom. The Londoners won it 2 – 0 without too much trouble and thus hauled themselves out of the bottom three which now consisted of Burnley and Sheffield United, still with just a point apiece, and then West Brom with three. Fulham had a point more than the Albion now they had a first win on the board.

With the first-team playing on Monday night, it meant the U23s fielded a side on Sunday without any of our big names featuring. Nonetheless they still walloped Crystal Palace 4 – 1 with a penalty from Joe Gelhardt and goals from Max Dean and Max McMillan together with an own goal to go second in the early PL2 Div. 2 table. In fact, 4 − 1 was a popular score this weekend for Leeds teams as the women bowed out of the Women's FA Cup at Barnsley by the same score. Now, a 4 − 1 win over the Foxes would be mint and would put us very nicely placed in third spot in the EPL; I wonder... I do love a good omen or a football coincidence and, looking back to the same day last season, November 2[nd,] 2019, I noticed that Leeds beat QPR 2 − 0 that day to go *third* in the Championship.

Leicester City, with what they'd achieved in recent years, had won the hearts of many fans outside of the immediate Leicester area and some, including our own chairman, saw them as a good blueprint to follow. In a recently published article on the sportspromedia.com website Radrizzani admitted as much saying: *"My model in football is Leicester; I think they have a good model, they run the club very well. That's what I aspire to do but also with the acknowledgement that Leeds United, with all respect, is a much bigger brand internationally. It's a big club."*[1]

Many Leeds fans expected the Leicester game to be similar to the Wolves match we saw a couple of weeks earlier. Both the Foxes and the Wolves had established themselves as teams amongst the elite of the middle section of the table; not anywhere near on a par with the big six but certainly better than most of the rest. Both teams tended to rely on the counter-attack too and both had plenty of pace; Leicester in particular had both Jamie Vardy and Harvey Barnes up front, both very quick and usually clinical finishers. It was going to be another big test for us but with that superb Villa demolition still fresh in the memory I guessed that, like me, many Leeds fans thought we'd give a good account of ourselves. Certainly the YEP Jury did; three of us went for a Leeds win and three, including me, went for the draw. The announcement of the Leeds team on Twitter, an hour ahead of the game, did nothing to diminish my expectations.

---

[1] *https://www.sportspromedia.com/from-the-magazine/leeds-united-andrea-radrizzani-interview-sportspro-issue-111*

Meslier
Ayling Koch Cooper (Capt) Dallas (Alioski 81)
Klich
Costa Hernandez (Roberts 67) Shackleton (Poveda 45)
Harrison
Bamford
Subs: Casilla, Davis, Casey, Struijk, Alioski, Poveda, Roberts.
Leicester City: Schmeichel, Justin, Fofana, Fuchs, Albrighton, Tielemans, Mendy, Thomas, Praet (Maddison 63), Barnes (Ünder 71), Vardy (Morgan 85). Subs not used: Ward, Iheanacho, Perez, Choudhury.
Referee: Andre Marriner.

The main change was signalled by my pal Kev W in a WhatsApp post on our Leeds United group chat, just seconds after 7 pm when the team was announced. Kev wrote simply: *"Hernandez starts"*. It was a surprise to me that was only explained when I saw the tweet from Phil Hay of 'The Athletic' who wrote: *"Rodrigo is out tonight, self-isolating after coming into contact with someone who tested positive for Covid. Raphinha absent after picking up an ankle injury."* *"Damn Covid!"*, I thought to myself, *"and damn these injuries!"* Having said that though, I was happy to see the return of our prodigal son Pablo, as I always felt he was the glue that held our play together, although recognising he was in the twilight of his career now and that he hadn't hit the high notes in the few minutes we'd seen him on the pitch this season. I was hoping we'd see the Pablo who almost single-handedly led us through those final nine games at the end of the Championship season. It was also fair to recognise that Leicester also had their share of injury problems with the whole of their first choice back line missing. In the following days it would be announced that Rodrigo himself had tested positive for Covid and, with case numbers soaring all over Europe, no one could be surprised that footballers were now being affected.

I settled down in front of the TV and watched as Jamie Carragher and the rest of the Sky team drooled over Mauricio Pochettino who was tonight's special guest on the show. The former Spurs manager was clearly putting himself in the shop window again, presumably looking for another crack at the EPL and, of course, he was full of praise in equal measure for both Brendan Rodgers and Marcelo Bielsa, the respective head coaches of Leicester and Leeds. It would be another couple of months before Pochettino landed a top job; he would become the new PSG manager on 3rd January, 2021 following the sacking of Thomas Tuchel; more about him later.

Our game was billed as a battle of wits between Rodgers and Bielsa, with Rodgers openly admitting in a brief pre-match interview that he'd be looking for the pace of Barnes and Vardy to undo Leeds on the counter-attack. *"Leeds very much play man to man which is different to what most teams will play"* he explained. *"What do you feel is the way to challenge what they present then?"* asked the interviewer. *"Well there's lots of space on the field"* he replied, *"They want to attack, and to attack in numbers but at times that will leave them exposed... and I would say that we have the best counter-attacking player in the league in Jamie Vardy"* adding that *"Harvey [Barnes] is super-fast as well"*. The camera cut away from Rodgers to a shot of the night sky over Elland Road showing the rains brought by storm Aiden pouring down. *"I wonder if that will also affect the game"* asked Sky presenter David Jones.

The rain was still lashing down as Liam Cooper and Kasper Schmeichel led their respective teams onto the pitch, each carrying a remembrance wreath. Cooper and his troops emerged from the tunnel and Leicester made their way down the steps of the West Stand to comply with one of the Covid Protocol stipulations requiring teams not to rub shoulders en route to the pitch from the dressing rooms. The wreaths were laid in the corners of the technical areas and the players lined up around the centre-circle as the *Last Post* was played by a lone bugler, in the usual Elland Road manner for this, the nearest kick-off ahead of Remembrance Sunday. The smiling face of Nobby Stiles also looked down from the big screen as he was remembered and the players all wore black armbands as a further tribute. Martin Tyler and former Arsenal and Leicester striker Alan Smith took up the commentary; Tyler making his usual *"It's Leicester at Leeds, and - it's - live!"* pre-match ritual announcement. Tyler reminded viewers of Nobby Stiles' strong connections to Leeds. His brother in law, Johnny Giles is a Leeds legend of course and not forgetting either that Nobby's son, John Charles Stiles played for Leeds between 1984 and 1989, scoring two goals. The scene was set; it felt like a big moment among many big moments we'd seen already this season but little did we know at the time that within three minutes it would turn into one of the many fiascos we have witnessed with Leeds on such big occasions. I have lost count of the number of times when our hopes and expectations have been built up to fever pitch ahead of a game only for Leeds to extinguish them with a piece of sheer stupidity or naivety within seconds.

All the players knelt at the referee's first whistle as the campaign against racism continued and then Leicester kicked off. Leeds were immediately on the front foot, pushing up the pitch towards the Leicester goal in front of the Norman Hunter Stand, with Leicester finding it hard to get the ball. The first minute passed with Leeds in possession as we played the ball all the way back to Illan Meslier who tapped it out again to Robin Koch who exchanged short passes with Luke Ayling and then Liam Cooper. Koch then played the ball to Ayling again, on the right touchline, and he, in turn, found Hernandez who quickly prodded the ball on to Costa on the right edge of the area. He had three Leicester players closing him down but managed to scoop the ball across to the back post where Harrison was in space. Jack nodded the ball back inside and there was Patrick Bamford, Harry Hot-Shot himself, six yards out with the ball coming straight to his head with just Schmeichel between him and the net. Bamford was in acres of space, all alone with eight yards to aim at but, incredibly, he nodded the ball straight at Schmeichel. It was already Bamford's fourth 'big chance' missed of the season, as folk who define and record such things would later report, and Patrick Hat-Trick now had his head in his hands as I fell back onto the sofa having momentarily jumped up, punching the air and just missing the light fitting hanging from the ceiling in our front room. It was a shocking miss (Bamford's not mine) but it was nowhere near as shocking as what was now unfolding on the screen in front of my eyes.

The speed with which Leicester moved the ball from the hands of Schmeichel to the back of our net took even the Sky camera team by surprise; they were still showing a replay of the Bamford miss before cutting back to the action just as Jamie Vardy pushed the ball across goal behind Meslier to Harvey Barnes who stabbed it into the empty net. We had to wait for a replay to see exactly what happened. Schmeichel rolled the ball out to his left and the Foxes' left-back launched the ball all the way down that left wing. It was too long for Ayling, still tracking back after the previous Leeds attack, and so it ran on behind to Robin Koch, now facing his own goal and near the west touchline midway in the Leeds half. Ayling pointed out the necessary ball back to Meslier but when Koch attempted to play it he under-hit it dramatically with the outside of his right boot, and Vardy was onto it in a flash. Cooper was left for dead near the 'D' not expecting there to be any need to get back. Vardy shimmied to the left going past Meslier while Harvey Barnes seemed instinctively to know where to run for the return ball and Vardy's pass behind the keeper gave him a simple tap in. From almost being a goal up to being a goal down took less than twenty seconds.

This was such a familiar feeling for me and I'm sure for any Leeds fan with a few years of Leeds in their blood. It was the same feeling we had on the first day of the season up at Anfield of course, albeit at least that one we could blame on a poor referee's decision. That came some three minutes into that game and it brought us all down to earth with a thump just as this one did now; the fires of hope extinguished so quickly. I don't have to think long to come up with many, many more examples. Millwall last season when I was privileged to be up on the gantry with my buddy Keith, again, such high hopes of a season-defining win and there again we were a goal down inside four minutes from a bloody corner; we did at least eventually win that one of course but when we conceded so early it was this same feeling.

I think it was doubly frustrating this time because we'd just made two diabolical errors, one missing in front of goal and the other giving the ball to Vardy. To give a side like Leicester a goal start was like signing our own death sentence; unforgiveable. It showed in Leeds' play for the next twenty minutes too, we were visibly shocked. That, and the conditions probably didn't help either but we were making errors all over the pitch. Even Pablo was passing the ball straight to the Foxes or curling a corner out of play on a regular basis while Jamie Shackleton looked completely lost and we were wasting more crosses than a Roman carpenter's apprentice. Maybe we were trying too hard. Meslier kept us in it with still only 11 minutes on the clock as he tipped a shot over the bar at full stretch; I almost moved to watch from behind the sofa;

this was more of a horror show than Halloween itself had been two days earlier!

It was no real surprise when Leicester sprang forward again in the 21st minute, a cross from the right beat Cooper at the near post, Vardy beat Koch to a diving header and Meslier could only knock the ball to the feet of Tielemans as it came off a glove and then his head. The Leicester man rifled the ball home from six yards. 0 – 2 with 21 minutes gone and I must admit I'd almost given up hope. The only thing keeping me going was thinking back to that Millwall game; we went in at halftime two goals down that night as well, but then a rip-roaring second half display saw us win 3 – 2. It did feel a bit like that one but Leicester were a tad better than Millwall of course and I knew that too.

Still the mistakes kept coming; Meslier almost fumbled a near-post cross into his own net as he juggled with it a la the proverbial bar of soap and then, when he rolled the ball out to Koch, our Robin fired the ball a good two yards wide of Ayling and out of play. It was getting embarrassing now! Seconds later and Meslier rolled the ball straight to a blue shirt! As Tyler and Smith discussed the mistakes on commentary the camera panned to Liam Cooper just as Smith spoke about the need for strong leadership on the pitch to settle the nerves. The one factor to cling to was that Leeds were still dominating the possession, having almost double the amount of ball Leicester were enjoying and, slowly, we did seem to calm the nerves. The feeling just started to grow in my mind that we only needed a goal to get us going, as we did eventually get in that Millwall game. We should have got it too as another big chance for Patrick Bamford went by the wayside. We were into the 38th minute.

Klich pushed the ball firmly to Luke Ayling who'd cut inside for once and he immediately threaded the ball through the line of six blue shirts to find Patrick Bamford suddenly behind them all and onside and only 12 yards out. His first touch though was heavy and that gave Schmeichel time to close him down and the second touch put the ball safely into the keeper's clutches. I was sure that would be big chance number five of the season once the statisticians got through their work. So, at halftime it was 0 – 2 but, poor as some of our play was and so plentiful and serious had been the mistakes, we were by no means dead and buried yet. I remembered what I'd said to Keith as we started the second half against Millwall that night; *"We need a goal in the first ten minutes of this second half..."* and we got one within three minutes of the restart. Blow me down, we only went and did it again.

I'd only just settled back down, now armed with a tumbler of malt having given up on finding any magic powers in the Red Stripe, when Leeds won a corner on the left as we attacked the Kop. Leeds now had Ian Poveda on the pitch, replacing the rather anonymous Jamie Shackleton. Matty Klich and Jack Harrison stood over the ball. Klich tapped it to Harrison who then knocked it all the way back to Stuart Dallas, some thirty yards out and level with the left edge of the area. Dallas took one touch and then curled the ball over towards the back post with his right foot. Schmeichel stood rooted to his line as the ball came across and a whole gaggle of players jumped for it but none got a touch and it merely carried on serenely to bounce into the far corner of the net. I glanced at the malt and made a mental note to try this more often!

Leeds were up for this now and suddenly it was the Foxes being hunted and chased for every ball. The only thing missing to help our cause was a noisy crowd of 36,000 Leeds fans, otherwise this was following that Millwall script pretty much line for line. In January against the Lions, it was a goal from Pablo Hernandez just after the hour mark that brought us level. This time it was a few minutes earlier when he almost did it again. Leeds had another corner on the left and Harrison and Klich initially both stood over it again. Eventually though Klich jogged away to leave Harrison to swing it across. The ball was headed clear of the box off a couple of Leicester heads, the second one ballooning it up into the air and it came down just outside the 'D'. It was the little magician who was under it and with an exquisite touch with his right foot he killed the ball stone dead and eased it around a Leicester boot to the left before getting it back on his preferred right side. Then he curled it almost perfectly towards the top right corner. It looked a goal all the way and Schmeichel could only watch and pray as it rose and then dipped but then struck the crossbar six inches from the right post and cannoned back to be hooked clear. Horizontally the sights were perfectly set, vertically they were six inches too high. It would have been a sumptuous goal but, this time it was not to be and, in hindsight, we knew that was the game gone in that one moment.

Had it gone in then I have no doubt we'd have gone on to win just as we did back in January in identical circumstances.

Having seen how close Pablo came to squaring the game through a wave of his magical right boot, it was a major surprise, to me at any rate, that Marcelo chose to substitute the Spanish genius on 67 minutes, turning instead to Tyler Roberts. Pablo was clearly annoyed and the cameras followed him as he trudged around the pitch shaking his head, tearing off his black armband and throwing it to the ground and then apparently kicking a water bottle near the dugouts, although we didn't get to see that on camera. I was sure Pablo would regret the slinging of the armband; that is something that is just not acceptable and would have upset many fans watching and goodness knows what Bielsa thought!

Whatever was in Bielsa's mind I don't think it worked. Roberts didn't really get too involved in the game before it was once again taken further from our reach as Leicester grabbed a third goal only nine minutes later and then sealed it in added time with a penalty. Their third was a classic Leicester counter-attack, made at lightning speed, set up by two of the Foxes' substitutes and finished by Vardy. The penalty was a soft affair as Klich got too close to the back of James Maddison on the right edge of the area. Maddison did the predictable triple salchow and, after an interminable delay and a visit to the VAR monitor, Marriner gave the penalty and Leeds shipped a fourth. Tielemans tucked it away in the top corner and that was that; the game did indeed end 4 – 1 just like that U23 game and the ladies game this weekend, but not the way we expected.

Initially, it was tempting to write this off as a poor Leeds performance, but on closer inspection there wasn't as much between the sides as the result suggested. Bamford had those two big chances that he missed and the first led directly to Leicester breaking away and scoring after the Koch-up. We'll never know what the outcome might have been had Bamford put that chance away as surely he ought to have done. The penalty was soft and, on another day, wouldn't have been given. Leeds had 68% of the possession and one more goal attempt than Leicester. Leeds won ten corners to the three earned by the Foxes. Leeds did have a very wobbly twenty-minute period at the start, possibly fuelled by the Koch mistake or the dire conditions or both, but apart from that, no, there wasn't a lot between these sides. It was a reminder above all else though that mistakes cost games and mistakes in the EPL are punished even more certainly than they are in the Championship. Marcelo had also warned after our first few games this season that a time would come when we wouldn't put away quite such a high proportion of our chances and hence why we needed to ensure we keep creating plenty. He freely admitted after this one that we didn't create enough. Bielsa told the BBC: *"In the first 30 minutes, we defended poorly and after that we didn't create enough danger. That is one of the main responsibilities of the manager. I am not taking the blame, just stating the players were not correctly distributed. The players are disappointed. Every game is an opportunity to recover, especially after a defeat."* That was as good a summary as any. Thankfully, we wouldn't have to dwell on this one for long; next up was a trip to Selhurst Park as soon as Saturday and I was going to miss not being at that one more than most.

I love the Palace trip; drinking before the game in the pubs of Thornton Heath and then walking up the road to the fine old Selhurst Park stadium to enjoy the magnificent eagle flying display on the pitch before the game and not to mention their fabulous cheerleader group, The Crystals! Google *"Crystal Palace Cheerleaders, I love it"* and watch their video of the Icona Pop song *"I Love It"* ... or the one of them as they *"Do Gangnam Style"*... or the one as they dance to the Crystal Palace anthem, *"Glad All Over"*... or another one as they do their version of *"Call Me Maybe"*... not that I've just spent much time watching them all... Ah, here comes the wife, now, where were we?

Leeds United 1 Leicester City 4 (Barnes 2, Tielemans 21, 90+1 pen, **Dallas 48**, Vardy 76,)

BCD. Round 7 League Pos: 12th.

Eagles Soar

T he big football news in the wake of our defeat on Monday night was the arrest of the Wales football manager Ryan Giggs. He'd been arrested on Sunday night regarding allegations of assault made by his girlfriend. Giggs denied all the charges but the Welsh FA immediately announced he would step down temporarily from his position as head coach ahead of the next international break that was looming after the weekend. It was unfortunate that, just as the Welsh national side was in a good place having gone ten competitive games unbeaten, along came this bombshell to potentially upset the apple cart.

There was chaos in America too as we waited for a definitive result in the US election which was so close that it took days to establish that 77-year-old (78 in less than a month) Joe Biden had err, trumped Donald to win a place in the White House.

As I waited for the first EPL games of the weekend to start on Friday evening, news filtered through on Twitter that the U23s had come unstuck at Newcastle. They'd raced into a 3 – 0 lead with two goals from Liam McCarron and a penalty from Joe Gelhardt inside the first half hour but lost the game 4 – 3. None of the regular first-team squad was involved.

The first two EPL games of the next round, game week 8, took place later that Friday, with both games ending in not unexpected results. Brighton and Burnley, both struggling at the foot of the table, played out a nil-nil draw while Southampton, the surprise package of the season so far, comfortably beat erratic Newcastle 2 – 0 to go top of the table with 16 points from their first eight games. I watched the Saints game and was impressed; they were in control throughout. Our game at Selhurst Park was the second game of four to be played on Saturday.

First off was the game between early pace-setters Everton and Manchester United who were struggling to find any sort of form, with Ole Gunnar Solskjær under pressure to quickly change their fortunes. The media vultures were gathering, believing he could well be the first EPL gaffer to bite the dust this season but we Leeds fans were adamant he should stay; we saw nothing wrong with their steady decline! The Red Devils comfortably beat a poor-looking Everton side that appeared to have peaked way too early this season; this 1 – 3 reverse being their third defeat on the trot having started with four wins from their first four games. Once this game was over I began searching the internet for a decent free stream for our game as it was another BT Box Office jobbie with that £14.95 price tag. The EPL had announced that the widespread boycott of these PPV games had caused them to reconsider the policy and they promised to drop the scheme after completion of this round of games. They hadn't though confirmed if we'd get all the future games as part of our Sky or BT subscriptions once they restarted after the break.

Our game at Palace was a rare Saturday 3 pm kick-off and, an hour before that, the team news came through on Twitter; there was a lot to absorb.

Meslier
Ayling Koch Cooper (Capt) Alioski
Struijk (Roberts 71)
Costa (Raphinha 45) Dallas Klich Harrison
Bamford
Subs: Casilla, Davis, Casey, Jenkins, Poveda, Roberts, Raphinha.

Crystal Palace: Guaita, Clyne, Kouyaté, Dann, van Aanholt, Townsend (Schlupp 71), Riedewald (McCarthy 77), McArthur, Eze, J Ayew (Benteke 85), Zaha. Subs not used: Butland, Sakho, Batshuayi, Cahill.

Referee: Chris Kavanagh.

We knew Rodrigo was still self-isolating and we knew Kalvin Phillips and Diego Llorente were still injured. What we didn't know was where the hell was Pablo Hernandez? There were only two possibilities; either Pablo too had picked up an injury, or, that show of dissent we saw at Elland Road on Monday had caused Bielsa to leave him out. There was no other explanation as to why he would not at least feature on the bench with Rodrigo known to be unavailable and, for me at least, putting Dallas in his place made us weaker; weaker in defence and weaker in midfield. The return of Pascal Struijk was not as contentious as we all knew he was only hooked from the Leicester game so early on account of that yellow card. The Leeds bench also showed we were still a bit light as a squad, with only Poveda and Raphinha inspiring much confidence as potential game-changers.

There were more wreaths and another rendition of the *"Last Post"* before kick-off as this was the nominated Crystal Palace Remembrance Day tribute and then I had a moment of panic when the commentary on my stream began… it was in Hindi! I was on releasesky.com on the laptop and they had two options; I'd obviously clicked on the Indian language version! I quickly closed that and switched to the other one and hey presto, picture clear as day, I had the game with an English commentary. As the camera panned around Selhurst Park I remembered back to my previous visit here, a 2 – 2 draw in March 2013 when Steve Morison scored a brace. Just looking back through my records as I write this, I also noticed that the game prior to that was, coincidentally, against Leicester City, just as it was this year. We drew that one as well, 1 – 1 at the King Power with a rare Sam Byram goal. A month earlier, still in 2013, I noticed we played Wolves and drew that one too. Just over seven years later and we were all plying our trade in the EPL not the Championship. The last time Leeds played at Selhurst Park in the EPL was as far back as January 1998 when Jimmy Floyd Hasselbaink and Rod Wallace both scored in a 2 – 0 win over a Palace side that included former Leeds man Tomas

Brolin. He was booed throughout the game by the traveling Leeds fans!

Leeds were winless on our previous 11 visits to the capital, having lost nine and drawn just two and, in fact, we only had one win in the previous 20 league games played in London, a 1 – 3 victory at QPR in December 2017 when Kemar Roofe scored a hat-trick. Those were all in the Championship though… this was a different era, surely? With both Palace and Leeds having near-identical records and locked together in 12th and 13th places in the table with ten points, this was a chance for either side to make significant progress back into the top half. It was a bright start from both teams too, almost as if they were well aware of the possibilities.

Both teams spent the first ten minutes or so just sparring with each other although Palace looked sharp with the likes of Wilf Zaha and Eberechi Eze both regularly on the ball. Leeds won the first corner during this period and Cooper sent a header over the bar from that one. Then, with eleven minutes gone, Palace won their first corner as the ball ricocheted off the legs of Luke Ayling. I sat up a bit straighter and shifted uncomfortably as dozens of goals Leeds had conceded from corners flashed through my subconscious. Had I of been inside the ground, I'm sure I'd have heard someone mutter *"Come on Leeds, for once f****** deal with it please…"*

That man Eze stood over the ball in the left quadrant and then curled it into the Leeds area towards the back post. Robin Koch was in front of Scott Dann and Liam Cooper came late from behind but Dann still got his head on the ball and it flew into the top right corner. That sinking feeling flooded over me again. Out of the TV speakers that damned Dave Clark Five tune *" Glad All Over"* was booming out while the Palace players celebrated wildly. Truth be told, I was already convinced we'd lose the game now, it just felt so 'Leedsy'. It was a game in London where we almost never win; we'd conceded from a corner as we always do; and we had neither Rodrigo nor Pablo to galvanise a recovery. Sure I had hope, but I had very little expectation. Five minutes later and I was totally convinced this would not be our day as we had another one of those extreme high, extreme low moments; another classic example of our infamous 'ups and downs'.

It started with a fabulous Leeds 'goal'. Leeds were bossing the possession as we always do and we moved the ball out to the left with Alioski and then back to Cooper who moved it out to the right side to Helder Costa. Costa, in turn, found Luke Ayling and he had Klich and Bamford with their hands pointing where they each wanted the ball, 'Bill' eventually picking out Klich on the edge of the box. Matty Klich took one touch, turned full circle to his right and flicked the ball through the Palace back line into the path of Patrick Bamford, still pointing where he wanted the pass. The ball was perfect and Bamford took a couple of strides before lifting it delicately over the keeper to nestle it inside the left post. It was a glorious move of nine passes with the perfect finish and, for a few seconds, I chastised myself for thinking so negatively just minutes earlier. Our luck in the capital was clearly changing. But, hold my beer, what's this? VAR was checking something; was Bamford offside? My TV showed the line as the ball was played by Klich and I breathed a sigh of relief; Bamford was clearly well *onside*, his feet well behind those of the defenders either side of him, although he was leaning forward with that left arm outstretched, pointing where the ball needed to go. Still VAR was checking and we saw the VAR screen with lines all over it trying to pick up the exact point where Bamford's short sleeve ended as this was currently the lowest point of the arm not considered handball – the so-called armpit rule - and therefore the furthest point forward that could be considered offside. It was going on so long that Mike 'Deadly' Dean, the VAR referee, clearly thought it was close.

But from what we could see on our TVs it was at worst level and it was impossible to know exactly where to drop the vertical lines from anyway, either on Bamford or the nearest defender let alone another defender who was mostly obscured by Bamford from the cameras although appeared to have his backside much nearer to goal than any part of Bamford's arm.

It's history now of course and you all know how it ended. The 'goal' was ruled out, with Bamford's arm said to be offside and it was the talk of the sports press and commentators all weekend. The likes of Robbie Savage called it the worst offside shout in the history of football, a comment echoed later that night on Match Of The Day. It was no consolation now though, it just got filed in that *"No fu***** luck in London"* file again. You decide…

All the players instinctively knew it was a perfectly good goal; Palace weren't complaining or appealing and everyone was waiting in position for the restart, but Mike Dean, with his set-square and Micky Mouse plastic ruler in Stockley Park, came to a different conclusion. The injustice would stay with me throughout the game and at the restart there was an air of *"what's the point?"* about Leeds' play for a while as they seemed to be going through the motions but gradually they settled back to the task in hand.

We moved on to the 20th minute and another strange moment as Mateusz Klich suddenly collapsed during a Palace attack, seemingly getting his studs caught in the turf. The attack was eventually halted as Eze was tackled by Robin Koch, a couple of yards outside our area. Eze, predictably, went down like the proverbial sack of spuds clutching an imaginary injured ankle, having done that thing when a player drags his back leg to make it look like he's been tripped. Chris Kavanagh bought it and gave the free-kick and every Leeds fan in the world knew what was coming…

It's a sad indictment of the modern game that too many matches are won and lost through cheating and poor officiating; if you get the rub of the green on such things you will usually win, particularly if the game is otherwise equal. It was Eze himself, miraculously recovered from the damaged ankle, who stepped up and curled the free-kick into the top left corner. Sometimes you just have to accept that the football gods are against you but I do admit it was one hell of a free-kick.

The game was still only 22 minutes old but it felt like we'd been playing for an hour, so much had already gone on and, although there was loads of time left, it just felt like it wasn't our day to me, even though my pre-match prediction of 2 – 2 was still perfectly possible. Even when Bamford did get on the score sheet, with still only 26 minutes on the clock, it sort of felt to me like a consolation. It was another fine piece of finishing from Paddy though, not dissimilar to the one chalked off. The ball looped into the area where Mateusz Klich headed it backwards into the path of Bamford and, on the first bounce, he took it on his chest and then volleyed it perfectly into the corner of the net with his left boot. His couple of misses against Leicester aside, the man was on fire.

For the next 15 minutes Leeds dominated the possession but our play was slower than usual and every attack seemed to lack something in the middle of the park. It was that vision and preciseness of a Pablo or a Rodrigo that wasn't there, meaning that the ball was moving straight from our back line up to Klich, just behind Bamford and too close to the Palace defence, almost every time. Sadly we were lacking in quality too. Time and time again we'd work the ball out to Harrison or Costa but just as often they'd get caught in possession or fail to get a cross worth the name into the box. By contrast, Palace had hardly any ball but when they did they oozed quality and I always felt we were only one attack away from another Palace goal. I was right, but the nature of it made even me look to the heavens; it was another goal that only Leeds in London could suffer.

Yet another slow, ponderous Leeds attack ended with yet another slack pass from Jack Harrison, giving the ball away in the final third out near the Palace right touchline. Alioski then gave a soft free-kick away in the centre of the pitch. Palace moved the ball out to their left and eventually it arrived with Wilf Zaha who went to and fro a few times before suddenly playing a reverse pass all along the touchline and deep into the Leeds right-back corner where Patrick van Aanholt was now behind the Leeds defence looking to cross. He had Helder Costa covering him and, as the Palace man struck the ball low towards goal, Costa's sliding boot deflected the ball straight as an arrow along the turf and inside the near post with

Meslier now wrong-footed and expecting the ball to be coming more towards his six-yard line. I have to say that, on the replay, it looked as though Meslier wasn't exactly on his toes but it was a freak goal and it sort of summed up the day.

3 – 1 down at halftime, Leeds swapped Costa for Raphinha for the second half and, once again he had a decent game, always looking bright on the ball but, overall, Leeds continued to look a bit like they did throughout the first half; plenty of perspiration but very little inspiration. It was difficult admittedly as Palace had a two-goal lead and they basically lined up in their own half in three lines in a 4 – 4 – 2 formation and said to Leeds: *"Try and get through that"*. Without the magic that Pablo brings, I couldn't see it happening and we just didn't create enough chances, in fact it almost looked like we were playing with ten men. Pascal Struijk put a header wide from a corner but that was pretty much the extent of Leeds' chances. We toiled and toiled and continued to dominate the possession but the final ball from Dallas, Struijk or Alioski, quite simply wasn't good enough. The situation was crying out for a Pablo or a Rodrigo patrolling that area outside the box looking for the incisive through-ball. I wondered again why on earth Bielsa felt it necessary to leave Pablo out as messages on my WhatsApp and Twitter feeds suggested that was indeed what had happened; Pablo had been available and fit but had been dropped, presumably because of that show of dissent against Leicester. Well, it looked short sighted to me.

To be fair, Palace were no better than we were in the second half but of course they didn't have to be so maybe they had more gears to use if needed. It took twenty minutes of the half for Leeds to get a strike on target – a long-range effort from Alioski turned low around the post by Guaita in the Palace goal – and then another followed quickly as Jack Harrison fired straight at the keeper, again from outside the box. There wasn't much going on at the other end either and only a weak Zaha shot straight at Meslier came from Palace but then, with just over twenty minutes left, Palace sprung the Leeds defence again much as we saw Leicester do.

A promising Leeds attack broke down midway in the Palace half with a couple of loose Leeds passes that left Klich clearly frustrated as his shoulders slumped and he swatted away an imaginary mosquito while Palace swiftly moved the ball to Zaha on the left corner of our box. Suddenly, the Leeds defence parted in front of Zaha, with Koch and Ayling to the left and Struijk, Cooper and Alioski on the right of a lovely clear corridor towards the penalty spot where Jordan Ayew was waiting. Zaha played the ball through the corridor to Ayew who let it run across his body and then lashed it past Meslier at his near post. It was the classic sucker punch again and it was terrible defending from Leeds. The body language of the Leeds players signalled that now, at 4 – 1 down, the ghost had well and truly been given up.

Tyler Roberts was immediately sent on for Pascal Struijk as Leeds tried to change their shape and presumably the intention was for Roberts to fill that vacant Pablo/Rodrigo role that was so obviously missing from the middle. It was way too late though and Palace easily saw out the remainder of the game although there was still time for the obligatory big chance miss by Patrick Bamford. This one came from a left-wing cross from Matty Klich that found the erratic Leeds striker in perfect position between two Palace defenders. Sadly, he got his jump all wrong and the ball connected somewhere between his head and his shoulder and looped harmlessly wide. As good as he'd been this season with his ballet-like feet he was still about as useless in the air as a lead balloon.

Palace had a couple of very good chances in the final minutes that could have made it a much worse day but Meslier saved one and Palace messed up another while Raphinha showed us he has a decent free-kick in his locker as he curled one inches wide. It was two very tired teams that shook hands at the end as Palace zoomed up the table to end this round of games 8th while Leeds slipped to 15th.

There were still six games to go in this final round before the next international break and after our game I watched as Chelsea beat Sheffield United with another 4 – 1 scoreline and then West Ham sneaked past Fulham with a late winner. Fulham's Ademola Lookman had the chance to level things up with an even later penalty in that one but he tried the infamous Panenka style dink and got it all wrong. He spooned the ball gently into the arms of the West Ham keeper for the funniest moment of the weekend. The Panenka is named after the Czech player Antonín Panenka, who introduced this technique in the 1976 UEFA European

Championship final when he beat West German goalkeeper Sepp Maier to claim the title for the Czechs. On Sunday, the final four games saw Spurs win by the only goal at West Brom and Leicester win, also by the only goal, at home to Wolves. Manchester City and Liverpool played out a 1 – 1 draw; and then, the shock result of the round, Aston Villa beat Arsenal 0 – 3 at the Emirates. All that meant Leicester went into the break at the top with 18 points, from Spurs and Liverpool with 17, and Southampton on 16. In Scotland, Rangers were romping away, with 38 points from just 14 games having this weekend walloped Hamilton 8 – 0, including two more Kemar Roofe goals. Celtic were trailing them by nine points but did have a couple of games in hand. That was it for now, some interesting international games to come, but for Leeds it was a well-earned fortnight off.

Crystal Palace 4 **Leeds United 1** (Dann 12, Eze 22, **Bamford 27**, Costa og 42, J Ayew 70
BCD. **Round 8 League Pos: 15th**

...And Pause Again

With much of the nation in lockdown again, those of us not working found ourselves at somewhat of a loose end as the next international break dawned, certainly until the competitive games came round anyway. For this second lockdown the Government decreed that fans were not allowed at *any* football grounds in England, not even the so-called non-elite clubs like Worcester City where I'd been able to get a bit of a football fix in recent weeks and which had escaped the ban until now. I was thus now effectively grounded. Parliament had at least been forced to debate the question of allowing fans back following the successful petition that passed the required 100,000 signatures, but the second lockdown meant there was no question of the rules changing at least until 2nd December when, all being well, the latest restrictions were due to be lifted. I read the transcript of the debate which consisted of a whole series of MPs virtue-signalling their support of their own local clubs without actually providing any sensible suggestions as to how we could get the fans back. In Scotland, the best story came from David Linden SMP, representative for Glasgow East. He declared himself to be a season-ticket holder at Airdrieonians and his emphasis was on the lengths clubs were going to so fans could at least see their teams on TV. His story came from an Inverness Caledonian Thistle versus Ayr United game, played recently behind closed doors. For this game, 'Caley' trialled a robot filming system whereby the camera was primed to track the ball without intervention from a cameraman, thus removing one more person from the crew required in an attempt to keep Covid exposure to the absolute minimum. Sadly, the liner on the near touchline was totally bald and that proved to be more of an attraction to the ball recognition software than the football! And we wonder why VAR is taking so long to bed in! The recent announcement that a vaccine could be ready to distribute to the public as early as December still seemed our best chance of seeing live football this season.

One piece of promising news coming out of Leeds as we waited for those international games was that it appeared the rift between Pablo Hernandez and Marcelo Bielsa might be coming to an end.

Pablo took to Instagram to begin the healing process by telling his followers in somewhat broken English: *"Apologies for my gesture the other day, it was a reaction that nothing describes my way of being or my way of thinking. I have always represented and will represent the values of this club and this fans as they deserve. #lestweforget"*. It was the least he could do having offended so many through the blatant disregard he'd shown for the Armistice black armband that he appeared to throw away.

Less good news was that our Under 21s had now bowed out of the EFL Trophy. Needing a win in their final group game at Blackpool, they were soundly beaten 3 – 0, despite the inclusion of Ian Poveda in the side. We'd earned just a single point for the 2 – 2 draw at Barrow and thus there would be no pizza glory in the Papa John's Trophy this year...

There were a few international friendlies taking place – ridiculous when you consider how much competitive football was being played to try to get everything squeezed into a shortened season – but the real interest was in the Euro 2020 play-off games. In the friendlies, Robin Koch played a full 90 minutes as Germany beat the Czech Republic and similarly Mateusz Klich played the whole game as Poland beat Ukraine 2 – 0. In the European Championship play-offs, Ezgjan Alioski was first to enjoy success as his North Macedonia side won by a single goal in Georgia to win their place in the finals next year. Next came Scotland, with Liam Cooper an unused substitute as the Scots edged past Serbia on penalties having drawn 1 – 1. I watched on TV as Northern Ireland fought bravely but went out after extra-time against Slovakia. Stuart Dallas injured an arm during the game but played on and all Leeds fans had their fingers crossed he wasn't about to join our ever-growing list of injured players. Thus it looked like Leeds could have six or seven players involved in the Euro 2020 finals next summer, with Rodrigo and Llorente both possibly representing Spain; Robin Koch likely to feature for Germany; Alioski an almost certain starter for North Macedonia; Kalvin Phillips for England; Tyler Roberts for Wales; and Liam Cooper for Scotland.

England of course had already qualified and so used this first international date for a hastily arranged friendly with the Republic of Ireland which they won at a canter, 3 – 0. The original game against New Zealand was cancelled due to the complications created by the latest Covid restrictions. There was no Kalvin Phillips of course but 17-year-old Jude Bellingham, now with Borussia Dortmund, became the 3rd youngest England player of all time when he came on as a 73rd-minute substitute. Who are the two ahead of him in the list? Answers at the end of the chapter.

They say 13 is unlucky but I doubt many folk would be shedding a tear over the news that broke on Friday 13th November; the so-called Yorkshire Ripper, Peter Sutcliffe died at the age of 74. He'd become infamous in the late 1970s when terrorising Yorkshire with a series of murders and attacks on women. He'd apparently succumbed to Covid-19 whilst serving his whole life order in jail. Sadly there were two more iconic names from my youth who met their maker this week and who *will* be missed; former Liverpool and England goalkeeper Ray Clemence and entertainer Des O'Connor.

I was lucky enough to see Ray Clemence play several times in the late 70s in games against Leeds and in the 1980 FA Charity Shield match at the old Wembley stadium when 'Pool beat West Ham. Once again a footballer of that era didn't make it into his eighth decade although one close to all Leeds hearts did make it this week; Johnny Giles turned 80. Des O'Connor made it to 88 and, as with Bobby Ball and Frank Bough who we lost recently, was also a constant face on TV screens when I was growing up. He also has a link with football as he once played professional football for Northampton Town... and no, that's not Cobblers, it's true! His first hit single was the classic *"Careless Hands"* and it topped the UK charts in 1967 just in time for the Liverpool Kop to serenade our own Gary Sprake in December of that year when the unfortunate Welsh keeper accidentally threw the ball into his own net in a 2 – 0 defeat at a snow-covered Anfield. It is said to be one of the most comical own goals of all time.

With the friendlies and Euro play-offs out of the way, the international sides turned their attentions to the UEFA Nations League; most teams had two games scheduled. In the first matches, Germany eased past Ukraine 3 – 1 with Robin Koch again playing the full 90 minutes, but fortunately both Matty Klich (Poland) and Gjanni Alioski (North Macedonia) were suspended for their initial games and Alioski was then also ruled out of the following game with a swollen hamstring so he returned to Leeds. Liam Cooper played the whole game for Scotland as they lost in Slovakia and Stuart Dallas did likewise as NI went down in Austria. Tyler Roberts got a few minutes at the end of the Wales game against the Republic of Ireland. The final games followed quickly, meaning that most nations had managed three games in seven days; a ridiculous schedule when added to the compressed domestic season and it was hardly surprising that a record number of muscle injuries were occurring. The schedule was clearly too much for Germany as they, with Robin Koch playing another 90 minutes, were hammered 6 – 0 by Spain and failed to record a single shot on target! Matty Klich returned to the Poland side and played the full 90 as they went down 1 – 2 to the Netherlands while Stuart Dallas also did the full game for NI as they drew 1 – 1 with Romania; a result that relegated the Irish to the 'B' section of the Nations League. Liam Cooper was an unused sub as Scotland lost again, this time 1 – 0 in Israel, and Tyler Roberts was only used as a very late sub as Wales continued their good run with a 3 – 1 win over Finland.

The four teams thus going through to contest the Nations League finals next summer were Belgium, who knocked England out with their 2 – 0 win earlier in the week, Spain, Italy, and France. England finished their games with a 4 – 0 win against Iceland. All in all it had been a satisfactory international break for Leeds as it looked like everyone had returned injury-free and several had the benefit of not playing the full three games, either through suspensions or not being picked. It had also soaked up some of the recuperation time for the likes of Kalvin Phillips and Diego Llorente and the Covid isolation time Rodrigo needed. Patrick Bamford should also have been in good spirits as he was named the PFA Fans' Player of the Month for September/October, coming out ahead of the likes of Jamie Vardy, Jack Grealish, Dominic Calvert-Lewin and the Spurs duo of Son and Kane; some achievement!

There was talk that the Government was considering the case for allowing fans back into grounds as early as December despite the current high levels of Covid but, for now, it was more TV football as we settled in for the next stint of the EPL; whisper it quietly but they were also pondering whether we'd be allowed to get together with our extended families for Christmas!

Quiz answer: Theo Walcott and Wayne Rooney.

Gunners Fire Blanks

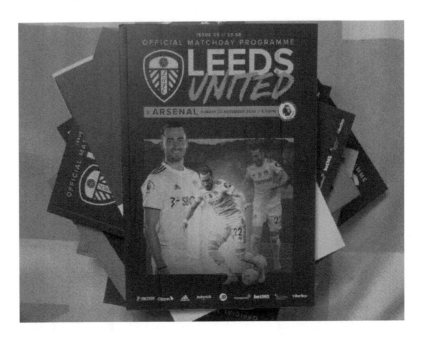

For the Arsenal game I was back in Edinburgh, exactly as I was on 17th July for the Father-in-Law's funeral and when promotion was secured as Huddersfield pulled off that magnificent and unexpected win over West Brom. Mrs W and I had driven up on the Wednesday ahead of the Arsenal game to be with the mother-in-law as she came out of hospital following a hip operation. We collected Mrs W's mum on Thursday morning and had an entertaining few minutes as we worked out how to get a walking frame, a toilet seat on legs, a bath seat and various walking sticks into an Audi A4 with three adults; suffice to say neither the walking frame nor the toilet seat fitted in the boot so Mrs W did the journey to the house on the other side of Edinburgh with a loo seat and its associated metalwork on her lap. We got some interesting looks from passers-by.

In the Friday press conference there was good news and bad from Marcelo Bielsa. The good news was that everyone who'd been away on international duty had returned injury-free and we had the additional boost of being told that both Kalvin Phillips and Rodrigo were now fit to resume playing. The bad news was that Pablo Hernandez now had another problem and Jamie Shackleton was also out. On Diego Llorente, Bielsa informed the journalists that he had recovered once but then suffered a relapse during training so they were now being extra careful about his latest rehabilitation. Bielsa confirmed that Phillips would start against Arsenal all being well but he was reluctant to confirm whether Rodrigo would.

Asked what he'd learned about his side following two 4 – 1 defeats, Bielsa launched into a long twenty-minute monologue about how he'd analysed every goal we'd conceded in the league this season, all 17 (it had to be didn't it?) of them, more than any other side in the EPL. He began by confirming the 17 number and comparing it to the best defensive record in the EPL, that of Spurs who'd conceded just nine. He went through each goal and discounted the four penalties we'd conceded, suggesting they were all doubtful and for which there wasn't much you can do anyway. He similarly discounted four more goals, including the freak Costa own goal and three others which he also considered were not down to any failure of his defence. Hence he considered the defence to be at fault for only nine goals... which, he pointed out, would be equal to the best defensive record in the division! I have to say it sounded a bit like one of my favourite sayings... *"If my auntie had been a bloke she'd have been my uncle!"* It was Bielsa's way of saying he didn't consider we were weak defensively, although he did consider that our worst defensive displays were the games against Manchester City and Liverpool, which most people considered were our best games! It was classic Bielsa. Mind you, he probably wasn't wrong about our defence; Leeds had amassed no less than 40 clean sheets in the 100 league games under Bielsa; that was more in that period than any other side in any of the four English league divisions.

The mother-in-law is not a huge sports fan and so there was no BT Sport or Sky on tap on the TV in Edinburgh so I was reconciled to having to watch the EPL games this weekend on the laptop. Pay Per View was at least now a thing of the past and we were back to the situation we had at the end of last season whereby every EPL game was scheduled for a different start time and all would be aired live either on BT, Sky or the BBC for the foreseeable future. The outcry against the £14.95 PPV fiasco had succeeded in bringing about the rethink. For BT games I'd have to log onto my son's BT account (or that of my buddy Cambridge Rob was another option) and for Sky games I could use the SkyGo feature so, in theory I could continue to watch every game pretty much as I'd been doing all season, albeit on the smaller laptop screen. First up, a 12:30 pm kick-off on Saturday lunchtime, was the Newcastle v Chelsea game which Chelsea won at a canter 2 – 0 to temporarily go top of the table thus becoming yet another side to win that accolade. Chelsea were looking very good and had scored 22 goals in their nine games, more than any other side at this stage and they had 18 points. My super-duper EPL spreadsheet also informed me that Chelsea already had 11 different goal scorers – 12 if you counted the one own goal they'd had – and that was also way more than any other side. It showed just what a decent squad they had this season. The second game saw Aston Villa host struggling Brighton. Villa started this one in the top six while Brighton were in the bottom six and yet it was Brighton that came out on top with a 1 – 2 score-line at Villa Park, thus continuing the yo-yo season Villa were putting together. They hammered Liverpool 7 – 2 remember, but then we went there and beat them 0 – 3. Then, before the break, they'd gone to Arsenal and beat them by three goals; they were totally unpredictable. In the final two games of the day I watched as Spurs beat Manchester City 2 – 0 and then Manchester United edged past West Brom 1 – 0. In general, the big six continued to build momentum.

To placate my other half, Sunday morning she had me walking into Edinburgh, my penance for then being allowed to sit behind the laptop for the rest of the day! It was a chance though to visit again one of my favourite places; Stockbridge Kitchen, a little bistro in Stockbridge on the outskirts of 'Auld Reekie' run by the lovely Allison and part-owned by her and big Leeds fan Paul R, aka @northbeach26 on Twitter. Allison was working in the shop but spotted us and recognised us from our previous visit back in early 2019. Maybe it was the Leeds badge on my coat she recognised, I'm not sure, but she waved and we went over to have a natter. The shop was open but only for take-away cakes and pastries due to the Covid restrictions and the fact that the shop is so tiny. Well worth a visit though if you're ever passing through Stockbridge on the way into the City via Kerr Street. Don't forget to mention that you know me and you may even get a discount on some of Allison's fabulous cakes! On a Sunday morning there is also a superb little food market just on the opposite side of the road.

Back at the house and the BBC had the first game of the day, a 12 noon kick-off between Fulham and Everton, much to the annoyance of the mother-in-law who was looking forward to her weekly dose of Songs of Praise which had now been pushed back a couple of hours! Another poor performance from the Londoners saw them go down 2 – 3 to the Toffees who remained in the top six. Fulham remained in the bottom four with only four points from their nine games and there was now a five-point gap to Brighton in 16th above them. Sheffield United v West Ham was next up and that went to the Hammers by the only goal to leave the Blades rock bottom with just a solitary point while West Ham were nicely placed in 8th. Finally, in the 4:30 pm slot on Sunday, it was time for Leeds.

I spotted the team selection on Twitter whilst watching the Blades game and, for a second or two, it was a surprise as the name Raphinha was listed. A quick check against the line-up we sent out at Crystal Palace last time out showed that Bielsa had brought in Raphinha at the expense of Helder Costa, which was the switch he made at halftime in that game at Selhurst Park. The only other change was that Kalvin Phillips resumed in his usual role in front of the back four, with Pascal Struijk dropping back to the bench. So actually, it was pretty much standard Bielsa to keep with what he had last time out although, for me at least, it didn't seem right that Rodrigo was only on the bench. He'd not been injured of course, just isolating having come into contact with the dreaded Covid, so surely he was ready to go? I still felt Leeds were a better team with Pablo in the middle pulling our strings and the next best thing, if he wasn't available, was to have Rodrigo on the pitch; he was just as Spanish if maybe not quite as magical! For Stuart Dallas it marked his 200th appearance for the club although I wasn't keen on him starting in midfield; that didn't seem to work in my humble opinion; he was a real workhorse but was neither Spanish nor magical. Raphinha was the first Brazilian to start a game for Leeds since Roque Junior back in 2003.

I was hopeful that in this game we might get a reprise of the famous old Test Match Special giggling session with the commentator possibly having to report: *"Right, here comes the corner and two players are grappling in the middle. The defender's Holding, the Leeds man's Koch...!"* Younger readers will have to Google *"The moment a BBC cricket commentator couldn't stop giggling"*. Both Holding and Koch were named.

Meslier
Ayling (Rodrigo 70) Koch Cooper (Capt) Alioski
Phillips
Raphinha Dallas Klich Harrison (Poveda 80)
Bamford

Subs: Casilla, Davis, Struijk, Poveda, Costa, Roberts, Rodrigo.

Arsenal: Leno, Bellerín, Holding, dos Santos Magalhães, Tierney, Ceballos, Xhaka, Pépé, Willock (Saka 57', Maitland-Niles 90+3), Willian (Nelson 45), Aubameyang. Subs not used: Runarsson, Lacazette, Mustafi, Nketiah.

Referee: Anthony Taylor.

The Arsenal line-up was full of the exotic-sounding names you associate with a big six side; Leno, Bellerin, Ceballos, Xhaka, the £75 million Pépé, Willian, and the dangerous Aubameyang up front. On the bench they had young Reiss Nelson who scored the goal that beat us down at the Emirates in January, as well as our old friend Eddie Nketiah who was now a regular first-team squad member at Arsenal. Eddie was seen having a laugh and a joke with the Leeds squad as the teams went through their respective warm-up routines. Arsenal and Leeds were coming into the game with similar records - both had lost three of their previous four games – and the Gunners sat four places and two points above us in the table. Of greater concern to Leeds though was that it was 17 (!) years since we'd beaten them and they had a pretty good recent record at Elland Road too. Arsenal had won on their previous four visits and three times the score was 1 – 4... yes, having lost to Leicester and Palace by that score I was a bit worried! Another statistic doing the rounds this week was that of away wins. Of the 80 EPL games played prior to this round, 34 had ended in victory for the away team with only 29 resulting in home wins. In the round nine games played so far, another four away wins had already been racked up with only two home wins. It really did seem that without fans in the grounds there was no real advantage in playing at home which I suppose should have come as no surprise. This was going to be no easy game against the current FA Cup holders and the side that beat Liverpool to secure the FA Community Shield less than three months earlier.

The first pictures of the Leeds team, sheltering from another biblical storm inside the players' tunnel, showed Liam Cooper holding an IPad that he was showing to the other players so they could wave to young Elliot Metcalfe and his sister who were connected via a live Zoom stream. 13-year-old Elliot is a cancer patient whose dream of being a mascot for Leeds United had been scuppered by the Covid-19 restrictions. But, in an ingenious initiative, the Make-A-Wish Foundation and the club had come up with the idea of live-streaming him at the game on the IPad. Coops carried the IPad onto the pitch for the line-up and Sky picked out the beaming faces of the two youngsters sat at home for our own TVs; a brilliant moment. Watching on in the stand was one David O'Leary, a former Leeds player and manager of course and now part of the Gunners backroom staff.

After the usual 'taking a knee' ritual which was still de rigueur before all EPL games, Arsenal kicked off attacking the Kop, although they didn't do much of that. Leeds dominated the game from the start and it was all very reminiscent of that cup tie in London back in January. Ceballos did fire an early shot just wide of Meslier's left post but from that point on it was all Leeds, just as dominant as in other games this season. Patrick Bamford had the first shot on target, toe-poking a cut back from Alioski but straight at Leno although Alioski looked suspiciously offside anyway on replays so it was probably as well we didn't put that one away or we might have been bemoaning another VAR decision. Next it was Raphinha showing us how good his left foot is as he curled another cut-back from Alioski just wide of the left post. Bamford had another half-chance as Luke Ayling got behind the defence to fire the ball across. It hit a defender amidships and Bamford volleyed the rebound towards the left post only for Leno to get a strong arm on it. Next it was Matty Klich, latching onto a low left-wing cross from Harrison. Klich stopped it with his right foot, moved it across a defender onto his left and then horribly spooned his shot over the bar. It has been a thing we've seen from Klich for as long as he's played for us; his shots are either brilliant or appalling, seldom anything between those extremes. The first half flashed by in a moment and, as the players trooped off, we were merely left to wonder if this would be another of those very familiar Leeds United days; total dominance of the game but nothing to show for it. It was almost a carbon copy of that FA Cup game in January and we know what happened then. Just to get me even more on edge, Reiss Nelson trotted onto the pitch for the second half replacing a tired-looking Willian.

The second half began in much the same fashion, with Leeds pushing forward but then, just six minutes after the break, we had a flash-point between Alioski and the £75 million man, Nicolas Pépé. For some reason Pépé and Alioski were pushing and shoving together midway in the Leeds half in the centre of the pitch and I suspected the reason was probably some mischief from the little North Macedonian. Suddenly, Pépé put both arms out and pushed Alioski in the chest and the little man half stumbled before getting back in the face of the Arsenal man as if to say *"What was that all about?"*. Pépé is slightly taller than Alioski and, as the two faced up to each other, Pépé just leaned in and gave Alioski a little tap on the forehead with his own. Alioski did the proverbial sack of spuds collapse as if poleaxed and began writhing on the turf as referee Taylor finally blew his whistle to halt the game. Sky were soon replaying the incident over and over again, even before Taylor trotted over to the VAR monitor at the side of the pitch. Taylor didn't take many viewings before returning and making the VAR screen signal with his hands before pulling out his red card. There was no real protest from Pépé or any of the Arsenal players or staff; Pépé had fallen for a very old trick and the Gunners were down to ten.

I can't say that the loss of Pépé made any real difference to proceedings really, Leeds continued to dominate and perhaps the blue shirts of the visitors sat back a little further but the game continued with much the same look about it; Leeds attacking with wave after wave of white shirts pushing towards the Kop. Leeds were getting closer with every passing minute but a combination of fine goalkeeping from Bernd Leno and the frame of the goal in front of the Revie Stand kept us out. Stuart Dallas hit a fabulous left-footer that was heading towards the top left corner before Leno threw out a big glove to push it around the post and then Luke Ayling messed up his first touch from eight yards out after some magical skills from Raphinha. Rodrigo, a 70th minute substitute for

Ayling, fired a left foot shot that arrowed inches over the left angle of post and bar but it was just another one to add to the mounting number of shots off target that Leeds were etching into the record books. Seconds later Rodrigo reprised that one with an almost identical effort following a lovely through ball from Robin Koch and this time the shot ricocheted off the angle and behind. There was always the worry in my mind that all these missed chances would merely be the prelude to an Arsenal break-away and a sucker-punch winner and it could so easily have been had Illan Meslier not been on his toes as Saka, on for Willock, was put clear through the middle. He dummied Meslier as he went to his left but somehow, scrambling along on his hands and knees, the Leeds stopper managed to lunge again as Saka finally tried a shot with his left foot and the ball was pushed away to safety.

With ten minutes left, Bielsa turned to Ian Poveda to try to unlock the stubborn Arsenal defence and he raced on to replace Jack Harrison. He was soon in the thick of the action too as he whipped a lovely ball towards the centre of the Arsenal area. Patrick Bamford leapt like the proverbial salmon and put what looked to be a perfect header down and wide of Leno only to watch as it bounced up onto the post and the rebound fell kindly for the Gunners. Seconds later and the ball fell to Raphinha and he also struck that same left post as he was found by a Dallas cross from the right wing. There were only a few minutes left now and it was crystal clear that we could have played for another hour and we'd not have scored today. It was just one of those days.

At the final whistle Leeds had recorded 25 attempts on goal; it was the most attempts by a side failing to score a goal since Manchester City hit 26 without success against Southampton at the back end of last season and was the third-best attempts total recorded in the EPL so far this season. We hit 27 at Villa Park a few weeks earlier of course but that day we managed to get nine on target and that was enough to create three goals. This time only four hit the target and none found the net. It was a reminder of one of the few shortcomings of this side of ours that we'd seen plenty of times in the Championship but then again it was only the third goalless draw we'd seen in the league since Bielsa took charge 101 games ago.

At the end of the day a point against Arsenal is not to be sniffed at but it was hard not to think it should have been more. Dominating the game as we did and with the Gunners down to ten for 40 minutes, we only had ourselves to blame, or maybe Lady Luck. On another day surely one of those shots that muddied the paintwork on the Kop goal-frame would have gone in, maybe it was to do with the fact we were not in that end sucking the ball in that made the difference. Anyway, at the end of round 9, Leeds were still in a safe mid-table position with 11 points; nine behind Spurs at the top and ten ahead of Sheffield United at the bottom. We'd all have taken that if offered it on day one, especially since we'd now faced three of the big six clubs. We were just about one quarter through the season.

Leeds United 0 Arsenal 0
BCD. **Round 9 League Pos: 14**th.

	Team	P	GD	Pts
1	Tottenham Hotspur	9	12	20
2	Liverpool	9	5	20
3	Chelsea	9	12	18
4	Leicester City	9	6	18
5	Southampton	9	4	17
6	Everton	9	3	16
7	Aston Villa	8	8	15
8	West Ham United	9	5	14
9	Wolverhampton Wanderers	9	-1	14
10	Manchester United	8	-1	13
11	Crystal Palace	9	-1	13
12	Arsenal	9	-1	13
13	Manchester City	8	-1	12
14	Leeds United	9	-3	11
15	Newcastle United	9	-5	11
16	Brighton and Hove Albion	9	-2	9
17	Burnley	8	-8	5
18	Fulham	9	-9	4
19	West Bromwich Albion	9	-12	3
20	Sheffield United	9	-11	1

Sticky Toffees!

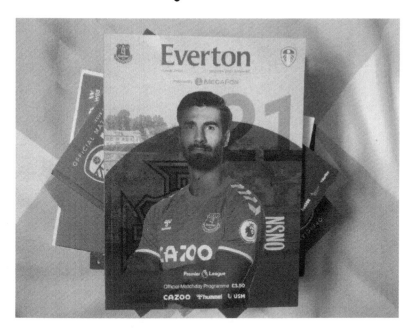

We all got a bit excited for a few minutes at the start of this week, the week between our nil-nil draw with the Gunners and our trip to play the Toffees the following Saturday. The reason was an announcement by the Government that fans would be allowed back into stadiums in limited numbers from the end of the current national lockdown, December 2nd. The excitement didn't last long though for Leeds fans as the limiting factor was going to be which local tier of restrictions applied where a stadium was located. Boris Johnson, still in isolation himself, informed the nation that once the national lockdown ended a new and more severe local regime would come into force with three tiers of restriction. In the lowest tier, a maximum of 4,000 fans would be allowed to attend a game, or half of the ground capacity if that was smaller than 8,000. In tier 2, the number was reduced to 2,000 and in tier 3, where infection rates were high or rising quickly or where hospital capacity was seen to be under threat, no spectators at all would be allowed. The current infection rate in

Leeds was amongst the highest in England and so we all quickly came to the conclusion no one would be inside Elland Road anytime soon. Fortunately, all the forthcoming Leeds games would be on TV as a whole raft of date or time changes for our fixtures through to the end of the year were announced, but there was a chance that 2,000 Chelsea fans would be allowed in for our game at Stamford Bridge on 5th December.

That spat between Pépé and Ezgjan Alioski was in the news this week again as both players were the targets for some vile and often racial abuse on social media. That directed at Pépé was for his ridiculous head movement into Alioski, while the man from North Macedonia was pilloried for his theatrical fall exaggerating the impact of the 'headbutt'. Both clubs released coordinated statements, in which they promised to work with the police and football authorities to identify those responsible. *"We utterly condemn the vile abuse directed at Nicolas Pépé and Ezgjan Alioski on social media,"* said Arsenal in their statement. *"This is completely unacceptable."* Leeds also called the abuse *"vile"* and said it would *"not be tolerated"*.[1]

The Under 23s were in action again this week and recorded another win; A strong team that included minutes for Casilla, Davis, Struijk, Casey, Rodrigo, Poveda, and Tyler Roberts beat West Brom 2 – 1 to go joint top of the PL2 Division 2 table along with Middlesbrough. Goals in the final ten minutes from Helder Costa and Tyler Roberts turned the game around.

On Wednesday 25th November, just under a month after his 60th birthday, footballing icon Diego Maradona suffered a heart attack and passed away. Argentina immediately announced three days of mourning and his coffin - draped in Argentina's national flag and a football shirt bearing his famous number 10 on the back - was on public display at the presidential palace on Thursday. By mid-afternoon, the queues stretched back more than a kilometre and police clashed with mourners as they tried to close off the palace in anticipation of the wake. There were reports of tear gas and rubber bullets being used as officers in riot gear struggled to hold back the crowd. They take their mourning seriously in South America!

---

[1] *https://www.bbc.co.uk/sport/football/55041052*

Back in Leeds and much of the Bielsa press conference this week was also devoted to Maradona as journalist after journalist asked Bielsa for his thoughts on his fellow countryman. Bielsa only worked with Maradona once, when he managed him in an Argentina XI against a Rest of the World XI for his testimonial 19 years earlier, at Boca Juniors' La Bombonera stadium. The match was Maradona's last before retiring and Bielsa said he will never forget the adoration and love the people showed him. He likened Maradona's football to a work of art, *"like the architecture of a great church to be admired"*, while also commenting that an idol such as Maradona helps others to dream and to believe they too can achieve great things.

Turning to the upcoming game with Everton at Goodison Park, Bielsa confirmed that Leeds would still be without Pablo Hernandez, Diego Llorente, and Jamie Shackleton who were all still on the injury list. He was asked to explain the importance of Mateusz Klich to his side and he gave an insight into how Klich had come to cement his position in midfield. Bielsa told the reporters that shortly after his arrival it was in his mind to ask Klich to play as a centre-back but then, for the Las Palmas friendly, he was forced to play him as a number 8 due to various injuries and absences. The rest, as they say, is history!

Bielsa was his usual beguiling self throughout another lengthy presser; he and interpreter Andrés Clavijo wore black Leeds puffer jackets but Bielsa seemed to have modified the sleeves of the grey training shirt he wore under his so he could stick his thumbs through a hole he'd torn in each cuff! He constantly looked down at the desk, periodically swept imaginary dust off the surface with his hand and had a good old scratch behind one ear every few minutes while taking his time to answer every question. At one point he was asked to explain what weaknesses he was aware of in the Everton make-up but he declined to answer. Instead he reminded everyone how long it had taken to go through his analysis of Leeds' defensive issues the previous week and he was already forty minutes into this conference! Bielsa did comment how honoured he was to have been nominated recently for FIFA Coach of the Year, although predictably he noted that any success he'd had at Leeds was purely down to the efforts of his players.

Match week 10 of the EPL began on Friday night with the game between Crystal Palace and Newcastle at Selhurst Park. I watched on the laptop, still at the mother-in-law's in Edinburgh, as the Toon squeaked past Palace with two goals in the final two minutes of normal time. Palace were without their talisman Wilfred Zaha who was self-isolating following a positive Coronavirus test and I reckon his absence was the difference. While watching the game I browsed through the Leeds website and spotted the news that the East Stand at Elland Road had now been formally named The Jack Charlton Stand, a fitting and lasting tribute to a Leeds legend. I did wonder though what would be left to name when the rest of the legendry Revie team eventually passes. I'm sure it was that thought that stimulated social media discussion this week about a group tribute, maybe a huge bronze of the famous *"Leeds wave"* from 1974 could be erected outside the ground. My pal Cambridge Rob has a tattoo of it around one thigh.

Saturday morning saw glorious weather in Edinburgh and my penance this time to be able to watch football all afternoon and evening was a walk up Corstorphine Hill with Mrs W. The views of Arthur's Seat overlooking the City to the right and across Murrayfield and Ravelston golf courses towards the Firth of Forth were stunning. I'd learn later that we were spoiled with the sunshine as England was apparently suffering another deluge.

I must admit that during the walk it was hard not to ponder about the upcoming game at Goodison and, as I trudged through the fallen autumn leaves, my mind strayed back to my previous visit to the blue side of Liverpool. I've had to look up the details since of course but, as far as I can remember, the last time I was there was on a cold Tuesday night in November 1979 for a Division One game; 41 years ago! At the time I was lodging in Toll Bar in St. Helens and working as a trainee accountant for the cable maker BICC, my first real job having graduated from university earlier that year. I would no doubt have driven my pride and joy, a turquoise Hillman Avenger (a £600 purchase during the summer) the 30-odd miles to Liverpool and I'm sure I would have had to part with a few coins for the local scallywags to: *"Look after yer car mate?"* I can't remember the specifics of the trip or much about the game but the record books show we were thrashed 5 – 1 and I remember the place was only about half full. The records show Bob

Latchford got a hat-trick with the other goals coming from Brian Kidd and a Paul Hart own goal and the consolation for Leeds was a last-minute Kevin Hurd goal. Not one of our finest hours.

In fact our record at Goodison is not great at all and it was thirty years since our last league win there; a 2 – 3 win in our first Division One game following promotion from Division Two under Howard Wilkinson. I can tell you exactly where I was for that game, and it wasn't at Goodison! I was in my then latest pride and joy, a silver Peugeot 405 Mi16 and I was testing its maximum speed returning from the North of Scotland where I'd been playing golf on my brother-in-law's annual stag reunion. There were regular score updates coming through the radio as we hammered down the A9! Gary Speed scored that August day in 1990 and of course he moved from Leeds to the Toffees in 1996; this weekend was the 9th anniversary of his passing,

I was back at the house in time to catch the final half-hour of the Liverpool game at Brighton, a game in which the Seagulls swooped and snatched a point with a disputed last minute penalty after Neal Maupay had already missed one earlier in the game. That put the Scousers top of the table by a point, with second-placed Spurs playing third-placed Chelsea the following day. The 3 pm game today saw Manchester City wallop Burnley 5 – 0 with goals from Torres, Mendy and a Mahrez hat-trick, a result that left City in mid-table and Burnley still rooted in the bottom three. It was midway in the second half of this one when the Leeds team was announced and I saw it first on Adam Pope's Twitter feed.

Meslier
Ayling Koch Cooper (Capt) Alioski
Phillips
Raphinha (Poveda 85) Dallas Klich Harrison (Costa 89)
Bamford (Rodrigo 90+1)
Subs: Casilla, Struijk, Davis, Poveda, Costa, Rodrigo, Roberts.
Everton: Pickford, Godfrey, Keane, Holgate (Bernard 82), Davies (Delph 61), Doucouré, Allan, Iwobi (André Gomes 67), Rodríguez, Calvert-Lewin, Richarlison. Subs not used: Lossl, G Siggurdsson, Mina, Tosun.
Referee: Chris Kavanagh.
Pope tweeted: *"Completely unchanged 18 for #lufc so Rodrigo remains on the bench"*. In those few words Adam Pope had

captured the inevitable bone of contention; exactly why was Rodrigo not in the XI? From my perspective, I thought he was excellent against Arsenal and I just felt we needed someone in the middle with some Spanish magic. There was the usual social media debate between those like me who felt Rodrigo should be in and the rest of the Leeds fans who were content to continue the IBWT mantra; In Bielsa We Trust; don't dare question the wise one!

We got our first sight of the team in the new third kit, an all claret or maroon ensemble, with Everton in their usual blue shirts with white shorts and socks as the teams arrived onto the pitch, Leeds from a Portakabin at the back of the main stand and Everton from the regular tunnel. The Z-Cars theme music boomed out as it has done for many years at Goodison. Z-Cars was a BBC police drama series that launched way back in 1962. I remember it well and the title music was based on an old Liverpool sea shanty called 'Johnny Todd', which dates back to 1891 and tells the story of a cuckolded sailor. The instrumental TV version was composed by Liverpool-based, Austrian-born musician and journalist Fritz Spiegl. A revamped version of the track was released as a single in March of 1962 reaching number eight in the pop charts on the strength of the popularity of the TV show. In November the same year, a few days before his tragic death, Toffees fan and Z-Cars actor, Leonard Williams from West Derby, the only genuine Scouser amongst the cast and who played Sgt. Percy Twentyman, was invited to watch Everton play Blackpool. Everton went on to win the First Division title that season and the song became synonymous with the success, so much so that it was adopted by Everton fans, not only in memory of the 1963 title, but also of their famous supporter, Leonard Williams.

Both teams lined up around the centre-circle to pay their tributes to Diego Maradona but all Leeds and Everton fans watching at home probably had Gary Speed in their minds too, as the few staff and media in the stadium joined in a minute's applause with the players. The players then lined up, took the knee, and then we were off.

Most people expected there to be loads of goals in this game; Everton and Leeds had a combined goals scored total thus far of 34 and a combined goals conceded figure matching that, also 34. Other things being equal therefore you might have expected to see something between three and four goals in the game if they were to keep up their averages. In hindsight, having watched the game, there should probably have been more than that with all the chances that were created.

Raphinha had the first half-chance within two minutes of the start as he broke through the middle of the Everton defence to latch onto a lovely headed touch from Patrick Bamford. Jordan Pickford raced out to narrow the angle but Raphinha was there first and stabbed a left boot at the ball trying to nick it past the Everton keeper. He didn't get enough on it though and merely scuffed it softly to the left and it was easily knocked away by a retreating defender. Six minutes later and it was the Toffees breaking away down their right side with Tom Davies as Liam Cooper unfathomably let the ball roll past him into the path of the blue-shirted Evertonian. He was now behind Alioski and had all the time in the world to look up, spot the run of Abdoulaye Doucouré towards the penalty spot, and then start to celebrate as the Everton striker connected perfectly with a left foot shot that had *"goal"* written all over it. Incredibly, Illan Meslier guessed correctly where the shot was going and flung himself to his right to block the initial effort and then was up and flying through the air like Superman to pounce on the loose ball. Within hours someone on Twitter had photo-shopped a picture of the second dive adding a Superman cape to Meslier's shoulders!

Two minutes after the Superman dive, Leeds broke quickly down their right wing with the impressive looking Raphinha again. This time he slid the ball perfectly across the penalty area, right into the path of the flying Harrison. It was another chance that looked too good to miss but somehow the City loanee managed it, sliding in to place the ball a foot wide of the left post. It was starting to feel like the Arsenal game already and we were only ten minutes into this one. It was like basketball, the action moving quickly from end to end, although no one was finding the basket. Richarlison had a shot saved by Meslier and then Klich had one blocked. Kalvin Phillips tried a long-range effort that was saved in the bottom left corner. Then, after 21 minutes, came another huge chance for Patrick Bamford. Sadly it was Bamford Mk I from the Championship who weakly fired a left foot shot from eight yards that Pickford got a leg to and not the deadly Mk II version we saw the previous month. For once a very animated Marcelo Bielsa showed his annoyance and it was picked up by the TV cameras.

On 24 minutes James Rodriguez had the ball in the Leeds net as our defence momentarily lost the plot at the back post. It was Stuart Dallas, who'd swapped positions with Alioski moments before, who allowed Rodriguez to gather the ball on the byline, check inside and lash it home but the VAR replays confirmed he was inches offside when the ball was played across. It was a let-off and a reminder that if we didn't put one of our many chances away there was always the possibility that Everton would bury one of theirs. We got another reminder minutes later as Michael Keane rose way above the Leeds defence to head over from a free-kick on the left, with Meslier rooted to his line.

Back came Leeds and the next big chance fell to Raphinha again who was all over the pitch. This time he leapt to meet a deep cross from Luke Ayling and I was out of my chair thinking this one was in, only to see a big gloved hand stretch out and knock it away. Ayling recovered the ball again and this time pulled it back to Harrison and his shot was blocked by Ben Godfrey almost on the line, sending it over the bar. Down the other end they went and another set-piece nearly undid us as once more a left wing free-kick sailed into the Leeds box. This time we allowed it to drop onto the boot of Mason Holgate but his volley was well saved by Meslier right on his line. Then Meslier was flinging himself away to his left to push away a Richarlison long-range shot. It was mainly Leeds having the chances but even so Meslier was earning his corn.

We were into the last minutes of the half but there were still more big chances for Leeds as Jack Harrison rose at the back post to thump a header against the woodwork and, while he held his head in his hands, Patrick Bamford hammered the rebound wide of the post. Then Luke Ayling tried a long-range shot that was blocked but it rebounded straight to Klich, edge of the area and perfectly on his right foot. Klich took aim and curled the ball towards the far post but got too much on it and it went a foot wide. It had been a wonderful half of football and the score could easily have been three or four each. Leeds had hit the target four times and Everton five while a further nine other Leeds efforts went high wide or not very handsomely away. Leeds had bossed the possession but Meslier had arguably been the busier keeper.

I felt sure we'd see Rodrigo line up for the second half but no, Bielsa was sticking to his guns and there were no changes. I suppose inevitably that meant we carried on as we ended the first period, with Leeds in possession and carving chance after chance but first I watched nervously as Calvert-Lewin broke free from halfway before hammering an angled shot straight at Meslier. Then Illan had a bit of a brain fade moment as he tried to clip the ball out to the Leeds left wing, something we'd grow to accept over the season was always in his make-up. Whether he mishit the pass or just didn't see James Rodriguez I'm not sure but Meslier's pass went straight to him, only six yards outside the Leeds area. Rodriguez, or 'James' as he has on his shirt, lobbed the ball straight back towards goal and Meslier just got back to retrieve it under his own crossbar. It was a moment when, for once, our keeper looked as inexperienced as he actually is! At the other end, Harrison tried another long-shot but it was all too comfortable for Pickford moving to his left and the clock moved on towards the final ten minutes. Everton had already made a couple of changes but Bielsa was still sticking and in the 79th minute, finally, his patience was rewarded.

It came from nothing really as Luke Ayling played a sharp one-two with Mateusz Klich out on the Leeds right wing. Ayling laid the ball inside to Raphinha who was poised about three yards outside the 'D' and clearly looking to shoot. He dummied to shoot but then took another step to his left and then he did let fly, right through the legs of a defender and pretty much all along the turf into the bottom right corner with Pickford a couple of feet short of reaching it. That was a real 'phew' moment! For a game in which Leeds had so many chances it was unthinkable we would yet again go home without all the spoils.

Leeds brought on Poveda, Costa, and Rodrigo for little cameo appearances late in the game and a combination of all three should have made it 2 – 0 right at the death. Poveda wriggled around a defender on the byline and pulled the ball back to Rodrigo who stabbed it further left to the unmarked Costa near the back post. It was there to be hit first time from the angle of the six-yard box but Costa took a touch and dallied and dithered and by the time he scooped it at goal Pickford was there to block it with his midriff. It mattered not, as shortly after that Chris Kavanagh blew the final whistle.

Leeds had played some excellent football throughout this game and were by far the better side and yet there had been good chances for the home side that could, on another day, have ruined it for us. We should have been able to find the target more often than six times with the 23 attempts we mustered and, had we done so, then I'm sure the score would have been more comfortably in our favour. Some of the efforts that missed were poor by EPL standards; the Harrison one he slid past the post, the Bamford shot from eight yards, the Klich shot when unchallenged should all have been buried. It was pretty much a replica of many Championship games when our shooting let us down. As a comparison, Everton hit the target eight times from only 15 attempts, a much more respectable ratio. As a game it was super exciting and I'm sure the neutrals watching would have been well satisfied; the 38 attempts recorded was the second highest in the EPL this season, only beaten by our own game at Villa Park which saw 39 attempts. At the end of the day this game left me overjoyed and yet still frustrated, frustrated that we couldn't record our brilliance in the stats books with a dominant scoreline.

In purely numerical terms, Leeds' football so far this season had been described as 'chaos football'. We'd created a high volume of chances; second only to Liverpool in shots, second in chances created and third in the number of touches in the opposition box. And yet, somewhat inevitably given the style of our play, we'd also allowed the opposition vast numbers of chances to score. Only Newcastle had faced more shots than Leeds and 62% of the shots faced were hit from within our own area which was also well above the average percentage. Many commentators had suggested this would be the way for Leeds this season and it was certainly panning out that way. The good news was that, for a newly promoted side, we were actually acquitting ourselves well, especially in the goal-scoring stakes. We'd tailed off a bit lately but in our opening six games we'd scored more goals than any promoted side since 1992! We were the neutrals' favourite side to watch at this stage of the season.

Everton 0 **Leeds United 1 (Raphinha 79)**
BCD. **Round 10 League Pos: 12**[th]

Chelsea

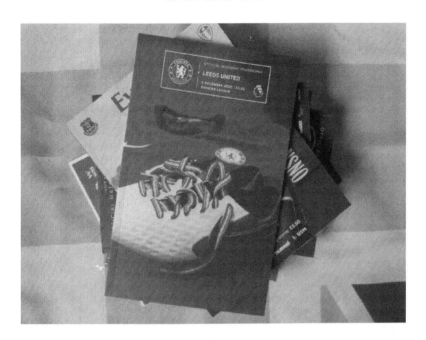

The final game on Saturday saw West Brom overcome Sheffield United in the bottom of the table clash at the Hawthorns. Albion won 1 – 0 but the Blades dominated the game, proving yet again that it's goals that win games not attempts or possession. On Sunday there were three more games featuring four of the big six and they suffered mixed fortunes. Manchester United looked to be heading for another defeat, this time at Southampton where they quickly went 2 – 0 down. It was a score that had the football equivalent of the Grim Reaper eyeing Ole Gunnar Solskjaer but, as they'd managed a few times recently, they came from behind to win 2 – 3. The second game was a more predictable nil-nil draw between two of the EPL heavyweights; Chelsea and Spurs. That kept them 3rd and 1st respectively, sandwiching Liverpool between them. The final game produced a surprising 1 – 2 win for Wolves at Arsenal in which there was a sickening clash of heads between Raul Jimenez and David Luiz that put the Wolves man in hospital with a fractured skull. Wolves climbed to 6th while Arsenal were labouring in 14th, a point and two places below Leeds. The final two games of match week 10 saw Fulham win 1 – 2 at Leicester, another game to go against form and then, finally, West Ham beat Aston Villa with more pantomime shenanigans from Jack Grealish captured on camera as he was poleaxed by another invisible sniper.

The main sporting news this weekend came out of the Bahrain Grand Prix during which the world witnessed a truly remarkable escape when Romain Grosjean crashed on the first lap. His car, which pierced the safety barrier, split in half and burst into flames but Grosjean managed to extract himself from the car and the inferno, suffering only burns to his hands and feet. Romain said he *"saw death coming"* but fought to get out *"for his children"*.

On Monday this week it was that marvellous time of the season when we get to know our opponents in the 3rd Round of the FA Cup. It's a competition that has not treated us well in recent seasons. In the 21 campaigns so far this century, Leeds had only progressed past the 3rd round on seven occasions and we'd suffered defeat at this stage to some right minnows! The names Hereford, Histon and Newport are guaranteed to cause the most hardened of Leeds fans to suffer nightmares. This time Robbie Savage put his hand in the big bowl and pulled out ball 19, Leeds United, right after he grabbed ball 48, Crawley Town. I confess I did suffer an involuntary shiver as I contemplated that game, although the saving grace was that we'd probably not be allowed to travel down there to see it in the flesh. It was, nevertheless, something to look forward to after Christmas.

It looked as though there would be fans at our next game, a trip to Stamford Bridge. London was currently in Tier 2 of the Covid cake in which clubs were now allowed to have up to 2,000 supporters inside the ground, or half their capacity if that was lower. We'd seen again this weekend how the lack of fans in grounds had clearly benefited the away sides as only three EPL matches were won by the home teams. I wasn't sure that a couple of thousand Chelsea fans would put us off our stride!

We might have been seeing fans go through the turnstiles again but Covid was still casting its evil shadow over all sports. In the EPL the scheduled Friday night opening game of match week 11 between Villa and Newcastle was postponed due to a 'significant increase' in Covid cases at the Magpies' training ground, with five players and two staff members succumbing to the virus. In Formula One, Lewis Hamilton tested positive and he was ruled out of the upcoming Grand Prix; young Brit George Russell would fill in.

When we do eventually get back inside Elland Road it will look a little different; this week new floodlight pylons went up outside the West Stand and the new diamond-shaped lights were a lovely nod to the famous old lights that shone over the ground between 1973 and 1993. Not quite as high, but the evocative shape of the lamps was sure to bring a dewy-eyed response from fans like me of a certain vintage. It was all part of the upgrade dictated by EPL regulations. Mimicking the famous lights from the past was apparently the idea of Rob Endeacott, author of several books with a Leeds United theme, and a fine idea it was.

In the press conference this week, Bielsa admitted that his team's defensive performance against Everton was nowhere near as assured as we saw against Arsenal the week before. He confessed that we conceded too many chances that could easily have resulted in a far more sticky Toffees' result than we eventually secured – my words of course, not his, although I bet he wishes he'd of thought of the phrase! Talking of the defence, when asked about Diego Llorente, Bielsa confirmed that he was now *"healthy"* but that ideally he'd now play a few Under 23 games to get himself match fit. The question was posed because of rumours doing the rounds suggesting that Robin Koch was now carrying an injury and might not be fit for the trip to Stamford Bridge. In fact, the word was that Koch had been suffering with a knee problem since the Liverpool game but that the medical staff thought it would hold out. Several times Bielsa noted that Llorente *could* play if necessary and that only further cemented the thought in our minds that Koch would struggle to be up for the Bridge. *"We hope we don't have an arising situation meaning we have to accelerate his process into the team"* Bielsa told reporters. It was a stop-start presser that was beset by technical issues with several questions cut short as internet connections continually failed. You'd have thought by now they'd have all got this remote presser thing sorted perfectly as we were all experts on Zoom, Teams and Skype.

The long-awaited deal between the EPL and the EFL to support clubs hardest hit by the ban on supporters attending games was reached this week. £30m was to be provided by the EPL to distribute amongst all League One and Two clubs with a part fixed sum and a part based on estimated lost gate receipts. A further £20m was then available for clubs to claim based on individual need. As long as clubs did not infringe EFL finance regulations the money need not be repaid. For Championship clubs, the EPL was providing access to a further loan of £200m, available interest-free to pay for PAYE liabilities up to a maximum of £8.33m per club. This money *was* repayable though, by June 2024, and was not available to any club in breach of existing EFL financing rules. No deal was ever going to be universally welcomed and this one was criticised for potentially supporting clubs that had been badly managed. I also had a sneaking feeling the real basis was to keep the Government at arm's length. They'd be assured of getting their tax and maybe that would be enough to keep them out of the affairs of the two football authorities, something threatened in the past more than once.

With that Villa v Toon game postponed, I found myself watching the Championship game between Barnsley and Bournemouth on Friday night. The Cherries walloped the Tykes 0 – 4 and the game featured starts for ex-Leeds colleagues Lewis Cook and Alex Mowatt while both Aapo Halme and Clarke Oduor got minutes for the home side as they made use of the five substitutes now allowed in the EFL; something voted down with a narrow majority by EPL clubs recently. It was thought by several of the also-rans of the EPL that five subs would only further strengthen the hold of the big clubs who inevitably had stronger benches.

Waiting for the Leeds game on Saturday, an 8 pm kick-off, took forever. Mrs W and I had driven back home from Edinburgh – that took five hours - but the afternoon still dragged on and on. I listened to the first game of the day on TalkSPORT Radio in the car; Everton grabbing a 1 – 1 draw at Burnley thanks to a Calvert-Lewin equaliser that helped my fantasy league side get off to a decent start. It was the Everton striker's 11th goal in 11 games. I watched the 3 pm kick-off on the laptop - Man City 2 Fulham 0 – and then switched on the TV to watch the Grand Prix qualifying. 22-year-old George Russell laid to rest the myth that it was all about the drivers as he drove Hamilton's Mercedes onto the front row, alongside regular Mercedes pilot Valtteri Bottas in the other

Merc. The week before, Russell had qualified only 14th in what was widely regarded as the slowest car on the grid, the Williams Mercedes FW43, now he was in the quickest and he was at the front. Funny that! We still had to endure one more game before ours started but I guess most Leeds fans gave it a miss; Man United were at West Ham. It started well enough, with Soucek putting the Hammers in front in the 38th minute and it stayed 1 – 0 until the 65th. Then it all went wrong. The lads in red from Mamucium got three late goals to win it 1 – 3. Mamucium, the original Latin name, means *"Hill shaped like a breast"*; I've always thought that was quite appropriate really for a team of..., well, let's just move on.

Around 7 pm the Leeds team was announced on the club's official Twitter account; there were no changes in the starting line-up from the one that faced Everton and Arsenal so all the rumours about Koch appeared to have been a figment of the imagination of Dave from Beeston on Twitter. There was however one change on the bench; Diego Llorente was there in place of Leif Davis.

Meslier
Ayling Koch (Llorente 9) Cooper (Capt) Alioski (Rodrigo 69)
Phillips
Raphinha Dallas Klich Harrison (Poveda 57)
Bamford

Subs: Casilla, Struijk, Llorente, Poveda, Costa, Rodrigo, Roberts.
Chelsea: Mendy, James, Zouma, Thiago Silva, Chilwell, Havertz (Kovacic 67), Kanté, Mount, Ziyec (Pulisic 30), Giroud (Abraham 79), Werner. Subs not used: Arrizabalaga, Rüdiger, Jorginho, Azpilicueta. Referee: Kevin Friend.

I had a few issues with the team selection this week: I thought it was a bit strange that Llorente was there when Bielsa had been so adamant that he needed Under 23 games so I have to say I did wonder if Koch was borderline fit and Llorente was the insurance. The other issue was that the starting XI was a bit light on Spanish magicians. OK, I accepted that Pablo was still injured (although rumours persisted that a falling out with Bielsa was the real reason) but why, oh why, was Rodrigo not starting? He'd looked so good every time he'd come on and yet Bielsa was only giving him bit parts. I doubt I'll ever fully understand El Loco.

The Chelsea squad for this game was said to have cost in excess of £500 million and we all knew it was going to be a stern test; our fitness, work ethic and organisation ranged against their undoubted individual talent. It was that equation that made me even more perplexed that *our* most expensive player, the £27m Rodrigo, was only on the bench. Chelsea were on a great run of form, unbeaten in 15 in all competitions and this was a chance for them to go top if they won.

There was also our London curse to think about; we never win down there! We had won a league game at Stamford Bridge more recently than we had at Goodison though before our previous game there and that turned out all right. Mind you, it was still 21 years since we last secured three points at the Bridge; a 0 – 2 scoreline with two Stephen McPhail goals propelling Leeds back to the top of the EPL in December 1999. These two clubs have history aplenty of course; we once destroyed their shiny new scoreboard. That was back in 1984 on the back of a 5 – 0 thumping at the hands of the Blues, and then there was the 1970 FA Cup final and replay that are considered two of the fiercest games ever seen in England. It's not for no reason that *"We hate Chelsea!"* is a familiar refrain often heard ringing around Elland Road.

8 pm finally rolled round and I was ensconced in front of the TV with the first bottle from my beer advent calendar courtesy of my lad Mark. I was a few days late starting it of course as we'd been up in Edinburgh but, if the first one was anything to go by, the rest of the box was going to keep my interest. Today's offering was 'Citra Dreams', a 7% IPA from the Captain Lawrence Brewing Company. I was feeling quite positive as Martin Tyler and Alan Smith took up commentary...

With London in tier 2 of the Covid pyramid, Chelsea were allowed to let 2,000 lucky home fans in for the first time this season, albeit socially distanced and with everyone wearing a face covering. They enthusiastically joined in with the ritual handclapping to the famous old tune *"The Liquidator"* by Harry J All Stars as the teams appeared. It's a tune I know well as it's been used by Worcester City and many other clubs over the years; West Brom use it. When the players dropped to one knee at the referee's first whistle, the fans broke into a polite round of applause, a gesture no doubt meant as a response to what happened at the New Den earlier in the day when some Millwall fans booed the players ahead of the game with Derby. Then we were off and the Chelsea faithful would have been well happy with what they saw for all of four minutes.

Leeds were in the all-claret ensemble again for the second week running and were no doubt hoping it would bring good luck again but, for those first few minutes, we were straight under the cosh. For 45 seconds Leeds hardly had a touch as Chelsea moved the ball around precisely and quickly until it fell at the feet of Hakim Ziyech, near the left corner of the Leeds six-yard box. He had Alioski close but still got in a powerful left foot shot that Meslier could only save with his left foot and put away for an early corner. I was cringing already, I'd lost count of the number of corners we've conceded to in recent years. We almost did again as Giroud beat Koch to the ball at the back post to fire a header into the side netting. As worrying as the near miss was, the fact that Koch was now holding his knee and limping away from the challenge was even more concerning. It was three minutes before Leeds had any meaningful possession and, in that respect, it was all a bit similar to our start against Man City when the opposition similarly showed their individual brilliance on the ball. But now the ball was with Kalvin Phillips, a clearance finding him right on the halfway line and near the left touchline. Kalvin had a couple of looks to see what was on ahead of him as he let the ball bounce twice and then he simply caressed a left foot pass in behind the retreating Zouma and into the path of the gambolling Patrick Bamford, looking a bit like a horny male alpaca chasing a female. Paddy stole in between Zouma and the onrushing Edouard Mendy, used his first touch to push the ball past the keeper and his second to steer it inside the near post. It was another superb piece of finishing from a man who seemed to have no middle way... he was either brilliant or awful! Bamford spent five years at Chelsea of course although he never played a first-team game there and was sent out on loan to no less than six different teams while under contract there. His celebrations were suitably conservative. It has to be said, the ball from Phillips was one of the finest passes I've ever seen; it was inch-perfect.

That knee of Robin Koch was still a worry as the German won a free-kick in the centre-circle following another clash with Giroud. Once again Koch winced as he limped away and already his inclusion looked like a plan that had badly backfired if this was indeed the same injury that caused the pre-match concern. He was then slow on the turn, allowing Giroud to pass the ball through to Timo Werner whose shot was deflected for another corner; more concern. But before the corner could be taken Koch had finally gone down holding that right knee and immediately Diego Llorente was stripped and jogging on. It was Llorente's debut of course and it was going to be a baptism of fire. The first question was whether his arrival would improve our ability to defend corners; no, was the emphatic answer to that!

The corner was floated in from the left wing, Giroud beat his man at the near post to flick the ball on and there was Timo Werner, the £47m Timo Werner, meeting the ball at the back post. Thankfully Werner got it all wrong as his first touch merely knocked the ball sideways and then his second flicked it up against the underside of the bar. There was a glove in there from Meslier as well getting an important touch to keep the ball out. Two corners from the home side and two near misses; we were riding our luck.

The next phase of the game though was pretty well balanced. The quality of the Chelsea players on the ball was obvious but it was matched by our own willingness to run and close down and by our own passing when we did have the ball. Every now and again though the difference in quality, and maybe experience, threatened to undo us. We saw another little lapse from Illan Meslier, similar to his brain fade moment at Goodison, as he almost lazily stroked the ball to the edge of our area, not spotting Giroud coming from behind Luke Ayling. To be fair, some of the fault must be laid at Ayling's door too, as he called for the ball, also not seeing Giroud. The big Chelsea striker was onto the pass in a flash but he shanked his left foot shot just wide of the right post; even £18m doesn't guarantee perfection! It was what the statisticians would call a 'big chance' missed.

Leeds were comfortable until around the 25th minute, but then Chelsea struck with lightning speed. The ball was played wide right to Hakim Ziyech who was being well marked by Alioski but Reece James was coming outside on the overlap. James was Harrison's man but Jack got the wrong side trying to tackle Ziyech, trying to 'Hakim' you might say, from behind and that left James in the clear behind the Leeds defence when Ziyech eventually pushed the ball deeper into the corner. James curled the ball low to the near post and Giroud was more aware than his Leeds marker to stick out a boot and divert it inside the near post. That was more like an £18m finish. Just under half an hour gone and it was all square at 1 – 1 but his part in the goal was Ziyech's last act as he now limped off to be replaced by Pulisic. That's a £33m player being replaced by a £58m player!

Still the game looked pretty even to me, although that beer was kicking in now and maybe it was flavouring my view positively. Another of those daft defensive errors then came from Llorente, doing pretty much what Meslier did earlier in giving the ball straight to Pulisic on the edge of the area. If he'd been on for longer he might have been sharper but, as it was, he was quickly closed down before he got a shot off. It was just another sign though that we were playing right on the edge of our abilities whereas Chelsea probably had something in reserve.

The one Leeds player who did look comfortable in this company was Raphinha; his touch was always assured and he was darting here there and everywhere; he looked worth every penny of his £17m fee. Kalvin Phillips with that 4th-minute pass showed his quality too. The rest of the Leeds men could not be faulted for their effort but I always thought any one of them could get caught in possession, play a poor pass, miss-control the ball, or wallop it over the bar; it was the first time this season that the quality of the opposition was so clear but we were still well worth the score as the halftime whistle was blown.

Within seconds of the restart we got another example of those random little mistakes we were making as Leeds kicked-off and moved the ball back to Llorente and then Liam Cooper. Coops seemed to think he had all the time in the world as he got the ball sort of trapped under his feet while Timo Werner raced to close him down. Only the quick thinking and quick feet of Kalvin Phillips saved the day as he slid in to knock the ball clear. Then Meslier dawdled over a clearance and again was a whisker from getting caught in possession. Somehow you didn't expect a Chelsea player to get caught like that; it's all about individual quality, awareness and skill; it's what comes with these big price tags; *"you get what you pays for"* as in most things in life. As we saw even in the Championship, these little errors are often punished and in the EPL they were almost *always* punished! I was worrying again as Chelsea won their first corner of the new half.

Once again it caused problems, bouncing around in the area before running through the box to where Alioski and Chilwell collided; Kevin Friend saw it as a foul by the little man from North Macedonia. We didn't deal with the free-kick any better, as Havertz rose higher than anyone else to thump a header over the bar. The game was now settling into one of attack v defence and it was the boys in blue doing most of the attacking. It was almost as if Chelsea were learning how to play us, adapting, another trait of the best players. Leeds' forays forward were rare now but we did win a corner as a Klich cross was diverted behind. From the left wing corner Raphinha hit a low volley that was blocked and then snatched at the rebound putting it over the top. A bit more composure and it was a good chance – the sort of effort you'd expect Werner to put away nine times out of ten. We were ten minutes into the new half now and Leeds made another change; on came the scurrying figure of Ian Poveda and off went Jack Harrison.

We were an hour into the game and we needed the agility of Meslier again as Timo Werner beat Alioski to the ball in the Leeds area to fire a low shot towards the near post on the angle. Meslier got down well to block that one and then was up and back down in time to keep the rebound out as well. This time Werner was there again picking up the pieces but his third effort was deflected over the bar. The danger wasn't over yet though as another corner-kick loomed, again from the right wing and again to be sent over by Mason Mount. It flew all the way to the back post and there was Kurt Zouma rising to power a header into the net. Liam Cooper protested that he'd been pushed but VAR checked it all out and found nothing extraordinary… apart from another Leeds corner catastrophe. For all the obvious gulf in quality between the two sides, it was only our old Achilles Heel that had done for us. I know how good Zouma is at corner situations – he's a mainstay in my fantasy team - you'd have thought our defenders would too.

One of the strangest aspects of this game was the treatment the Chelsea fans were handing out to Diego Llorente. For most of his time on the pitch the Chelsea fans wailed at him in a high pitched pantomime squeal every time he got on the ball but no one seemed to have any idea why! The best explanation came from former Blue, Pat Nevin, writing in the Chelsea Chronicle: *"When Leeds substitute Diego Llorente made a noise so high-pitched that it caused mayhem all the way over in Battersea Dogs' Home, the Blues supporters weren't having it,"* he explained. *"For the rest of the game, they reminded him of his screeching every time he touched the ball. There are a hundred reasons why I want the fans back in the stadiums, but that humour is right up there with my favourites."* [1]

Why it took the best part of 70 minutes for Bielsa to turn to Rodrigo, I will never know. He cost Leeds a reported £27m, on a par with many of the Chelsea players on show tonight, he was fit and Leeds needed inspiration and yet all he got was 20 minutes. Very strange. He replaced Alioski as Leeds shuffled Dallas to left-back with Rodrigo slotting into midfield. He made a marginal difference but Leeds were not having enough ball to give him any real chance to impress. At the other end, yet another corner was met by Giroud's head unchallenged as he lost Llorente but he put that one over the bar. Poveda was perhaps making a better impact as he put in some decent crosses and then let fly from the edge of the box. Replays would show he was unlucky not to win a penalty as a stray Chilwell boot clattered against Poveda's ankle when he crossed the corner of the box; we'd all seen similar ones given by VAR this season but Poveda hadn't taken a dive and was more intent on getting his shot away. Maybe that's naïve in this league, true to our luck in London, nothing doing from VAR this time. It was fine margins as always; on another day it's given, Bamford slots the penalty in and we all go home happy as Larry, even accepting that Chelsea were head and shoulders above us in the quality stakes. As the game moved into the final ten minutes, yet another home corner was won by a Chelsea head. Reece James this time sending a header wide. The home side would win eight corners in total and I don't think we properly defended any of them! Leeds tried in vain to create a definitive late chance but Chelsea opted to soak up such pressure as a now tired Leeds could

---

[1] *https://www.thechelseachronicle.com/news/pat-nevin-explains-chelsea-fans-high-pitched-squealing-at-leeds-diego-llorente/*

muster by keeping eleven men behind the ball and then, almost inevitably, they were able to break up-field and finish us off. Leeds were enjoying a long spell of non-stop possession but were simply unable to break down the Chelsea defence and then Patrick Bamford was dispossessed as three blue shirts surrounded him. Substitute Kovacic came away with the ball, slotted it inside Dallas for Werner to run onto and he crossed low for Pulisic, another sub of course, to sweep home from close range; it was almost identical to their first goal. It was the classic smash and grab that we succumbed to against Leicester and Palace. That was it, Leeds were well beaten by a side we are not yet resourced to battle with on level terms. To do that we'll need to spend many tens of millions more and we'll probably need a couple of EPL seasons behind us to even contemplate doing that. For now, we were not really in competition with the likes of Chelsea, or any of the big six, even though in our four encounters against them so far we'd always been in the games until the final whistle. No, the league we had to concentrate on was the one in the middle of the division, games like West Ham and Newcastle perhaps, and they just happened to be our next two opponents at Elland Road.

At the end of the game, Frank Lampard went over to applaud the 2,000 happy West Londoners who, in turn, warmly saluted their players as they trotted off down the tunnel. One fan held up a banner that said simply: *"It's great to be back!"*. That was another positive we could all take from this game, maybe we'd be back at Elland Road soon.

After the match, Bielsa told the BBC that the game was an opportunity to learn; *"Always defeats are an opportunity to learn something"* he said. For me though, the thing that we didn't seem to be learning was how to defend corners and set-pieces. Leeds had now conceded five goals from set-pieces (excluding penalties) in the EPL this season, only Leicester had conceded more from such situations (six). As big as the gulf in individual player quality was, had we defended that Zouma header better and had VAR given us that penalty shout, then we'd have at least drawn with a team that went top of the table. I know it's all ifs and buts, but it's also such fine margins.

Chelsea 3 **Leeds United 1** (**Bamford 4**, Giroud 27, Zouma 61, Pulisic 90+3) Attendance: 2,000. **Round 11 League Pos: 14**[th]

Hammers Nail Set-pieces

O n Sunday I spent most of the day in front of the TV again as four more games took place. West Brom's difficult start to the season took a turn for the worse as they were thrashed 1 – 5 by Crystal Palace for whom talisman Wilf Zaha was back after his Covid isolation. Next, another side at the bottom, Sheffield United suffered yet another defeat as a 90th minute Jamie Vardy goal sent them to a 1 – 2 defeat to Leicester. Blades remained rock bottom, still with only one point. Leicester were flying again and shared the top four places with Spurs, Liverpool and Chelsea. Spurs went top with a 2 – 0 win over North London rivals Arsenal who continued to struggle and then Liverpool joined Spurs at the top again with a 4 – 0 demolition of Wolves.

The final game was on Monday night, a south coast derby in which Southampton came out on top with a 1 – 2 score at Brighton. We were now more than a quarter of the way through the season and Leeds were one of seven teams covered by just three points from West Ham in 8th to ourselves in 14th spot. Effectively, I reasoned, we were currently bottom of that seven team mid-table group. The two upcoming games against West Ham and Newcastle would see us battling teams we really had to compete with. So, we had the top seven comprised of five of the big-six and gate-crashed by Leicester and Southampton; the next seven; and then the bottom six, the only surprise being that Arsenal were in that final group.

In the Sakhir Grand Prix this weekend George Russell pretty much proved to the world that F1 these days is all about the cars; any current F1 driver, if put in a Merc, would be in the top two. Russell should have won the race but a late cock-up by the Mercedes pit crew putting the wrong tyres on his car and then an even later puncture ruined his day. The proof was there for all to see though; Lewis Hamilton had a huge advantage driving a Silver Arrow.

On Tuesday, we Leeds fans were dealt a huge blow as we learned that the injury to Robin Koch was so serious that he'd need surgery on that right knee. The initial prognosis was that he'd be out until the spring. We were all waiting to hear how serious the problem was that Llorente had too; he was picked out by the cameras limping off the pitch at the end of the Chelsea game. Also on Tuesday, the whole country was celebrating; no, not because Manchester United were knocked out of the Champions League with defeat at RB Leipzig, good as that news was. No, not that, but in Coventry a 90-year-old lady called Margaret Keenan became the first person known in the world to have been given the Pfizer Covid-19 jab as part of a mass vaccination programme that was being rolled out in the UK. Bizarrely, the first *man* to receive the vaccine went by the name of William Shakespeare. For me it was all Much Ado About Nothing but the prospect of a return to normality was at last on the horizon and footy fans could finally dream of seeing their heroes at close quarters again. Who knows, it could happen before Twelfth Night. No? OK, As You Like It!

There were more famous deaths reported this week, once again names that were prominent throughout my youth. Former Leeds player Alex Sabella passed away aged just 66. Alex made 27 appearances for the Whites back in 1980, scoring a couple of goals, but he became more famous later in his managerial career which took him to the very top as he led Argentina to the 2014 World Cup finals. We also lost Paulo Rossi who died at the age of only 64. Rossi shot to fame in the 1982 World Cup in Spain when he scored six goals and won Player of the Tournament as Italy went on to win it. He famously faced Diego Maradona in the second group stages as the Azzurri beat Argentina 2 – 1 in the Estadi de Sarria, home of RCD Espanyol in Barcelona. Not only have we now lost both Rossi and Maradona but the old Espanyol stadium has since been demolished too...

Then, on Thursday 10th December we lost Dame Barbara Windsor. For anyone of my era she was a household name back in the late 60s and early 70s as a main character in the Carry On films that pretty much defined that era of entertainment. For younger TV viewers she was similarly well known for her role as Peggy Mitchell, landlady of the Queen Victoria pub in EastEnders. I thought she'd carry on for ever...

Marcelo Bielsa held his weekly press conference on Wednesday this week ahead of our game on Friday night; another one being shown live on Sky TV. He reported that the Koch surgery, never a pleasant experience, went well but the big German defender was still expected to be out until next spring. Worse news was that our other expensive centre-back, Diego Llorente, was now also injured; that muscular injury that saw him limping at the end of the Chelsea game was now expected to see *him* sidelined for two or three weeks. Better news was that both Jamie Shackleton and Pablo Hernandez were fit again.

Bielsa was questioned about what he was doing to try to improve our defending at set-pieces. *"I haven't yet found the tool which will prevent this from happening"* he told reporters, but he said he was doing everything he could to find an answer. He wasn't concerned about the loss of Koch and Llorente and he reaffirmed that he could call on Ayling, Struijk, Phillips and, hopefully by February, Gaetano Berardi to play at centre-back so he would not be looking at bringing in anyone in the January transfer window.

In another wide-ranging and rambling presser, Bielsa also confirmed that he'd supplied Patrick Bamford with video analysis of Erling Haaland, at Paddy's request to help him develop his technique. Now, if Paddy turns into Erling Haaland then we might start to fly! In a final unexpected twist, one journalist asked Bielsa if he'd decided who would play alongside Cooper at the back. *"It could be Ayling or Phillips"* Bielsa replied and then when the journo pressed him with *"Will you keep West Ham guessing?"*

Marcelo reeled off the entire team! The interpreter, Andrés Clavijo couldn't resist a smile as he repeated the names: *"Meslier, Dallas, Ayling, Cooper, Alioski, Phillips, Raphinha, Klich, Moreno [Rodrigo], Harrison and Bamford."* That created quite a stir on Twitter but I particularly liked the summary of @pnxbioia on Twitter: *"The hissy fits and hysteria other managers go to, to keep their teams secret... Bielsa couldn't give a flying fig."*
And so it was exactly that line-up that was announced at 7 pm on Friday night:

Meslier
Dallas Ayling Cooper (Capt) Alioski (Shackleton 45)
Phillips
Raphinha Rodrigo Klich Harrison (Costa 45)
Bamford (Roberts 74)

Subs: Casilla, Struijk, Poveda, Hernandez, Costa, Shackleton, Roberts.
West Ham: Fabianski, Coufal, Balbuena, Ogbonna, Cresswell, Rice, Soucek, Bowen (Johnson 85), Benrahma (Noble 84), Fornals (Snodgrass 90+5), Haller. Subs not used: Randolph, Lanzini, Dawson, Fredericks. Referee: Michael Oliver
So, Rodrigo got the start that most Leeds fans had been calling for and he effectively came in for Robin Koch compared with the starting XI the previous week. Dallas went to right-back, Luke Ayling to centre-back and Rodrigo slotted into midfield. This was the 113th game in charge for Marcelo Bielsa, a number that was significant only in as much as that was the most number of games he'd ever spent at any club in his career; he also achieved 113 games for Athletic Bilbao.
I'm not going to spend too long on this game: suffice to say it fell into that category of huge hope and expectation disintegrating rapidly into despair and disappointment. The YEP Jury that I'm part of, that gives little previews and reports on the Leeds games, were unanimous that Leeds would win this game. We all felt, as I'm sure most Leeds fans did, that we were possibly the best team in that middle section of the table, those seven teams separated by just three points. If that was the case then we had to be picking up points against the other sides around us and West Ham currently led that particular pack. If we could dull the Hammers we could go

level on points with them and they were generally assessed to have had a good start to the season. The game got off to the perfect start for us too as Patrick Bamford was put clear through the centre of the West Ham defence after a tackle by Cooper won the ball in midfield after only two minutes. He slotted the ball down the centre, Paddy touched it past Fabianski, much as he did with Chelsea's Mendy the previous week, and the Hammers' keeper brought him down. It was one of the least controversial penalties of the season and Fabianski was booked. Up stepped Mateusz Klich to take it. Now, do you remember the one he took against Derby the previous season at Elland Road? The one where he gave the keeper the eyes and then rolled the ball tamely past the left post. Well, this was the same technique, except this time it was hit so tamely that Fabianski had time to dive to his right to easily gather it. I was apoplectic and nearly knocked my beer over! What a stupid way to miss a penalty! But wait, what's this? The Sky cameras were now replaying a still image of Fabianski as the ball was kicked and his feet were clearly already an inch or so in front of the goal line. Sure enough, after a quick VAR check, Michael Oliver is doing the TV screen sign (bet these refs are brilliant at Charades) and then pointing at the spot again! *"Please don't let Klich take it again!"* I'm shouting at the screen but there he is, ball tucked under his arm, with a chance to make amends. Fair play to him, he put the second one away neatly enough inside the right post with Fabianski guessing correctly again but this time just too late to reach the ball. Me, I'm still a fan of putting boot through t'ball.

The first penalty attempt sort of summed up the whole Leeds performance this evening; we were just out of sorts. We dominated the possession as usual but our use of the ball was awful. We constantly got the ball wide to the wings but then we hardly ever got it across into the danger area and, even if we did, it was easily dealt with by the Hammers' heads. At the other end it was crystal clear that however much work Bielsa had done on our set-piece defending, it was nowhere near enough. West Ham, like Chelsea before them, dominated the corner-kicks and free-kicks all night and it was no surprise that the equaliser, when it came, was from a corner; we'd lasted 25 minutes.

It was the first West Ham corner, taken from the north east quadrant, and it floated across to the back post. There was the giant Soucek climbing above Stuart Dallas to power a header at Meslier and he couldn't stop it crossing the line. Yet another corner, yet another goal conceded; this was old school Leeds, a problem we've been tussling with for years. We'd already had a couple of let-offs from crosses not dealt with from open play and, if anything, we appeared to be getting worse at this part of the game, not better.

In fact most things Leeds did today were poor. Our crossing was dire, our shooting when we did find an opening was weak (Rodrigo for example cut inside and had a clear view of goal but his shot wouldn't have troubled a five-year-old, never mind a giant Polish stopper like Fabianski) and we somehow just looked lacklustre all over the pitch. We might have had a second penalty too when Ogbonna seemed to 'cup' the ball with his arms as he battled with Bamford to get on the end of a cross. It would have been harsh on West Ham though and would have papered over some disturbing cracks seen during this performance. We were lucky to go in at halftime still level, although neither side was playing particularly well. Once again, when it mattered, West Ham had that little bit of quality in some of their players that perhaps we were lacking. We were working as hard as usual, running further, having twice the possession but creating very little. For me it was a game that would have suited Pablo Hernandez and, if the intention was that Rodrigo was performing that creative role in the centre of the pitch, then it wasn't working. I was sure we'd see Pablo on at halftime, but I was wrong.

Bielsa did make changes at the break; he sent on Helder Costa for the underperforming Jack Harrison, and young Jamie Shackleton for Alioski. Bielsa had clearly not been happy with that left side. Not that the changes seemed to make much difference as the second half had exactly the same feel to it. Leeds passing the ball about but seldom creating a chance, while West Ham waited for a set-piece to sling the ball into our box knowing we wouldn't cope with the size and strength and knowhow of their taller, stronger players.

Klich hit one volley cleanly enough but straight at Fabianski as we finally made something from one of our own corners but that was pretty much it from Leeds. Fornals should have put the Londoners ahead when he was left clear on goal after Cooper slid in and completely missed the ball but thankfully the Hammer dragged his shot wide with Meslier well beaten. Then we gave away another free-kick, out on the West Ham right wing in front of the dugouts. The ball was curled in behind the Leeds defence and yet again a West Ham player was there unchallenged to hammer a header at goal. This time it was another giant, the 6ft 2 inch Fabian Balbuena, but Meslier made an amazing save on his line to thwart that one. It was another warning though and we just did not heed it. Either that or we'd given up, knowing we had no answer to the West Ham height.

We survived with various scares until the 80th minute but then an identical free-kick was conceded on the West Ham left wing. Again it was curled in behind our back line, again it was a West Ham head that was highest, and this time the forehead of Ogbonna smashed the ball into the top corner. This time it was Cooper marking him but Coops hardly got off the ground and might not have been there at all for all the good he did.

Only the agility of Meslier prevented further humiliation as Heller suddenly found himself back to goal and six yards out. The overhead kick was well-placed and powerful but Meslier again defied the laws of physics and gravity as he somehow anticipated where it was heading and pushed it away. The one unwavering aspect of this Leeds team had been the form of the 20-year-old Leeds keeper this season. Yes, we'd seen his immaturity on occasion with a few misplaced passes, but his shot-stopping was generally top class. He was my man of the match again today which also says something about our performance. He was almost beaten late on as West Ham finished the stronger, hitting the post with a glancing header that, another inch or two to the right, would have gone in. Having said all that, in the dying moments we could have snatched an unlikely-looking equaliser as Luke Ayling swept the ball into the middle. Rodrigo got himself in the perfect position between two defenders and only six yards out but his header was straight at Fabianski. To be honest it would have been an injustice.

The post-match press conference was a tense affair as the journalists tried to coax information from Bielsa. Adam Pope led the charge about our set-piece defending costing us the game. *"There are no mysteries about the problem"* Bielsa sighed. *"The set-pieces can be affected by continuing to train for them. We have had this problem before and sorted it and now it is happening again".* I thought back to those early Barbara Windsor Carry On films; Carry On Regardless maybe? Bielsa then chastised one journo who suggested that the games we were losing were generally close-fought affairs. *"That's not the case"* he asserted. *"We have lost 4 – 1 twice, 3 – 1 and today the result should have been by a bigger score-line".* You had to hand it to him, he was not sugar coating the issues. The phrase coming to mind about Leeds was that we were flattering to deceive. Playing well and entertaining the TV audiences and yet taking just eight points from our last nine games and just one from our last four home games. The problem defending set-pieces was costing us dear with seven such goals now conceded. Bielsa had some thinking to do.

On Saturday there were four more games; Villa won by the only goal at Wolves to maintain their decent start; West Brom's troubles increased as they lost 2 – 1 at Newcastle; the two Manchester clubs played out a tedious goalless draw; and Everton beat Chelsea 1 – 0 to put themselves back into the top seven. On Sunday there were another five games, scheduled so it was actually possible to watch four of them; I managed it! Southampton kept up their amazing start as they thrashed hapless Sheffield United 3 – 0, leaving the Blades still adrift at the bottom with just that one point. Next, I watched as Crystal Palace drew 1 – 1 with Spurs, halting their good run. With the chance to gain a significant move on their faltering rivals, Liverpool also messed up as they could only draw against a spirited Fulham side that belied their lowly position; that one ended 1 – 1. The final two games both kicked off at the same time; Arsenal hosting Burnley and Leicester hosting Brighton. Burnley pulled off the surprise of the round as they won 0 – 1 at the Emirates while Leicester strengthened their case for inclusion as title candidates with a solid 3 – 0 win over Brighton. There was another round of games coming up in mid-week with Leeds having another game against one of those mid-table sides: Newcastle. Another chapter would soon be written and the season was already full of intrigue in the week we lost another name that was ever present for us baby boomers: John le Carré, author of the George Smiley spy thrillers died aged 89.

Leeds United 1 West Ham Utd 2 (**Klich 6 pen**, Soucek 25, Ogbonna 80) **BCD. Round 12 League Pos: 14**[th].

Beer 52

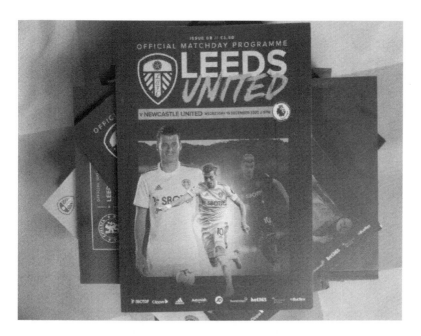

The first-team may have been struggling of late in the Premier League but the Under 23s were still going great guns in EPL 2, Division 2. The 13th December was far from unlucky for them as they came back from two goals down to beat Aston Villa 3 – 2 to go top of the table. Mind you, with Pablo Hernandez, Ian Poveda and Tyler Roberts all getting 45 minutes we did have a pretty strong side out; all came through without incident while the goals came from Bobby Kamwa and then two penalties, one from Sam Greenwood and one from Tyler Roberts.

Hardly a day went by now without another famous name from the worlds of sport or entertainment shuffling off this mortal coil. This week began with the news that Gérard Houllier had left us. Houllier managed Liverpool from 1998 until 2004 and then had shorter spells with French side Lyon and Aston Villa. For the last eight years he'd overseen the rise and rise of Red Bull on the world football scene. He was just 73-years-old but had suffered with heart problems for many years following the discovery of an issue back in October 2001 when he was rushed into hospital with chest pains during the halftime break of a Liverpool versus Leeds EPL game. Danny Murphy equalised a first-half Harry Kewell goal in that one. In Bielsa's pre-Newcastle press conference he was inevitably asked about Houllier but, disappointingly, Marcelo confirmed that they'd never met and so two of the most intellectual managers of the modern era never got to exchange ideas. Had they met, then perhaps they might have discussed how to defend set-pieces. It was inevitable that this topic cropped up again following our defeat to West Ham in which another two set-piece headers flew into our net to put Leeds at the top of the table for set-piece goals conceded with seven in all so far including five headers. Bielsa still didn't seem too worried about it and claimed it was only being raised because we'd conceded such goals in our two most recent games, with Zouma for Chelsea and Ogbonna and Soucek for the Hammers all getting the better of us. He did get his numbers a little wrong though in that he claimed the only other such goal was the header by van Dijk for Liverpool, thus completely ignoring the Scott Dann header from a corner for Palace. His point was probably well made though in that those were the only five examples all season of set-piece headed goals compared with twice that many being conceded from open play and almost as many from daft penalties! He also defended his players, noting that all the players who'd scored against us in the air were some of the best, and the tallest, players in the EPL, while we'd recently been without our own aerial experts – Koch and Llorente. I couldn't agree with him though when he claimed we'd scored a similar number of set-piece goals to the number we'd conceded. By my reckoning we only had three set-piece goals to our name, and none of them were headers!

There had been a bit of a furore after Bielsa's previous pre-match presser when he proceeded to name his starting XI, so this time Bielsa told the listening journalists that he would no longer *"... continue to give answers on which players can or cannot play on weekends."* BBC Leeds' Adam Pope then chanced his arm asking if Patrick Bamford was injured but Bielsa did answer that, responding simply: *"No!"* It was another rumour doing the rounds.

All of the midweek EPL games for match week 13 were being shown live courtesy of Amazon Prime Video who were trying to muscle in on the lucrative top table of English football. It was a bit of an issue for me though as I'd always resisted paying the monthly fee to subscribe to Prime. For the first two games, played on Tuesday evening, I watched on one of those dodgy illegal streams on the laptop while continuing to work my way through my Beer 52 Advent calendar. The beers were all so strong that I was resisting the temptation to try to catch up to the correct day but I must admit I did sneak an extra one in for these games. Wolves surprisingly beat Chelsea 2 – 1 with a winner in the 5th minute of added time at the end of the game and then, in the second match, West Brom ruined many an accumulator by getting a point at the Etihad in a 1 – 1 draw with Citeh. As soon as that game was over the media was awash with rumours that Albion boss Slaven Bilic was about to be sacked and, sure enough, it was confirmed the following day with the added news that Sam Allardyce would be making yet another comeback starring as Red Adair with the carrot of another million quid bonus dangling if he could keep the Baggies in the EPL this season. It was the first managerial casualty of the season in the top league.

Our game against the Toon was one of three starting at 6 pm on Wednesday, with another three following at 8 pm; all available on Amazon Prime Video which I didn't have of course. Fortunately, my good buddy Cambridge Rob, who is part of our little crowd from the White Hart, does and he somehow managed to get me hooked up to his account and I was able to settle down in front of the TV in the sound knowledge I wouldn't suffer the regular picture freeze and loss of connection that is part and parcel of watching on the illegal internet streams. I picked out the next beer – a foul looking orange concoction called 'Orange Crush Gose' brewed by the Brick Brewing Co. in London – from my Beer 52 crate and checked the team on Twitter.

Meslier
Dallas Ayling Cooper (Capt) Alioski
Phillips
Raphinha Rodrigo (Hernandez 82) Klich (Shackleton 89)
Harrison
Bamford (Roberts 84)
Subs: Casilla, Struijk, Poveda, Hernandez, Davis, Shackleton, Roberts.

Newcastle: Darlow, Murphy, Fernández, Clark, Lewis, Hendrick (Krafth 62), S Longstaff, Hayden, Fraser (Almirón 75), C Wilson, Joelinton (Gayle 74). Subs not used: Gillespie, Carroll, Shelvey, Ritchie.

Referee: Simon Hooper.

So, it was another unchanged starting XI and just the one change on the bench where Leif Davis took up the space previously occupied by Helder Costa's bum. In fact, five Leeds players had started every EPL game – Meslier, Ayling, Dallas, Klich, and Patrick Bamford, six if you include Jack Harrison who only missed the Man City game due to not being eligible to play against his parent club. Once again my only disappointment was that there was no room for Pablo Hernandez. As the teams came out, Liam Cooper was again holding an iPad against his chest showing a happy little chappie experiencing another virtual mascot experience.

This was the 114th game in charge of Leeds for Marcelo Bielsa, one more than he'd managed anywhere else in his career, with this one going past the figure he achieved at Athletic Bilbao. For the best part of 80 minutes, it was much like many we've witnessed over the past 29 months or so; Leeds dominated the possession and carved out chance after chance as we peppered the Newcastle battlements. Leeds had their first corner after only six minutes but of course nothing came of that and then we saw a Matty Klich shot blocked and then the first big chance went begging as Rodrigo skied a shot over the bar that should have at least tested the goalkeeper. Klich then missed with a header and then, from our second corner, Liam Cooper did put in a decent back post header that Darlow, in the visitors' net did well to block. Raphinha was having a busy game and he had another shot blocked and then blazed one over the bar as did Klich seconds later. You start to get the picture yeah? Leeds were up around 70% of possession but the commentator sagely noted *"It's what you do with it that counts!"* and, in the 26th minute, Newcastle proved his point for him.

Newcastle worked the ball out to their left wing and Ryan Fraser easily went outside Klich to swing the ball over to the near post. Callum Wilson beat Ayling in the air to flick it towards the back post and there was Jeff Hendrick, unmarked, to steal in and stab the ball past the scrambling Meslier. OK, this wasn't a set-piece, but it was a cross ball and a header that had ultimately undone us.

The game resumed to exactly the same MO, Leeds constantly on the front foot and creating chances. The ball looped up in front of Raphinha after one of Harrison's crosses finally made it past the front man and Raphinha caught it perfectly on the volley, albeit into the turf only to see it fly straight at Darlow who reacted well to push it away. Stuart Dallas then missed the target and later Raphinha put a header over the bar and Alioski headed into the arms of Darlow; I was sinking lower and lower into the sofa. Then, suddenly, our luck turned.

It started with a Darlow goal kick that Stuart Dallas met in the centre of the pitch, heading it forward to Bamford with his back to goal. Paddy laid it back along the turf to Klich who immediately sprayed the ball right to Raphinha who had not always been accurate but had certainly remained busy. Now he had a quick look into the middle to see what was on and spotted Rodrigo who'd found space between a couple of Newcastle defenders near the penalty spot. Darlow had initially been tempted to come for the cross but suddenly realised he wouldn't get there and Rodrigo had spotted he was now off his line and tried a little dinked header over the stranded keeper. Darlow had absolutely no chance of getting to it but still flew through the air thinking he was Superman. The ball bounced against the crossbar and there was Bamford, unchallenged, following up to nod it home with Darlow still on the ground inside the net. It was nothing less than Leeds deserved for dominating the game but, as we know only too well, sometimes you never get what you deserve; years of good behaviour whilst waiting for Santa proved that to me! It was Bamford's 35th goal whilst playing under Marcelo Bielsa for Leeds and that was the most goals anyone had ever scored while playing in his teams, surpassing the 34 scored by Fernando Llorente for Athletic Bilbao whilst the great man was in charge there.

Leeds equalised after 35 minutes and, for the remainder of the first half, neither side really created anything of note. But, as Simon Hooper blew his whistle to end the first period, Leeds could only wonder how this game was still level. Leeds had recorded 14 attempts at the Newcastle goal – the highest first-half total in the EPL so far this season – while the Toon, looking a bit like the All

Blacks in their changed away strip and most of them just as well built as the rugger boys, had managed just four, of which only two hit the target. It was another totally dominant performance by the men in white but, once again, we'd not converted that dominance into goals. Newcastle trudged off the Elland Road pitch looking a tired unit and their energy had probably been sapped by an unusually threadbare and sticky looking Leeds pitch as well as the chasing about they'd had had to endure.

As the players returned after the break, the sounds of Marching on Together could be heard blasting out from the PA system and it was another reminder of what we'd been missing for so long; it was almost nine months since we'd been inside the ground; you could make a baby in that time! Neither side had made any changes although Jack Harrison did have his name and number back on his shirt having played part of the first half in an unmarked top after dripping blood as well as sweat and tears on his original one; he got a smack on the nose from somewhere. Those new floodlights were obviously working well too as the quality of the picture I was getting from this Amazon Prime Video broadcast was superb, the bright yellow Nike Flight winter football shining like a small sun.

An early second-half Newcastle attack saw a booking for Kalvin Phillips to go with the one Matty Klich picked up in the first half and then I watched nervously as Ryan Fraser swung the free-kick into our box in front of the South Stand. Predictably it was a Toon head that got to the ball first but this time Joelinton's forehead sent it well over the bar. Newcastle were clearly placing all their chips on another set-piece goal while relying on defending their way through the game. It was pretty much their normal approach under Steve Bruce and usually yielded them the minority of the possession as it was doing now.

In the 53rd minute we had the first real VAR intervention as they studied a challenge by Liam Cooper on Callum Wilson in the Leeds box. Referee Simon Cooper hadn't spotted anything but now the replays were being run and run on our TV screens and I have to say I'm surprised we got away with it. Those replays showed that Coops just slid into the left ankle of Wilson and, on another day, it might easily have been called as a penalty. Had it of been, I'm sure VAR would have backed it up. This time we got that little bit of a break and VAR agreed with the referee's first call. In the EPL, and the Championship without VAR for that matter, it is often these decisions that determine the outcome of a game. Steve Bruce was livid about it in interviews afterwards, claiming it could well have altered the outcome in their favour. As it was, Leeds came away with the ball and soon we were planning our next attack with Newcastle about to make their first substitute; a white '17' on the back of Emil Krafth waiting on the touchline giving me a little shiver. I still hate that number even though it's a while since anyone wearing it really hurt us.

Stuart Dallas cut out a cross-field ball, nodding it to Alioski who, in turn, played it short to Klich and on to Cooper and then Ayling as the ball moved out to the Leeds right. Eventually it came to Stuart Dallas again who hit a long diagonal ball into the box but it was easily headed clear as far as Rodrigo. The Spaniard battled to get control of the ball and then launched it out towards Harrison who was racing down that left wing again. He had no right to reach the ball really but, stretching out his left foot, he got a toe to knock it further forward towards the byline, almost in the north west corner. Harrison still didn't give it up and he just managed to wrap his left foot around the ball to lash it across the area on the second bounce. There was Rodrigo diving forwards to head the low ball into the bottom right corner to complete a fabulous Leeds move, another Bielsaball move, and Leeds at last had their noses in front.

Newcastle finally got to make their sub and there was plenty of time left as we'd only just gone past the hour mark and Newcastle now had to be a bit more positive if they were to salvage anything from the game. It was Leeds though who had the next effort on goal as Patrick Bamford let fly from a tight angle forcing Darlow to block it away for another Leeds corner. Kalvin Phillips went across to take it. Now, Leeds have been notoriously bad at corner-kicks at both ends of the pitch for quite some time but we were about to plumb new depths as Phillips struck the ball with his right foot. I have no idea what Kalvin was intending to do but he effectively passed it straight to Ryan Fraser on the edge of the box and he was able to hare off down towards the South Stand with eight Leeds players committed at the other end waiting for the corner! Fraser slid the ball down the right wing for Jacob Murphy who evaded Alioski and crossed low towards Callum Wilson who met it on the full on his left foot. Somehow he could only kick the ball into the turf but it ballooned up towards the top right corner and only the most acrobatic of saves from Meslier just eased it over the bar. It would have been the ultimate embarrassment to have conceded a goal from our own corner! The danger wasn't over yet of course as we were now going to be tested with another Newcastle corner which Ryan Fraser swung in. Patrick Bamford got himself under this one and, facing the wrong way, could only head it behind for a second one. The second corner was a high looping one towards the back post and I watched incredulously as Ciaran Clark rose above a static Luke Ayling to nod it down and inside that back post to square the game up again. Oh my! That was a painful one and even Marcelo Bielsa looked distraught as the cameras showed him shouting something at his players while stomping around his technical area. It was all too easy for Newcastle and now we had to do it all again. The lead had lasted just four minutes.

The players had to do it all themselves of course as there were still no fans allowed inside Elland Road. Changes to the various tiers were due to be announced the following day but no one expected Leeds to move down to tier 2; most of the country was seeing Covid cases, hospital admissions and deaths rising again and there had even been talk of *"cancelling Christmas"*. The Prime Minister had not gone that far yet, merely wishing everyone a *"merry little Christmas"* in his TV briefing earlier in the evening. The emphasis being on the 'little' meaning we were being asked to keep our gatherings as small as possible and for as short a time as possible to avoid another big spike in cases after the holiday. The vaccine had arrived and the roll-out had begun but it was still going to take months to get round to everybody.

It took a wee while but eventually the natural positivity in this side of ours shone through again and forward we drove. Time and time again the Magpies would clear their lines but they had eleven men behind the ball so it was easy for Leeds to collect it again and start the next attack. Newcastle looked to be trying to be positive too as they completed their substitutions with the arrival of Dwight Gayle and Miguel Almiron onto the pitch. There was still time on the clock – the best part of quarter of an hour was still left.

Leeds had a scare as Murphy suddenly sped into the box with the threat of Rodrigo bringing him down from behind. Thankfully I think Rodrigo was almost running on empty and Murphy got away from him only to run into Cooper whose challenge was sufficient to allow Meslier to pick up the loose ball; he rolled it out to Coops and then Kalvin Phillips strode forward with the ball at this feet. He played it wide left to Harrison who's cross was cut out but collected again by the Leeds number '22' as he moved infield. This time he threaded it into the box to Patrick Bamford who knocked it wide again to Klich on the left edge of the area. Klich took one quick touch and then clipped it over towards the back post. Raphinha jumped for it with a defender but neither got to it and instead it dropped behind them to where an unmarked Stuart Dallas was running in to head it wide of the keeper on the first bounce! 3 – 2 and hope sprung eternally that this time we could hang on!

Well, as it happens we didn't hang on at all, instead we pushed on and, in an inspired move, Bielsa chose this moment to introduce Pablo Hernandez into the action. Pablo replaced the very tired-looking Rodrigo while Paddy Bamford was also given the hook to be replaced by the fresh legs of Tyler Roberts. It was all too much for Newcastle.

If there was an award for Man of the Final Eight Minutes, this one would have gone to Pablo. In his short time on the pitch he stamped his authority on the game and performed 12 successful passes; four of which were in the final third. He made three ball-recoveries and recorded two assists and he looked a class above anyone else out there. He'd been on the pitch three minutes when he set up Alioski to score and, with delicious irony, it came pretty much from a Newcastle left wing corner!

It took three attempts for Leeds to clear their lines but eventually the ball was hacked clear by Kalvin Phillips to Raphinha who set off through the inside right channel from deep in his own half. Pablo's little legs were going at ninety to the dozen behind Raphinha and pretty much along that right touchline as the two of them sprinted the length of the pitch while, to their left, we had Alioski, Klich, and Harrison all completely unmarked as they arrived at the edge of the box. Raphinha got the call from Pablo to his right and laid the ball off and then Pablo just waited for the perfect moment to roll the ball along the edge of the box. It was Alioski who it went to and two little touches got the ball where he wanted it and the third saw him smash the ball into the corner of the net. It was another lightning-quick Bielsaball break but it needed that sprinkling of Pablo magic-dust just to make it look easy. It was also a further example of just how fit this Leeds team was as six Leeds players sprinted from one end to the other while Newcastle could only muster three to try to do the same. Just a couple of minutes later and we pretty much repeated the example.

It was another corner for Newcastle, this time on their right wing and it was won by Stuart Dallas who nodded it down into the path of Pablo who seemed to be everywhere; wherever the ball broke free, Pablo was there to gather it and this time he had a look up and then clubbed the ball down the centre of the pitch right into the path of Jack Harrison. Harrison had Klich to his right as he continued to motor towards the Newcastle area with three black shirts backing away ahead of him. None of them seemed interested in closing down the Citeh loanee so Jack kept going, veered slightly to his left and then suddenly unleashed a left foot shot that fizzed into the top right corner. It was a stunning goal that capped a stunning last quarter of an hour by Leeds during which everything came good; everything we touched in this period turned to gold.

So dominant were Leeds that the 25 attempts we racked up was our third entry into the current top five of that stat, with Manchesters City and United having the other two and it was only fitting that it was accompanied by a goal haul to match. It was by no means the perfect performance of course and we had to remember that the game was in the balance for almost 80 minutes and there was that penalty shout that could so easily have gone against us and turned the game. But, if ever a result was deserved, then this was that result.

For me this result was welcome reassurance that we were indeed at least good enough to mix it with the middle order sides of the EPL and that, if we could merely sort out those set-piece wobbles, then we might even worry a few at the top. The lack of points from recent weeks had sown seeds of doubt in the minds of many Leeds fans but this was pretty much back to business as usual.

I grabbed myself another beer from my Advent Calendar and had a little chuckle as I spotted the logo on the side of the box: 'Beer 52' it read; now, if that wasn't an omen, I don't know what is!

There were five other games played on Wednesday night and the final two took place on Thursday, again all of them exclusive to Amazon Prime Video subscribers:

Wednesday:
Arsenal 1 Southampton 1
Leicester City 0 Everton 2
Fulham 0 Brighton 0
Liverpool 2 Tottenham 1
West Ham 1 Crystal Palace 1
Thursday:
Aston Villa 0 Burnley 0
Sheffield United 2 Manchester United 3

All of that meant Leeds were up to 13th in the table, level with Newcastle on 17 points and with a nice eight point cushion to the first of the relegation places, currently filled by Fulham on nine points. West Brom and Sheffield United filled the final two places on seven and one point respectively. At the top, Liverpool with 28 points now had a three point advantage over Spurs and four over Southampton and Leicester City. Then came Everton and Man United on 23 in fifth and sixth places and Chelsea a further point adrift with 22. I still considered we were in the mini-league from West Ham in eighth to Newcastle in 14th all covered by just four points.

Leeds United 5 Newcastle United 2 (Hendrick 26, **Bamford 35, Rodrigo 61**, Clark 65, **Dallas 77, Alioski 85, Harrison 88**).
BCD: Round 13 League Pos: 13th.

A Rivalry Resumed

Even though we'd played as recently as Wednesday night, the wait until the Sunday afternoon game with Man United seemed interminable. Everywhere you looked in the media there was talk of the upcoming game and, in particular, the perceived rivalry between these two great footballing institutions. The journos involved in the latest Bielsa presser did their best to get the great man involved in hyping up that rivalry even more but, in his normal measured and objective manner, he seemed far more interested in seeing it as just another chance of adding points.

Leeds had not been to Old Trafford for a league game for almost 21 years, when we were last in the EPL, although we had met twice in that time in cup competitions. *"On January 3rd, remember the date, we beat the team that we f*****g hate!"* That was the famous FA Cup 3rd Round game in January 2010 of course when we played the role of giant-killers as a League One side. Then, some eighteen months later, we were humbled 0 – 3 in the League Cup at Elland Road; another famous meeting when we took the mickey out of

Ryan Giggs for his alleged extramarital affairs only for him to bang a goal in and then give us some back! Michael Owen scored the other two that night, a night when a double decker bus full of Reds fans famously pulled to a halt outside Billy's Bar and all hell broke loose, both in the bar where I was and on the upper deck of the bus as the two factions tried to get to each other despite the inconvenience of two glass barriers!

Bielsa did have first-hand knowledge of what it takes to win at Old Trafford and he was asked in the press conference to explain what it was like when his Athletic Bilbao side went to Stretford in 2012 and famously beat the Red Devils 2 – 3 in a Europa League Round of 16 game. Athletic also won the second leg to go through the tie. It was a typical Bielsa team performance in the Old Trafford game, with Bilbao recording 61% possession by halftime (57.8% over 90 minutes), out-working and out-passing the hosts; even then Bielsa was the high priest of the high press. Bielsa's main memory was *"... of 8,000 Basque fans in the away end"*. For the Athletic fans it must have been a similar experience to our FA Cup victory there.

A full-page article in The Daily Telegraph on the eve of our game did its best to explain where the fierce rivalry between the Reds and Whites really came from and, as if to dispel any doubt that it truly exists, they recalled the 2011 Champions League Final at Wembley when Man United faced Barcelona. *"But, just before the teams come out from the tunnel, what are the Manchester United fans singing to the tune of The Piranhas' Tom Hark? "We all hate Leeds scum!""* In fact, the Telegraph suggested, hardly a game still goes by at Old Trafford when you can't hear that refrain at some point. [1]

It's quite neat and therefore often suggested, that the rivalry goes back to the 15th Century and the Wars of the Roses; Red Rose v White Rose, the House of Lancaster v the House of York, but in reality that has probably only been a convenient addition to the spice seized upon since the rivalry on the pitch and between the two sets of fans began in the 1960s. In 1964 a newly promoted Leeds beat top of the First Division Manchester United 0 – 1 at Old Trafford, a game in which Nobby Stiles for the Reds and Bobby

---

[1] *https://www.telegraph.co.uk/football/2020/12/18/man-utd-v-leeds-inside-story-english-footballs-toxic-rivalry/*

Collins for the Whites adopted the role of chief aggressor for their respective sides; George Best in particular was on the receiving end of some tasty challenges from Collins. It was the only time that good friends and in-laws Johnny Giles and Nobby Stiles fell out, with Stiles refusing to speak to Giles after the game! Ten years later, on the day Leeds were crowned champions of England, Man United were relegated and that probably further angered and irritated their fans. It was a time when hooliganism anyway was rife in the English game but various events conspired to pitch our two clubs against each other more than most. The transfers of Joe Jordan and Gordon McQueen in 1978 ramped feelings up another notch in LS11. I can still vividly remember the pain of those announcements myself and that was before McQueen came out with his parting comment: *"Ask all the players in the country which club they would want to join and 99 per cent of them would say "Manchester United". The other one per cent are liars"* Talk about waving a red flag!

There were more traitorous moves too, as Eric Cantona, Rio Ferdinand, and Alan Smith followed the path trodden by Jordan and McQueen, albeit in various different circumstances and we could argue that we got just as good a deal if not better when we persuaded Johnny Giles and Gordon Strachan to go the other way. Some tasty FA Cup clashes over the years have also all added to the rivalry but for me, I have to say, the clashes with Chelsea, Arsenal and Liverpool are just as important and tasty.

The Saturday games came and went without too much of note. Liverpool began this match week 14 with a thumping 0 – 7 result at Crystal Palace although Palace actually played quite well! The difference was some astonishing finishing from the Reds who scored from 50% of their attempts at goal proving yet again how money buys quality in front of goal. Liverpool, playing first of course, thus went six points clear at the top of the table. Next came a Manchester City win at Southampton by the only goal, a result that kept them nicely placed and with a game in hand still against all their main rivals. Arsenal's dire run continued as they lost 2 – 1 at Everton, thereby keeping the Toffees in a sweet spot near the top. The final Saturday game saw Newcastle and Fulham draw one apiece.

Sunday dragged on and on. The weather was most un-Christmas like, wet and mild, while the news was all about the latest surge in Covid-19 cases that had now caused the Government to: *"cancel Christmas"*, something not altogether unprecedented as they did it in the 17th Century during the Civil War too! The new variant of the disease was apparently transferring itself from person to person at a rate 70% higher than the first strain and daily new cases were fast approaching 30,000. Daily hospital admissions were topping 2,000 and deaths of five or six hundred each day were common. The Government had banned all travel out of the South East where the rate was rising most quickly but unless they had roadblocks on the M25 I didn't quite know how that worked! We were still expecting our lad Adam to do a Chris Rea and drive home for Christmas from Surrey in the coming days. Lorries were parked for miles and miles around Dover and filled the disused airfield at Manston as the port was effectively closed for 48 hours with the French refusing entry while they assessed the threat posed by potentially importing more Covid cases than they already had. The bottleneck had already started well before the latest Covid outbreak as companies tried to stockpile goods ahead of an expected Christmas rush and in case no deal was reached between the UK and Europe as the Brexit deadline approached. Football remained one of our few mental escape routes from the logjam of bad news.

So the football continued, with the EPL game between Brighton and Sheffield United starting the Sunday programme on Sky Sports. That ended 1 – 1, with the Blades surviving despite playing the whole of the second half with ten men. That doubled Sheffield United's points haul for the season to two. In the second game, Leicester City strengthened their position near the top of the table with an eye-opening 0 – 2 result at White Hart Lane and then it was our turn.

Meslier
Dallas Ayling Cooper (Capt) (Davis 72) Alioski
Phillips (Struijk 45)
Raphinha Rodrigo Klich (Shackleton 45) Harrison
Bamford

Subs: Casilla, Struijk, Davis, Casey, Shackleton, Costa, Hernandez, Poveda, Roberts.

Manchester United: de Gea, Wan-Bissaka, Lindelöf, Maguire, Shaw (Telles 60), McTominay, Fred, James, Bruno Fernandes (van de Beek 71), Rashford (Cavani 71), Martial. Subs not used: Henderson, Bailly, Pogba, Mata, Greenwood, Matic.
Referee: Anthony Taylor.

The Leeds squad was the same one that saw service against Newcastle but, with two additional subs now allowed following an EPL vote earlier in the week, Leeds added Oliver Casey and Helder Costa onto the bench. Although increasing the number of named subs to nine, the EPL once again voted down the option of allowing five subs during the game. Bielsa was thus, perhaps not surprisingly, keeping to the side which so thoroughly demolished the Toon in midweek, although I still felt we ought to be trying Pablo Hernandez from the start, just to see how that went. For Manchester United, all the big guns were there and the one thing you couldn't argue against was that they had some serious talent at their disposal; I wondered how good they'd be if they had a Marcelo Bielsa to organise them and if they could be persuaded to get themselves as fit as we were, although something told me they'd never achieve that; a couple of 'Murderball' sessions and I was sure they'd be handing in transfer requests to go back to Europe for an easier life with the money they were on!

You will all have watched this game and will no doubt remember how it went so I'm not going to regurgitate it all again here. Suffice to say it began in a manner that is so familiar to us. I'm sure all Leeds fans, like me, had been looking forward to this game for weeks, probably since the fixtures were announced. All that hype about the rivalry and the chance for Leeds to demonstrate again just how good we were had many of us salivating like the proverbial Pavlov's dogs; the expectation of a thrilling battle with them from over the hills was tantalising. I suppose therefore, we should have known what was about to happen.

Within four minutes of the start, Leeds were two goals down as we simply didn't get going. Scott McTominay scored both, becoming the first man in history to score two goals that early in an EPL fixture. The first came after Raphinha got his legs in a tangle as he was mugged on the Leeds right by Luke Shaw and Marcus Rashford. Rashford touched it to Bruno Fernandes who, in turn, shifted it to his right and there was McTominay, completely free just outside the 'D' with Matty Klich ball-watching having let him get away and then running as if in treacle trying to get back. He never made it and McTominay smashed a perfect low drive with the outside of his right foot that curved its way into the bottom right corner. Alioski was in front of McTominay but merely turned his back, hoping to block the shot. It was the sort of clinical finish you get from players at this level; it was no more than a half-chance really but that's what you need to prosper in the best league in the world. I was slumped back in the chair, screwing up my eyes in anguish and shaking my head thinking how absolutely typically 'Leeds United' this sort of a start to a game had become. I almost didn't believe it though when McTominay knocked in a second literally seconds later!

Man United took a throw on their left, level with the edge of the 'D' and it reached Martial who had Ayling practising social distancing and Cooper only mildly interested. Meanwhile McTominay was allowed to run past them all, again with Klich in his wake. Martial threaded the ball between Coops and Bill and right into the path of McTominay who slid it effortlessly past Meslier. Had that of been one of my lads getting the wrong side of McTominay and looking as asleep as Klich was... well, I'm not sure what I've have done but I'm sure I'd now be serving a life sentence for it!

I think we all knew it would be nigh on impossible to come back from that start; we knew we'd make chances once we settled down but the way Man U were outwitting our defence it was hard to see how they wouldn't get a few more as well. And that is pretty much how it panned out. Leeds did make chances, Bamford in particular had one glorious opportunity similar to the second McTominay finish but, whereas the Man U man found the corner of the net, Bamford could only steer his effort wide of the post. He also had a clear header that he wasted over the bar and did get one in the net with a nice finish that was ruled offside. The problem was we were AWOL in the middle of the pitch – it was that Pablo-sized hole I'm always going on about – and Man U were quick-witted and slick. The third Man U goal came when a suicidal Rodrigo pass was cut out, fed forward to Fred who tried to put Martial in inside the Leeds box. Ayling did stop Martial but the ball broke to Fernandes who walloped it home low past Meslier. That was in the 20th minute. In the 37th it was four and it was our old friend the corner-kick. A left wing corner was swung in to the near post; Martial left a statuesque Bamford as he took a few steps towards the ball and then beat Ayling to glance it across the face of goal and there was Victor Lindelof losing Phillips, who was doing more ball-watching at the back post, to tap it home. Shocking, shocking, shocking.

Leeds got one back with a sharp Cooper header at one of our own corners to make it 4 -1 and, clinical as Man U had been, we should still have gone in only the one goal down had we put our, much better chances, away. We'd dominated the possession too, so it was nowhere near as one-sided as the score suggested but boy had we been naïve at times at the back and in midfield.

We only lost the second half 2 – 1 and it was a closer half than the first with Bielsa having hauled off Phillips and Klich who had both had shockers; Struijk and Shackleton came on and had decent games. We could have scored when Rodrigo found Raphinha at the back post but, this time David de Gea somehow parried the volley into the air and it bounced against the foot of the other post before being chested away for a corner by Maguire. Remember, had we put our chances away as well as they did, that would have levelled things at 4 – 4. Sadly, we hadn't improved at the back and McTominay then gave Rodrigo the run around on halfway before sliding the ball through another huge hole in the Leeds defence for Dan James to run onto and rifle it through the legs of Meslier for 5 – 1 after 66 minutes. Then it was a half dozen four minutes later, as Rashford carried the ball to and fro in the Leeds area before Martial took it off his toe, saw Pascal Struijk place his foot down and made sure he toppled over it and went down like the first spruce for sale at Christmas. Fernandes put the penalty away with his usual hop skip and jump for 6 -1.

Still Leeds continued to play the only way we knew though and within three minutes Stuart Dallas pulled one back with his very familiar curling right foot shot from the edge of the area finding the top right corner after Jack Harrison clipped the ball in from the right and Raphinha stunned it back to Dallas. I remember Dallas doing that twice in quick succession at Guiseley one pre-season. And that was that really: the record books will show that Man United beat Leeds 6 – 2 in the last game before Christmas but, like many Christmas stories, there was more to it than that. Yes, the quality on show from the Man U players was undeniable and some of their passing and finishing was of the highest order, but that's what you expect for the tens of millions these players cost and the hundreds of thousands they get paid every week. Leeds dominated the possession and created more than enough chances themselves but when we needed that clinical finish it wasn't there and our regular set-piece woes and a soft penalty flattered the home side.

After the game there were plenty of reporters – and some fans – ready to crucify Bielsa for not changing his approach to this game. The argument was that he needed to tweak his approach for only a few opposition teams but that this was one of them. The Daily Telegraph's James Ducker didn't err, duck the issue, when he noted: *"Leeds have plenty of pace and threat themselves on the break and, while a Bielsa team were never going to sit in, the space they routinely left for Ole Gunnar Solkjaer's blistering red arrows to attack undermined all attempts to penetrate the home team's goal."* Even Patrick Bamford didn't sound totally convinced about his boss's approach as he told the Telegraph: *" But it is our style of play. It's fine margins. Sometimes it works but if you're one yard out of place, you get picked off against the best players. Ultimately, if we play exactly the way the manager wants we'd win, but we're human, we make errors. It could have been 6 – 6 if you're an optimistic Leeds fan or it could have been 10 – 2. We couldn't do ourselves justice."* For me it was all about individual quality. If Bamford was Rashford he'd have got a couple of goals for Leeds. If we'd had Koch or Llorente fit and Ayling in his natural right-back slot then we may have been more solid at the back in those opening three minutes. Maybe an experienced Harry Maguire would not have planted a boot so close to Martial as the young Struijk did and we'd not have succumbed to that penalty and, on another day, that Raphinha volley would have gone in. Say what you like, and many did, we were not far away from grabbing a point in this game or at least eking out a result not dissimilar to the Liverpool, Citeh or Arsenal games. As always though, you are only ever as good or bad as your most recent result and this one was a 6 – 2 defeat.

There was one more game to come on this pre-Christmas Sunday and that saw Sam Allardyce take charge of his Albion side for the first time. It's hard to know if he made any difference in this one though because West Brom sort of self-destructed against Aston Villa when Jake Livermore got himself sent off in the 37th minute with the Albion already a goal down. They fought bravely throughout the second half and only conceded again in the final ten minutes with a tap in and a penalty to go down 0 – 3, leaving the Baggies still in deep trouble in the bottom three.

The final two games of the round took place on Monday evening with our next opponents, Burnley hosting Wolves and then Chelsea facing West Ham in a London derby. Burnley grabbed a vital win, 2 – 1 over the Black Country side and then Chelsea edged past West Ham 3 – 0 with a couple of late goals from Tammy Abraham. The early-season pressure on Frank Lampard seemed, for the time being, to have gone which disappointed many a Leeds fan hoping for him to be sacked. The win kept the West London side in touch with the leaders in 5th, behind Liverpool, Leicester, Man United, and Everton; six points covered the top six including Spurs on 25 points level with Chelsea. Leeds were back in that familiar 14th spot we grew to know and love in the Championship for so many years!

Manchester United 6 **Leeds United 2** (McTominay 2,3, Fernandes 20, 70 pen, Lindelof 37, **Cooper 42**, James 66, **Dallas 73**)
BCD. **Round 14 League Pos: 14th**

Showing Bottle for Clarets

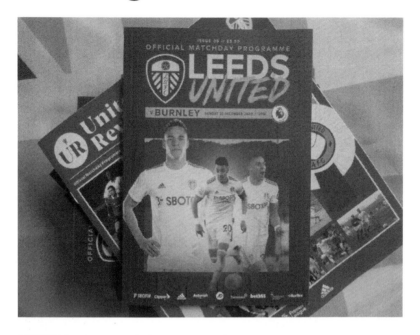

This close to Christmas you often get some outrageous scores in football at all levels; though I've never really understood why; Christmas parties perhaps? But there weren't any of those this year due to Covid restrictions. With the first-team going down 6 – 2 at the weekend, on Monday it was the turn of the Under 23s; they hammered Fulham 7 – 1 at Thorp Arch to maintain their lead at the top of the PL2, Div.2 table. It was another strong team, with Roberts, Hernandez, Leif Davis, and Helder Costa all featuring and the goals came from seven different players; Roberts, Cresswell, McAvoy, Hernandez, Kamwa, Gelhardt and Costa.

It might have been an awful year, and this Christmas was shaping up to be the most dismal in all of my personal history but at least we still had Jesus; Gabriel Jesus that is. He scored the opening goal as Manchester City thrashed Arsenal 4 – 1 in the Carabao Cup quarter-final to put the Cityzens a step closer to an incredible fourth consecutive title in the competition. In the other games, Brentford beat Newcastle 1 – 0, Spurs won 1 – 3 at Stoke, and Manchester

United won 0 – 2 at Everton. In the semi-final draw, the two Manchester clubs were drawn together, leaving Spurs to face Brentford, the only non-EPL side left in the last four.

Did I just suggest that Jesus was the salvation of this awful year? Before we could even get as far as Christmas *he* suddenly went down with Covid! Gabriel that is, not the Son of God. He, Kyle Walker, and a couple of the Manchester City backroom staff all tested positive in the aftermath of the EFL Cup win at Arsenal and so there would be no Jesus this Christmas after all!

Boxing Day is usually a magical day in the football season; it always seems to be played out in a haze after the excesses of Christmas Day and the fixture computer tries to get everyone a local fixture to allow even more time for an alcohol top-up. When the fixtures originally came out and I saw we had a home game against Burnley I was more than happy; a game that should be winnable to keep the Christmas merriment going a few days longer. But Covid messed up any chance of being there and then Sky TV decided to move our game to Sunday 27th anyway. About the only saving grace was that Storm Bella, the latest winter storm to hit the UK, whipped up the wind and dumped loads of rainwater on much of England meaning many areas were once again subject to flooding. If we hadn't had enough to cope with already this year at least we'd not be battling Bella on our way to Beeston.

Boxing Day was thus spent in front of the TV (again) watching the six EPL games still left on the traditional day. I was joined by Adam, my younger son, who was in our domestic Covid 'bubble'; another term that had come into common parlance in this extraordinary year. We watched as Leicester and Man U drew 2 – 2 to leave them second and third in the table respectively, at least until the other games were completed. Next came another Aston Villa win, 3 – 0 over a disappointing Crystal Palace, despite Villa going down to ten men just before halftime. Fulham and Southampton drew 0 – 0 and then we watched as Arsenal finally got another win on the board, surprisingly beating Chelsea 3 – 1 and in the process shifting the spotlight from Mikel Arteta to Frank Lampard who became a potential managerial casualty again. Arsenal went one place above Leeds on goal difference but we could put that right with a win the following day. The final two games on Boxing Day, played at the same time, were shown on two different BT Sport channels. Manchester City eased past Newcastle 2 – 0, without help from Jesus of course, while Sheffield United looked in dire need of divine intervention as they lost to Everton 0 - 1; their 13th defeat in 15 EPL games. We had to wait overnight for our game; a 12 noon kick-off on Sunday.

Our Leeds United WhatsApp group had a Skype call at 11 am and by the time I joined, a few minutes late, the team had already been announced. I was surprised when Kev explained that Diego Llorente wasn't playing. In the pre-Burnley presser on Christmas Eve, we were informed that Liam Cooper wouldn't feature as he was still getting over an abdominal strain but that Llorente was *"in condition to play"*. Quite why now the team was published there was no sign of Diego in it, none of us had any idea! It was a strange one but not the first time there had been a slip 'tween presser and match line-up. We were starting to think that Llorente was just the Spanish way to spell Forshaw...

Meslier

Ayling (Capt) Phillips Struijk

Dallas   Klich (Shackleton 66)   Alioski

Raphinha (Poveda 70) Rodrigo (Hernandez 59) Harrison

Bamford

Subs: Casilla, Poveda-Ocampo, Roberts, Hélder Costa, Hernandez, Davis, Shackleton, Jenkins, Casey.

Burnley: Pope, Lowton, Tarkowski, Mee, Taylor, Benson (Stephens 74), Brownhill, Westwood, Pieters (Rodriguez 74), Wood, Barnes. Subs not used: Peacock-Farrell, Norris, Bardsley, Long, Dunne, Mancini, Mumbongo. Referee: Robert Jones.

So, one change in the starting XI from the Old Trafford line-up; Pascal Struijk replacing Liam Cooper in the side and that left a Jack Jenkins sized spot available on the enlarged bench. For Burnley we had a chance to renew old acquaintances with Chris Wood and Charlie Taylor who both started, and Bailey Peacock-Farrell who continued to warm the bench for the Clarets. Experienced Burnley full-back Matthew Lowton also had a Leeds connection; he started out in the Leeds youth set-up from the age of ten and was with the club for almost five years.

Burnley is not a game of the standing of your Liverpool or Manchester clubs and we've had a few recent battles with them so this wasn't a rare meeting either; definitely not the renewal of an old rivalry. In fact, since I've been attending almost every Leeds game over the last ten years, I've been at no fewer than eleven meetings with them.

The win against Newcastle, another of the sides like Burnley occupying the middle section of the table, sort of restored our faith in believing we could more than hold our own with that quality of team and hence we ought to be able to hang around in the EPL for at least another season. Then, the scale of the defeat at Old Trafford, if not maybe the nature of our performance which I felt was better than the score suggested, just sowed a few seeds of doubt. Beating Burnley would clarify, or maybe 'claretfy' things again and cast out any lingering doubts, at least for me anyway.

I was with my lad Adam again for this one, not where we should have been at Elland Road, but in my front room watching the telly. It was the first of four games this Sunday afternoon all being shown live on Sky. As the players emerged into the stadium, the most surprising thing was the dire state of the Elland Road pitch. I'd noticed how bad it looked for the Newcastle game and it looked just the same now; very little grass and threadbare in places. It was the subject of much debate on social media but I never did see a satisfactory answer other than the amount of rain Leeds had been subject to lately and the fact we knew it was overdue for a complete renovation, as noted by Angus Kinnear way back in February. The Covid pandemic meant it didn't happen in the summer as originally planned.

I'd lost count of the number of times this season that a goal had featured in the opening minutes of our games but here we were, only five minutes into this one, and we had our first of the day. It was a scenario we'd seen a few times this season. Luke Ayling clipped a long diagonal ball over the top of the Burnley defence from out near the right touchline. It beat the back line and Patrick Bamford was alert to chase it down as Nick Pope, the Burnley keeper, raced out towards him. Both arrived at the ball at pretty much the same time but Bamford got enough on the ball to ensure it broke loose to his left but he couldn't then go after it as by this time Pope had clattered into him and both went to ground in a crumpled heap. It looked like a penalty and referee Robert Jones thought so too; VAR didn't raise any objections. My immediate thoughts turned to whether Klich would be a bit more confident this time when he struck the penalty, having missed that first one against West Ham before he was reprieved, but then the camera showed it was Patrick Bamford who had the ball tucked under his arm. After the game Bamford explained that it should have been Klich's since technically he did score his previous one; they each keep the responsibility until someone misses and then hand it over, but Klich didn't fancy this one and Bamford said he was happy to oblige! He also said he'd been practising his penalties a lot this season in training and it showed big-time as he calmly struck an unstoppable shot into the top right corner; Pope didn't have a prayer...

I thought there might then be an avalanche of goals in this game but the one thing I'm quickly learning about the EPL is that it is nothing if not unpredictable in the extreme. We ought to have gone in at halftime two or three goals to the good but, once again, despite dominating the possession and fashioning numerous really good chances, our finishing just wasn't up to scratch. At the other end there was just one moment that could have upset our day.

Burnley were unfortunate not to be level after 20 minutes when Ashley Barnes appeared to capitalise on Illan Meslier's mistake to spin inside the area and fire the loose ball into the roof of the net despite the best efforts of Luke Ayling who stretched to try to get his head to it. The Leeds' goalkeeper was awarded a free-kick by referee Rob Jones, despite spilling the ball after what, if anything, looked like a foul *by* Meslier jumping through the back of Ben Mee. It would be a major talking point on the TV show and from Burnley manager Sean Dyche after the game. Dyche was apoplectic as he told the BBC: *"... the keeper goes through with his knee in Ben Mee's back. Ben has got nothing other than eyes for the ball, that is all he is concentrating on... Even in my day, if you put your knee in someone's back like that when they are trying to head the ball, you're not only giving a foul away, you're going to get booked, and nowadays you're probably in trouble. So I have no clue where the game is at physically at the moment."* I have to say I tend to agree with him but, for once, we got that little break you often need to sway the game towards you. The best Leeds chances fell to Harrison, Raphinha and Rodrigo.

Harrison was all on his own, twelve yards out, as Raphinha cut the ball back but Patrick Bamford was in the way and blocked the Harrison shot that was otherwise destined for the bottom corner of the net. Raphinha then didn't quite strike the ball well enough as he met it for a half volley from the edge of the box and Pope saved easily. Finally, we had Rodrigo finding space between two defenders to meet a fabulous left-wing cross from Harrison but the Spaniard got it all wrong and the top of his head sent the ball miles over the bar. Once again, it was hard to dismiss the thought that top-quality players would have buried all those chances and we'd have been going in for a suck on our oranges with a four goal lead. Would we rue the missed opportunities?

Well, no, not this time, although the second half was a totally different game. For maybe the only time this season so far, Leeds were penned back in their own half and Burnley dominated the possession. Corner after corner rained in on the Leeds six-yard box and time after time we managed, often more by luck than judgement, to scramble the ball away. We may lack technique at the back, especially with a makeshift centre-back pairing, but boy did we show spirit and determination to keep a clean sheet. Kalvin Phillips was playing as a third centre-back as Bielsa set up his team to deal with the two Burnley strikers, Wood and Barnes. Kalvin was quite simply majestic. Either side of him, Pascal Struijk and Luke Ayling worked like Trojans while Illan Meslier, his one early mistake apart, was positive and courageous. After the game even Pontus Jansson messaged Luke Ayling on Instagram: *"Understand why I had to leave when the RB is better CB than me, ha-ha love it bro."* 12 Burnley corners and numerous other set-piece situations came to nothing, despite the Clarets being a side well known for their own ability in the air and Leeds' poor record at the back that had been well publicised during the lead up to the game. Leeds had conceded more goals than any other side in the EPL this season and we'd conceded more from set-pieces, more from crosses, and more headed goals than anyone else. This felt like, and very much looked like, a team determined to start to put that record behind them. We were helped by the fact that Burnley's record at the top end of the pitch is as dire as ours is at the back. The Clarets were the joint lowest scorers in the league, with only eight goals so far this season (Leeds started this game with 24) and that lack of a clinical edge was evident after the break. From ten second-half attempts, only four were on target, as Barnes produced two good Meslier saves from their best opportunities.

So, Leeds held on and put another three points on the board against a side now seven points behind us. It was another win against the sort of team we were fighting with in the mid-section of the table, but, more importantly, it was a performance that showed that, if need be, we have the bottle to defend for our lives even if we needed a lucky break or two. It was also a quick response to the media, many of whom criticised Bielsa for not changing his style of play when faced with teams coming at us. Speaking before the game, Marcelo Bielsa said: *"Normally, when there is adversity, what the press do is try to weaken the one who is facing adversity or to ridicule the style of play of a team."* It was one of the few times I could remember Bielsa having a pop at the media but it seemed to pay off. The 'us against them' mentality he thus created and which we often thrive on as a club seemed to shine through as we fought a rearguard action for much of the second half. It was a spirit we might well need in the next game coming up in just over 48 hours; West Brom at the Hawthorns. Now under the leadership of the wily old fox Sam Allardyce, Albion gained their first point since he took over with a remarkable draw at Anfield later in the day, while the two other Sunday games also finished all square: West Ham drew 2 – 2 with Brighton and Wolves held Spurs 1 - 1.

Leeds United 1 Burnley 0 (**Bamford 5, pen**)
BCD. Round 15 League Pos: 12th.

Baggies Battered

With match week 15 completed on Sunday, we were straight into the next round on Monday. Three games were scheduled but only two were played. I watched as Crystal Palace and Leicester City drew 1 – 1 and then Adam and I settled down to enjoy the Chelsea v Villa clash. Before it began though they announced on Amazon Prime Video that the final game of the day, Everton v Manchester City, was now off; it was Covid again. Citeh had suffered further positive Covid tests and had applied to the EPL to have the game postponed. With so many players now isolating and the training ground closed indefinitely it would have been harsh had the EPL insisted the game go ahead. In the UK generally the situation continued to deteriorate; reported daily cases now exceeding 40,000 and the NHS sounding warnings that they now had more Covid patients in their care than they did at the height of the first wave back in April. There was talk of another national lockdown and, whisper it quietly, there was even talk that elite sport could be stopped again.

So, Chelsea v Villa was the final stint of the day. It was yet another 1 – 1 draw, in fact all five games played since our win over Burnley ended all square, highlighting yet again how close this year's EPL was going to be. Leeds, in 12th, could conceivably end the next round of games just three points off the top six. To have any chance of that of course we first needed to beat Big Sam's Baggies.

We'd awoken on Monday to a light covering of snow at home in Shropshire and then, on Tuesday morning, we had another substantial load dumped on us; the Hawthorns is just 40 miles south of here so I was slightly worried the game might be in doubt. There were five EPL games scheduled for the Tuesday; four of them kicking off at 6 pm and the final game, Man United v Wolves, at 8 pm; every game was shown live on Amazon Prime Video. I'd got quite used to watching all the games so it was a minor irritant that I'd not be watching the three other 6 pm kick-offs live; it looked like Match Of The Day for those.

Despite it not being mentioned at the Bielsa press conference this week, a rumour went round social media again that Patrick Bamford was injured, although no one seemed to know where the rumour came from. I guessed since it was the same rumour we heard ahead of the Burnley game that it was some twonk on Twitter trying to stir up a reaction and, sure enough when the team appeared on the club's official Twitter account, it was unchanged.

Meslier
Ayling (Capt) Phillips Struijk
Dallas   Klich (Shackleton 58)   Alioski
Raphinha (Costa 81) Rodrigo (Hernandez 70) Harrison
Bamford

Subs: Casilla, Poveda-Ocampo, Roberts, Costa, Hernandez, Davis, Shackleton, Jenkins, Casey.

West Brom: Johnstone, Furlong Ajayi, O'Shea, Peltier, Sawyers, Robinson, Phillips (Ivanovic 45), Gallagher, Diangana (Krovinovic 72), Grant (Costa Pereira 61). Subs not used: Button, Grosicki, Austin, Harper, Kipré. Referee: Lee Mason.

With Cooper, Koch, and Llorente all injured, the selection for Leeds just about picked itself. Big Sam was intending to adopt the same policy after seeing his new charges gain that priceless point at Anfield last time out but he was thwarted when Kieran Gibbs was reportedly injured by a stray ball in the warm-up and former Leeds player Lee Peltier was given the late call. 'Pelts' was recruited by Neil Warnock and was a regular for Leeds between 2012 and 2014 making 66 appearances, some as club captain. He scored one goal; a looping header in a 1 – 1 draw at Blackpool on Boxing Day 2013 from a Danny Pugh cross.

The Albion game, as with all the round 16 games, was exclusive to Amazon and we had Jimmy Floyd Hasselbaink and former England Women's international Karen Carney giving their expert puntry on our game. They reminded us that Leeds' first game of 2020 was also against the Albion; a 1 – 1 draw when we sat 1st and 2nd in the Championship table on New Year's Day, with Semi Ajayi scoring at both ends. I was at the Hawthorns for that one of course but now, for the final game of 2020, I was again watching at home with my son Adam while the ladies busied themselves in the kitchen trying to come up with yet more ingenious ways to use the mountains of turkey we still had left over. The game was only nine minutes old, (the match that is not the turkey), when the women folk were brought scurrying in to see what was going on as both Adam and I jumped up and exclaimed simultaneously: *"What the hell has he done there?"*

The pitch was in superb condition by the look of it, despite little remnants of snow lying against the perimeter advertising boards that was highlighted on camera as the players arrived to that tune 'The Liquidator' again. The match began in familiar fashion with Leeds mostly in possession and camped near the West Brom area but a series of woeful final balls meant no real chances were created and each Leeds attack would end with the Baggies trying to play their way out of their own final third. They were doing just that in the 9th minute after Raphinha gave the ball away, right on the edge of the Albion box. Conor Gallagher collected the loose ball and then gave it to Grady Diangana but he had to turn back as Stuart Dallas was already in his face on the Leeds right touchline. Diangana pushed it back to Romaine Sawyers who took a couple of touches and looked to be about to play it to another Albion player on that touchline. Then, with his route blocked by the presence of Rodrigo, he suddenly turned 180 degrees to his left and swept the ball back towards his own goal, presumably thinking that's where Sam Johnstone, his keeper, was waiting. Except Johnstone had already come off his line and was backing up Sawyers in case he wanted to play it back near the touchline! The ball rolled straight between the posts with Johnstone stranded and only able to watch it glide past. It was one of the most absurd own goals I've ever seen, although it did remind me of a similar one scored in this same city some 18 years earlier. That was when Aston Villa's Olof Mellberg aimed a throw-in back towards his own keeper, Peter Enckleman, in a derby game against Birmingham City. The ball scooted under the keeper's boot and into the net and the goal was awarded; Enckleman being adjudged to have touched it. This one, from Sawyers, was right up there with the best and, as the cameras panned around to Big Sam, we saw him slump back in his seat with a resigned look on his face. On his club jacket was the Ideal Boilers logo, just below the club crest. Ideal was the main Albion sponsor but this was far from an ideal start for the men from Sandwell. It's true what they say, when you're at the wrong end of the table struggling to find a result, you can almost guarantee all the breaks will go against you.

That goal pretty much set the trend for the night; things would continue to go in our favour throughout the game but we were also clinical in the way we took advantage. Leeds played superbly throughout with maybe the exception that our final ball could have been better. Leeds were two goals up by the half-hour mark as Rodrigo fired in a cross from the right wing with his left foot; a better one this time that was somehow headed away by a defender. The header was poor though and the ball dropped perfectly onto the left foot of Ezgjan Alioski, near the edge of the box and he sent a screamer curling away into the top right corner and in off the post. Adam and I were up on our feet again and the ladies were soon rushing back in to see what the noise was about. Five minutes later and they were back again…

Alioski was involved again, this time collecting a pass from Pascal Struijk, out on the left touchline. Jack Harrison was just ahead and Alioski pushed the ball forward to him as he set off infield towards the 'D', with Darnell Furlong tracking alongside him. Ten yards outside the area Harrison pushed the ball to Bamford on the edge of the 'D' and kept running to neatly collect the wall-pass from Paddy. Furlong was still there but Harrison, now on the penalty spot, stopped, cheekily played the ball with his right foot behind his left, and then lifted the ball into the top left corner with his left foot.

Still we weren't finished with this avalanche of first-half goals and it was only four minutes later that a long aerial pass from Kalvin Phillips reached Stuart Dallas on the right wing, level with the edge of the Albion box. Dallas nodded the ball down to Matty Klich with the most subtle of cushioned headers and Klich just rolled the ball along the edge of the area. Rodrigo had played the original ball to Phillips but was now steaming in to meet the Klich pass and he stabbed out his left boot. It was another fabulous Leeds move but it still needed another helping hand from Lady Luck as the ball cannoned off Dara O'Shea's outstretched right boot completely wrong-footing the hapless Sam Johnstone who was once again diving away to his left. The ball passed him the other way to nestle in the opposite corner. 4 – 0 and it had been an astonishing first half of football. Two sumptuous goals from Leeds, an incredible own goal and a cruel deflection had left the Albion wondering who'd smashed a mirror over Christmas and even VAR appeared to be on our side as it lingered over a scramble in the Leeds area at an Albion corner. They apparently replayed it over and over again, as they did on the Amazon coverage and it showed Rodrigo putting a headlock on an Albion striker; on another day that was a penalty but today the decision went our way. Good as Leeds had been it was impossible to ignore how the breaks had gone in our favour at every turn.

West Brom made one change at halftime, introducing the former Chelsea defender Branislav Ivanovic for Matt Phillips; hardly a sign they were going to try to get back in the contest. There were enough warnings though early in the second half that the game wasn't over quite yet and, for whatever reason, Leeds took a little while to get going again. We certainly got a wake-up call early in the new period as we seemed to have mentally switched off. We were defending in our own right-back area with Raphinha on the ball facing his own goal; he knocked it back to Matty Klich, right where the edge of the area meets the byline. Klich stopped the ball and then looked unsure what to do next. He had Luke Ayling three or four yards away, also near the byline, and Karlan Grant nearby keeping us honest. Klich decided, after a second's thought, to slide the ball across the face of goal to Illan Meslier. We've seen Illan make suicidal passes a few times this season and we were about to see one of his worst. It was as if he didn't see any Albion shirts as he decided on his next pass. He had Kalvin Phillips outside the area calling for the ball, but Grady Diangana saw that pass coming well before Kalvin did and he was to it first, nipping in front of the Yorkshire Pirlo. We then saw the better side of Meslier as he managed to block the shot from the Albion man and then have the speed of reaction to leap and push away the looping ricochet for a corner. It was a let-off and just another example of how Lady Luck was well and truly batting for Leeds this time.

The first Leeds substitution came shortly after the Meslier brain fade moment; Klich limped off, with a strapping on his right leg giving away that he'd picked up an injury in the first half; he was replaced by Jamie Shackleton and I thought it was well overdue. Whether it was the injury I'm not sure, but Klich had been poor today despite Leeds dominating the game. His passing was off and his shooting was, well, his shooting was very Klich-like! West Brom made their second change on the hour mark with Matheus Pereira replacing Karlan Gant. Even at 0 – 4 I was still not convinced we were yet safe and Pereira had often been a decent player against us in the Championship. Quite why he didn't start for the Albion I'll never know.

It was noticeable how the Baggies were working much harder now to close Leeds down and that, and I guess the inevitable shifting down a gear or two by Leeds, meant the second half didn't produce much in the way of goalmouth action. In fact there was an element of going through the motions for much of it and that led to the odd careless moment; Luke Ayling stumbled over a throw-in and gave a needless corner away and the passing was never quite as sharp as we saw earlier in the game. Meslier also whacked the ball out for a throw-in when trying to launch it up-field, and sliced another one into the corner; it was just a bit like a training game now. Both sides made full use of the 'Ayling Flop' free-kick at every opportunity as well, to sort of kill the game. It was gone for the Albion and there was nothing much to be gained for Leeds by us busting a gut. We made the usual Hernandez for Rodrigo change with twenty minutes to go and his movement was as classy as ever and started us ticking again. It took just a few minutes for another Bielsaball goal to materialise.

It started with a long clearance from the boot of Sam Johnstone that was eventually won by the footballing ferret that is little Jamie

Shackleton, winning a ball he had no right to win against a taller, stronger opponent. Shacks played a short pass inside to Harrison who, in turn, knocked it further left to Phillips and on to Alioski on the left touchline. Then Leeds moved it back the other way to Struijk and then he played it through the legs of Ayling to Stuart Dallas, again near the right touchline; then it started to heat up. Dallas played it short to Raphinha who played it back and then set off down the right wing. Dallas played a one-two with Shacks and then a first time ball into the path of the rapid Raphinha. The Leeds number '18' cut inside and moved along the edge of the Albion box from right to left and then, as the Albion defence took social distancing to new extremes, he simply rifled the ball into the top left corner with his left foot. It was the culmination of ten unanswered Leeds passes and, as the cameras lingered on the face of Sam Johnstone, lip readers could clearly see him telling his defence they were: *"fu****g sh**!"*

There was still time for more careless clearances from Illan Meslier who'd looked strangely out of sorts all night, but nothing came of them and the presence of Pablo meant there was even more class about our actions on the pitch. West Brom were totally gone now, all resistance had been quashed with that rapier-like run of Raphinha. He got a hug and a kiss on the cheek from Alioski as he was replaced by Helder Costa for the final ten minutes which became a masterclass in passing and showboating reminiscent of those halcyon days of Don Revie's side.

It was a 0 - 5 result, a resounding result earned through a near faultless display by Leeds. The only holes I could pick in it were a lack lustre performance from Matty Klich and those few wobbles from Illan Meslier. On reflection though, it was worth also remembering how the EPL is a league of such fine margins. Against Manchester United a couple of weeks earlier we'd lost 6 – 2 and yet there were a couple of glaring big chances missed by Leeds in that one and a soft penalty for the Reds that, on another day, could have seen that game as close as 5 – 4, not dissimilar in fact to the 4 – 3 Liverpool game. Yes, both those sides had players in every position with oodles of quality that made the most of their chances but our work rate and organisation ran them close and, had we had the rub of the green, we'd have been even closer. Similarly, today was a day when Leeds had all the breaks go our way. West

Brom were soundly beaten by the better side and, with the likes of Rodrigo and Raphinha we had players of quality of a different level to the Albion but, on another day, Sawyers would not have put through his own goal, that Rodrigo shot would not have been deflected into the net, a better striker than Diangana would have punished that Meslier clanger and, maybe the Albion would have had that penalty given. 0 – 5 could easily have become 2 – 3 and it could have been as tense as that Newcastle game was for an hour. I know it's all ifs and buts, and I know you do get luckier the harder you work, but it's just worth reflecting on it for a moment. It was often the case in the Championship that games would be decided on the rub of the green; a referees call, a deflection, a slip, and EPL games were often just as tight.

For now though this was more confirmation that Leeds were easily good enough to see off most teams in the bottom half of the table and we would, luck permitting, give the top sides a run for their money too, accepting that their players, on average, are probably better than we have.

In those other games played while we were thrashing the Albion, there were wins for Arsenal at Brighton, Burnley against Sheffield United who still had only two points, a nil–nil draw between Southampton and West Ham and then, later the same night, Manchester United beat Wolves 1 – 0.

On Wednesday night there were due to be two more games but the London derby between Spurs and Fulham was the latest to fall to the rising Covid case numbers as the Fulham camp was struck down. The final game this side of the New Year therefore took place at St James' Park where the Toon held Liverpool to a goalless draw. Hence, in the eight games that went ahead in this 16th round of matches, only one team managed to score more than a single goal. In fact, of the 12 goals scored in this round of games, Leeds hit five of them. Yep, Leeds United were the entertainers. We'd now scored 30 and conceded 30 in our 16 games; only three sides had scored more (Liverpool, Man United, and Chelsea) and only one (West Brom) had conceded more. What a season it would have been to be there inside the grounds watching.

West Bromwich Albion 0 Leeds United 5 (Sawyers og 9, Alioski 31, Harrison 36, Rodrigo 40, Raphinha 72)
BCD. Round 16 League Pos. 11th.

Quality Counts

In the immediate aftermath of our superb win at the Hawthorns, social media wasn't actually full of awe and wonder over our performance; rather there was indignation and anger. It was all directed towards Karen Carney, the Amazon Prime Video pundit who, at one point during the coverage, opined on Leeds that her only concern about our season was whether we'd fade towards the end. *"I actually think they got promoted because of Covid"* She said and went on to explain that the pause in the season *"gave them a bit of respite"* and that she was not sure the team *"would have got up without that break"* It was not the first time a pundit or reporter had mentioned this hypothesis of course and the 'Bielsa Burnout' theory has been promulgated by many over the long years of Bielsa's managerial career. This time though the Leeds United social media team got involved, tweeting a video of Carney including her saying the club had been *"promoted because of Covid"* and pulled that sentence out into their tweet. Unfortunately that got the post huge coverage, with over 13,000 retweets and

55,000 likes and it started a tsunami of sexist abuse towards Carney. The club eventually came out and *"completely condemned"* the abuse Carney was receiving, as did many other folk, but the damage was already done. Apparently the likes of Carney and Alex Scott are regularly on the end of such abuse every time they appear on TV, their views being seized on by trolls as evidence that women have no place in the game, whereas with male pundits they are merely dismissed as poor pundits. It was just a shame that much of the shine of our win was hidden in the shadow of this social media storm. A lot of people took the view that women, to be treated equally, should be just as subject to ridicule as men for their comments but I now understand the difference here.

Anyone or any organisation with a significant following just needs to be aware that, in society at the moment, there are just too many trolls hiding behind their keyboard anonymity waiting to heap sexist abuse at any women put in the spotlight so, the consequences for a woman are entirely different to the consequences for a male recipient. A bloke will merely be castigated as a plonker, but it seems a woman will draw abuse for the entirety of the female sex.

Leeds were in a tricky situation but Radrizzani came out and took full responsibility for the club tweet although others in the club did worry that, with hindsight, it was probably not the smartest post they'd ever made.

I suppose social media is just a fashion of our time really and fashion was in the news this week as another icon of my era, designer Pierre Cardin, passed away at the age of 98. His death was followed by news that Tommy Docherty had passed away and then a couple of days later we learned that Gerry Marsden, lead singer of the iconic 60s group Gerry and the Pacemakers, had also left us.

In the Queen's New Year Honours list published this week the fashionable cry for Lewis Hamilton to be knighted was finally heard, although I was less happy about that than about the MBE awards made to Rob Burrow and Spurs legend Jimmy Greaves. Hamilton has a fantastic record of F1 victories, but is he really that much better a driver than anyone else in F1? I was still firmly in the camp that believed F1 was all about the cars these days, not the drivers, as amply demonstrated by George Russell recently. When he got a chance to drive Hamilton's Mercedes in anger he would have won first time out but for the strange pit bungle by the

Mercedes crew which spawned many conspiracy theories that his race was actually sabotaged to protect Hamilton's market value. With everything we've seen in F1 over the years, nothing would surprise me!

Match week 17 was upon us on New Year's Day, or New Year's Day evening to be precise. There were very few games taking place this year on Jan 1 but two EPL games were scheduled; Everton faced West Ham at 5:30 pm and then Man United took on Aston Villa at 8 pm. With my lad Adam having returned to work, I was on my tod again as this TV football lark continued. I'd now not been at a professional game for more than nine months with only that handful of Worcester City games and a Stafford Rangers cup tie to my name in that time. It was starting to irk me more than I thought it would. This weekend would be particularly annoying as we were playing in that super-duper new Spurs stadium. When the fixtures came out I was sure we'd be back in the grounds by now.

West Ham pulled off a surprise 0 – 1 result at Everton to stop the Toffees' sweet run while consolidating themselves in mid-table, three points ahead of Leeds. Man United then joined Liverpool at the top with 33 points as they beat Villa 2 – 1 after a minute's silence before the game in tribute to the memory of Tommy Docherty. The flags at Old Trafford were also flown at half-mast for the Doc who managed both sides during his long career. Mind you, he managed 12 other teams too, as well as his home nation, Scotland. He once said of himself that he *"had more clubs than Jack Nicklaus!"* Docherty's first game in charge of Man United was, funnily enough, against Leeds at Old Trafford in December 1972, a 1 – 1 draw, with Allan Clarke scoring for Leeds and Ted MacDougall for the Red Devils.

Saturday dawned and there was more snow in our village so it was no real chore to be sat in front of the TV again for another day of couch football. It was depressing seeing the wonderful shots of the new Spurs stadium though and wondering just what sort of a day I might have been having but for Covid, but at least I hadn't had to be up at the crack of dawn clearing the snow off the car. Our game was a 12:30 pm kick-off and it was the first game of four scheduled throughout the day so it was possible to watch them all just about back to back.

An hour before kick-off, as usual the team sheet appeared on Twitter and, unsurprisingly there were no changes; it was the same starting XI that put the Baggies to the sword. On the bench there were a couple of differences as Leif Davis and Tyler Roberts were missing, with rumours that Roberts was the subject of interest from Bournemouth for a possible loan or permanent transfer in the January window. Their places were taken by centre-back Charlie Cresswell and left-back Niall Huggins, two more from the regular Under 23 squad to add to Jamie Shackleton, Jack Jenkins and Ollie Casey that helped give the bench a very youthful look.

Meslier
Dallas Ayling (Capt) Struijk Alioski (Shackleton 64)
Raphinha Rodrigo (Hernandez 65) Klich Harrison (Poveda 61)
Bamford

Subs: Casilla, Poveda-Ocampo, Cresswell, Costa, Hernandez, Shackleton, Jenkins, Casey, Huggins.

Tottenham: Lloris, Doherty, Alderweireld, Dier, Davies, Winks (Sissoko 76), Højbjerg, Bergwijn, Ndombele (Lucas Moura 78), Son Heung-Min, Kane (Alves Morais 87).

Subs not used: Hart, Reguilón, Rodon, Alli, Tanganga, Carvalho Fernandes. Referee: David Coote.

This was of course another trip to London for Leeds and it was now more than three years since we'd won a game in the capital after 12 attempts; maybe this was to be our lucky 13th, although Spurs were a top side and could consolidate their position in the top four with a win.

Leeds had not played Spurs in a league game of course since we were last in the EPL, as Spurs had not been out of the top-flight since 1978. We'd met them three times though in the FA Cup since our own relegation in 2004; we had one win, one draw and one defeat in those games. The most recent meeting was the victory at Elland Road in 2013 when Luke Varney and a brilliant solo effort from Ross McCormack sent us through to the 5th round of the cup; it was a Spurs side that included Gareth Bale. That was the year we had our 'snooker' side with Green, White, and Brown in the team.

I'd been to the old White Hart Lane a few times when working in London in the late 70s but I'd not seen Leeds there since Valentine's Day in 1970 when I was just 12-years-old! That was a 1 – 1 draw when Leeds were top of the First Division and Spurs were mid-table. It was the season after we won our first top-flight title and we'd only be pipped for a consecutive one by Everton. Peter Lorimer scored that day for Revie's team against a Spurs side including Pat Jennings in goal and Martin Chivers up front on a snow-covered pitch with Leeds playing in all red. Just reading the match-day programme again from that game, I'm struck by how revered that side of ours was at the time. In the programme they wrote: *"The power of Leeds is so universally acclaimed, and their record is so eloquent of past and present achievement, that the strength of the Yorkshire team is never underestimated. Every club knows that a match against Leeds provides a searching test of skill, resource and tactical know-how, and it is in this mood that we tackle the reigning League champions today."* We were at that time simply the most feared side in the land.

Back to the present and I could only despair at being sat on the sofa as the TV cameras relayed pictures of the new Tottenham Hotspur Stadium; some of the aerial shots they had of the golden cockerel sat proudly above the new South Stand were incredible. The new cockerel is actually a replica of the one that first graced White Hart Lane in 1909 and, at 4.5m tall, is almost twice the height of the original. It's been made complete with all the dents and blemishes said to have been present on the original, many of them made by an air rifle fired by none other than former Spurs legend Paul Gascoigne[1], or so the story goes.

For half an hour Leeds more than matched their wealthy London opponents in their plush new stadium. As almost always we dominated the possession and created several chances that, arguably, top EPL strikers might have scored. For once it appeared that the missed chances were causing Marcelo Bielsa some discomfort, as he could be seen stomping around his technical area clearly annoyed at our profligacy as Alioski drove the ball into the side-netting and then a Harrison cross eluded everyone in the middle as it fizzed across the face of goal. Then Matty Klich leaned back and lifted the ball over the bar from six yards and Patrick Bamford could only head Raphinha's seemingly perfect cross over

---

[1]   *https://talksport.com/football/420585/new-tottenham-stadium-white-hart-lane-golden-cockerel-gazza-air-rifle/*

the top. As always, I'm sure I wasn't alone in thinking we'd rue these missed chances as the game went on.

The ruing started in the 29th minute and Illan Meslier was in the frame for this one. I've mentioned before how in almost every game he seems to have at least one moment of madness, usually a poorly directed pass out of his box that often looks like he hasn't seen the opposition player lurking. So it was this time that, under no pressure at all, the young keeper side-footed the ball from his six-yard line straight past Kalvin Phillips who was just outside the 'D' and instead right to the feet of Harry Winks. If Winks had been wearing the burgundy Leeds shirt it would have looked perfectly normal but now it looked an awful pass. Winks took one touch and made a couple of yards before sending it forward to Steven Bergwijn near the edge of the area. As often happens when one mistake is made another can soon follow in the moment of panic and Bergwijn was now goal side of Alioski who, spotting the danger, had raced back. Inevitably, as soon as Begwijn felt the merest puff of breath from Alioski on his neck, down he went and David Coote was pointing at the spot. It looked close to the edge of the area and the VAR replays were not conclusive as to whether the contact, such as it was, took place inside or outside the box, the best guess was outside but the VAR officials were still loathe to overturn a referee's call so they let it stand. Harry Kane strode forward to smack the penalty straight down the middle as Meslier dived away to his right. It was, in many ways, a case of Leeds not getting the rub of the green, but then again you have to say that none of it was necessary had Meslier not made the daft pass in the first place. He is a fine young goalkeeper who is an excellent shot-stopper and yet he has this one foible he needs to rid himself of and he needs to do it quickly.

So, half an hour in and the big team were ahead with a stroke of good fortune and from there on in the game was much more even. The difference came down to that little bit of stardust these top EPL players can call on. In the 43rd minute, Harry Kane sent in a right-wing cross, Stuart Dallas was left ball-watching as Son nipped in ahead of him at the near post and stabbed it past Meslier. It was hard to shake the thought that if we had a Son or a Kane we'd be converting many more of the chances we created; often our chances were easier than those these top players were converting against us.

It was merely left in the second half for another of our regular Achilles Heel moments to finish us off, as Toby Alderweireld stooped to head home a near-post corner to cap a disappointing day for the Whites. Fingers were pointed again at Meslier for that one too, as he appeared to be well-placed but seemed to fumble it over the line and the referee's wrist device signalled it was a goal. Meslier then went on to make a few decent saves in the rest of the game but it had not been a great day for him.

To some extent most Leeds fans expected this sort of a result; it was now pretty widely accepted that we had the resources to mix it with most sides in the EPL and, on occasion and when the breaks went for us, we'd comfortably win against most of them. Against the top teams though, the ones stacked full of top-quality world-class players, then it was more likely that we'd struggle to make our domination of the games pay. As we saw in this one, if we had better finishers we may well have taken the lead, and that, in turn, may have made it a much different game. But equally, we had to learn that every mistake at this level is likely to be punished by players that are, put simply, better than we have, players that cost the earth because they make less mistakes than we do, put in better crosses more regularly, score more difficult chances and defend better than we do. You get what you pay for in football. It was really too much to ask for our players to constantly play without mistake, to finish every chance, put every cross on a sixpence. We were well drilled and organised but that little bit of star quality was in short supply. We saw the usual substitutions late in the game as Hernandez replaced Rodrigo and once again we saw how his class shines through, but there was still the worry that his game time was now going to be limited by his age although I still felt he was worth a start to check that hypothesis out properly. Rodrigo may well be a top player, but he plays number '9' for Spain not number '10' and what this side of ours clearly needed, as shown when Pablo is on the pitch, was a proper '10'; a Strachan, a McAllister, a Pablo, a Johnny Giles type player to complete the jigsaw and pull everything together. We had Jamie Shackleton replace Klich again and he also looks ready for a start while Poveda replaced Harrison and perhaps looked less ready.

So, we had to accept we were not yet in a position to battle with the mega-rich sides. Part of me still felt we could possibly do more with our existing squad just by experimenting with some of the fringe players we already had; it was not something Bielsa was known for though. Unless one of his preferred XI was injured it seemed highly unlikely he would change any of them; it was hard to think of any occasions when Bielsa had effectively 'dropped' or 'rested' anyone; this was the criticism heaped upon him when he stubbornly refused to try out Eddie Nketiah for so long. We had an FA Cup tie against lowly Crawley Town coming up next week which would be the ideal chance to do some experimenting but last season we merely put out an Under 23 side and then reverted back to the regular XI in the following games. For me, it would be a chance to maybe just swap a couple and see how that played out.

At the end of the day though it was hard to criticise; Bielsa had crafted a team more than capable of holding its own in the EPL and we were the most entertaining team in it. We were getting established and hopefully building a war chest to be used in future transfer windows to get some of those world-class players who could take us to the next level. The likes of Spurs and Chelsea and Man United were not the teams we were battling yet, the next few games though would see us facing Brighton, Southampton, and Newcastle again and they were well and truly in our sights. Before then though there was that trip to Crawley Town.

In the remaining games of this match week 17, there were wins for Crystal Palace, who beat Sheffield United 2 – 0, Arsenal, who won 0 – 4 at West Brom, and Brighton and Wolves drew 3 – 3; those games following ours on Saturday. On Sunday, Leicester continued their great run as they won 1 – 2 at Newcastle while Manchester City overwhelmed Chelsea 1 – 3 to start rumours that Abramovich would soon be ditching Frank Lampard, much to the great joy of many a Leeds fan. On Monday night a bad weekend for Liverpool culminated with them losing their game at Southampton 1 – 0, but the sadness Liverpool fans would feel over that was but nothing compared to that news about Gerry Marsden passing away the previous day. Marsden made famous the Rodgers and Hammerstein musical song *"You'll Never Walk Alone"* when it topped the charts in 1963 and it's been the Liverpool anthem ever since…

Tottenham Hotspur 3 **Leeds United 0** (Kane 29 pen, Son 43, Alderweireld 50) BCD. **Round 17 League Pos: 12th.**

The Misery of the Cup

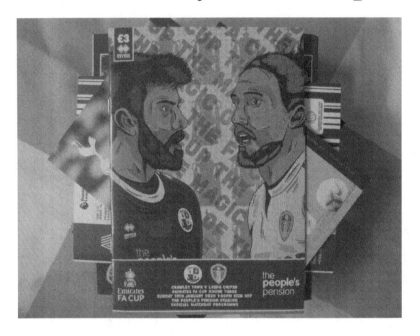

Coronavirus was still ripping through Europe and in the UK the figures were showing it was bordering on getting out of control. Daily positive test cases were now topping 60,000, daily death figures were often above 1,000 and there were said to be more than 30,000 hospital intensive care beds filled with Covid patients. These figures were all much higher than we saw at the peak of the first wave back in April. With the outlook so bleak, Mrs W and I drove to Edinburgh to take the mother-in-law home before the inevitable next lockdown came into force. We were only just in time. It was vital we got Mrs W's mum home so that she was there, ready in the queue when the vaccine was available as she was in one of the first groups scheduled to receive it being 88-years-old. But, having driven up on the Monday we had to come straight back on Tuesday as Boris Johnson announced the next national lockdown would become law on Wednesday morning.

Leeds were doing their bit to help the nation overcome the Covid crisis as the club agreed to allow the Centenary Pavilion to be used as one of the many vaccination hubs being set up around the country. NHS England considered the Pavilion was ideally placed near the motorway network and with space under normal conditions to host 2,800 patrons it was one of the largest arenas in the North of England. The club readily agreed when approached.

Around this time there seemed to be news of the death of a celebrity or a famous sports icon every few days and, so soon after the news about the deaths of Tommy Docherty and Gerry Marsden, another one was reported. The passing of Tommy Docherty had prompted a minute's silence at Old Trafford for their game on Sunday against Aston Villa but now Manchester City were preparing for a tribute to one of *their* all-time greats; Colin Bell, the 'King of the Kippax', died on Tuesday 5th January.

It was EFL Cup semi-final week and Spurs had beaten Brentford 2 – 0 in the first semi on Tuesday night. Before a Manchester derby in the second semi on Wednesday, various tributes were paid to Colin Bell. City won the game 2 – 0 to reach their 4th consecutive EFL Cup final, a fitting tribute in itself to the player who also earned the nickname 'Nijinsky' after the famous Derby-winning horse. All the City players lined up for the pre-match presentation wearing retro City shirts adorned with Bell's famous number '8' on the back, before a minute's silence ahead of the game.

I was lucky enough to watch Bell play for City many times between 1975 and 1978 when I was a student in Manchester, living just around the corner from their old Maine Road ground. In fact, I was there in November 1975, stood on the Kippax terracing, watching as City thrashed Man United 4 – 0 in the 4th round of that year's League Cup, with more than 50,000 fans packed inside the ground. Tommy Docherty was the manager of Man United, having got them promoted the previous season, but City had a tremendous side with the likes of Joe Royle, Dennis Tueart, Willie Donachie, Asa Hartford, Mike Doyle, Alan Oakes and, of course, Colin Bell; all names that will be very familiar to any bloke of my vintage who would, like me, have stuck their pictures in the sticker books of the day and played Subbuteo games involving them all. It was sadly not all smiles for City that night though as it was the game in which Bell suffered a horrendous injury following a bad tackle by Martin

Buchan, a tackle that snapped Bell's knee ligaments and severed blood vessels and, despite several aborted comebacks, he was never the same player again. The last time Bell played against Leeds for Man City was another infamous game, played in January 1978 in the FA Cup 3rd Round. City won it 1 – 2 but it was a feisty game with trouble on the terraces, a pitch invasion and it even saw Gordon McQueen throw a right hook at his own keeper, David Harvey! It was only weeks after that of course that McQueen jumped ship to go to Old Trafford, probably a wise move having earned the wrath of big Dave Harvey!.

The January transfer window was now open and there were the usual rumours involving Leeds. We were linked with a number of players even though we'd been told all along we were unlikely to be doing any business; there were players Bielsa and Orta had agreed we wanted apparently, but none of them were said to be available until the summer. One Leeds player making a move though was young Jordan Stevens; his loan to Swindon was curtailed and he went off to join Bradford City instead on a new loan for the rest of the season.

The world seemed to be on the brink of collapse around this time, with the pandemic, weird weather all over the world including heavy snow in Spain, and political chaos in the USA. Donald Trump was acting ever more manically as we moved towards the last few days of his presidency with him still refusing to accept defeat at the hands of Joe Biden. At one point Trump urged his supporters to march on Capitol Hill but that ended with hundreds of them actually storming and ransacking the famous Capitol Building. Five people died during the siege which Biden would describe as an act of insurrection and which many saw as an attack on democracy itself. Trump meanwhile was seen as such a danger in whipping up anti-establishment feeling that Twitter and Facebook cancelled his accounts and politicians in the US were desperately seeking ways to ensure his access to the big red nuclear button was denied... just in case!

Against this background, football once again seemed a bit of a guilty pleasure, an irrelevance that perhaps should be postponed for a while. In fact some were calling for just that. Newcastle's Steve Bruce said: *"Financially it's right to play on but, for me, morally it's probably wrong."* His side Newcastle was the first to see games postponed due to his players testing positive for Covid. Continue it did though, even though this weekend's FA Cup 3rd Round ties often looked like Under 23 games as various teams lost first-team players to positive Covid tests or isolation. All the football authorities could do was stress again how important their own Covid protocols were to maintain, and they demanded that clubs punish any players found to be contravening the rules. The FA stressed again that handshakes and high fives at games were now banned but it still went on in every game.

Aston Villa was the latest team to announce they'd suffered positive Covid tests, including Jack Grealish, although the joke quickly did the rounds that it was typical of him that he'd gone down with it despite having had no contact with anyone! A very young Villa side held Liverpool for an hour before the Merseyside club ran away with the tie in the final 30 minutes to win 1 – 4. Shrewsbury's game at Southampton was called-off with many of the Shrewsbury players in isolation, while Derby also had to field what was mostly an U18 side as they went out to non-league Chorley at their quaint little Victory Park ground. Along with West Brom going out at Blackpool on penalties, the Derby defeat was the only other major surprise in the games played on Friday night and Saturday; our game was a Sunday lunchtime kick-off.

This FA Cup weekend so far had been a pretty miserable one all round; there was still snow on the ground at home and temperatures had been at or below zero for days on end and Covid meant there was nowhere to go anyway. Then my buddy Kev W sent me a message on Twitter informing me of the death of a mutual friend, Liz, yet another of our Leeds United family taken far too early at just 46-years-young. I first met Liz on a trip to the Amex in Brighton several years ago when she lived and worked down there and later, when she moved to Yorkshire, she was a regular in the Pavilion with us before home games. It was Liz who introduced me to the Fiddler's Elbow, a delightful little pub in a back street of Brighton where, I can confirm as she once promised; *"They serve the best pint of Guinness this side of the Irish Sea!"* RIP Liz...

FA Cup 3rd Round weekend has always been magical for me, as I'm sure it is for most folk of my age. A break from the sometimes turgid repetitiveness of the league programme and with the prospect of a giant-killing always on the cards. Sadly, for Leeds, we'd been on the wrong end of more giant-killings than most big clubs over the years and especially during our time in exile away from the top-flight. The only saving grace had often been the phrase: *"At least we can now concentrate on the league!"* Defeat at Arsenal last season was one of our more pleasurable cup exits; we outplayed the Gunners for 45 minutes and should probably have won, but at least we could then *"concentrate on the league!"* which we finally did successfully. The year before we all travelled to Loftus Road expecting to beat QPR but threw the game away and travelled home saying the same thing. But before that we'd had disasters at Newport, Sutton United (that was a 4th round game having scraped through at Cambridge United) and Rochdale all in recent memory and Histon and Hereford not that much longer ago. All still left a bad taste in the mouth. In fact the FA Cup just didn't seem to be our thing anymore; if we didn't go out embarrassingly to lower league opposition we'd have the misfortune instead to be drawn against one of the top sides, usually Arsenal, but also Man City and Spurs within the last thirteen years. I was convinced this year would be different.

This year we were going well in the Premier League, looking safe enough in mid-table and we'd been drawn away at League Two Crawley Town. They were having a decent season, unbeaten in nine and sitting 6th in the table, but we didn't have to *"concentrate on the league"* this year did we? Marcelo Bielsa told us he would respect the competition and that no one *"who hadn't played"* would take the field against the Red Devils so that meant a strong side that ought to win. None of the real major disasters had occurred under Bielsa either, so he wasn't tainted; this was a new era. We certainly couldn't consider ourselves immune to any more 3rd round defeats but surely Bielsa could be regarded as the vaccine? Crawley had the second-lowest budget in the whole of the football league and Kiko Casilla's annual salary of £1.8m was about the same as that for the whole Crawley squad put together. That small but raucous crowd you usually get at these games was also missing of course and that had to be another advantage for Leeds.

Casilla
Phillips Cooper (Capt) (Casey 45) Davis (Greenwood 58)
Shackleton   Struijk (Jenkins 45)   Alioski

Poveda (Raphinha 58) Hernandez Costa
Rodrigo (Harrison 45)
Substitutes: Caprile, Casey, Huggins, Jenkins, Raphinha, Harrison, Greenwood.
Crawley: Morris, Francomb, Tunnicliffe, Craig, Dallison-Lisbon (M. Wright 90+1), Matthews (Davies 71), Hessenthaler (Doherty 90+1), Powell, Tsaroulla (J. Wright 72) Nadesan (Watters 72), Nichols. Subs not used: Nelson, McNerney, Frost, Galach.
Referee: Peter Bankes.

When I first saw our team selection I was fairly happy with it and still confident it was more than strong enough to win this tie. There were some predictable inclusions like Kiko Casilla, Pablo Hernandez, and Jamie Shackleton who I think we'd all have guessed would start; Kiko because he'd not had a Premier League start at all this season, Pablo to see how he coped with 90 minutes these days and Shacks as he was now a regular sub in the EPL campaign but seldom got the full 90. The top men being rested completely were Meslier, Ayling, Klich, Dallas, and Bamford, none of whom was even named on the bench, although that in itself did look a bit odd as we only named seven substitutes when nine were now allowed; five could be used in the FA Cup. Liam Cooper was back after injury, with Ollie Casey on the bench in case Coops broke down, or maybe he'd be rested at halftime if all was going well. The Crawley side were an unknown to me with the exception of course of Mark Wright on their subs bench. He was the former TOWIE star and part-time footballer in some of the big charity games and was currently the subject of his own TV documentary, *"The Last Chance"* following him through his attempt to finally make it as a pro footballer. His brother Josh was also on the bench. My only other information came courtesy of my lad Adam who works at a school in Surrey. He informed me that Crawley forward Ashley Nadesan was a former pupil from his school and he was: *"bloody quick!"*

It was a cold day, albeit the forecasters told us it was finally warming up after the prolonged spell of freezing weather. The pitch looked OK if a little bare in places but only marginally more so than Elland Road had looked the other day. Leeds were all in white, with the Red Devils looking more Liverpool than Man United in their all-red strip as we kicked off.

The first half was OK for Leeds, nothing more than that but we were the better side, dominated the possession of the football, and created the odd half-chance once we'd seen off a couple of early corners and a free-kick that Crawley won in the first three minutes; all safely dealt with by Casilla. Pablo Hernandez was our midfield general calling all the shots and looking mostly back to his old self, albeit still giving the ball away now and again. He always does to some extent of course, it's that 'omelette' concept; you can't make one without breaking a few eggs just as you can't make a telling pass without a few going astray. Rodrigo was taking time to settle into his number '9' role and was caught offside a few times. It was fifteen minutes before Leeds had the first shot in anger when Ian Poveda rifled a low shot from the corner of the six-yard box that the keeper blocked with his right boot to send the ball spinning agonisingly across the face of goal. There was a shout for a penalty too as Rodrigo was pulled around by the shoulder to prevent him getting onto a volleyed Costa cross, but with no VAR available it was down to the referee and he was pleading the Arsène Wenger. For all that Leeds dominated the play, only that Poveda shot needed any intervention from the home keeper and, five minutes before the break, we needed Casilla to foil what was an equally good chance at the other end.

It came, predictably, from a left wing Crawley corner, won after a sloppy loose pass in midfield by Kalvin Phillips led to a breakaway and a shot blocked by Liam Cooper. The corner was whipped in towards the back post and Tom Nichols rose highest to thunder a header at goal but Casilla was alert enough and got both hands behind it to push the ball away from the line. That was it for the first half, Leeds on top with Hernandez and Poveda looking our best players but little in the way of chances created. At the other end just that one set-piece effort from Crawley.

I was confident Leeds would remain unchanged at halftime; why would we change anything when we were on top and we'd given everyone the chance to settle into an unfamiliar line-up? The obvious thing was to go again and then maybe utilise Raphinha and Harrison if we hadn't found a way through by the hour mark. But what do I know? As I sat back down in front of the TV with another beer I could see three Leeds substitutes waiting near the dugouts. Jack Harrison, Oliver Casey, and Jack Jenkins were coming on and eventually we could see that Rodrigo, Cooper, and Pascal Struijk were coming off. With the three coming off all expected to be involved in the next Premier League game, probably starting, it could only mean that Bielsa was protecting his 1st XI. It seemed a risk though, with this game still in the balance, putting two such inexperienced players as Casey and Jenkins into the fray. It was tempting to think that maybe Bielsa was not quite as committed to the FA Cup as he suggested before the game.

The biggest worry about the new line-up was that it looked as though Jack Harrison was playing the number '9' role. He had done this once or twice before in similar situations, but with Rodrigo, a Spanish international striker, failing to make much of a mark in the first half, why would Harrison be a better bet? Once again I was sure this was only happening because Bielsa had more concern about his next Premier League game. For me that was all wrong for all the reasons I noted above; there was no need to rest players with no game for another six days, our position secure in the table, and the chance to get some momentum going. After the game I saw some folk even suggest on social media that they felt Bielsa had 'thrown' the game, not even wanting to have the future distraction of further matches in the competition. We'll never know I guess but I don't think Bielsa would do that... Whether he'd not thought this through and come up with the wrong substitutions though I could believe. Some of our fans think the great man is infallible and won't have a word said against him, but of course he is not.

Within eight minutes of the restart the game was as good as lost as Leeds gave away two soft goals. The first came following a Pablo Hernandez shot that cleared the roof of the little stand at one end of the ground. Glenn Morris launched the goal kick down to the other end and Leif Davis won the header but then the ball bounced around before it was eventually collected by Nick Tsaroulla, back to goal and fully 35 yards out. Tsaroulla spun away from the attentions of Pablo and Jamie Shackleton and then headed into the Leeds area where he swept past both Casey and Phillips before letting fly with a left foot shot that seemed to go under the outstretched hands of the diving Casilla. It was a catalogue of errors from at least five Leeds players and the joy on the faces of the Crawley players was in marked contrast to the worry now etched on the faces of the young Leeds squad. With the line-up Leeds now had it was hard to see how we'd fight our way back. Three minutes later and it looked impossible. Leeds were rattled and it showed in our passing as Leif Davis played a risky ball forward to the feet of Jack Harrison expecting him to be as adept at holding it up as Patrick Bamford. He couldn't and the ball was poked off his toes to set Crawley off on the counter. Tom Nichols raced after the ball and touched it on past the retreating Casey who was outsprinted in the inside right channel by that man Ashley Nadesan (I told you he was quick!). Nadesan took one further touch and then drove the ball towards the near post. It could be argued that Casilla ought to have stopped the first goal but there was no argument about this one. Sure it took a wicked bounce just in front of him but to allow it to cannon off his knee and into the net was unforgiveable; if he'd had his body behind the shot it couldn't have gone in. It was another awful goal to concede and, for all that I'd complained about Illan Meslier's regular loose pass every game, boy did I wish it was Illan and not Casilla between those posts today.

Now it didn't look as if Bielsa was happy losing this game, in fact his next move looked like sheer panic! Within a few minutes he threw on his final two substitutes with Raphinha and young striker Sam Greenwood replacing Poveda and Leif Davis. But the damage was done and Leeds were a team full of square pegs trying to fill round holes. We were all over the place and still had Harrison playing ahead of Greenwood which seemed ridiculous. Remember, Leeds now only had four of their recent regular 1st XI on the pitch; Phillips, Harrison, Alioski and Raphinha, and all of them were playing out of position.

After 70 minutes Jordan Tunnicliffe fired into the roof of the net after Casilla parried a shot from Nadesan following a right wing free-kick. It looked like more sloppy goalkeeping and it was now 3 – 0 and Crawley could have had a fourth after top scorer Max Watters came off the bench to round the keeper, only to be denied by the covering Ollie Casey. The second half was quite simply a car crash. Crawley even had the luxury of bringing on reality TV celebrity Mark Wright in stoppage time for his debut, having only signed for the club on non-contract terms in December. That would no doubt be for the benefit of that TV documentary.

It was, in many ways, a similar cup exit to the EFL cup defeat to Hull City earlier in the season. That was an even more inexperienced side than we started here but eight of the players involved that day played at least a part in Crawley. Against experienced opposition, of whatever level, a team largely made up of our Under 23s usually isn't up to the job. We also saw that in the way our Under 21s were mostly played off the park in the EFL Trophy games against the likes of Blackpool and Accrington earlier in the season.

After the game, Marcelo Bielsa said: *"the result generates a lot of sadness and disappointment for us"* which I could certainly relate to... I was fuming! For me this was a chance missed, needlessly missed, and I could only hope that the hangover from it didn't affect the team going forward as we'd seen it do in previous seasons. Often momentum is underestimated as a powerful driver of football results; embarrassing defeats like this one somehow fester in the minds of the players, whether or not they were involved. Either way, they possibly feel they have to make amends and that sometimes means they don't play their natural games. We wouldn't know whether that was going to impact us this time until the next game, against Brighton at Elland Road. If we won that and played well then even I'd reluctantly put Crawley out of my mind, but any slip-up would surely raise more questions as to what exactly Bielsa was trying to achieve this weekend. For the FA Cup that was it for Leeds for another year and for that reason I also had a lot of sadness and disappointment. So often in recent seasons it had been only misery the FA Cup had brought us, not magic. Bielsa had changed a lot at Leeds United but this cup misery lingered on. There were no other cup shocks in the remaining games so ours took centre stage on all the news broadcasts for the next 24 hours and on the back pages of all the papers and folk I'd not heard from for months were suddenly texting and messaging to take the Mickey. Our next opponents in the Premier League, Brighton, almost faltered at a place where we did once, Newport, but they eventually came through on penalties. Ourselves and West Brom were the only two Premier League sides to go out to lower league opposition this weekend and keeping that company didn't feel great!

Crawley Town 3 **Leeds United 0** (Tsaroulla 50, Nadesan 5, Tunnicliffe 70)

BCD FA Cup 3rd Rd.

Brighton

The first-team might have been stuttering but the Under 23s continued to go from strength to strength at the top of the PL2 Division 2 table. 24 hours after our crash at Crawley they battered Burnley 1 – 4 with a Crysencio Summerville hat-trick to go six points clear at the top. Summerville has a name worthy of fame and is a clever player but boy does he look small! None of the regular first-team squad were included of course as most were involved at Crawley the day before, but Sam Greenwood played an hour after his minutes in the cup and he also scored the opening goal.

There was still plenty of tinkering going on with our fringe players; Robbie Gotts' loan at Lincoln was cut short and he moved instead to Salford City, presumably with the hope he'd get more game time there. Meanwhile Ryan Edmondson joined Northampton Town having returned from his spell at Aberdeen. I thought the 19-year-old was sufficiently different to anything else we had at the club to deserve being brought back inside but he was still very young despite his size that often made folk think he was much older.

There were six Premier League games played this week in what should have been week 18 of the programme, but with cup commitments and Covid postponements the schedule was starting to go awry with some teams having played two games more than others. The early-season goal-fest had also disappeared and most games were now being won by the odd goal or drawn. Tuesday, 12th January saw Sheffield United finally get their first league win of the season at the 18th attempt as they squeaked past Newcastle 1 – 0. That was also the score as Man United edged out Burnley at Turf Moor and then Everton beat a faltering Wolves 1 – 2 at Molineux. On the Wednesday, Manchester City narrowly beat a battling Brighton 1 – 0, while the two other games this week, Spurs v Fulham and Arsenal v Crystal Palace, both ended all square; 1 – 1 and 0 – 0 respectively. Game-week 19 then started on Saturday with a lunchtime Black Country derby that saw Sam Allardyce pick up his first win, with West Brom defeating Wolves 2 – 3; a 6th Premier League game without a win now for the Molineux side who were sliding down the table. There were a couple of three o'clock kick-offs today, our home game with Brighton and West Ham's with Burnley. Fortunately our game was live on Sky Sports while Amazon Prime Video covered the West Ham game.

Brighton was seen as another must-win game by most Leeds fans; not in terms of it being vital for our safety this season – it was too early for that - but in terms of showing that there was no hangover from the Crawley defeat. Brighton were also exactly the sort of side we ought to be beating and indeed *had* been beating this season. We'd not won against any of the fancied sides this term with the exception of our 1 – 0 win at Everton who continued to go well. Other than that we'd only beaten one other side in the current top ten; Aston Villa (10th) in that amazing game at Villa Park in October. Contrast that with the fact that we'd already beaten five of the current bottom six; Brighton was the one we hadn't yet played. Add to that the fact that Brighton were going to be missing several first-team players and the odds seemed to be tipped in our favour, although we would still be missing Koch and probably Llorente through injury and Kalvin Phillips with his one game ban following a 5th yellow card received in the game at Tottenham. Tariq

Lamptey, Adam Lallana, Danny Welbeck, Alireza Jahanbakhsh, and Aaron Connolly would all miss the game at Elland Road for the Seagulls. There was one other rumour knocking around on social media; it was being suggested by some supposedly 'in the know' fans that Meslier was ill... but I assumed that was maybe someone not quite finishing his name off correctly or maybe it was a rumour of the same origin as the weekly one telling us Patrick Bamford would be missing, which he never was of course. But, as I settled down in front of the TV, beer at hand, scrolling through Twitter on the laptop to find the team; there it was with Kiko Casilla at the top of the list.

Casilla
Dallas Ayling Cooper (Capt) Alioski (Hernandez 67)
Struijk
Harrison Rodrigo (Roberts 62) Klich Raphinha (Poveda 75)
Bamford

Subs: Caprile, Llorente, Davis, Shackleton, Jenkins, Hernandez, Roberts, Poveda, Costa.

Brighton: Sánchez, Webster, Dunk, Burn, Veltman, White, Groß, March, Trossard (Tau 73), MacAllister (Bissouma 63), Maupay (Pröpper 81). Subs not used: Walton, Alzate, Zeqiri, Sanders, Jenks, Khadra.

Referee: Kevin Friend.

No one seemed certain what the issue was with Illan. In his press conference ahead of the game a couple of days earlier, Bielsa had confirmed that everyone apart from Phillips, Koch and Forshaw (obviously!) was available. Then, when pressed just before the game, Bielsa would only say Illan was *"unavailable"*. For his part, Meslier posted on his Instagram story board: *"Sorry to miss today's [match], behind you all the ways boys. Thank you to the fans for all the support, I'm recovering well,"* We could only assume it was Covid but quite why the club seemed so reluctant to confirm it I wasn't sure unless it was to avoid scrutiny by the FA who'd told the clubs they would be investigating the circumstances behind any reported positive cases to make sure their protocols had been followed to the letter. Whatever the reason, Casilla was the beneficiary and that sent many fans searching for the Valium.

The Brighton team included some familiar names, none more so of course than Ben White who'd played such a major part in our Championship winning side last season. He was now employed by Brighton in more of a midfield role and he was flourishing just as much there as he did for us at centre-back. Up front for the Seagulls was the striker Neal Maupay who'd scored many a goal against us in the past as a Brentford player.

The first thing I noticed as the teams emerged out onto the Elland Road pitch was how green it was; the turf now looked lush and thick compared with the threadbare mud flat we saw against Burnley three weeks earlier. As the cameras zoomed in to show a close-up of the surface though, it could be seen that even during the warm-up the pitch had cut up quite badly; it was very soft and the grass was quite long. It had probably been thickened up on purpose but then the recent snow and rain had turned it into a bit of a gloopy bog!

I'd been really nervous about this game, I was convinced we were on a path we'd seen us tread so often before at this time of year. In most recent seasons we'd been fine up to the Christmas period and then, having gone out of the cup at the first attempt, we often seemed to suffer some sort of mid-winter hangover. We did it last season even though our cup exit to Arsenal was no disgrace but we then didn't win a game until the 28th January and that only when we managed to come back from a two goal deficit to Millwall. We then lost the next two including a 0 – 2 result at Nottingham Forest after which Luke Ayling gave his now infamous shell-shocked interview. Eventually of course we got it out of our system and we won five in a row up to the first Coronavirus suspension. It was remarkably similar the year before too, when despite two amazing come-backs, at Villa and at home to Blackburn before Christmas, we then lost five of our next seven. It just seemed that we didn't like the cold short days of mid-winter and I thought we'd most likely do the same this year. I even predicted we'd lose 1 – 2 in my Super Six pick although I chickened out of telling the Yorkshire Evening Post readers I thought we'd lose, so I plumped for a 1 – 1 draw in my piece for the YEP Jury. The other five jurors all went for a Leeds win but Leeds fans of my vintage just know we tend to follow history very closely…

And so it would prove to be the case this year. Leeds made a decent enough start on the difficult pitch and should arguably have gone ahead in the 7th minute when Alioski hit a glorious ball across the face of goal that was begging for a touch. Rodrigo had a defender right with him, five yards out and in front of the near post, but the defender missed the ball and so did our £27m Spanish striker. I was starting to understand why Rodrigo had scored only seven or fewer goals in four of his six seasons with Valencia in La Liga. He was a bit of a conundrum, but we had been warned when he joined us that his forte was in creating goals not scoring them but, if he was neither a goal scorer nor a creative midfielder, what exactly was he bringing to the party?

After 14 minutes another decent chance went begging as Matty Klich leaned back and spooned a left-footer well over the bar, not for the first time this season. Then, in the 17th minute, my least favourite minute of the game, Leeds went behind.

It started, predictably enough, with Ben White marauding forward across the halfway line and then he gave it to Alexis MacAlister in the inside right channel. MacAlister played a one-two with Leandro Trossard to his left, marked by Cooper but not tight enough to stop the wall-pass being returned to MacAlister who was now behind the Leeds defence to the right of goal. Stuart Dallas tracked him all the way, but again nowhere near tight enough to his man. Meanwhile, at the back post, Neal Maupay was all alone behind the oblivious Luke Ayling who'd watched the ball all the way through the move, never once looking behind to see where Maupay might be. Maupay side-footed the low cross into the empty net. It was a goal that, had we scored it, we'd have been lauding Bielsaball again but to concede one like this looked very naïve indeed.

Leeds could have gone a further goal down in a first half in which neither side had many real chances; on this occasion though the luck was with us as Trossard tried to hammer the ball across goal only to see it deflect up off the boot of Luke Ayling. The ball flew past Casilla who was wrong-footed but struck the crossbar and rebounded to safety. Leeds looked as stodgy as the pitch for most of the first 45; we were, as always, dominating the possession, but we really weren't doing much with it.

It was similar in the second half for the first fifteen minutes before any changes were made; the closest Leeds came was a curling effort from Harrison who was now plying his trade on the right for some reason. Raphinha, now on the left, created the opening for Bamford but he wanted one more touch than time allowed and the ball was knocked away straight to Harrison. He set himself nicely and curled the ball towards the far post but it just didn't turn enough. At the other end Brighton wasted a good chance as they blazed over after Alioski gave the ball away.

Just after the hour mark Bielsa made his first change; Tyler Roberts, another player we'd assumed had gone missing through Covid recently, trotted on to replace the ineffective Rodrigo Moreno. To be fair, Roberts looked eager and was soon buzzing around and was far more involved than Rodrigo had been but still Leeds laboured in vain to create chances. It was interesting to note that when Roberts replaced Rodrigo, Leeds then had ten players on the pitch who were part of our Championship winning squad. Only Raphinha could be said to be part of any strengthening of that side. It was still the same minutes later when Hernandez replaced Alioski and then, when Poveda replaced Raphinha in the 75th minute, all our players were of Championship vintage. It was starting to be the story of our season. We all knew that our Championship squad had to be improved to make real inroads at the next level and yet, for one reason or another, we were still largely relying on last year's men. We'd spent a fortune on Llorente, Koch, Raphinha, and Rodrigo and yet none had yet made any significant impact either because of injury or form. Most observers believed Koch and Llorente would eventually be our preferred centre-back pairing but whether either of Rodrigo or Raphinha would provide the quality boost we needed was a question being asked during most games.

This one ended 0 – 1 and that mid-winter malaise was seemingly with us once again. We now had ten days without a game due to our match with Southampton being postponed to allow them to fit in their rescheduled FA Cup 3rd round game with Shrewsbury, itself postponed the previous week due to the Shrews squad suffering a number of positive Covid tests. The Shrews manager, Steve Cotterill, was even in intensive care for a few days as he was struck down with the virus and he'd be out of action for many months to come suffering with the ongoing complications of the disease that were often experienced and known as 'long Covid'.

For Leeds it was hard to put a finger on what was wrong, other than to shrug and suggest it was just what always happens at this time of year. The pitch didn't help our usual slick passing and quick tempo but you can't explain it all through that as Brighton showed with their goal. The whole Leeds team just looked lethargic, tired even, despite many having had that break for the cup tie. Two efforts on target from seven attempts in this game simply wasn't good enough. Some credit had to go to the Seagulls of course.

The manner of the defeat left Marcelo Bielsa saying he was *"worried"*: *"Of course it worries me, these are three games that we could have resolved in a different manner,"* said the Argentine master. *"The game against Tottenham less, but the game in the cup and the one today leave me worried."* [1]

The trend for games to be settled by fine margins applied to all the games played this Saturday. After the West Brom game and ours were settled by the odd goal, so too West Ham edged past Burnley by a single goal and then Chelsea did the same at Fulham. Leicester kept up their good run and went 2nd in the table as they beat Southampton 2 – 0, but their second goal only came in the 5th minute of added time.

On Sunday, Liverpool and Man United played out a nil-nil draw while two of the other top five, Spurs and Man City, had more comfortable wins over Sheffield United and Crystal Palace respectively. Leeds thus finished this round of games still in a respectable 12th spot in the table. Man United remained top with their point at Anfield.

Leeds United 0 Brighton and Hove Albion 1 (Maupay 17)
BCD, **Round 18 League Pos: 12th**

---

[1] *https://www.bbc.co.uk/sport/football/55598708*

Halfway There... For Most!

The Leeds United Under 23s had another good win this week, opening up a six-point gap behind them in the table after a 1 – 0 win over Stoke City. Several regular first-teamers had a run-out including Costa, Roberts, Poveda, Llorente, Davis and Kalvin Phillips. The winning goal came in the first half, with Llorente heading home at the far post from a Phillips cross. Diego only played the first 45 minutes but looked sharp and, to me at least watching on the laptop, ready to play his part with the big boys.

On Wednesday this week the world watched as the 46th president of the USA, Joseph Robinette Biden Jr. was sworn in, while Donald Trump flew off for one last hurrah in Air Force One, awarding himself a military send-off and a 21-gun salute. The inauguration ceremony was, like pretty much everything else these days, 'behind closed doors' or at least there were no members of the public thronging around the Capitol Building; just 25,000 National Guards making sure there was no further trouble from the Trump supporters. I watched the ceremony unfold on TV; Lady Gaga sang the national anthem and Jennifer Lopez and Garth Brooks also performed, but it was 22-year-old Amanda Gorman who stole the show. Gorman, chosen at age 18 to be the nation's first National Youth Poet Laureate in 2017, recited *"The Hill We Climb,"* the poem she composed for the event; it was spellbinding!

Round 19 of the Premier League programme was blank for Leeds due to that Southampton v Shrewsbury cup game being rescheduled, a game Southampton won 2 – 0. In the rest of the games the results mainly went with form:

Arsenal 3 Newcastle United 0
West Ham United 2 West Brom 1
Leicester City 2 Chelsea 0
Manchester City 2 Aston Villa 0
Fulham 1 Manchester United 2
Liverpool 0 Burnley 1
Aston Villa 2 Newcastle United 0

	Team	P	GD	Pts
1	Manchester United	19	11	40
2	Manchester City	18	18	38
3	Leicester City	19	14	38
4	Liverpool	19	15	34
5	Tottenham Hotspur	18	16	33
6	Everton	17	7	32
7	West Ham United	19	5	32
8	Aston Villa	17	13	29
9	Chelsea	19	10	29
10	Southampton	18	5	29
11	Arsenal	19	4	27
12	Leeds United	18	-4	23
13	Crystal Palace	19	-11	23
14	Wolverhampton Wanderers	19	-8	22
15	Burnley	18	-12	19
16	Newcastle United	19	-14	19
17	Brighton and Hove Albion	19	-7	17
18	Fulham	18	-12	12
19	West Bromwich Albion	19	-28	11
20	Sheffield United	19	-22	5

The one result that raised eyebrows was that Burnley win at Anfield, a result that really damaged Liverpool's title pretentions, even at this early stage. It was a 5th consecutive league game for Liverpool without a win.

Leeds were right in the heart of the mid-table battle, just six points adrift of Aston Villa in 8th and well clear of the bottom three. Fulham, Albion and Sheffield United already looked good bets for relegation. Manchester City, after their relatively slow start, had now moved ominously up to 2nd place and looked to be right in the hunt for another title while Liverpool's recent poor form had left them a lot to do.

Leeds' next test was a tricky looking visit to the North East.

Game of Two Halves

In the FA Cup games played on the weekend of the 23rd/24th January there were no major shocks. Chorley came close against Wolves but the last remaining non-league side went out to a magnificent 12th minute Vitinha 30-yard shot that almost burst the net and Cheltenham Town briefly led Manchester City before going down 1 – 3. It was perhaps a surprise that Southampton knocked out the holders Arsenal in a tight game at St Mary's but can hardly be classed as a giant-killing with Saints riding high in the Premier League. In the big clash between Man United and Liverpool, a repeat of the Premier League clash a week earlier that ended in a goalless draw, it was United that came out on top 3 – 2.

Leeds might have been having a little break due to the Crawley cup exit and that Southampton v Shrewsbury cup tie being moved, but the club was still busy. They spent £300,000 on a transfer for starters… not a player but a pitch! Leeds persuaded Tottenham to sell their spare pitch that they kept for NFL games played at the stadium, which of course were all cancelled due to Covid. Leeds reckoned the 17-day gap between the Brighton and Everton games was sufficient to lay the new pitch and get it established. It was a sign as to how important a factor the pitch had been maybe in that Brighton defeat. It was hoped the Spurs pitch would take us through to the end of the season when a complete reconstruction of the Elland Road playing surface, including new undersoil heating and incorporating all the modern developments of pitch construction, could be carried out in the summer; the first such reconstruction in 25 years.

Then, on Monday 24th January, the news broke that Andrea Radrizzani had sold another tranche of the club to the San Francisco 49ers. The 49ers bought an initial 15% stake back in 2018 for a rumoured £10m but had now increased their shareholding to 37% with, it was said by Radrizzani *"something more than £50m"* being paid for the additional 22%. This valued the club at something between £230m and £250m, more than twice what Radrizzani paid for it. The 49ers had therefore also already made a substantial paper profit on their initial investment with promotion to the Premier League being the biggest driver of the increased value. Radrizzani still retained a majority 60% of the share capital and would remain as Chairman, with Paraag Marathe, the 49ers representative and already a board member, becoming vice-chairman. It was believed the move by Radrizzani was primarily to take advantage of the 49ers experience of building a worldwide sports brand and of course they had recent experience of building a new state of the art stadium for the San Francisco based NFL outfit which would be of interest to Leeds as they contemplated the expansion of Elland Road. For Radrizzani, it freed up capital to pursue other interests which he'd openly stated included involvement in other football projects around Europe and of course it was a nice return on his own investment. The increase in the 49ers shareholding didn't in itself mean any more cash for the club to spend as it was thought to be a purchase of shares already owned by Radrizzani who thus received the cash, but it was a sign of the ability of the club to attract future investment when needed.

The 49ers clearly saw Leeds as a route into the major and very attractive Premier League market and were following the several other examples of US-based investments in EPL clubs I mentioned earlier in the book. The attraction of Leeds cannot be overstated and was highlighted in a recent paper published in the US by Samford University in Birmingham, Alabama.

The paper highlighted the *"explosive growth amongst Generation Z football fans"* that had already taken place since our promotion. According to Darin White, Executive Director of the Center for Sports Analytics, *"Generation Z has replaced Millennials as the most coveted demographic group for brands ranging from Coca-Cola to Visa to Nike. Sports teams around the globe are scrambling to attract this generational cohort which has proven difficult because of their decreased interest in watching live sports."*[1]

Generation Z are those born since the mid to late 1990s, the first generation that has grown up with the internet and therefore they don't respond to the marketing strategies of previous generations. Also known as 'Digital Natives' they were shown in the Samford study to make up more than half of some 55,000 people who only started to follow Leeds on social media in the three months following our promotion. Many are based in America and Asia, two important markets for Premier League clubs seeking to expand their financial clout. Hence the fact that Leeds were seen to be attracting so many of exactly the sort of consumers the world's top brands were clamouring to attract, partially explained the 49ers interest and it boded well for the club's future revenue generation. The reasons why Leeds were such a pull for the digital natives could be many and varied but essentially, having been out of the top-flight for so long, we were a bit *"novel"* to millions of EPL watchers across the globe. We'd also had the perfect start to capture their interest, playing cavalier football, scoring and conceding lots of goals and playing in exciting games. The club also seemed well aware that it needed to cultivate these new followers with innovative marketing strategies, and it might explain why some activities of the club look a bit strange to folk like me who've been supporting the club for donkey's years! The array of unusual third kits for example; we've often been told how red is a colour that sells well in Asia… ask Cardiff City who tried to change their club

---

[1]   *https://www.samford.edu/sports-analytics/fans/2020/Leeds-Uniteds-Explosive-Growth-Amongst-Generation-Z-Football-Fans*

colours to grab some of that market. We may have been testing the water with our 'maroon' ensemble.

Someone for whom the future, or even the present, didn't bode well was Frank Lampard; he was sacked by Chelsea after 571 days in post and with Chelsea 9th in the table. Suffice to say there were not many Leeds fans mourning his fate. Within hours he was replaced by Thomas Tuchel. The German coach previously led PSG to a domestic quadruple and a Champions League final, which followed spells at Borussia Dortmund and Mainz. Tuchel took over from Jurgen Klopp at Borussia Dortmund in the summer of 2015.

It had felt much like an international break waiting for the next Leeds game; I had about as much interest in the FA Cup since our early exit as I did in those internationals. The next round of the EPL was officially week 20 although few teams had managed to keep on schedule due to the various knock-on effects from Covid postponements. Leeds were about to play their 19th game, exactly halfway through our season.

The Newcastle trip was another one I was really going to miss. Any game in the North East has usually been a chance to stay with our friends who live in Darlington, Sheila and Brian, who regular readers will remember Mrs W and I met on our honeymoon in what was then Czechoslovakia back in 1984. Brian is the manic Chelsea season-ticket holder who travels down from Darlington for most home games. Now that is dedication! Anyway, it was not to be this season of course and it would once again be a TV experience – or at least a laptop experience since all the round of 20 games were being shown on BT Sports.

Our most recent trip to St. James' came on Good Friday in 2017, in a Championship game as we were battling to sneak into the play-offs and the Toon were already pretty much sure of promotion. The Magpies pecked us senseless for 90 minutes but only got the one goal, a Jamaal Lascelles header after 67 minutes. A subdued Leeds following of over 3,000 out of a capacity 52,000 crowd was ready to escape with just the one-goal deficit as we went into the 5th minute of added time. Anyone there will never forget the final few seconds. Hernandez wiggled past one player before feeding the ball wide left to Kemar Roofe, back to goal, near the left corner of the Toon box. Roofe swivelled round to his left and clipped the ball into the middle and there was Chris Wood to volley in the equaliser! The Leazes Stand erupted in amazing scenes as hairy arsed blokes hugged and kissed and punched the air while the Leeds players all gathered on the byline miles below us. It was a huge goal that kept alive our play-off hopes and so the celebrations carried on all the way down the 14 flights of steps and spilled into the streets of Newcastle; it was right up there with some of our most famous escapes.

This year I didn't think the game could possibly live up to that sort of excitement but, in a way, the game this year was just as important. Leeds didn't make the play-offs in 2017 and it took us another three years to win promotion. Now the challenge was to not lose our hard-earned place at the top table. Newcastle were in dire form, having lost eight of their previous ten games in all competitions and having won none; a sequence that began with our 5 – 2 cull of the Magpies in mid-December. Leeds' recent record wasn't that much better of course; we'd lost six of our previous nine in all competitions, including all three games so far this calendar year without scoring. Newcastle was just the sort of team we expected to beat if it was true that we were a solid mid-table side. So far we'd generally beaten sides in the bottom half of the table but had only beaten two of the current top half; Everton and Villa.

In the Bielsa pre-match press conference he told reporters that Illan Meslier had recovered from his *"health issue"* and was cleared to play and only Koch and Berardi (and Forshaw of course) remained side-lined; even Berardi was expected to start training again shortly. He actually said that Adam Forshaw wasn't far off either... but no one believed that! It was widely thought therefore that the centre-back pairing this week would be Cooper and Llorente.

Meslier
Ayling Llorente (Struijk 10) Cooper (Capt) Alioski (Klich 56)
Phillips
Raphinha Dallas Rodrigo Harrison
Bamford (Roberts 60)
Subs: Casilla, Struijk, Davis, Shackleton, Costa, Klich, Hernandez, Roberts, Poveda.
Newcastle: Darlow, Hayden, Lascelles, Schär, Lewis, Murphy, (Saint-Maximinat 64), Shelvey, Hendrick, Almirón, Fraser (Gayle

77), Wilson. Subs not used: Dubravka, M Longstaff, Carroll, Joelinton, Ritchie, Krafth, Manquillo.

Referee: Anthony Taylor.

With Meslier fit, Llorente considered ready to start, and Kalvin Phillips back after his one-match ban, this was the team most expected to see... except Mateusz Klich was only on the bench; that was unheard of! It was only the second time in Marcelo Bielsa's reign that the Polish international had not started a league game. It would be Stuart Dallas playing a midfield role again taking Klich's place. The only good news for us in the Newcastle line-up was that the exciting Allan Saint-Maximin was only on the bench as he continued to regain match fitness following a bout of Covid, as was Dwight Gayle who'd scored four against us in five previous appearances.

As the players appeared from within the bowels of St. James', I settled down with a few nerves and plenty of beers. The pitch looked first class so that didn't look like being a factor while the referee, Anthony Taylor, always might be.

For 45 minutes Leeds looked pretty much back to our dominating best while Newcastle sat deep and played into our hands, or more appropriately, our feet. The only set-back came ten minutes into the game when Diego Llorente plonked himself down on the turf with a grimace and a rub of his right hamstring. He couldn't continue and it was hard not to think we'd got ourselves an injury-prone centre-back as he limped off and young Pascal Struijk jogged on. The debate about Llorente would no doubt rage after the game but already comments were flying about on social media as to whether we'd ever get much game time from him. Stories quickly emerged about how he'd missed sizeable chunks of previous seasons when with Real Sociedad; 23 games in two seasons missed apparently. This would now be his third spell of injury in his short time with Leeds and, as a man expected to be a regular member of the back-line, it was a worry.

It didn't seem to matter today though, as Pascal Struijk slotted in seamlessly and, in any case, most of the action was at the other end in the first half once we'd negotiated a scrappy first five minutes and the Llorente stoppage. The clock in the bottom left corner of the screen had not long ticked over past '16:00' so we were into the 17th minute but, fear not, Leeds were on the attack. Alioski made a successful challenge on halfway and poked the ball forward to Patrick Bamford who strode forward with it in the centre of the pitch. He had Rodrigo to his right near the corner of the area. Bamford's pass was a touch heavy truth be told and it ran past Rodrigo onto his weaker right foot so rather than take on the shot he stopped and, using his left foot for three little touches, he assessed what was on. What was on was that Raphinha had found space on the edge of the area and was now calling for the ball. Rodrigo rolled the ball to him and after one touch to get the ball out from under his feet Raphinha swept it majestically through a crowd of players to nestle in the bottom left corner. It was a lovely move and an exquisite finish.

Rodrigo himself had another couple of half-chances, perhaps taking too long with the first that was blocked and then dragging a second just wide of the right post. Those were the best efforts from Leeds despite dominating the half. Newcastle looked a very poor side and, whereas Leeds had finally scored after a barren spell of 304 minutes of football, it was hard to see Newcastle doing so as they reached 442 minutes without a goal of their own as the halftime whistle sounded. The only time they'd looked dangerous at all was from three corner-kicks and a couple of other set-pieces around our box that were virtually all won in the air by Jamaal Lascelles; the same Jamaal Lascelles who did us in the air the previous time we were in Toon. That particular Achilles Heel would not go away.

Almost from the start of the second period it was obvious this was not going to be easy. Newcastle had clearly been whipped into action during the break by some stern words from Steve Bruce and they looked a totally different proposition and suddenly Leeds seemed to lack the composure they had earlier. Those characteristic traits started to emerge of loose passes and silly mistakes, possibly as the home side were now pressing as well as if not better than we were meaning everything we did was now rushed. This all came though after we had the ball in the net just a couple of minutes into the half. A quick break down the Leeds right ended with Raphinha pulling the ball back across the area to where Stuart Dallas was racing in. Dallas stretched out a right boot and poked the ball at goal only to see it ricochet straight back at him off a defender's legs. Incredibly, the ball then cannoned against Dallas' left arm as he fell, back to goal, and the ball sailed into the net off the underside of the crossbar. Anthony Taylor was alert though and spotted that one without the intervention of VAR and the 'goal' was chalked off. It was one of very few efforts Leeds would fashion after the break.

By contrast the home side was now racking up numerous efforts. A Jacob Murphy shot was blocked and Miguel Almiron had a shot saved by Meslier following another badly defended corner. Alioski then had to grab the ball with his hands to stop another Newcastle break that rightly got him a yellow card. From the free-kick Lascelles yet again rose highest to plant a header wide. Whether it was the booking or whether Bielsa felt we needed to change anyway, I'm not sure but, almost immediately, Alioski was subbed and Klich resumed duty in midfield as Dallas dropped into the left-back slot. Leeds were still reorganising for that change-round when the Toon finally got their goal and it was a bit of sloppy play from Patrick Bamford, deep in his own half that started the move.

Bamford tried to play a ridiculous short pass into the feet of Luke Ayling who was immediately tackled and lost the ball. It ran to Jonjo Shelvey who, quick as a flash, moved it left to Wilson who, in turn, stunned it first time inside to Almiron who was then behind three claret-shirted Leeds players. Almiron set himself and then drove the ball low towards the left post. The keeper had no real right to get near it, so well was it hit, but he almost stopped it, only to see it cannon up into the net behind him. Bielsa immediately gave Bamford the dreaded hook and he was replaced by Tyler Roberts and I did wonder whether the sloppy play from Paddy made Marcelo's mind up for him. Within seconds of this latest change, Leeds were ahead again, albeit against the run of play. It was though another sumptuous phase of football.

Rodrigo, on halfway, clubbed the ball diagonally out towards Raphinha, almost without looking, knowing the Brazilian would be lurking near that right touchline. Raphinha was only 12 yards short of the Newcastle area but there were five other Leeds players ahead of him, Ayling to his right and four others, including Rodrigo who'd sprinted after making his initial pass. Raphinha ran with the ball parallel to the edge of the area, right to left, as no fewer than eight Toon players kept an eye on him and marked Ayling and three of the Leeds attackers... but no one had picked out the movement of Jack Harrison on the left corner of the area. Raphinha lifted the ball over the Toon back-line and, cool as you like, Jack stopped it with one touch of his left boot, let it bounce, and then struck it gently with the outside of his left foot to curl it around Darlow and inside the far post. It couldn't have looked more nonchalant had he been practising in his own back garden!

So, Leeds were back in the lead within four minutes but it didn't change the way the game was being played and, the longer the game went on, the more likely it looked that we'd concede again. Time after time we'd give the ball away, often in daft circumstances, and Bielsa was clearly tearing his hair out on the touchline at our lack of game management. On one occasion Raphinha launched the ball back towards his own goal from almost on halfway to concede another corner! We weren't helped by the fact that Newcastle had now introduced Allan Saint-Maximin into the game as a 64th-minute substitute and his pace and tricky ball control was causing us all manner of problems. Each time he arrived in the Leeds box it was clear he was just waiting for the merest touch to go down to win a penalty, while the rest of the time he was just slaloming around the burgundy shirts like a downhill skier. It reminded me of a previous trip to the North East when Adama Traore did a similar job for Middlesbrough on that night when Bamford scored three against us. We just don't deal with pace very well. Shots continued to rain in on the Leeds goal and more corners were won. Lascelles headed one onto the top of the crossbar and then Shelvey headed one that Meslier tipped acrobatically over the bar. Every corner was met by a Newcastle head. Somehow the Leeds goal remained intact by a combination of good saves from Meslier and sheer good luck. At the final whistle many Leeds players collapsed onto the turf in total exhaustion while Marcelo Bielsa embraced Steve Bruce and was clearly giving him some compliments as to his team's second-half performance.

After the game Steve Bruce said he might have been on his worst run of results in 20 years as a manager but he was encouraged by his side's second-half display. For his part, Bielsa commented *"We expected a difficult game. There was a 20-minute spell after Jack Harrison's goal where it was difficult to control the game. For us it was a game we needed to win and it was very difficult but we managed to do it."*

The star of the show for Leeds was without doubt Raphinha, with his fine goal and the perfect pass for Harrison; throughout the game he looked well worth his £17m fee. For Leeds and the fans it was another comforting win that showed again that we had the wherewithal to hold our own in the Premier League by usually managing to beat the sides in the bottom half of the table, however difficult we might make it sometimes. We'd cemented that 12th place in the table now, three points behind Southampton and three ahead of Crystal Palace; not bad company to be keeping at all in our first months back in the big time.

After the game a picture circulated on social media of the Leeds United players in the dressing room at Newcastle holding up a white shirt with the name 'PRICE' on the back. It was a message of support for Rob Price, Head of Medicine and Performance. Liam Cooper tweeted: *"When one suffers we all suffer. Condolences to Rob and his family. That was for you and yours mate."* No details were released as to the loss the Price family had suffered but it was another sign of the unity of this Bielsa family of players and staff.

In the other games played in this round of matches there were wins for West Ham at Palace, Arsenal at Southampton (thus getting some revenge for their FA Cup defeat at St. Mary's at the weekend) and Manchester City who walloped West Brom 0 – 5. Poor old Sam Allardyce had thus presided over four home games for the Albion and had seen them ship 17 goals without reply, including the five we scored there. Those games were all played on the Tuesday night and then on Wednesday there were five more; Burnley beat Aston Villa 3 – 2 while the games between Chelsea and Wolves, Brighton and Fulham, and Everton against Leicester were all drawn. In the final game on Wednesday we had what was probably the biggest upset of the Premier League season so far as Sheffield United, with one win all season, beat top of the table Manchester United 1 – 2 at Old Trafford. That result meant Manchester City went top of the table for the first time this season; the 9th different team to lead the Premier League up to this point.

Newcastle United 1 **Leeds United 2 (Raphinha 17**, Almiron 57, **Harrison 61)**
BCD. **Rd 20 League Pos: 12**[th].

Bamford's Back!

Round 21 of games came round quicker than you could say Raphael Dias Belloli aka Raphinha and the next challenge for Leeds was a daunting one; high flying Leicester City at their King Power Stadium.

Spurs and Liverpool were still completing their round of 20 game on Thursday evening this week, a game that saw the Reds storm back to form with a resounding 1 – 3 victory. The game also saw Harry Kane limp away at halftime too and everyone knew how important he was to Tottenham. Liverpool were back into the top four and only four points covered those clubs; Man City, Man United, Leicester and Liverpool.

The transfer window was slowly closing but so far there had been hardly any significant business for the Premier League clubs. Just four permanent signings had occurred with only a couple of days to go before the window slammed shut at 23:00 on Monday 1st February. It was not expected that there would be any late business involving Leeds although there were rumours that Gjanni Alioski might possibly move on despite him making noises about wanting a new contract with the Whites.

The first batch of six round 21 games took place on Saturday while Leeds' game was one of four more scheduled for Sunday. On Saturday we started with Newcastle, fresh from losing to us, going to top-seven placed side Everton and comfortably beating them 0 – 2. It was the first of a number of surprising results that showed again just how tight the Premier League was in this peculiar Covid ridden season. We then had more-routine wins for Crystal Palace, 1 – 0 over fast fading Wolves, and Manchester City by the same score over Sheffield United. The Blades were still in dire trouble but they virtually always only lost by the odd goal! They had lost no less than 12 of their 17 defeats by the odd goal and eight of them by the only goal in the game. West Brom and Fulham drew 2 – 2 in a bottom of the table clash and then Arsenal and Manchester United played out a nil–nil draw. In the final game on Saturday evening, Aston Villa won by the only goal at Southampton in a game where VAR rescued Villa from a blatant handball and then an offside call that denied the Saints a goal by less than a pixel's width.

Sunday is a day I will never forget as I took a call from an old school pal. He and his wife were part of a small group of friends that had known each other from school and we'd shared holidays and get-togethers for almost fifty years. We were dreading the call as we knew his wife, the lovely Carmel, was battling Covid in hospital and had been for some weeks. She passed away earlier in the day. It was as close as the virus had yet come to our family but the official death figures had now passed the awful milestone of 100,000; a figure once recorded for deaths during the great London plague in 1665, proving once again that there is little new in this world of ours. The race to get the nation vaccinated was going well and by this weekend that figure was up to almost nine million; sadly, it was too late for Carmel. RIP, we'll miss you.

That news meant that football didn't really seem very important anymore and the day's games served only as a distraction, something to occupy the mind and stop it wandering back to days gone by...

Chelsea and Burnley were first up, the Londoners beating the Clarets 2 – 0 to give new manager Thomas Tuchel his first win. Then it was our turn.

The appearance of the team selection on Twitter was only surprising in that, once again and for a second consecutive game, Mateusz Klich was only on the bench. Hence Bielsa had gone with the same side that started in Newcastle apart from the inclusion of Pascal Struijk for the injured Diego Llorente.

Meslier
Ayling Struijk Cooper (Capt) Alioski
Phillips
Raphinha (Costa 80) Dallas Rodrigo (Klich 21) Harrison
Bamford

Subs: Casilla, Davis, Cresswell, Shackleton, Poveda, Costa, Klich, Roberts, Hernandez.

Leicester City: Schmeichel, Castagne, (Ricardo Pereira 37), Fofana (Ünder 79), Evans, Justin, Tielemans, Mendy, Albrighton (Söyüncü 45), Maddison, Barnes, Pérez. Subs not used: Ward, Amartey, Choudhury, Iheanacho, Fuchs, Thomas.

Referee: Chris Kavanagh.

Hence the Leeds line-up was pretty much what we'd expected considering who was available. For Leicester, we'd known all week that Jamie Vardy would be missing, he'd undergone a hernia operation the previous weekend and would likely be missing for a few games. They still had some decent players though and were on a great run with only one defeat in their previous 13 games in all competitions. A win today would put them second in the table and leave them only two points behind Man City. There was also the slight matter of that 1 – 4 humping they delivered at Elland Road to keep us on our toes. I couldn't see any way we could win this game if Leicester played to their normal level; they were a top team this season and Leeds had only taken one point from the current top six sides; that 1 – 1 draw with Man City at Elland Road. Some folk were more positive though; my son Mark had installed Patrick Bamford as his Premier League Fantasy League team captain. I had to chuckle when I spotted that...

I've said it for most of our away games this season but this was another one that I'd have loved to be at; the normal routine for Leicester was to drive down, park near the ground, have a few pints in the Counting House, hoping they had that fantastic automatic lager dispenser on the go – the one that fills the glasses from the bottom - and then buy a burger from the van on the corner opposite the ground. Today I was in front of the TV again watching Sky and I didn't even fancy a beer.

Leicester looked sharp from the opening moments of this game and tried a cheeky free-kick when spotting Meslier out of position, the ball went over the bar but it showed they had their thinking heads on. Leeds were taking longer to find their range and Harrison wasted a good opportunity as he over-hit a through ball aimed for Patrick Bamford. Then, with only 12 minutes gone, Leicester ripped through the heart of the Leeds defence to take the lead.

Liam Cooper played a loose diagonal ball left to right in his own half that was easily intercepted by the head of James Justin before it could reach Raphinha. The speedy Harvey Barnes then took over and ran with the ball back along the same route Cooper's pass had just taken. Luke Ayling was running with him but didn't ever try to tackle him. As Barnes reached the edge of the area he played a quick one-two with Maddison who had Kalvin Phillips notionally marking him but again nowhere near tight enough to block the wall pass. Barnes collected the return, still with Ayling close by, but the Leeds defender allowed the Leicester man a couple of touches and then he simply threaded the ball inside the left post wide of the diving Illan Meslier. It was a move which sort of caught Leeds cold, but one which was typical of the way Leicester can cut through sides. I merely shrugged and sat back further on the sofa; it was no more than I expected really so there was no point getting annoyed by it. I was sitting up a bit straighter though within another two minutes as Leeds suddenly out-foxed the Foxes.

A Leicester attack was broken down as a loose pass was easily intercepted by Luke Ayling and 'Bill' immediately made up 50 yards taking him from deep in our half to midway in theirs, still on that right flank. He had Patrick Bamford inside, near the right corner of the Leicester box, and the ball was slid through for Paddy who took one touch and then stroked it further forward with the outside of that cultured left foot of his into the path of the Irish Rover, Stuart Dallas, who was racing onto it. Dallas hit the ball first time all along the ground with his right foot and it beat Schmeichel and nestled inside the far post. It was a classic counter-attack goal. On 'Match Of The Day 2' later that night, former Bournemouth manager Eddie Howe was waxing lyrical about the move saying how, for a counter-attack to work well, it really had to be achieved in four passes or less. This one took just two passes and a slick finish to go from one end to the other.

That goal put an altogether different slant on this game and you could tell by the body language of both teams that it had made everyone just reassess the possibilities. It sowed a seed of doubt in the minds of the Foxes while it clearly bushed up the tail feathers of the Peacocks; I think it was enough to just instil the belief into the Leeds lads that Leicester were actually not that special. We were still in the first 15 minutes of the game and it was all square but with Leeds probably in the better mind set, but then we suffered yet another injury setback. Rodrigo Moreno stretched to reach a ball and immediately winced and sank to the turf.

He was tended to by the physio and then gave it another couple of minutes, but then it was clear that he'd pulled something in his groin or upper leg and his day was done. I have to say I wasn't that disappointed as I assumed we'd now see Pablo Hernandez and I was looking forward to seeing if he still had anything left in those legs of his with well over an hour of the game to go. Shock horror though, it wasn't Pablo stripping off, it was Matty Klich! This represented a major change of tack by Bielsa as far as I was concerned; Marcelo was nothing if not predictable and all season he'd treated Rodrigo and Pablo as interchangeable; early-season Pablo had the starting spot but would then be replaced by Rodrigo, then, after the infamous armband strop from Pablo and the rumoured muscle injury, he gave way to Rodrigo in the starting XI and then, once fit, it would always be Pablo replacing Rodrigo late in the game. A little bit of me wondered if the rift between Bielsa and Hernandez had never actually been healed, but pictures later in the game of Hernandez celebrating joyfully with the rest of the players seemed to knock that idea on the head. Anyway, for now, it was Matty Klich back in the saddle.

While Rodrigo was limping around the pitch trying to decide if he could run off the injury or not, Leicester had the ball in our net again and it was almost a carbon copy of their first goal. A loose forward pass from Struijk, intercepted, Barnes and Maddison playing a one-two on the edge of the area and this time the ball went through to Perez who fired home from close range near the left post. Thankfully, my favourite assistant referee, Sian Louise

Massey-Ellis MBE, had spotted that Perez was offside. Why is she my favourite liner? I just have this memory of her flagging a Preston 'goal' offside in the pouring rain at the far end of Deepdale one dark night and ever since then I've regarded her as a sort of lucky omen. That was the game when Billy Paynter finally got his debut goal for us, another special memory of celebrating amongst thousands of Leeds fans in the Bill Shankly Stand up there.

Patrick Bamford should probably have done better with a chance in the 25th minute when a Jack Harrison left-wing cross looped into the air off a defender's boot. It seemed to drop perfectly, six yards out, and there was Bamford who'd read the flight and jumped unchallenged but then missed the ball completely! Schmeichel was able to claim it on the first bounce but it was a huge chance albeit one of the first big chances Bamford had missed in a while. His conversion rate had improved no end this season. Most of the other chances in the first half also fell to Leeds. Jack Harrison blasted a volley that Schmeichel did well to push around the post for a corner. From the corner we scored! Well, no, not really, although we did get the ball in the net. Patrick Bamford met Phillips' corner perfectly with his head, Schmeichel clawed the ball from under the crossbar and then Klich knocked in the rebound from two yards. Sadly, Klich was offside when Bamford made the initial contact.

Bamford was on fire today and next he played a delicious one-two to put Raphinha through on goal in the inside right channel. The Leeds number '18' rifled a shot at goal but again Schmeichel got down with a strong arm to push it away for another corner. Leeds were making a mockery of struggling against top-six sides; we were the better team. Just before halftime, we did need Meslier to be sharp – and lucky – as a low ball was fed into the Leeds six-yard area where two Foxes were foraging but Meslier just managed to grab it at the second attempt. Halftime and, on points at least, Leeds were ahead and we'd bossed the possession too with 53%.

Leicester made their second change at halftime as they decided to re-jig things to try to wrestle back the impetus. They'd already had to replace the injured Castagne with Ricardo Pereira ten minutes before the break, and now they sent on Söyüncü for Albrighton. It seemed to do the trick too as Leicester were far more impressive in the second period although still without making many clear-cut chances. We had one heart in mouth moment minutes after the restart as the cameras lingered on a tussle in the Leeds area at another Leicester corner. Leicester had spent the first three or four minutes in the Leeds final third and a James Justin shot was blocked away for a corner. That one was blocked away too but then, after the second corner was cleared, the referee halted the game while VAR looked at something going on in the area. What had gone on was a grappling session between Cooper and Fofana, during which Cooper clearly got a handful of the Leicester man's shirt and pulled him over. Mike Dean was the VAR today and he'd already been involved in those two dodgy calls in the Southampton v Villa game the previous day. This time we got away with it, and the game moved on, but it was another reminder of just how fine the margins can be; on another day it could easily have been seen as a penalty but, presumably, we were helped by Chris Kavanagh not spotting it on the pitch in real time.

The action was halted again shortly after that, this time as Luke Ayling picked up a cut on his forehead and was shedding blood. He had to go off eventually to be given the traditional *"Kisnorbo"* bandage all around his head. Leeds were thus down to ten men for a short while. Then, comically, with Ayling patched up but still awaiting the ref's signal to come on, Meslier threw the ball over to him! Thankfully that ended OK, but Leeds had hardly ventured into Leicester territory yet and the second half was now ten minutes old. Leicester had switched to a back three (or five however you wish to describe it) with two wingbacks, and they dominated the possession now and would eventually overturn that statistic in their favour for the whole game; the first time this season any side had done that to Leeds. All the Foxes had to show for it though was a couple of long-range shots easily gathered by Meslier. Leeds were steadfastly sticking to their defensive shape and pretty much nullifying the possession Leicester were amassing. It was more of a chess match now than the basketball game that Brendan Rodgers had hoped it wouldn't turn into; he knew Leeds' fitness would then come into play so this suited Leicester and their new formation. We reached the 70th minute in this mode and then, out of the blue, Leeds struck again with another superb phase of football.

Leicester, for once, were pinned in their own final third and tried unsuccessfully to get the ball away several times before it was hacked into the midfield area where Pascal Struijk, who was having a fine game, was first to dart in to intercept the ball once more. He pushed it forward to Raphinha and the razor-sharp Brazilian turned the ball round the corner through the Leicester back line and onto Patrick Bamford's left foot; who doesn't appreciate a razor-sharp Brazilian? Bamford let the ball run across his body and then let loose with that left boot of his and thumped the ball over the outstretched hands of Schmeichel to dip into the net off the underside of the bar and into the far top corner. It was another fabulous strike from Bamford and yet another contender for the Leeds United goal of the season.

The Leicester body language told the story again, shoulders were suddenly hunched and a degree of interest seemed to be lost as they contemplated the end of their recent good run. They did test the usual Leeds Achilles Heel as we continued to look shaky at set-pieces of course. A Maddison free-kick was allowed to drop behind Kalvin Phillips and that created a chance for Fofana that was blocked over the bar and then, from the resulting corner, Söyüncü inevitably won a header that skimmed past the back post, with two Leicester men just failing to turn it into the net. A long-range Perez shot then tested Meslier as it was heading for the bottom corner but the Leeds keeper turned that one round the post. From the corner Meslier, for some reason known only unto himself, punched away the corner when my Gran could probably have caught it one-handed. It fell perfectly for Mendy on the edge of the area and Meslier had to react sharply to get down to smother the resulting shot. It was a little purple patch for the Blues but Leeds continued to defend stoutly if not prettily. It was a bit like the second-half pressure we withstood at Newcastle.

Bielsa was very animated on the touchline during this period, either barking instructions or crouched on his haunches studying a little patch of turf between his feet, but clearly not convinced the game was won yet.

There was another injury worry too as we moved towards 80 minutes on the clock. Raphinha, already sporting one of those skin-coloured kinesiology patches all over his left thigh, went down holding the top of that leg and was soon limping off to be replaced by Helder Costa. There was no obvious gash showing but there was clearly an issue with the Brazilian… It meant that all four of our big-money signings from last summer were at that precise moment injured: Koch, Llorente, Rodrigo and now Raphinha. For the final few minutes of the game therefore it was a Championship XI Leeds had in this Premier League match and indeed eight of the side had been present in Marcelo Bielsa's first competitive game in charge back in August 2018!

Leeds almost got their third, unlikely as it seems, from another Kalvin Phillips left wing corner. It dropped right in the six-yard area in front of Pascal Struijk but, just as he swung a boot at it, Pereira nicked it off his toe. In the 84th minute though we did put the game out of the reach of the Foxes and, once again, it was a copy of what Leicester did to us at Elland Road.

Leicester won a free-kick, not far outside the Leeds box and when it was swung in it was Pascal Struijk, falling backwards, who acrobatically nodded it out wide towards Stuart Dallas. Dallas controlled the ball, gave a Leicester player a hefty shove with his shoulder, and then flicked it further down that left touchline towards Matty Klich. Klich just got to the ball before a Blue shirt and was able to poke it over the halfway line and into the path of Patrick Bamford who now had fifty metres of open grass to run into. He did have Jonny Evans chasing him, but he also had Jack Harrison keeping pace on his right and, with Schmeichel in front on his six-yard line and Evans inches behind, Bamford merely touched the ball across and Harrison stabbed it into the unguarded net. It was a real smash-and-grab goal and that was the game won.

There was the obvious temptation to suggest that if Leicester could be considered title contenders playing the way they do, then so could we, as we'd pretty much played them at their own game; OK, they were missing the influence of Jamie Vardy, but we were missing Llorente and Koch and, by the end, Raphinha and Rodrigo too. Perhaps talk like that was premature but, at the very least, this win restored any flagging belief that we were entitled to consider ourselves at least mid-table fodder if not better.

After the game, Patrick Bamford was most fans' choice for Man of the Match and he did the post-match interview. He joked that he was *"fuming"* that he'd removed himself out of his own fantasy league side. It reminded me that, not for the first time this season, I'd been outwitted by my lad in the fantasy league stakes. I'd loaded my team with three Man City players and had Foden and Gundogan as captain and vice-captain; City of course only scraped past the Blades with one goal from Gabriel Jesus; I should have had more faith!

Marcelo Bielsa also had plenty of praise for Bamford after the game, he had of course been involved in all three goals: *"What I value most is for 3-1 he passed to Jack Harrison when a goal scorer would normally go for goal,"* said Bielsa. *"He was very generous and thought more of the team. He preferred the team got a third than he got a second."*[1]

In the final two games this Sunday, I watched as Liverpool again showed they were over their little slump as they beat West Ham 1 – 3 at the London Stadium and then Spurs showed that they were not over theirs as, without Harry Kane, they slumped to a 1 – 0 defeat at Brighton. Leeds ended this weekend still in that solid 12th spot in the table, now 15 points above the bottom three and only 6 points adrift of West ham in the Europa League position.

Leicester City 1 **Leeds United 3** (Barnes 13, **Dallas 15, Bamford 70, Harrison 84**)
BCD. **Round 21 League Pos: 12th**

---

[1] *https://www.bbc.co.uk/sport/football/55769208*

Toffees Again

The January transfer window closed as expected without any significant Leeds United news. We did learn that Conor Shaughnessy had left the club to join Rochdale on a permanent deal, another promising young player who we'd seen glimpses of in the first-team squad in the past but who'd faded out of the picture. It was a similar story for Rafa Mujica, the 22-year-old who arrived with a bit of a fanfare back in July 2019. He immediately got a run out in a friendly at York but then just as quickly was loaned out to various Spanish clubs and now his latest loan was to Las Palmas for the rest of the season. Finally, Jay-Roy Grot left the club to join VFL Osnabruck. Jay-Roy was another signing who was initially talked up as our next centre-forward but, after 23 appearances, most from the bench, his time was over. Grot scored just one goal in his time at Leeds, when coming off the bench in the 1 – 2 home defeat to Sheffield Wednesday in 2018. There were no Premier League games on Monday but our Under 23s were in action again and they put another three points on the board to go a full ten points clear at the top of PL2 Division 2. It was Sunderland this time that failed to dent our recent record and goals from Tyler Roberts from the penalty spot and Niall Huggins gave a comfortable 2 – 0 win at Thorp Arch. That was despite an injury to Ian Poveda early in the second half that left Leeds with only ten men for the rest of the game.

The Premier League action started again on Tuesday. This week's games were all being covered by BT Sport so I was there on Tuesday tea time logging into my son's BT Sport account and the first game I watched was the next bottom of the table clash; this one between Sheffield United and West Brom. The Albion took the lead just before halftime, giving big Sam some optimism, but then in the second half the Blades cut through the Baggies' defences and scored twice to win the game. At the same time, on a second BT Sport Channel, Wolves were beating Arsenal 2 – 1 with more VAR controversy. Arsenal scored in the 32nd minute and had by then also hit the woodwork twice and had a 'goal' disallowed as they battered the Wolves. Then, just before the break, David Luiz was adjudged to have brought down Willian Jose; Luiz was sent off despite the VAR replays showing that any contact was absolutely negligible. A penalty resulted that was scored and the game was turned on its head. The second two games kicked off at 20:15 and those who chose to watch Crystal Palace win 1 – 2 at Newcastle instead of the Man United game with Southampton probably now regret their choice!

Saints had Alexandre Jankewitz sent off after only two minutes and that allowed the home side to bang in nine goals to equal the Premier League record score of 9 – 0; a record that Saints were already holding following their similar decimation against Leicester City back in October 2019. Ipswich, Marcelo Bielsa's favourite tongue-twister, also shared the record of course having also been beaten by the Red Devils 9 – 0 in 1995. The Saints' game this season was riddled with refereeing controversy, with Bednarek sent off late in the game for allegedly bringing down Martial. It caused Southampton to formally request that no more of their games this season were refereed by Mike Dean, or Lee Mason who was in charge for their similarly controversial home defeat to Aston Villa. Saints appealed the Bednarek red card and Arsenal appealed the red handed out to David Luiz as general discontent with VAR continued to be voiced. For reasons known only to the FA, the Saint got off while the perennial sinner, David Luiz did not. You had to wonder if Luiz's reputation had gone before him.

Tuesday's news was all about the death of Captain Sir Tom Moore, the man who'd done so much in the last few months to raise both national spirits and money for the National Health Service. He shot to fame when he decided to try to do 100 laps of his garden before his 100th birthday on 30th April 2020, with the modest initial aim of raising perhaps £1,000. By the end of the year, he'd raised around £39 million once all the Government tax rebates were included; recorded a version of *"You'll Never Walk Alone"* with Michael Ball which became a number one single; and was knighted by the Queen. Sir Tom was a Yorkshireman of course, being born in Keighley in the West Riding where he was schooled at the Local Grammar School. One hundred years old eh? When Tom was born in 1920 there was no television, the first sets only being sold in Selfridges in 1928. Thank God John Logie Baird came up with that invention in the intervening years or this pandemic would have been insufferable. Captain Tom's oft-quoted phrase was the optimistic hope that *"Tomorrow will be a good day"* and everyone was drinking to that in hope every evening these days!

The Wednesday night football schedule was a bit crowded; two games kicked off at 6 pm, then Leeds and Everton started at 7:30 pm and then the final two games, between Aston Villa and West Ham and Liverpool v Brighton, started at 8:15 pm. As you can quickly work out it was not possible to watch all the other games if, as we Leeds fans would all be doing, we watched the whole of ours. So, I started with Burnley v Man City, hoping again that Gundogan could earn me some fantasy league points. City won 0 – 2 with one Gundogan assist so that was better than nothing. The simultaneous game to that one was another away win, again 0 – 2 as Leicester won at Fulham. Both those games were still going on though when I eventually clicked on to the BT Sport 3 channel which was showing the Leeds game.

Meslier
Ayling Struijk Cooper (Capt) Alioski (Hernandez 78)
Phillips
Raphinha Dallas Klich (Roberts 69) Harrison (Costa 87)
Bamford

Subs: Casilla, Davis, Cresswell, Shackleton, Huggins, Jenkins, Hernandez, Roberts, Costa.

Everton: Olsen, Holgate, Mina, Godfrey, Digne, Doucouré, André Gomes, Iwobi (King 87), G Sigurdsson (Davies 89), Richarlison (Keane 80), Calvert-Lewin. Subs not used: Subs not used: Neves Virginia, Delph, Nkounkou, Rodriguez, Bernard, Coleman. Referee: Michael Oliver.

The sight of the Leeds line-up on Twitter didn't cause any palpitations; we knew we'd be without Rodrigo and, with Koch and Llorente still out as well, this was almost the logical team. I say almost as I was still perplexed as to why, with Klich having not started the previous two games, it was he and not Hernandez who was brought in to replace the injured Rodrigo. Bielsa had always said that Rodrigo and Hernandez were the two players vying for that creative midfield role and yet, here we were with another defensive and far from creative midfielder now being chosen. Was Hernandez really still that much out of favour with Bielsa?

Everton had their injury problems too, with Jordan Pickford out with bruised ribs and midfielders Allan and Jean-Philippe Gbamin out with hamstring and Achilles injuries respectively. Reading some of the posts on an Everton fans forum though it was by no means clear they thought the absence of the erratic Jordan Pickford was a disadvantage.

Everton's record to date was a bit of a mishmash not dissimilar to that of our own. They'd started really well, winning their first four EPL games to go top of the early table, but then they'd lost four of their next six. Then they went on another good run winning four on the bounce again. Like Leeds they didn't often draw but, encouragingly, their previous two games saw them draw and lose to Leicester and Newcastle, two sides we'd just beaten. Leeds were messing with my head lately though, winning when I doubted we could but losing games I expected to win. I genuinely had no idea how this would go. Everton were still touted as possible claimants for a European place and yet Leeds started this game only four points behind them and some Leeds fans had started to talk up our own European chances after those wins at Leicester and Newcastle.

I'd been flicking through the match-day programme earlier in the day and the highlight was once again provided by the Leeds United wordsmith, the Beeston Bard himself, Angus Kinnear. His target this week was VAR and, in particular, the incident where Danny Ings had been ruled offside by the width of a gnats whisker when comparing the position of a Villa backside with Ings' sleeve. Kinnear wrote that there must be something wrong when a goal is *"denied by a geek over a hundred miles away frenetically trying to align his cross-hairs with an arse and an elbow while simultaneously demonstrating he doesn't know one from the other."*

In the lead up to the game, pictures were shared on social media of the new Elland Road pitch and, at first glance it looked pretty much perfect, despite having been down for less than two weeks. It would still be interesting to see how it stood up to a night of Yorkshire rain and twenty-two blokes running around on it. The players all lined up around the centre-circle before the start in tribute to Captain Sir Tom Moore. His picture shone down from the big screen at the south end of the ground together with those now famous optimistic words of his: *"Tomorrow will be a good day."*

The BT commentary was provided by Rory Hamilton and former Everton player Leon Osman who quickly alienated the whole of the Leeds United fan base with his constant references to *"Marco Bielsa"*. Quite where that came from, none of us knew, but it grated all through the game.

Leeds started well enough; we had our first corner within a minute of the start after Raphinha collected a throw-in from Luke Ayling, got to the byline and then tried an audacious shot from a tight angle that was blocked away. In fact, eight minutes passed with Leeds in total command of the ball without actually creating anything and then, well, then we succumbed again to our own adventure.

Leeds had seven men in the Everton half as Jack Harrison slipped on the new turf, one of many such slips we'd see from Leeds players throughout the game. He thus spooned his pass straight to Richarlison near the Everton left wing. Richarlison had Luke Ayling closing him down but of course that meant Ayling was still in the Everton half as the ball was shifted to André Gomes who, in turn, launched it down the Everton left wing deep into the Leeds half. It went straight to Lucas Digne who'd spotted the opportunity by racing up that left wing with only Raphinha spotting the danger. The Brazilian never got close enough though to prevent Digne swinging the ball into the Leeds area, low along the edge of the six-yard box. Pascal Struijk looked as if he could have cut out the cross but he left it and then, on reflection, it looked as if Meslier could have come for it. Neither did and Gylfi Sigurdsson, who'd somehow been allowed the freedom of the Kop end, strolled onto the ball to tap it into the net past the stranded figure of Illan Meslier with Liam Cooper a good two yards adrift of Sigurdsson. You could argue the ball had been played into that infamous 'corridor of uncertainty' but I have to say in all my years of watching the game, such uncertainty I've never before seen. It was a shocking goal to have conceded with at least five Leeds players guilty of errors in the build-up.

Whether the goal unsettled us or whether it was just time for the regular 'Meslier moment' I'm not sure, but the next chance for Everton came when our young stopper threw the ball out towards Stuart Dallas who had no less than three blue shirts hunting him down. Inevitably Dallas was dispossessed, the ball was moved inside to the dangerous Calvert-Lewin and he, with a lucky bounce off a Leeds defender, had a free shot at goal. Thankfully he scuffed his attempt and Meslier saved easily and he, and we, could breathe a sigh of relief.

From that moment though we finally started to get our act together and next it was Klich firing in a right foot shot that Olsen pushed away for another Leeds corner. From the corner, delivered as an in-swinger by the left-footed Raphinha right onto the left boot of Alioski, we saw what might well be the shot of the season. Alioski watched the ball all the way onto his boot and simply lashed it on the full towards goal; he was so unlucky to see it crash against the left post and not the net.

Leeds had the game in their grip now and next it was Pascal Struijk flicking on a Phillips free-kick. It just took a nick off a defender's head and was going under the bar until Olsen tipped it over. We had one of those situations developing where a stand-in keeper was having the game of his life. Leeds were playing quite well now and I didn't even flinch when Everton won a corner, their first, five minutes before halftime. Perhaps it was the beer that had numbed my senses but I didn't even consider that we'd mess up again.

But mess up we did, conceding our eighth goal to an opposition corner as Sigurdsson swung the ball in towards the near post from the left wing. Godfrey beat Liam Cooper and Stuart Dallas at the front post, flicked the ball backwards with his head towards the back post, and nobody stopped Calvert-Lewin who stooped to head home. I wondered if there was a Guinness Book of Records entry for the number of goals conceded to corners...

Two-nil down at halftime to a side that was knocking on the door of a European place felt like a tough situation to me, but we'd been in similar situations before and had come through. That incredible game with Millwall the previous season came to mind again, as it probably always will whenever we are in this situation. That night we got a goal back within a few minutes of the restart and, in that respect at least, this game followed the same script. It was a goal from nothing as Stuart Dallas merely lobbed a speculative ball into the Everton box that fell somewhere near the penalty spot. Two defenders were there with Jack Harrison as the ball hit the ground and then bounced up in the middle of the trio. As it came down again it brushed the knee of Mason Holgate and then off the boot of Harrison it cannoned off Holgate's nose. Patrick Bamford then got involved to make it a foursome that was trying to get hold of the ball as it pinged about. Whether he meant it as a pass or whether his touch was too strong, we'll never know, but the ball came off Bamford's boot and ran a few yards away to where Raphinha was waiting for just such a break of the ball. The lightning reflexes of the Brazilian were apparent again as he simply steered the ball all along the turf through the legs of Ben Godfrey and into the bottom corner of the net. It was a super cool piece of finishing from a player who was rapidly earmarking a little place for himself in that big book of Leeds United legends.

Leeds huffed and puffed throughout the rest of the game in search of at least an equalising goal and we came close on several occasions but, this time, we couldn't find it. There was one almighty scramble following some more wing wizardry from Raphinha. He eventually clipped the ball into the middle looking for the head of Patrick Bamford but that was headed clear by Doucoure but only as far as Alioski. Gjanni was on the left edge of the box and he spotted Klich free near the 'D' and whipped the ball across. Klich, not for the first time, got his shot all wrong and merely kicked it into the turf, but it took a deflection as it bounced and wobbled its way towards goal. The deflection wrong-footed the keeper and yet he still managed to get down to block it and then even managed to push it away again as it spun back towards the line. This time it fell for Raphinha a few feet from the post and the Brazilian rifled it back at goal only to see Olsen get in the way of that one too. The ball was knocked clear but it was picked up by Leeds in the shape of Kalvin Phillips again on the right wing, in front of the vast empty spaces of the East Stand. Raphinha then launched it into the middle again and once more an Everton head cleared it away but only as far as Jack Harrison's left foot. The volley was swerving and dipping but yet again Olsen was equal to it and eventually the ball was hacked up-field. The Everton goal was under siege but, in much the same way that the famous old Lock-Up Tower on their badge was designed to keep the guilty in, so now they had effectively locked Leeds out. 'Nil Satis, Nisi Optimum', *"Nothing but the best is good enough"* is the Everton motto and this evening Leeds just couldn't better their defences.

Leeds had other chances; Patrick Bamford stretched to head the ball onto the top of the crossbar at one point and Bielsa tried to increase the pressure with Tyler Roberts replacing Klich on the hour mark and then Hernandez replaced Alioski. Dallas went to left-back but neither of the subs really added the spark of invention we were looking for to get through what was now a very tight and secure Toffees wrapper. Indeed, when Pablo tried one risky pass just outside the Everton area it was intercepted and should have brought the Blues a third goal had Calvert-Lewin not been foiled in a one-on-one with young Meslier. And the best chance of all was squandered by Roberts when Bamford cut the ball back to him, 16 yards out, but he horribly mishit the volley over the bar and the cameras picked out an exasperated Bielsa looking to the heavens and slapping his sides in frustration.

In many respects this game was another reminder of what we all really knew; we were just that tiny bit short of the quality needed to turn a solid performance into a winning one. Playing much of the second half with a midfield pairing of Stuart Dallas and Tyler Roberts it was hard to see us unlocking a decent defence and the arrival of Pablo Hernandez showed us that maybe he is now past his best, although expecting him to work his magic in fifteen minutes on an unfamiliar surface was again perhaps not a fair challenge to expect him to overcome.

The fundamental problem was of giving a decent side a two-goal lead. Not that we did it intentionally of course, but with our regular failure to deal with set-pieces and our cavalier attacking MO it is always a possibility. That Everton scored from their only corner of the game makes that particular goal even more annoying and it was just the latest of 17 (Ha!) goals we'd conceded this season from set-pieces, more than any other EPL side. Sometimes we'll score enough to overcome those issues and sometimes we won't. Many argued that we probably *"deserved"* at least a point from the game but, as we well know, it's not a phrase you'll find in the rule book. After the game Bielsa accepted that: *"The two goals they scored were preventable."* He also lamented the fact that giving Everton a two-goal lead meant they could sit back and defend but he still felt we ought to have taken something from the game. *"After they were winning by two goals they gave us the ball and started defending in their own half. The amount of goal scoring opportunities we created makes us think we should have had a draw or win."*[1] When asked why so many Leeds players seemed to be slipping on the new playing surface, Marcelo refused to blame the pitch, saying only that *"It's better than the old one!"* but, remembering that we bought this pitch from Spurs, a few Leeds fans pointed out the irony that, once again, we couldn't win on a London track.

In the final games of the day, Villa lost 1 – 3 to West Ham and Liverpool, in another shock result, went down 0 – 1 to Brighton. The next evening Chelsea continued their revival under Thomas Tuchel with a 0 – 1 win at Spurs, albeit with another soft penalty where you'd have needed a powerful magnifying glass to spot any contact on Werner. Jose was justifiably annoyed by that one.

That was the end of the latest round of games and Leeds had gone up a place to 11th courtesy of that 9 – 0 drubbing Southampton were handed meaning that their goal difference was now significantly worse than ours. We could all have Friday off but then the action started all over again on Saturday; the pace of the season was unrelenting.

Leeds United 1 Everton 2 (Sigurdsson 9, Calvert-Lewin 41, **Raphinha 48) BCD. Round 22 League Pos: 11th.**

---

[1] *https://www.bbc.co.uk/sport/football/55820959*

ER Palace Freeze

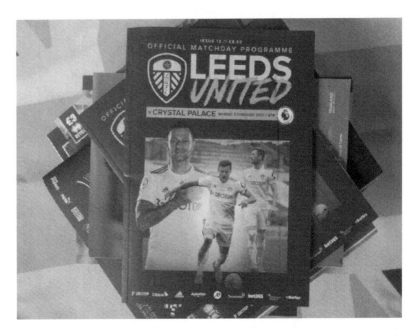

I f we needed a reminder of how things had changed at Leeds over the last three years, we got it this week. It was the third anniversary of the appointment of Paul Heckingbottom on 6th February 2018, although to me it felt like a lot longer with so much having changed. Leeds finished 13th in the Championship under 'Hecky' and meanwhile, 13th in Serie B in Italy this week was Massimo Cellino's Brescia. Cellino sold up before Heckingbottom arrived of course, that was a rare Radrizzani mistake, but Cellino was still his same old self. This week he appointed Pep Clotet as his 5th manager of the season. Clotet, was assistant to Gary Monk at Swansea, Leeds and then Birmingham, before the two had a much-publicised falling out after Monk was sacked by the Blues. Clotet himself eventually landed the Birmingham job but that only lasted a year. Now he was raring to go again telling the press: *"I thank the president Massimo Cellino, with whom I have a wonderful relationship since the days of Leeds..."* It will be interesting to see how long Clotet's *"wonderful relationship"* lasts; the tenure of the previous four Brescia managers had been two, none, one and ten games.

Round 23 of Premier League games began on Saturday, 6th February, with just the one day's break since the final game of round 22; it was Premier League football now virtually wall to wall including all afternoon and evening on Saturdays and Sundays. Even I was starting to get a bit of footy fatigue. The games began with Aston Villa beating Arsenal by a single Ollie Watkins goal at Villa Park in a 12:30 pm kick-off. Then came two games at 3 pm; Burnley and Brighton drew one apiece at Turf Moor while, in the game I watched on BT Sport, Newcastle United edged out Southampton 3 – 2. That point for Burnley and the three for the Toon opened up an eight-point gap between Burnley and the bottom three sides, a gap that was only reduced by one point as the fourth game of the day, Fulham v West Ham, ended in a goalless draw. It really did start to look as if the bottom three – Fulham, Albion, and Sheffield United - were already doomed, although Albion and Blades were still to play this weekend. The Fulham game was only notable for yet another controversial VAR decision as Lee Mason called Mike Dean over to look at a stray elbow from West Ham midfielder Tomas Soucek that caused Mitrovic to throw himself to the turf holding his face. It was clear to everyone that a) any contact was minimal and accidental and b) Mitrovic was feigning injury. Nonetheless, after numerous replays Deadly Dean marched back onto the pitch and sent Soucek off! The game was fast becoming a pantomime.

The final game on Saturday saw a dramatic conclusion as Everton grabbed an equaliser in the 5th minute of added time at the end to secure a 3 – 3 draw with Man United, despite having gone two goals down in the first half. The loss of the extra two points meant Man United failed to overhaul City at the top.

On Sunday the two bottom sides – Albion and Blades – both lost, Albion 2 – 0 at Spurs and Blades 1 – 2 at home to Chelsea, results that confirmed the thought that they and Fulham were in dire trouble. In the wildlife derby, the Wolves and the Foxes played out a goalless draw and then we watched as Liverpool played Man City in a game that many commentators thought would go a long way towards deciding the title; it was a game that turned on two mistakes by Liverpool keeper, Alisson. He single-handedly gave

City a couple of goals as he twice made appalling clearances that were easily intercepted to ensure City won the game 1 – 4. Sky went to their advertising break after the game with an *"Alisson Blunderland"* headline. It was a not so subtle reminder to Leeds fans that those two errors were just the sort of mistakes that our own Illan Meslier had been guilty of with his distribution a few times this season, so far without being punished. We could only hope that in our game on Monday night against Crystal Palace we didn't give that Sky headline writer any more ideas.

There was good news and bad news again this week on the Covid front. The good news was that over 12 million people in the UK had already had their first jab and it was now a Government target to get everyone over the age of 50 the offer of a jab by mid-May. That would be me then, hopefully sorted by mid-May and on the strength of that I booked a concert in London for early August (obviously having first checked to ensure that the new Premier League season wouldn't have started by then!). I was fully expecting our rescheduled The Who gig, moved from last year to March 17th (it had to be the 17th didn't it?) this year to be cancelled any time soon but at least there was light at the end of the tunnel.

The bad news was that scientists were now saying it looked very much as though we'd all need to be having a Covid vaccine jab every year for the rest of eternity, just like the flu jab. I could see my left arm looking like a second-hand dartboard if I managed to reach the age of 80.

The Leeds United Under 23s continued to move serenely through their Premier League 2 programme with another win. This time they saw off Middlesbrough 2 – 4 having raced into a four-goal lead by halftime. Goals from Max Dean, Nohan Kenneh and two from Joe Gelhardt made the headlines but the star of the show was undoubtedly the little winger from the Netherlands with the long name; Crysencio Jilbert Sylverio Cirro Summerville. He ran rings around the Boro defence and, at 19-years-old, looked ready for a try in the match-day squad to me. His only shortcoming is that he's, well, short, although it looked to me like his agent had been editing his Wiki page as that suggested he was five foot eight.

As always with these Monday night fixtures, it seemed like an age until it rolled around and it looked like it would be the one game not to escape the arrival of the Beast from the East II, aka storm

Darcy. She was heaping large dollops of snow all along the East of England. Fortunately, the worst of it was restricted to the south, in Kent and East Anglia. The bitterly cold temperatures would be a test though for our new southern softie London sourced pitch.

There were no surprises in the pre-match press conference which suggested that the match-day squad for the Crystal Palace game would be unchanged from the Everton defeat and yet, by the time the squad was announced, there was a name missing. Pablo Hernandez was not in the 20 man group.

Meslier
Ayling Struijk Cooper (Capt) Alioski
Phillips (Shackleton 88)
Raphinha Dallas Klich Harrison
Bamford

Subs: Casilla, Davis, Cresswell, Shackleton, Jenkins, Huggins, Costa, Roberts, Gelhardt.

Crystal Palace: Guaita, Clyne, Dann, Cahill, Mitchell, Eze, Milivojevic, Riedewald, van Aanholt (Townsend 45), Mateta (Batshuayi 65), J Ayew (Benteke 76). Subs not used: Butland, Kouyaté, Kelly. Referee: Andre Marriner.

The word on Pablo was that he was *"injured in training"* but I have to say I was getting more and more suspicious that something was going on we weren't getting to hear about with Pablo mysteriously dropping out of a squad at the last minute yet again. For the rest, it was as per the Everton group, with young Joe Gelhardt filling the space on the bench left by Pablo. Once again our lack of depth in the squad was highlighted by the nine subs with only Casilla, Costa, Roberts and, to a lesser extent Jamie Shackleton, having much first-team exposure. Palace had injury problems too; they only felt able to name six substitutes. Their main man, Wilfred Zaha was their biggest miss; Palace had not won a game without him in the side in 19 attempts but that was just the sort of statistic Leeds often go out of their way to correct. Zaha was to Palace what Vardy was to Leicester and Kane was to Spurs or even Kalvin Phillips to Leeds. The one danger man left in the Palace side was Eberechi Eze, a player Bielsa respected very much indeed. This was a milestone game for Kalvin Phillips who was recording his 200th appearance in all competitions for the club, a record already achieved by both Liam Cooper and Stuart Dallas in the current squad.

As I settled down in front of the TV again to watch the game, the first thing that struck me was that our new pitch still didn't look that flat! Whenever there was a close-up it looked to have a lot of grass on it but also lots of bobbles – like you get when you mow your lawn when it's too wet. That may well have been the case of course with all the recent bad weather but in any case the Leeds players looked to be sliding about less than we did against Everton. In fact in the first couple of minutes Palace hardly had a touch; just one excursion up towards the Kop while Leeds generally passed the ball to and fro looking for an opening. Leeds amassed dozens and dozens of short passes up and down the pitch in the opening couple of minutes with Palace restricted to a couple of interceptions and one catch by their keeper. With the counter on the screen showing 2:30, two minutes and thirty seconds, Palace cut-out the ball in their left-back area and immediately lost it again with a poor clearance that Pascal Struijk got to first. He pushed it forward to Matty Klich, back to goal who, in turn, just nudged it inside to Stuart Dallas. Dallas quickly pushed it to Harrison, now just outside the 'D' in front of the South Stand. Cool Boot Jack took one, two touches getting the ball onto his right foot, and then just hit it. The ball flew over the futile grasping of thin air by Guaita and into the net off the underside of the bar. Replays would show Guaita may have been unlucky in that the ball just took a nick off the outstretched boot of Gary Cahill that may have deceived the Palace keeper; maybe it was Lady Luck paying back the first instalment after having given us nothing at Selhurst Park. It was a fine shot though, with Harrison's 'wrong' foot. Leeds had taken the lead with the first shot of the match, the third time this season we'd managed that, more than any other side in the Premier League. It was the perfect start and I was immediately wondering if this would be another goal-fest.

Well, it wouldn't be as it happens, although Leeds should certainly have been three to the good by halftime. We continued to boss the game throughout the first 45 minutes with only very rare spells of possession for the Eagles and we soon abandoned the 'five at the back' formation that we might have expected to employ with Palace notionally playing 4 – 4 – 2; effectively our constant possession forced Palace to adopt two lines of five. The only thing still giving concern was the pitch; after only five minutes Mateusz Klich suddenly slipped with no one near him, performing a creditable gymnast's 'splits' manoeuvre that brought tears to my eyes never mind his. Thankfully, he got himself upright again and seemed none the worse for wear.

It was fully eight minutes before Palace got into the Leeds box and then it was an over-hit pass easily gathered by Meslier and it was as one-sided a game as we'd yet seen this season. Gradually the chances started to fall to Leeds too, the first, a clever glancing header from Patrick Bamford that Guaita managed to stop at the foot of a post. The first 'big chance' that went begging came after 21 minutes and it was one of those familiar one-on-one situations we saw Patrick Bamford mess up several times in the Championship. He did brilliantly in the first place to create the chance when he read and then intercepted a Palace pass aimed for Gary Cahill, right on the halfway line. Bamford cleverly knocked the ball past Cahill to his left while running himself round the other side of the Palace defender. It was then a straight race down the pitch on his own but, as Guaita came to close him down, he tried to curl the ball with his left foot into the top left corner, much as we saw him do with his third at Villa Park this season. This time though, with far more time and no opposition player near him, he got it all wrong and spooned the ball way over the bar. It really was a bit of déjà vu from the Championship when he always looked more comfortable acting on instinct, when he had no time to think. Give him too long to think about where to put the ball and he invariably messed up the chance. It was hard to criticise him too much though as he'd put away some stunning strikes already this season and he did only cost £7m. Sure, Mo Salah would have scored it 99 times out of 100… but he cost Liverpool £37m and he's probably now worth twice that.

Our second 'big chance' fell to Pascal Struijk just before halftime. Raphinha won a corner that was taken by Kalvin Phillips on the left. The initial corner was bundled away by the Palace rearguard but only as far as Phillips again who lifted it back into the middle. Somehow Pascal found himself a couple of yards of free space between the Palace centre-backs and, falling forward, he only had to place his header either side of Guaita on the line. Incredibly, he seemed to dive too early for the ball and it squirted off his head past the front post. He smashed his fist into the turf in anger at that one and, just for a few seconds I did wonder if maybe Lady Luck wasn't taking this balancing up thing as seriously as she should. Surely we wouldn't rue these missed big chances would we? Once again it was easy to forgive Pascal for this one; if it had been Virgil van Dijk going for the header and not Pascal it was a goal, but, that sort of certainty comes with a price tag of about £75m... So, it was only 1 – 0 at halftime, but it was a very one-sided 1 – 0. The game felt in the balance still despite the dominance Leeds had shown.

The nerves were eased a little just minutes into the second half. A Palace clearance was intercepted by a strong challenge from Kalvin Phillips that sent the ball spinning back towards the visitors' penalty area where Matty Klich collected. He set off moving to the right while Raphinha cut back the other way calling for the pass and Klich delivered a lovely little reverse ball into the path of the Brazilian. He took one little touch and then smashed his left foot through the ball but Guaita read it and did well, moving to his right to stop the shot but pushing it into the path of Bamford. Paddy didn't have any time to think about this one as it came towards his left foot and he instinctively steered it into the bottom right corner. It was his 100th career goal and his 38th for Leeds with the others coming for M K Dons (21), Derby (8), and Middlesbrough (33).

At 2 – 0 it should have felt comfortable but I confess I was agitated throughout the second half. It wasn't that we gave Palace any real chances, but passes would regularly go astray giving up possession cheaply and there was always that feeling that this could still turn into one of those typically 'Leedsy' days where we make a couple of mistakes and sacrifice a couple of points. At times our passing was awful and I did wonder again whether the pitch had anything to do with that; we were not generally slipping over but several times we seemed to lose our footing just as we struck the ball. As it was we survived although, like we did in the first half, we did squander what looked like some good chances. Bamford seemed to meet an Ayling cross perfectly but headed weakly into the keeper's arms and then Pascal Struijk somehow failed to score from almost on the goal-line as he met another Phillips in-swinging corner but again failed to get the right contact. At least we were, for the first time in years, now looking dangerous at our own corners and it was surely only a matter of time before Pascal bagged himself a goal.

There were other chances; Dallas hit one towards the bottom corner that Guaita stopped and Harrison walloped one that bounced on top of the bar while, at the other end, Townsend, a Palace substitute, hit one straight at Meslier. But it ended 2 – 0 and it was, despite being nervy at times, a really good performance from Leeds with little to complain about. Yes, it should have been four or five nil probably, but maybe Lady Luck decided she could save her energies for another day. Towards the end of the game Kalvin Phillips limped off to just tarnish what was otherwise a near perfect evening. Looking back on the game it was only a lack of clinical finishing that really spoiled a near-perfect performance, albeit against a very poor and injury weakened Crystal Palace; that and the loose passing we saw throughout the game. It did seem that the pitch did have something to do with that as Patrick Bamford joked afterwards that he'd taken to using rugby studs on his boots to try to help get some grip. Roy Hodgson also commented on the pitch noting: *"I didn't think our passing was as good [as usual]. The pitch was difficult for both teams... they may be more used to it. It's not the reason we lost the game but it may have affected the way we were able to pass the ball which I didn't think we did well enough."*[1]

The win put Leeds up to 10th in the table on 32 points, 17 ahead of the bottom three. Looking up the table, we were only 7 points adrift of Chelsea in 5th and that had some Leeds fans talking up our chances of a Europa League campaign next season again. For me it was merely satisfying that, once again, we'd shown we were quite capable of regularly getting strong results against the bottom half sides; whether we could now push on and start to get some encouraging results against the top sides was another matter. Arsenal were next up, another test to see if we were yet ready to get that London hoodoo off our backs; we'd at least shown that we could do it on a pitch brought up from London.

Leeds United 2 Crystal Palace 0 (**Harrison 3, Bamford 52**)
BCD. Round 23 League Pos: 10th.

---

[1] *https://www.bbc.co.uk/sport/football/55882704*

London Again! Shrug...

I'd somehow managed to miss the fact it was the Super Bowl on Sunday night; I was probably all TV'd out after watching the Premier League games all weekend. Anyway, a re-run of the highlights suddenly appeared on BBC late on Monday night after the Leeds game. It was the usual spectacular sporting occasion despite the limitations of the Covid regulations. It was billed as the match between two of the all-time great quarterbacks; six-time winner of the Super Bowl, 43-year-old Tom Brady who led the Tampa Bay Buccaneers, and the young pretender, 25-year-old Patrick Mahomes for the Kansas City Chiefs. Tampa won it 31-9 against most predictions. The game was played in front of 25,000 spectators, including 7,000 vaccinated health workers, together with 30,000 crowdies - cardboard cut-outs bought by fans for a hundred bucks a time. Brady, the oldest player to ever play in the Super Bowl, threw three touchdown passes to win the game and claim his 7th winners ring in his 10th Super Bowl appearance. Mahomes probably isn't too bothered though; after leading Kansas

City to their first Super Bowl win in 50 years the previous season, he was rewarded with a 10-year contract making him the *"first half-billion dollar player in sports history"*.

The other news coming out of the States this week was sad news; Mary Wilson, a founding member of the US Motown group 'The Supremes' died suddenly at the age of 76. Formed two years after I was born, they were a huge act in the 60s and 70s and then continued as 'Dianna Ross and the Supremes' before co-founder Dianna Ross left to pursue a solo career. It was a little bit more of my past being dismantled.

It was the next round of the FA Cup this week with all the games played to a finish to decide the quarter-finalists. In the fifth round ties there were wins for Bournemouth, Man United, Man City, Leicester, Sheffield United, Everton, Southampton, and Chelsea. I confess I didn't watch any of the games as I think my mind was still scarred by that crappy Crawley caper.

The Leeds United news this week, such as it was, concerned Marcelo Bielsa's court battle with Lille over his alleged wrongful termination from the club back in 2017. He 'appeared' in court via a video conference and was allowed fifteen minutes for a presentation, twice that by the time his answers were translated. He was claiming some 19 million euros in compensation and the case was due to be adjudicated in July this year.[1] Bielsa was in charge for just 13 games before he was first suspended, and then had his contract terminated by Lille in December 2017. It wouldn't be a Leeds United season without a bit of court action now would it?

It was another long weekend for Leeds United fans as we had to wait until 4:30 pm on Sunday for our game which would be the 7th of the weekend. On Saturday there were wins for Leicester City, Burnley and Manchester City who all scored three goals. Leicester beat Liverpool 3 – 1 who thus slumped to their third consecutive defeat, hardly the stuff of champions. Compare that with Manchester City's 3 – 0 win against Spurs which was their 16th consecutive win in all competitions. City had lost just two of their 36 games this season and their latest win took them a whopping 13 points ahead of Liverpool and maintained their seven-point lead

---

[1] *https://onefootball.com/en/news/marcelo-bielsas-day-in-court-32372047*

ahead of Leicester at the top of the table. They still had a game in hand as well. Burnley's win was a 0 – 3 scoreline at a faltering Crystal Palace who were still without Wilf Zaha, while in the final match on Saturday Brighton and Aston Villa fought out a nil-nil draw. Sunday's games began with Wolves winning 1 – 2 at Southampton, a game between two sides struggling to find their form again having both started the season well. For Southampton this was a 6th consecutive league defeat for the first time in their entire history while, for Wolves, it was only their third win in nine. I then watched as West Brom drew with Manchester United before settling down for our game.

The team news was not totally unexpected, although the absence of Kalvin Phillips, signalled as possible in Bielsa's press conference, was still a disappointment. Knowing that Phillips could be missing, fans had speculated all week as to how Bielsa would respond, with many putting forward their hope that he'd just bring in Shackleton and leave the back four alone. But Bielsa once again opted to shuffle his pack by moving both Ayling and Struijk, a move that surely risked another little spell of re-acclimatisation and a slow start to the game.

Meslier
Shackleton Ayling Cooper (Capt) Alioski (Huggins 53)
Struijk
Raphinha Dallas Klich (Roberts 45) Harrison (Costa 45)
Bamford
Subs: Casilla, Davis, Huggins, Cresswell, Hernandez, Jenkins, Costa, Roberts, Gelhardt.
Arsenal: Leno, Bellerín, David Luiz, Gabriel, Cédric Soares, Ceballos (Holding 89), Xhaka, Saka, Ødegaard (Elneny 78), Smith Rowe (Willian 62), Aubameyang. Subs not used: Ryan, Lacazette, Pépé, Chambers, Marí, Ryan, Martinelli.
Referee: Stuart Attwell.

This was of course another game in London to try to lay that particular hoodoo to rest; we'd won just one of our previous 23 league games played in the capital and it was an albatross that not even Marcelo Bielsa had been able to wrestle from around our necks. Arsenal were fresh from two defeats on the road, at Aston

Villa and Wolves, and their home record was not that great. Towards the back end of last year the Gunners lost four in a row at the Emirates and some saw this as a great opportunity to start to address our poor London record. I didn't! I always thought we'd come unstuck in this one for many reasons, some logical and thought through and others just based on a hunch and our history in games like this. The logic was that we were a few men down; Kalvin Phillips now joined Rodrigo, Koch, and Llorente on the sidelines, all players you'd think were nailed on for the 1st XI. In contrast Arsenal, although coming into this one on the back of two defeats, at least now had the dangerous Aubameyang back after he'd missed a couple of games due to a family illness. I also reasoned that a team full of quality players like the Gunners was unlikely to suffer a third defeat on the trot, although acknowledging that Liverpool had just done exactly that. The other reasons had no logic at all. We were always poor in London and usually suffered bad luck or somehow managed to shoot ourselves in the foot every time we played south of Watford Gap and too many fans were talking up our chances of breaking into the top six in the table and grabbing a place in Europe next season. Every time this season when that looked a possibility we'd lost the next game. No logic I know, but I just had this bad feeling...

And so it proved to be! I'll not dwell on the first half; you will all remember it only too well. A goal down inside the first 15 minutes when that man Aubameyang was allowed to cut inside onto his right boot (as if the whole of the football world didn't know he always does that!) to fire the ball inside the near post with Meslier looking decidedly out of position. We then escaped a penalty decision when VAR suggested that Stuart Attwell's call was perhaps harsh as Liam Cooper toppled over on the falling Saka only for Meslier to then, within minutes, give away a stone-waller as he dawdled over a clearance, not for the first time this season, and then caught Saka on his ankle. Aubameyang walloped the penalty into the top corner. Still we weren't finished with our generosity and next it was Hector Bellerin firing a shot past Meslier that deceived the young stopper at the near post again, albeit from the opposite side to the Gunners' first goal. Leeds had started so sluggishly that it was easy to think that maybe Bielsa had got this wrong today, maybe we were all having to re-learn our defensive roles and maybe it was not coming as easy as it should. Whatever the reason it was a dire first half and it fitted perfectly into the 'cock-ups in London' portfolio.

Bielsa made two changes at halftime signalling that he knew things weren't going well. Off went Matty Klich and Jack Harrison and on came Roberts and Costa. Quite why Bielsa didn't think it was worth giving Pablo Hernandez a try in this situation, I failed to understand. I had to admit that Pablo had not looked great during the few minutes he'd been given this season, but if ever there was a time to give him another chance; this was it. It confirmed in my mind beyond all doubt that his lack of game time was now more to do with the fall out with Bielsa than any injury or form issues. In fact a video would do the rounds on social media after the game showing Bielsa discussing his attitude to player dissent. Although dating from well before the infamous 'armbandgate' episode against Leicester, he described perfectly a similar situation and he firmly denounced any player dissent against his coach. He suggested that if a player is allowed to criticise the decisions of the coach then it follows that the coach can criticise his players but that, he said, completely undermines the trust in the playing group. I paraphrase but that was the gist. I doubted we'd ever see Pablo again and Pablo himself posted a cryptic message on Instagram after the game that seemed to suggest he'd given up on Bielsa. His post seemed to mimic another well-known Bielsa speech that he gave to his Marseille players back in 2015 after his side lost a crucial game to PSG. Pablo's post was translated as: *"Even if it's impossible for you, don't ever complain about anything, swallow the poison of hatred and accept injustices, rest assured that everything is balanced in the end"*.[1] The implication was clearly there that Pablo believed he was suffering an injustice, but presumably his gist was that he would keep his council but that in the end fate would tilt in his favour. Make of it what you will, but I certainly thought it was the end for Pablo under Bielsa.

Quite what Pablo thought as he watched us concede a fourth goal within two minutes of the restart, when Costa carelessly lost the

---

[1] *https://motleedsnews.com/news/pablo-hernandez-posts-cryptic-insta-message-after-clash-v-arsenal/*

ball and then Pascal carelessly lost Aubameyang at the back post, we'll probably never know. Pablo's mood definitely wouldn't have improved though when Bielsa then turned to 20-year-old Niall Huggins and not him for his final substitution. Huggins replaced Alioski, with Stuart Dallas dropping into the left-back spot, Huggins at right-back, and Shackleton moving into his more usual midfield role.

The only surprise in this game is that, once that fourth goal went in, Leeds started to play. It may well be as Luke Ayling said in a post-match interview that *"it's quite easy to play when you're 4 – 0 down and run around and look like you're doing alright 'cos the game's pretty much done by then"*. Arsenal had probably started to ease off too I guess. Nevertheless, Leeds did show their undaunted spirit; it was as if we just pressed the reset button and started from scratch as if there was no score. It helped that more of our players were now in their best positions too. It started with a Raphinha right foot shot that stung the hands of Bernd Leno who pushed it out for a corner. Then, from the left wing corner driven across by Raphinha, it was Pascal Struijk attacking the ball at the near post like all Leeds fans have desperately wanted to see it done for years. Struijk was well above the experienced David Luiz and the ball was thumped into the top corner. What with his several near misses last week and now this, it really did start to look as if we may have found the answer for our own corners. That came in the 58th minute and there was a little glimmer of hope that, even if we couldn't save the match, maybe we could at least remove it from the 'embarrassing' list and put it instead in the 'close-run things' column. It was only 11 minutes later that we made that even more likely as we grabbed a second goal and it was so easy you wondered how we'd made this trip to London so difficult for so long. The two subs were crucially involved though so maybe more credit to Bielsa and he wasn't as daft as some of us thought when he made the changes!

It started with Stuart Dallas pushing up that left wing and he moved the ball inside to Raphinha. The Brazilian then played the incisive ball through the inside left channel into the path of Tyler Roberts, taking Bellerin out of the game at the same time. Tyler got to the byline, pulled the ball back perfectly and Helder Costa was there to stab it home with his right instep, just inside the post. 4 – 2 and I'm sure all Leeds fans were suddenly sitting up a bit straighter. Within another few minutes it could have been, and many will argue should have been, 4 – 3 as Leeds suddenly reverted to the confident, slick passing side we knew we could be. Patrick Bamford touched the ball to his left to Tyler Roberts who immediately played a clever reverse pass back with his heel into the path of Bamford. Patrick then repeated the exercise with an even shorter touch to his right to Jamie Shackleton who took one touch as Bamford carried on his run and then threaded the ball through into the striker's path again, now between two Arsenal defenders. The two red and white shirts sandwiched Bamford and then one threw himself in his path to ensure he wasn't getting that return ball. Down went Paddy who was immediately appealing for the penalty. It wasn't to be though as Attwell waved the claims away and any VAR check, if indeed one was made, was over quickly deciding there was no clear and obvious problem with Attwell's eyesight... although every pundit commenting on the clash would tell us it looked like a penalty to them. Just a standard 'trip to London' decision against Leeds really. I think it's just too far for Lady Luck to travel from Yorkshire to the capital; it must be, she never turns up down there.

That penalty shout, had it been given, could have made the final minutes very tense, although Arsenal also had the chance to go 5 – 2 as Aubameyang crashed a shot against the angle of post and bar with Meslier merely watching and hoping with that one. In a frantic final few minutes, Leeds then had another chance as Niall Huggins poked the ball through for Luke Ayling to get to the byline to the right of goal. His cut-back found Bamford at the near post but he just couldn't get enough on it to turn it home.

That was it. It was another defeat in London, another defeat against Arsenal who we'd not beaten now in nine attempts, and another four goals in the conceded column; the fifth time this season we'd conceded four or more. This Leeds season continued to be a real mishmash of scores with those five heavy defeats but almost as many big wins. By the end of this one I was feeling a lot better about the world than I did when that fourth Arsenal goal went in. At that point I was fretting that it could turn into a total embarrassment. In the end it wasn't and, in fact, for the majority of the second half we showed we were just as good as the home side but we had just given ourselves too much to do Why was that? Well, in short we'd made too many mistakes. Poor Illan Meslier had a bad day, there was no denying that and, depending how harsh you wanted to be, he was at fault for one, two, or even three of the opening goals. For the fourth the finger was pointed at Helder Costa for getting caught in possession and then Pascal Struijk for losing his man at the back post. All four goals were preventable. At the other end, once we got going, we looked sharp and even in this defeat there were a few positives to recognise. That Pascal Struijk header I will remember for a long time; Tyler Roberts looked sharp; Helder Costa, that one error aside, also showed that he was worthy of inclusion, while young Niall Huggins did his future chances no harm at all with a faultless performance showing some nice touches. In many respects, to me, it felt like so many of our trips to London in recent years; we've so often travelled down there in great spirits with great hope only to put in a performance laden with mistakes.

No harm done, we again swapped places with Arsenal in the table but we needed to put this behind us quickly, as the next challenge would be upon us as soon as Friday night, at another of my favourite stadiums; Molineux, in the Black Country.

In the final game played on Sunday, Fulham pulled off the surprise of the day by beating Everton at Goodison with a 0 – 2 scoreline. It was a result that just gave the Cottagers a glimmer of hope that maybe they were not dead yet having spent the first half of the season seemingly on life support along with West Brom and Sheffield United. Then, in the two games on Monday night, we watched as the Blades couldn't do their cause any good as they went down 3 – 0 at West Ham who, for a couple of hours went 4th in the table. Then they were overtaken by a resurgent Chelsea under new manager Tomas Tuchel; they beat Newcastle 2 – 0. The Toon were now looking nervously over their shoulder as Fulham were only 7 points behind them and the Londoners had a game in hand. Leeds were still a comforting 14 points above the bottom three.

Arsenal 4 **Leeds United 2** (Aubameyang 13, 41 pen, 47, Bellerin 45, **Struijk 58, Costa 69**)
BCD. **Round 24 League Pos: 11**th.

Luck 1 Leeds 0

The UK was slowly edging towards the end of lockdown. Daily reported cases of Covid were back down below 10,000 and the daily death figures were falling week on week, although there were still more than 20,000 unfortunate folk in the nation's hospitals with Covid. The vaccination programme continued apace, with the number of adults who'd now had the jab topping 15 million this week. An offer had already been made to every adult over the age of 75, although not all of them had opted to have it. The roll-out was now continuing with the over 65s and, in some areas, the over 60s... that was me of course but our area hadn't started that group yet. It was all good news though and, for football fans, there was a little glimmer of hope that our enforced abstinence from the live game might be coming to an end. Talks were ongoing between the FA and the Government as to when and how fans could be allowed back into grounds with the FA Cup Final and EFL Cup Final being suggested as possible pilot events.

On Monday lunchtime this week I watched on the laptop as the Leeds United Under 23s won again, this time a comfortable 3 – 0 win over Reading with a goal from Liam McCarron and two from Stuart McKinstry. It was the U23s eighth win on the trot and, for a few hours at least, it took them 13 points clear at the top of the table from Stoke City. The Potters then won their game against Norwich 2 – 1 later that evening to close the gap back down to ten points with only eight games left for Leeds to play.

It wasn't all good news this week, for the third time in just over a month I had news of the death of a friend. My buddy Keith messaged to say his wife Gill had died. I've been meeting up with Keith for several seasons at various games, he and Gill had been season-ticket holders for many years and they'd travelled all over Europe following the Whites in days gone by. In recent years Mrs W and I often met up with them before games and we'd shared some memorable times together. They were present when I completed my '92' at Southend one year and another time we shared a table at the Leeds Player of the Year Awards. 2020 had been an awful year for so many people but it was 2021 that had already taken three lovely ladies from us, two of them from the Leeds United family and all of them far too soon... And then we learned that yet another member of the Leeds United family had passed away: Kalvin Phillips posted on social media to say his beloved gran, Granny Val, had died.

A couple of the games postponed from earlier in the season were played this week; Burnley and Fulham drew 1 – 1 in another bottom of the table clash, a result that did more for Burnley than the Londoners as it kept the gap between the Clarets in 15th and Fulham in the bottom three to eight points, although Fulham were looking the most likely of the bottom three to perhaps put a life-saving run together; West Brom and Sheffield United looked to be already gone. In the second game, Manchester City beat Everton 1 – 3 at Goodison to go ten points clear of rivals Man United at the top of the table.

In other football taking place this week, in the Round of 16 Champions League games, there were wins for Liverpool at RB Leipzig and a huge 1 – 4 result for PSG at Barcelona. There were also wins for Porto and Borussia Dortmund. In the Europa League there were good away wins for Manchester United, Tottenham and Rangers, while Arsenal and Leicester both drew, also in away ties. In the Bielsa press conference, on the eve of the Molineux game, we learned that Matty Klich and Diego Llorente were both fit enough to be considered for the game, while the news on Kalvin Phillips and Rodrigo wasn't quite as positive. They were touch and go, but more likely would be kept back until the rearranged Southampton game the following Tuesday. When asked if Pascal Struijk would again play the Phillips holding midfield role, Bielsa declined to answer, which was intriguing although in keeping with his recent comment that he'd no longer be giving out his selections ahead of the games. In another comment though he did sort of intimate that he was in the Leeds project for the long haul. He commented that: *"To have a complete squad in your first year in the Premier League is very difficult. So it's very important to develop some players."* He mentioned this in respect of Pascal Struijk and Jamie Shackleton in particular. Bielsa also noted how expensive it would be to buy a complete team fully competitive for the Premier League saying: *"We have to make reference to how much it would cost to get good players in these positions. The example is Leeds wanted to buy Ben White for £30m and we weren't able to. We have to go in a careful manner and try to evolve the group."* It certainly sounded like he was aware how long this project might take. Leeds boss Andrea Radrizzani wasn't going to be caught unprepared though if Bielsa decided not to do another season; this week he told CBS Sports: *"If he stays, we are really delighted to continue... If the group is happy with him, I am also happy and we should continue. So, it's up to him. We wait on his decision but in any case, myself and Victor [Orta] have already analysed the options and what to do in case Marcelo does not want to be with us."*[1]

The other big news this Thursday, 18th February 2021, was that NASA landed their latest mission on Mars. To say Leeds fans were getting bored waiting to see the Whites in the flesh again was an understatement; tonight my regular travel buddy Kentley and I were

---

[1] *https://www.cbssports.com/soccer/news/leeds-owner-andrea-radrizzani-explains-his-teams-success-welcomes-san-francisco-49ers-investment-and-more/*

both watching the Mars landing on YouTube while messaging each other on WhatsApp! It was a bit of a laugh, Kentley telling me at one point that *"I suppose they can't really take people to Mars can they, what with there being no facilities, runways, immigration and the like"* I replied, *"Yeah but they do have a bar..."*

It would have been nice to be spending Friday afternoon in a bar in Wolverhampton waiting for the game, but Wolverhampton might as well have been Mars for all the possibility we had of being there during this pandemic. No, for Leeds fans everywhere it was still off-limits and so I spent Friday afternoon watching the Leeds United Under 23s on the laptop as they continued their seemingly unstoppable march to Premier League 2, Division 2 glory. This time they beat Norwich City U23s 0 – 2 with a goal from Max Dean and a penalty from Crysencio Summerville to remain ten points clear at the top of the table with only seven games now remaining of the season. It was a feisty affair for an U23 game; there were seven yellow cards and three dismissals, including Nohan Kenneh for Leeds. There was a second penalty for Leeds too but that was slid past the right post by Bobby Kamwa.

It wasn't long before I was settled in front of the TV again ready for the big boys and this time I'd finally worked out how to Bluetooth the laptop to the TV so that the BT Sport broadcast I was logged into via my lad's BT subscription could be cast to the television. It was the best solution I'd so far come across to get a crystal clear picture on the TV screen. I'm sure football fans all over the country were regularly fiddling with their TVs, laptops and phones to get their own optimum solutions to this now very familiar challenge.

Meslier
Ayling Struijk Cooper (Capt) Dallas
Shackleton (Hernandez 66) Klich (Alioski 81)
Raphinha   **Harrison (Costa 81)**
Roberts
Bamford

Subs: Casilla, Alioski, Huggins, Llorente, Davis, Costa, Jenkins, Hernandez, Gelhardt.

Wolves: Rui Patrício, Dendoncker, Coady, Saïss, Nélson Semedo, Neves, João Moutinho, Castro Otto (Marçal 60, Aït-Nouriat 82), Neto, Da Silva (Fábio Silva 87), Traoré.

Subs not used: Ruddy, Hoever, Gibbs-White, Vitinha, Kilman, Otasowie.

Referee: David Coote.

When we first saw the team selection it was still unclear who was going to play the Kalvin Phillips role; even on the LUTV team graphic for example Pascal Struijk was shown in front of a back four of Shackleton, Ayling, Cooper, and Stuart Dallas, exactly as we started at the Emirates. Once the game started though, it was obvious Bielsa had changed it around as some of us thought he might, listening to him evading those questions in the press conference. In fact, Pascal was back in what most people now considered was his best position, centre-back, with Ayling also in his most efficient role at right-back. This meant Jamie Shackleton could also play in his more familiar midfield role alongside Mateusz Klich.

This was a third consecutive game against a side locked in mid-table alongside Leeds. We'd overcome Crystal Palace, lost to Arsenal, and now faced Wolves who started the game one place and two points behind us; very similar to where Arsenal were before the game the previous week. I'd been confident we could win this one, in contrast to how I felt about our trip to London. Wolves had been erratic all season, as evidenced recently when they lost at home to Southampton in the FA Cup only to go to St Mary's three days later in the league and win. All I felt we needed was the rub of the green, something we didn't get in the reverse fixture at Elland Road last October. That was the occasion you will remember when Leeds dominated from the off but then succumbed to a 70th-minute Jimenez shot that deflected wildly off Kalvin Phillips' bonce. Lady Luck just had it in for us that day which was another reason I thought we'd be OK today; these things even out over time don't they? In fact, the only thing just concerning me a little bit was the absence of Phillips today; Leeds had lost the previous four games when he'd been missing. That wasn't quite so bad as that Crystal Palace record when playing without Wilf Zaha (Palace had lost 18 of their last 20 Premier League games without the 28-year-old featuring, failing to score in all but two of those 18!) but everyone acknowledged how important Kalvin was to us.

Wolves kicked off with the brand new white Nike Flight football making its Premier League debut; the third different ball to be used this season. The design featured: *"a bespoke graphic designed to reflect the intensity of the final stages of the Premier League, when the focus of the teams and players narrows and the Premier League Trophy is in sight."* or so the official Premier League website told us. I just hoped it would bounce nicely for us.

The first half was a fairly even half of football. Patrick Bamford had an early effort blocked after a good run from Tyler Roberts while, at the other end, Illan Meslier pulled off a superb finger-tip save to prevent a Ruben Neves shot, deflected off the boot of Stuart Dallas, finding the top left corner. Then, with twenty minutes gone, the first big chance came for Leeds as Liam Cooper found space 12 yards out to meet a Raphinha right wing free-kick but directed his header straight into the gloves of Rui Patrício on the first bounce.

It seemed that every Premier League game for months on end had been played in pouring rain and this was no different, plus there was a wicked wind blowing around Molineux to make conditions even more tricky; maybe that's a small excuse for the Cooper header not finding the net. That new ball wasn't exactly helping us either; a Raphinha right wing corner eventually led to a shot from Matty Klich from a very acute angle. It beat Patrício but struck the post and somehow then bounced away from goal and not in off the fumbling keeper as it could so easily have done. It fell for Pascal Struijk who walloped it with his right foot only for the keeper to push that one back out and then Pascal had a go with his left foot but that one was blocked. Roberts then blasted the loose ball past the far post. In some games, those four shots would have resulted in four goals!

Back at the other end again and Illan Meslier was looking very assured this week, twice denying Nelson Semedo from a tight angle, clearly intent on not being beaten again at his near post. At halftime therefore it was still 0 – 0 with little between the two teams. Wolves had nine attempts, Leeds eight, although Wolves had hit the target with five of theirs compared with only three for Leeds. There had been four corners apiece and Leeds had looked far more comfortable than usual in defending theirs while Pascal Struijk was our new hope in attacking them at the other end.

The second half began in the same manner, with both sides trading long-range shots but most ending up in the stands. Then, in the 62nd minute, Raphinha lined up another free-kick out near the right touchline and midway in the Wolves half. The Brazilian was taking every Leeds set-piece in the absence of Kalvin Phillips and most were right on the money. This one was perfect too; curling in behind the old-gold shirts of the Wolves back line right onto the head of Liam Cooper. Coops met it on the full and powered the header at goal but it was straight at the keeper who was able to push it straight back out. This time Patrick Bamford got his head to it but again a combination of a defender and the keeper pushed it away. It was tempting to think that, had that been one of the multi-million pound Premier League centre-backs instead of our Coops, that was a goal all the way and maybe it was just that little bit of quality that was preventing us winning some of these close encounters. I was still blaspheming about the header as Wolves collected the ball again from a hefty heave down the middle by Stuart Dallas and they then moved it steadily up-field towards the Leeds goal. It was a goal out of nothing but it showed how important it was to have Lady Luck on your team.

Traore had the ball tight to the Wolves left wing, right on the touchline across the pitch from where we ought to have been and near halfway. He spun and motored away leaving Luke Ayling in his wake, tacking across the pitch like a little sailing boat using a strong wind. He had Pascal Struijk in close attention as he reached the centre of the pitch but he was still 25 yards from goal when he got just the yard he needed to unleash a powerful right foot shot. The ball looked destined for the top right corner as Illan Meslier took off with a mighty leap to his left; the ball struck the woodwork right in the angle of post and bar, bounced down, and then cannoned of the back of the prostrate Meslier and rolled gently into the net. Once again Leeds had been undone by an unlucky bounce of the ball; we'd watched earlier when Matty Klich's shot had beaten Patrício but Lady Luck had steered that rebound past the keeper but now this one had bounced back in the net. I immediately thought back to that deflected shot at Elland Road and I sat shaking my head at the unfairness of it all. It was unfair on Illan Meslier too, he'd surely suffered enough the previous week and yet now he'd been undone like this.

Leeds battled away to try to find an equaliser but Wolves were now content to sit back and defend for their lives. This new ball seemed to have a magnet in it that was attracted to Liam Cooper as most of our chances fell to him. Another Raphinha free-kick found him at the back post but his stretching leg could only poke the ball straight at the keeper and then he mistimed another header from a Harrison left wing corner. Leeds had made one change just after the Wolves goal as Pablo Hernandez replaced Jamie Shackleton and Pablo looked back to his old self while not often enough unlocking a stubborn Wolves defence and, when he did, that little bit of luck we needed just wasn't there. He pushed the ball through for Tyler Roberts who then sent it along the turf into the path of Bamford. Paddy creamed the ball into the top right corner but then, once VAR had it's say with a myriad of lines criss-crossing the screen, he was adjudged to be offside. It was the Crystal Palace nonsense all over again and if he *was* offside it could be by no more than an inch. On such moments and fine margins games turn.

Alioski and Costa got minutes towards the end, replacing Klich and Harrison, and Costa will still be kicking himself for fluffing a great chance right at the end to score against his former club. Raphinha was the provider again as he lofted the ball down the middle into the Wolves area. Helder Costa was under it with a Wolves defender but did brilliantly to trap the ball and shift it onto his right foot but then weakly scuffed his shot straight at Patrício who saved with his legs; that wasn't luck, that was poor finishing.

So, Wolves became the first side to complete a league double over Marcelo Bielsa in a top-flight game since Montpellier and Paris St-Germain defeated his Marseille side home and away in Ligue 1 in 2014-15; it was a sixth loss in nine games for Leeds and several of those games were against sides in our mid-section of the table. But, whereas some of our recent defeats had been of our own making, there was little to criticise about this one. Sometimes it doesn't matter how well you play, how much you dominate a game, sometimes a result is just down to bad luck. It's what makes predicting football results so difficult. You can always weigh up one side's qualities against another, look at current form and which side is struggling most with injuries, all of that stuff, but by its very nature, you cannot forecast what part luck will play. They say it evens out in the long run but it clearly doesn't even out over home and away matches in the Premier League. Wolves had got away with six points from Leeds this season when all logic would say they should only have had two at most. There is a school of thought in the game, the fatalist view I guess, that says you have to ensure that luck plays no part in a match; if you do everything right, take your chances and not make mistakes then, other things being equal, any odd bad bounce of the ball shouldn't define the final result and I have some sympathy with that view. Marcelo Bielsa also refused to blame luck after the game saying: *"Luck is not a factor in the result. It's clear the result was defined by their efficiency. Luck and what you deserve is not always the same. Look at the chances we had, we had double [what] they did, and we defended well, we attacked well. There were only a few moments in the game where we didn't dominate. We had 10 chances and we weren't able to score a goal, they had five and scored one. That explains the game."*[1]

Wolves boss Nuno Espirito Santo recognised the luck his side had benefitted from but felt they deserved it: *"There's luck with the goal but the strike of Adama is fantastic. It was almost unstoppable and I think we deserved that luck."* No Nuno, you didn't, and I don't think we deserved to be beaten by a strike that won't even feature in the shots on target statistics, think about that! Perhaps it was the absence of Kalvin Phillips that was the most crucial factor; with him in the side, we had a 50% win ratio this season; without him it was now just 17% - it would be wouldn't it?

With our game taking place on Friday night, the first of this round of matches, we were then able to watch the rest of the weekend's games in a fairly detached manner; albeit interested to see if any of the sides below us could close the gap we had between ourselves and the three relegation slots. On Saturday, the first game saw Southampton, our next opponents, draw 1 – 1 with Chelsea to end the Saints' record-breaking run of six defeats on the trot. Trust them to find some form just before arriving at Elland Road! Burnley and West Brom then played out a nil-nil draw that was far more useful to the Clarets than the Albion who were left mired in the bottom three, nine points from safety. Liverpool then continued to destroy accumulators as they lost a fourth consecutive game at Anfield – something not done since 1923 – going down 0 – 2 to

---

[1] *https://www.belfasttelegraph.co.uk/sport/football/premier-league/marcelo-bielsa-bemoans-missed-chances-after-wolves-edge-victory-over-leeds-40111808.html*

local rivals Everton. That result left Liverpool and Everton in 6th and 7th places in the table, both with 40 points and therefore both just three points adrift of Chelsea in the fourth Champions League place. The final game of the day saw two of the bottom three fighting it out, with Fulham just edging it 1 – 0 over Sheffield United who were therefore pretty much beyond redemption. Fulham however were really making a fight of it and this result put them only three points behind Newcastle, the first of the sides above that all-important relegation drop zone. It also had Leeds fans searching their cupboards for their lucky rabbits' feet as the gap to Leeds was down to ten points, although if we were in trouble, so were the five sides between us in 12th and the Londoners in 18th.

On Sunday there were four more games and, stoically, I watched all four. West Ham beat Spurs 2 – 1 to grab that fourth Champions League spot from Chelsea while leaving Mourinho's Spurs down in ninth and only four points ahead of Leeds. Leicester City then consolidated their top-four credentials with a 1 – 2 win at Aston Villa for whom Jack Grealish was out injured. Grealish was almost as influential for Villa as Zaha was for Palace or Kalvin Phillips was for us. Most teams seemed to have one crucial player; Fernandes for Man U, De Bruyne for City, Vardy for Leicester etc. etc. Talking of Kevin de Bruyne, he returned after injury to help City win 0 – 1 at Arsenal to keep the Blues on track for the title.

In the final game on Sunday, Man United beat Newcastle 3 – 1, a result that pushed the Reds back into second place, displacing Leicester on goal difference. The result was another blow for the Toon though who were still just those three points ahead of Fulham. There was still one final game of this 25th round of games to go and that was on Monday night with Brighton hosting Crystal Palace in the so-called M23 Derby!

Wolverhampton Wanderers 1 **Leeds United 0** (Meslier 64 og.)
BCD. **Round 25 League Pos: 12th**

Saints on the Slide

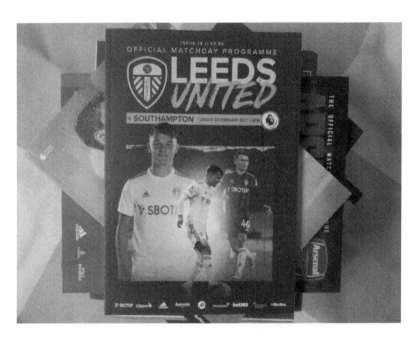

I watched the M23 derby on Monday night, an incredible game in which Brighton absolutely battered Palace with 75% of the possession, a massive 25 attempts on goal to a meagre three from Palace, and 13 corners to none. Yet Palace won it 2 – 1 with a 95th-minute Benteke volley. It was yet more proof, if proof were still needed, that goals win games; nothing else really matters. Palace thus hauled themselves above Southampton to join Leeds on 32 points; the Saints being our next visitors the following night in the match rearranged from five weeks earlier.

The sheer one-sided nature of the Brighton v Palace game and the fact that Palace managed to steal the points, reminded me very much of the last time Southampton were at Elland Road for a league game. Saints' last visit was in October 2012 in the League Cup when they sent a weakened side and were well beaten, but the last visit in the league was a Championship game the previous March. Southampton were on their way to promotion, sat top of the table, while Leeds were desperately trying to scrape into the play-offs, a task we failed in partly due to dropping three points to the Saints. We'd gone behind to a Rickie Lambert volley in the first quarter of an hour and then proceeded to batter Saints' goal for the rest of the game. We hit the woodwork twice and Southampton keeper Kelvin Davis was inspired, so much so that his teammates mobbed him at the final whistle. It was just one of those games when we could have played for another hour and not scored. However well you play, however dominant you are, sometimes you just need that little rub of the green. We were due some luck this week I reckoned after that Wolves annoyance...

Earlier on Monday, Boris Johnson hosted the latest Downing Street press conference, this one outlining his 'roadmap' out of lockdown. It was going to be a while yet before we got back to anything like normality but at least the way was clear now for a staged relaxation of restrictions over the coming weeks and months. Schools would be going back on 8th March; after 29th March the 'stay at home' rule would cease to apply and two households could meet outdoors; and on 12th April all shops could reopen and pubs could start serving outdoors. Then, 17th May was the big one: pubs could serve indoors and major sports stadia could reopen up to a maximum of one-quarter capacity or 10,000 people, whichever was the lower. Leeds fans quickly assessed that Elland Road would be able to host around 8,000 or 9,000 fans but there was only currently scheduled to be one game after 17th May; the final day of the EPL season was 23rd May when Leeds would host West Brom. All the dates were subject to the figures on infection rates, hospital numbers, and the vaccine roll-out all continuing to go in the right direction but there were some obvious perils in opening grounds just for the final game of the season. What if a team playing away on the final day needed points to survive? Was it fair that, for the first time in the season, for perhaps their most crucial game, there would be a hostile home crowd to face albeit a small one? There was a significant amount of cash applied to each position in the table too, so every point was vital and a home crowd could make a difference. How would a club like Leeds with 22,000 season-ticket holders choose the lucky fans? And did the club not realise the likelihood, if pubs were open, that tens of thousands of Leeds fans would travel to the ground anyway and celebrate outside just for the craic? Would that be safe? Lots to ponder for the authorities and the clubs there.

Southampton arrived at Elland Road on the back of a dire run of results that had completely derailed what, at one time, looked like being a tremendous season for them. They lost just four of their first 17 (they should have been wary!) Premier League fixtures and at that point were sitting pretty in 6th place, level with Manchester City in 5th on 29 points. Then they lost six in a row including that 9 – 0 drubbing at Old Trafford and only halted that sequence at the weekend when they drew with Chelsea. Had we caught them just after a turning point?

This felt like another big game to me; it was not worth any more or less than three points of course but I just felt we needed an injection of confidence again. We'd gone through the whole season so far without putting together a run of any particular results; we'd at most won two on the trot and at worst only lost two on the trot and we'd still only drawn two games all season. Each time we won a couple, we got ourselves to within a few points of a Europa League spot and Leeds fans were checking the expiry dates on their passports. Each time we lost a couple, Leeds fans were seeking out their lucky rabbits' feet and checking the Fulham fixtures. Once again we'd go into this game on the back of two defeats – one pretty much self-inflicted at Arsenal and one that Lady Luck played a huge part in - so we certainly didn't want to damage confidence further by stringing three defeats together for the first time.

In the press conference this week Bielsa confirmed we'd still be without Phillips and Rodrigo but that Llorente was fit and available. Bielsa was a bit coy when he was asked if Pascal Struijk would play the Phillips role again after the experiment of using Jamie Shackleton as a second defensive midfielder alongside Matty Klich. I sort of got the impression Bielsa was contemplating something different again but wasn't sure what it might be. When the team was announced ahead of the game, all became clear.

Meslier
Llorente Struijk Cooper (Capt)
Ayling   Dallas
Raphinha Roberts (Hernandez 75) Klich (Alioski 59) Harrison
(Costa 45)
Bamford

Subs: Casilla, Alioski, Cresswell, Huggins, Jenkins, Hernandez, Roberts, Gelhardt, Costa.

Southampton: McCarthy, Bednarek, Vestergaard, Salisu, Bertrand, Armstrong, Ward-Prowse, Romeu (Djenepo 70), Tella (Minamino 58), Adams, Redmond (Ings 58). Subs not used: Forster, Stephens, Ramsay, N'Lundulu, Jankewitz, Chauke.

Referee: Andre Marriner.

So it was to be Diego Llorente playing the defensive midfield role or, if need be, we could go with three at the back. The introduction again of Llorente was the only change from the Wolves defeat with Shackleton missing out.

This game was a live on Sky 6 pm kick-off and so I was settled down in front of the TV by 5:30 pm to watch all the preamble. When the Leeds players emerged from the tunnel the cameras were trained on Patrick Bamford, who this week was holding an iPad to give some kids the semblance of a match-day mascot experience via a Zoom conference. It was all part of a scheme whereby Bamford had donated £5,000 to Beeston Primary School to buy 20 new iPads to be loaned out to families for remote learning during the pandemic. Patrick then set up a little competition for the kids that resulted in 11 lucky winners taking part in the live zoom call ahead of the game.

The first half resembled the Wolves match; it was tight and both sides had chances but, for once, when we needed the rub of the green we got it. The first big chance fell to Leeds in the 24th minute when Raphinha slalomed through the Saints back line to pull the ball back perfectly for Tyler Roberts. Sadly, Roberts' finish left a lot to be desired and he smashed it well over the bar. Ten minutes later though and that first rub of the green moment arrived.

Former Arsenal academy winger Nathan Tella was making his debut for the Saints tonight and he was certainly causing Leeds some problems. Tella was part of the 2015 scholarship intake at Arsenal along with the likes of Eddie Nketiah and Joe Willock who also made the grade in the EPL this season with Newcastle. He'd already got through earlier in the game to fire a shot at Meslier but now he was being shepherded down the side of the Leeds area by Diego Llorente. Suddenly, Tella appeared to trip and went down, while Llorente threw up his arms as if to say *"I didn't touch him ref!"*. Unfortunately, referee Andre Marriner wasn't persuaded by our man and he immediately pointed at the spot. After Sky showed a couple of replays it soon became clear why Llorente was so adamant he wasn't guilty; replays showed clearly that Tella, young as he may be, was already skilled in the strikers' dark art of diving. It was Tella who'd kicked his right boot out at Llorente as he went past and when he felt the contact the Saint took a dive. It was clear the Saint had sinned but there was now the wait with bated breath to see if Kevin Friend, the man on VAR duty today, had seen what we'd now all been shown. Thankfully he had and, rather reluctantly I thought from his mannerisms, Marriner made the VAR screen sign with his hands and then pointed for the free-kick to Leeds. It was such a big moment and we've all seen similar situations where obvious dives are still given as penalties, but this time they got it right; on such moments do games turn. The one disappointment, echoed by Graeme Souness in the Sky studio at halftime, was that no disciplinary action was taken against Tella for clearly trying to con the ref. There was one more big moment just before the break.

Southampton won a free-kick midway in the Leeds half, just to the right of the centre of the pitch. Referee Marriner walked away to take up his position near the 'D' while James Ward-Prowse, waited to take the kick. He looked like he wasn't ready and was looking everywhere but towards the Leeds goal. Suddenly Ward-Prowse stabbed the ball straight into the Leeds box all along the turf and the only player awake was Che Adams who let it slide past before slamming it into the net past a dumb-struck Meslier. Marriner was now blowing his whistle and holding it up explaining he wasn't ready and the kick had to be taken again. Replays would clearly show the referee had his back to the action and had only just started to raise his whistle to his mouth as Ward-Prowse took the kick but it was such a close-run thing that you had to conclude we'd got away with one; Leeds' defence was asleep and had Saints waited just a fraction of a second I'm certain Leeds had not read what was about to happen.

So, the two big moments in the half both went our way; yes they were both absolutely correct decisions, but so often we've seen such things go unchecked. Apart from those incidents, the sides were pretty even and there were a couple of decent half-chances at either end; a break from half-way saw Raphinha tackled brilliantly just as he was about to pull the trigger and Stuart Dallas stretched to poke a shot that was tipped over the bar after a clever Raphinha free-kick found Llorente unmarked. For their part, Saints had a shot from Tella saved by Meslier and a Vestergaard header flashed wide. The one other significant aspect of the first half was that both sides found the new Elland Road pitch to be more like a skid pan on a snowy day than a billiard table as most players lost their footing at one time or another. It really did seem like the top surface was unstable, as if it hadn't bedded down properly. If anything, and surprisingly, it seemed to affect Leeds more than the visitors for some reason.

I didn't know what to think as I refilled my glass at halftime: it had been a close-run thing and we'd got some breaks but I still felt it was important to use that good fortune now and get a result out of the game, otherwise it would feel like we'd wasted it. Fortunately the second half was only a couple of minutes old when we did indeed stake our claim for the points.

Leeds had made one change at the break as Helder Costa was given another run-out in place of a subdued Jack Harrison. In fact, there was general agreement amongst Leeds fans on social media (an unusual state of affairs) that Jack had been 'below par' for a couple of weeks now while Costa had always looked sharp when he'd arrived on the pitch. The ball spent most of the first 90 seconds of the second period in the Leeds half, with the only real worry being one of Illan Meslier's poor clearances that went out for a Saints throw over the west touchline. Fortunately that Southampton attack then ended with a tame shot straight into the arms of the Leeds keeper. This time he quickly rolled the ball out to Diego Llorente, who was actually playing more as the right side of a three-man back-line with Struijk and Cooper. That wasn't unusual of course since Southampton were playing with two strikers; Redmond and Che Adams. Llorente weighed up his options and then played a diagonal ball all along the turf to Tyler Roberts who'd found himself a few yards of space in the centre-circle. He struggled to stay on his feet on the slippery surface as he turned almost full circle but then he spotted a run through the centre by Patrick Bamford and managed to send the ball right into Bamford's path, dissecting the two Southampton centre-backs. Paddy let the ball run across his body onto his left foot and then struck it through the legs of the challenging Vestergaard to find the perfect spot just inside the right post. It was a fine accurate strike for Bamford's 13th goal of this profitable season for him.

For whatever reason, going a goal up only made me more nervous as the second half developed. I suppose it was the fact that, having worked so hard to get the lead and having ridden our luck in the first half, it would now be doubly annoying if we wasted the opportunity. Tyler Roberts almost made me a lot more comfortable as, within minutes of the Bamford goal, he almost doubled the lead. It was that magician Raphinha again who brilliantly collected a long ball over the top of the Saints back line from Liam Cooper in the inside left channel. He got almost to the byline, pulled the ball back all along the turf and there was Roberts steaming in. Sadly he made great contact with his right instep but the ball curled inches past the right-hand post.

Southampton weren't giving this one up quite yet and next we needed Illan Meslier again to be sharp as he saved a Stuart Armstrong shot down near the foot of his right-hand post. I cringed just before Armstrong shot as I could clearly see the big white number '17' on the back of his red shirt. Back came Leeds and another big chance for Patrick Bamford as Stuart Dallas found him unmarked on the right corner of the six-yard box. Bamford thumped it at goal with his right boot but that was pushed straight back to him by Alex McCarthy. This time Bamford shifted the ball inside to Roberts but his shot was tame and easily collected by the Saints' keeper. Leeds had hit a little purple patch now and next it was Llorente of all people arriving in the box to stab a snap-shot that McCarthy was lucky to get a boot to and knock it clear. Helder Costa had made a real difference operating down the right hand side and Leeds had taken to playing regular long balls down that wing that he was gobbling up. Leeds also now had Hernandez and Alioski on the pitch for Roberts and Klich. Costa was onto another long pass as the clock ticked onto 78 minutes.

Stuart Dallas carried the ball a few yards deep in his own half before sending it out wide for Costa to chase after again; Dallas meanwhile continued to jog forward. No one had gone to mark Dallas so, as he arrived on the edge of the area, he had plenty of time to trap the return pass from Costa and then spear it with a sort of angled left-foot toe-poke inside the left post before the Southampton rearguard could get to him. 2 – 0 and I was feeling a lot better, although some of that comfort was no doubt coming from the tumbler of Penderyn single malt I'd grabbed a few minutes earlier. As Dallas celebrated with the rest of the team he pointed to that big toe that had done the damage and then he grabbed a shirt from somewhere that had the name *"GRANNY VAL"* printed on the back; he briefly held it up for the cameras.

If we thought the evening was good already there was still one more magic moment to come as Leeds were awarded a free-kick about 27 yards out in the inside right slot. Raphinha stood over it and then clipped a stunning left foot shot that just scraped inside the left post, bouncing right on the goal line with McCarthy's arms just not long enough to reach it. As part of his celebration, Raphinha whipped off his shirt to reveal an undershirt with a long message written on it as he stood facing the TV cameras. Later the message was translated as: *"Much strength for the Assis Moreira Family. Rest in Peace Donna Migudina"*. It was a message of support for the family of his fellow Brazilian, Ronaldinho, after the passing of his mother. When the final whistle blew all the Leeds players gathered for a group photo with that 'GRANNY VAL' shirt again and Liam Cooper would later post it on social media with a message of support for Kalvin Phillips.

And that was that; in the end a superb and ultimately comfortable 3 – 0 victory that pushed Leeds back into the top half of the table on 35 points; a point ahead of Arsenal and only one behind Tottenham. We were only five points adrift of Liverpool and Everton in 6th and 7th places. Every team apart from Everton and Spurs had now completed their first 25 games, so the table was pretty much representative of the season to date.

I'd been nervous throughout the first 77 minutes of this game, until that Dallas toe-poke went in, but now I could relax and finish another glass of malt. We'd got close to those European places a few times before already this season and usually then lost our next game so I wasn't going to get carried away this time, but the key thing was we were almost secure for another tilt at the EPL next season. Most Leeds fans thought one more win would probably do it; it would be nice to do it on Saturday against Aston Villa.

Leeds 3 Southampton 0 **(Bamford 47, Dallas 78, Raphinha 84).**
BCD. Round 25 League Pos: 10th.

Villa but Familiar

If there was any doubt about the magnitude of Leeds' achievement in holding down a mid-table place in the Premier League in our first season back, then you only had to look at how both Fulham and West Brom were still mired in the muddy waters of the relegation zone; Leeds had clearly done something better than our fellow promoted clubs. Some empirical evidence was also published this week on the excellent Planet Football website. It has long been recognised that probably the best indicator as to where a club will finish in the Premier League is their wage bill, a hypothesis put forward back in 2009 by Simon Kuper and Stefan Szymanski in the excellent tome 'Soccernomics'. This week 'Planet Football' published the current list of estimated wage bills and compared it to the current Premier League table. The big six were obviously way ahead of the other clubs in terms of spend, and four of them were pretty much where you'd expect them to be amongst the top six in the table. Only Arsenal and Spurs were currently out of position. All of the big six had a wage bill of more than £100 million per year, with Manchester United topping the lot at a staggering £183 million. Only Sheffield United were spending less on their playing squad than Leeds, so you could argue that the Blades were only really getting what they were paying for while Leeds were clearly over-achieving by some distance. It was estimated that the current wage bill at Leeds was around £22 million. If you think about it, there is logic in this theory; the best players ought to command the highest wages, almost by definition, and the highest-paid squads should therefore be the best teams, although a highly paid squad still needed to be organised into an efficient unit. There's a bit of chicken and egg too, in that obviously a club needs to have the money in the first place to pay the higher wages and that was exactly the state of play Leeds were now in; if we could consolidate our position in the Premier League for a few seasons then we'd have the Premier League TV money to invest in better players who cost higher wages. If some of the young players could also be developed to become top players then that helped as well, as you can save the extortionate transfer fees and take a little time before having to pay top dollar wages to them.[1] For now, Leeds appeared to be steering an excellent course; we'd invested in a few top-quality players, and they, in conjunction with the work ethic of the bulk of the Championship squad and some talented young players coming through the academy, had been ably moulded into a solid mid-table team by El Loco himself, Marcelo Bielsa. This had been achieved despite a string of injuries too; In terms of games missed by first-team squad players due to injury, Leeds were third in that particular table with only Crystal Palace and Liverpool having suffered more.

Someone who'd not done quite such a good job this season was Neil Lennon. This week Lennon resigned as Celtic manager with the Hoops 18 points adrift of Rangers at the top of the Scottish Premiership and seemingly destined not to achieve a tenth straight title win.

---

[1] *https://www.planetfootball.com/quick-reads/how-every-premier-league-clubs-wage-bill-compares-to-their-league-position/?fbclid=IwAR1dfNbMf4AhhgI_kUSWX8ppDjaRt56ekrzo6snkrW GMnXhJJSbij-wB_04*

On Friday, the eve of the home game with Aston Villa, there was sad news doing the rounds on social media and confirmed in a statement from Leeds United. The club announced that Peter Lorimer was in a hospice *"battling a long-term illness"*. 'Lash' was the club's all-time record goal-scorer, having bagged 238 goals in all competitions for Leeds in a career with us lasting more than twenty years. I was digesting this bad news as Mrs W and I watched online the funeral service of our good friend Carmel who'd been taken by Covid at the end of January. It was a sad day all round...

On Wednesday and Thursday this week there were more European games played. In the Champions League, Manchester City continued their relentless pursuit of four trophies this season as they comfortably beat Borussia Monchengladbach 0 – 2 in a game played in Budapest due to German Covid restrictions prohibiting arrivals from nations with cases of the new variants of Covid. It was City's 19th consecutive victory in all competitions. In the second game played this week, Real Madrid won 0 – 1 in Atalanta. In the Europa League, Spurs beat Wolfsberger AC 4 – 0 to record an 8 – 1 aggregate score as they went through to the last 16. Wolfsberger were actually listed in the results as 'RZ Pellets WAC' as part of some peculiar sponsorship arrangement. On Thursday, Arsenal, Rangers, and Manchester United joined Spurs in that final 16 while Leicester City bowed out of the competition as they surprisingly lost 0 – 2 against Slavia Prague.

Premier League round 26 kicked off on Saturday lunchtime, with yet another Manchester City win. This time they beat West Ham United 2 – 1 at the Etihad, their 20th consecutive win in all competitions and one that took them 13 points clear at the top again. Next came the three o'clock kick-off, a crunch bottom of the table game between West Brom and Brighton. This was another game with the dangerous combination of Lee Mason as referee and Simon Hooper on VAR duty; predictably the game turned into a complete farce. It was won by West Brom by a single early goal, a goal that just about kept the Baggies' hopes of survival alive, but there were three other big moments featuring Messrs Mason and Hooper. There were two penalty awards to Brighton. The first, one of those dubious ones where the ball brushes a raised arm, could have gone either way to be honest but Mason gave it and VAR agreed; Pascal Groß smacked that one against the crossbar though. Then, just before the break, Brighton were awarded a free-kick outside the Albion area. It was all a bit reminiscent of the disallowed Saints' goal against Leeds earlier in the week. West Brom were slow getting ready to defend the kick with Sam Johnstone still stood at one post finalising his wall as Lee Mason blew his whistle. Lewis Dunk was alive and alert and struck the ball at goal just a nanosecond after the whistle and it flew into the unguarded net. Mason clearly realised that the keeper wasn't ready as soon as he blew the first whistle so immediately blew it again and disallowed the 'goal' only to then panic and award it after protests from the Brighton players. Enter stage left Mr Hooper on VAR. Hooper the Blooper had spotted that the second whistle had possibly been sounded before the ball crossed the goal line and so he called Mason to the monitor and, for a third time, Mason the Mystified changed his mind and ruled the 'goal' out. It was farcical and what Mason was lacking was the self-belief and awareness shown by Andre Marriner at Elland Road. Mason wasn't finished yet though and in the second half he awarded Brighton a second penalty, this time believing Pascal Groß had been brought down by Conor Townsend. Replays showed it was a ludicrously soft award with Townsend clearly getting the ball and Groß collapsing like a dying swan. Did VAR spot that? Well, if it did Hooper kept quiet and the penalty stood. Fortunately Danny Welbeck smacked that one against a post. If Brighton hadn't had bad luck, they'd have had no luck at all. If Brighton do subsequently get relegated this season I mused, they will only have themselves to blame. As to the performance of Lee Mason, it was not as if the football authorities hadn't been warned before. Wolves' boss Nuno Espirito Santo picked up a £25,000 fine after he complained about Mason after the Wolves defeat against Burnley last December. Nuno's words at the time now seem prophetic: *"The referee does not have the quality to whistle a game in the Premier League. It is not about the crucial mistakes or decisions, it is about the way he handles the game. The players get nervous, too much voices, he whistles by the voices when some players are shouting... I hope he doesn't whistle a game of ours again because all the games we have with Lee Mason are always the same. He cannot control the players, the players are constantly arguing – both teams. With all the other referees the game flows, there's dialogue. He's just not ready to do it.*"[1]

Nuno refused to apologise for his comments so convinced was he about the truth of them, but here we were again just weeks later with another embarrassing Lee Mason episode. Maybe this time some lasting action would be taken. Incidentally, an interesting comparison between football and rugby came to light today following the Six Nations rugby clash between Wales and England. An ultimately emphatic Welsh victory was shrouded in controversy after French referee Pascal Gauzere awarded two controversial Welsh tries inside the opening 30 minutes, the first of which former England captain and boss Martin Johnson described as: *"absolutely appalling".* But England manager Eddie Jones refused to condemn the referee in the way Nuno did about Lee Mason, noting only that: *"We can't debate it, we are not allowed to debate it. All I will end up with is a fine and that won't help anyone,"* He continued with tongue firmly in cheek: *"The dog won't be able to eat its food, the wife won't be able to eat, so I can't say anything."*

Finally, 5:30 pm arrived and our game with Villa, live on Sky TV, was next up and Leeds fans were hoping for better from referee Peter Bankes.

The talk about maybe some fans getting to see the last game of the season in the flesh was still doing the rounds and I felt I was a little step closer having had my first jab along with Mrs W this week. The Government was apparently reviewing the possibility of vaccine passports for things like international travel, sports events and even visiting the pub, so I was happy to have the vaccine just in case. Thankfully I suffered no side effects whatsoever and so was in good fettle as I settled down in front of the TV again.

The team news was not entirely unexpected; it was the same team that started against the Saints with the one exception that Helder Costa got the nod over Jack Harrison who he'd replaced at halftime in the win at Elland Road on Tuesday. Most Leeds fans agreed that Harrison had been quiet in recent games although some were not convinced Costa was the better player. The good news for Leeds

---

[1] https://www.theguardian.com/football/2020/dec/31/fa-charges-nuno-espirito-santo-over-comments-about-referee-mason

fans was that Jack Grealish had not recovered from a muscle injury and would not feature; Villa's record without their talisman was not great. In fact they had won only three games out of the previous 18 when Grealish hadn't played which was a record getting towards the extremes of Crystal Palace without Zaha. We had our own talisman still missing though of course; Kalvin Phillips was still out and our record was not great without him in the side.

Meslier
Ayling Llorente Cooper (Capt) Dallas
Struijk
Raphinha Roberts Klich Costa
Bamford
Subs: Casilla, Alioski, Davis, Cresswell, Jenkins, Huggins, Hernandez, Harrison, Gelhardt.

Aston Villa: Martínez, El Mohamady, Konsa, Mings, Targett, McGinn, Nakamba, Ramsey (Sanson79), Traoré, Watkins, El Ghazi (Trézéguetat 88). Subs not used: Heaton, Taylor, Douglas Luiz, Barkley, Engels, Davis, Hayden.

Referee: Peter Bankes.

I thought Leeds were odds-on to win this one; Villa didn't have that man Grealish, Leeds had got back to form and had tamed the skid pan of Elland Road on Tuesday night, and Villa had a poor record at Elland Road; they'd gone six games in Leeds without a win with their last victory being back in December 2000. I suppose the only inkling I had that we might lose this game was the fact that all six members of the YEP Jury had predicted a Leeds win; we have an awful record every time that happens.

Villa were no longer one of my favourite teams, although they were once upon a time. When I first started going to games, Villa Park was a favourite destination. That was back in the early 70s when I lived in Worcester. Then, in the 80s and 90s, a very good friend of mine, the owner of a supplier we used at work and a vice president of Villa, would sort me out with tickets whenever they played Leeds; I was even entertained in the Villa directors' box on a few occasions as well as being invited to some extremely risqué men-only evenings at Villa Park; you don't get those anymore! But, the turning point for me was that awful game at Elland Road two years ago when the Villa players lost their collective rags after Matty Klich scored having played on with a Villa player rolling around on the turf feigning injury. It was not only the way they reacted after the goal was scored but also their lack of humility or even acknowledgement of the gesture Bielsa then made by insisting we gave them the goal back. Their response was almost as if it was their divine right to be given the equaliser. Since then I've been constantly annoyed by the appalling way all of their players behave on the pitch. It's not only the diving and cheating from Grealish, they all seem to do it, and they are constantly play-acting or trying to get away with horrible tackles or challenging with a leading elbow. I know all teams do it to some extent but they seem to be the masters at getting away with it. Beating them was therefore high up my required list of positive results when the fixtures first came out and the Patrick Bamford hat-trick at Villa Park was still one of the highlights of the season so far.

When the players emerged onto the pitch, the Sky cameras spotted Marcelo Bielsa in conversation with Emi Martinez, the Villa keeper, and after the game he was asked by journalists what the conversation was about. Bielsa commented; *"We just said hello. We're compatriots."*

Ultimately our game with Villa had a very familiar and 'Leedsy' feel about it and Martinez didn't have a lot to do. Leeds did go close in the first minute when Patrick Bamford slipped on the slippery surface while striking at goal. The ball was sliced across to the back post and the bounce just evaded the stretching Raphinha. But at the other end the Leeds defence was looking shaky. A first Villa corner was allowed to drop right in the centre of the Leeds area and appeared to brush the arm of Luke Ayling; that one was checked but cleared as OK by VAR, but a second corner quickly followed. This time it sailed over everyone in the box, was collected by Jacob Ramsey on the left edge of the area and he moved it to his right to Ollie Watkins. Watkins looked up, played a little wedge shot over the Leeds defensive line as he slipped and there was Anwar El Ghazi nipping in ahead of Helder Costa, free as a bird to stretch and stop the ball with his right foot and still have time to sweep it past Meslier with his left. He actually had time for a selfie and a sandwich if he'd wanted.

It was that same old Leeds feeling; we'd literally only just started, we'd switched on our TV sets full of hope and anticipation and here we were, less than five minutes in and already a goal down. If I had a pound for every time I've felt like this... well, I'd have had a few quid. The real annoyance was that we'd played right into Villa's hands; they had one of the best defences in the Premier League; only Manchester City and Chelsea had conceded fewer goals and I just knew they would now sit back and defend for their lives with little interest in going for a second goal that might have left them exposed. We'd seen it so many times already this season when we'd conceded early; we'd actually conceded first no less than 14 times this season, with only West Brom, Sheffield United and Wolves doing worse than that. We'd also conceded 27 first-half goals and that was more than any other side. Villa were set up to be efficient away from home and only Manchester City had conceded fewer goals on their travels, while Villa's record away from Villa Park was amongst the best in class. In short we'd given ourselves a Herculean task and it was a task that would prove too great.

Leeds would dominate the possession as we almost always do, but on the still slippery Elland Road pitch we had little penetration and too many players looked no more than average. We would complete more than twice as many passes at the visitor's but we rarely threatened the Villa goal and their excellent Argentine keeper, Emi Martinez had a quiet day. In the first half we had that first-minute back post chance that Raphinha couldn't reach and then later Tyler Roberts latched onto a rebound from another Raphinha effort that was blocked. This time Roberts caught the shot well enough but hit it straight at Martinez. Roberts had a better chance later that he skied horribly over the bar from the edge of the area. Villa offered very little apart from one El Ghazi long-range shot that Meslier easily turned over the bar. In the second half Leeds failed to record a single shot on target while the Villa defender Matt Targett should probably have been sent off for numerous sneaky fouls. He was booked early in the second half but then proceeded to go through the back of Raphinha scraping his studs down the Brazilian's ankle and later was caught on camera throwing Patrick Bamford to the floor at a corner; VAR for some reason declined to get involved on either occasion. Villa meanwhile were content to waste time and try to break up the flow of the game in any way they could.

It was the first time I can remember Illan Meslier going up for a corner, as Leeds loaded everyone in the Villa box. It was a bizarre sight with Meslier in his bright pink strip marking Martinez in all green. Nothing came of the corner other than Tyrone Mings going down as if shot to waste more time and Bamford looking totally bemused by the wrestling antics of the Villa defence.

Leeds' best chance of the second half came just before that when Raphinha was picked out at the back post. His header was almost too good though as he rammed the ball into the turf only to see it bounce up and over the bar. Leeds had thrown Alioski, Harrison, and Hernandez on during the second half replacing Struijk, Costa, and Roberts, but to no great effect. Pablo did have one sniff of a chance late on but his first touch let him down before he could shoot inside the Villa penalty area. The removal of Pascal Struijk from the action was later said to be due to an injury which was another worry.

Looking back on this game in the future there were so few moments of excitement that the abiding memory might well be when Luke Ayling's hair came loose when he was buffeted in a challenge by a couple of Villa players. It brought back memories of that unforgettable goal celebration against Huddersfield last season, almost exactly a year earlier and the last time any of us watched a game in the flesh inside Elland Road. Following this very annoying game with Aston Villa that was a very sobering thought.

So, that was that. It was another home defeat for Leeds, our 6th of the season; only the bottom three had lost more on their own patches. For the umpteenth time this season, just when it looked like we could inch further up the table, we'd shot ourselves in the foot. I thought it was a stodgy performance on a stodgy pitch but Marcelo Bielsa refused to accept that we'd played badly. He told BBC Sport: *"We dominated 80% of the game and the goal they scored was opportunism. In the first half we created enough chances to score a goal but in the second half we couldn't finalise the attacks."* It was still considered sacrilege to question what Marcelo said but I was still of the opinion we'd thrown this one away. Why we'd been so impotent I wasn't sure. The pitch hadn't helped of course, our passing game really needed a smooth slick surface and that was clearly the reason for laying the new turf. But, for whatever reason, it hadn't worked and it continued to look a very difficult track to play on. The use of Pascal Struijk in that defensive midfield role again also didn't work if you ask me. We'd tried this several times before and when we ditched it against Southampton I thought that would be the last time we'd see it, yet here it was again. We'd clearly missed Kalvin Phillips of course, but we'd played much better without him on Tuesday. It was all a bit of a mystery really.

In the final game of the day Newcastle and Wolves drew 1 – 1 at St James' Park, a result that left Newcastle tied with Brighton on 26 points just above the relegation zone. Fulham could have got to within a point of both of them had they won at Crystal Palace in the first game the following day but the Cottagers could only draw 0 – 0. Then, in the second game on Sunday, Arsenal surprisingly won 1 – 3 at Leicester and in the process the Gunners went above Leeds yet again to push us down to 11th. Tottenham then walloped Burnley 4 – 0 to leave the Clarets in a spot of bother just two points ahead of Newcastle and Brighton. In the final two games of this round of matches, Chelsea and Manchester United played out a dull 0 – 0 draw; not the first time this season members of the big six had cancelled each other out, and Liverpool won 0 – 2 at Sheffield United. It was perhaps significant that none of the big six lost this weekend and I wondered if by the end of the campaign they would all be in their predicted top six slots in the table.

The next round of games was scheduled for mid-week but Leeds were without a game so, by the time we faced West Ham in ten days' time, we'd have a game in hand over most teams as we reached the three-quarter point in the season.

Leeds United 0 Aston Villa 1 (El Ghazi 5)
BCD. Round 26 League Pos: 11th

Short Of A Bit Of Quality

There was another trio of celebrity and sporting deaths as February morphed into March. The passing of Glen Roeder was announced at halftime during the TV coverage of the Chelsea v Man United game. Roeder was one of the nice guys in the game and had a long career as a cultured defender with the likes of QPR, Newcastle, and Watford and then went into management with Gillingham, Watford, West Ham, Newcastle, and Norwich. It was while he was at West Ham that he was diagnosed with a brain tumour in 2003 and he died following a relapse ending an 18-year battle with the cancer. Roeder was just 65. Our game at West Ham would be the first opportunity that the Hammers would have to pay tribute to their former manager.

Also on 28th February, the TV world lost Johnny Briggs aged 85. Briggs was best known as Mike Baldwin, the loveable rogue and factory owner in Coronation Street and appeared in no less than 2,348 episodes between 1976 and 2005. When Mike had an on-screen affair with Deirdre Barlow, her husband Ken (played by another Corrie stalwart, William Roache) became his arch-enemy and almost 20 million viewers watched the episode in which Deirdre and Ken were reconciled. Such was the public interest that the electronic scoreboard at Old Trafford – where Man United were playing Arsenal – informed the 56,000 fans inside the stadium: *"Deirdre and Ken united again!"*

On 1st March, the death was announced of former Liverpool and Scotland winger, Ian St John, who died aged 82. It was St John of course who scored the extra-time winner against Leeds in the 1965 FA Cup Final. Us oldies also remember 'Saint' as one half of the excellent football TV show 'Saint and Greavsie' that he presented with Spurs legend Jimmy Greaves between 1985 and 1992.

Most of the Leeds United Under 23s wouldn't even have been born in time to see 'Saint and Greavsie' of course but there was one old face in the side we put out for the next PL2, Div. 2 game away at Crystal Palace; Gaetano Berardi completed his recovery from his ACL injury by playing the first half. Leeds were looking for a tenth consecutive win and were hoping to stretch their lead at the top of the table but, in typical Leeds fashion, it didn't quite go to plan. I watched the game on Crystal Palace TV for the princely sum of £3 and it was a tremendous game, only spoiled by an officious referee. He booked Crysencio Summerville early doors when our young winger offered some pithy advice about where a free-kick should be taken from and then argued over the measurement of the ten yards. Whether the ref had then made up his mind that he was going to teach young Crysencio a lesson I'm not sure, but in the 20th minute the Leeds player made an innocuous tackle from behind and immediately got a second yellow and a red card for his troubles. The Leeds lads fought bravely but succumbed to goals at either end of the second half to go down 2 – 0. They remained ten points clear at the top of the table though and were thus still on course for promotion

There were another eight EPL games scheduled this week, with Everton actually playing twice as they started to catch-up with their match schedule. They beat Southampton at Goodison 1 – 0 on Monday and then won by the same score on Thursday at the Hawthorns to beat West Brom. The scores this week were peculiar in that, of the 15 sides involved, the only one that could manage more than a single goal in a game was Manchester City. They walloped Wolves 4 – 1 although spookily, three of their goals only came in the final ten minutes. The full results this week were:

Monday 1st March: Everton 1 Southampton 0
Tuesday 2nd March: Manchester City 4 Wolves 1
Wednesday 3rd March: Burnley 1 Leicester City 1
                        Sheffield United 1 Aston Villa 0
                        Crystal Palace 0 Manchester United 0
Thursday 4th March: Fulham 0 Tottenham 1
                        West Brom 0 Everton 1
                        Liverpool 0 Chelsea 1

It really did look as if the pressure was beginning to tell as we moved inexorably towards the climax of the season. Either that, or every team was now so knackered, one goal was all they could muster. It was a far cry from those heady days last September and October when most teams were scoring for fun.

The games continued to come thick and fast at all levels and on Friday the Under 23s were in action again. This time they came through a tough game at Wolves to win 0 – 2 with two first-half goals from Rodrigo; a nicely struck shot from the edge of the box and a penalty after Max Dean was brought down. At halftime, both Rodrigo and Berardi were withdrawn but both came through this latest test without any issues. The only disappointment for me was that the game was played at Aggborough, home of Kidderminster Harriers where my beloved Worcester City played while in exile for a few seasons. I've been there many a time and, had there been no pandemic restrictions, I would have been there again watching it in the flesh. As it was, I had to make do with LUTV.

As for the Premier League, that resumed again after just a one-day break with the next four games, the first of round 28 for most teams, taking place on Saturday. The trend for all the games to be closely fought continued as Burnley and Arsenal drew 1 – 1, Aston Villa and Wolves drew 0 – 0, Leicester sneaked a 1 – 2 win at Brighton and only Southampton could post more than a single goal victory; they won 0 – 2 at hapless Sheffield United. The Blades must surely have now accepted they were as good as relegated as they remained 12 points from safety with only ten games to play.

Another four games were scheduled for Sunday and it felt like our game on Monday night would never arrive. I sat and watched the four Sunday matches and once again they were all very tight. The first saw West Brom and Newcastle battle out a dour stalemate, 0 – 0, a result which did neither much good. Albion were left eight points from the safety of 17th place, a place currently occupied by Brighton with 26 points. The Toon now had one point more in 16th. Newcastle's plight then looked even more worrying as Fulham continued their renaissance by winning 0 – 1 at Anfield. That result meant the Cottagers were now level on points with Brighton and, for the first time, it looked like Fulham could actually achieve what had looked impossible only weeks earlier and save their EPL lives. For Liverpool, astonishingly the Fulham defeat was a sixth consecutive home defeat as their title defence continued to crumble. The third game on Sunday saw the latest Manchester derby end with Manchester United coming out on top 0 – 2 to end a 21 game winning streak for City. It still left Man U 11 points adrift of their neighbours at the top of the table though. It was not until the last game of the day that we finally saw a decisive, clear-cut scoreline as Spurs beat Crystal Palace 4 – 1, but even that one looked much closer when Palace equalised just before the break. Two goals and two assists for Harry Kane saw him accumulate 38 points as captain of my Fantasy League side, while Gareth Bale continued to show he was back in form with the other two Spurs goals.

This Sunday also saw Rangers finally end Celtic's rule in Scotland as they claimed their first Premiership title in ten years. Celtic could only draw 0 – 0 at Dundee United, a result that left them 20 points behind Rangers with only 18 left to play for. In England, it was a bad news day for an Australian as Harry Kewell was *"relieved of his duties"* by Oldham Athletic; news that wouldn't disappoint many Leeds fans who will never forgive him for choosing to play for Galatasaray. It also meant Leeds fans could now give their unequivocal support to young Alfie McCalmont, now a regular in the Latics' midfield. The hate for all things Galatasaray by many Leeds fans was in the news again this week as rumours spread that Gjanni Alioski had turned down a new contract at Leeds and was eyeing a move to the Turkish club. Overnight Alioski was transformed from likeable clown to despicable traitor in many fans' eyes. For me, I couldn't harbour such hate for so long and certainly wasn't going to turn against a player who'd added so much to our cause in his time with us. It's a bit like the complete distaste that some fans insist on showing for anything coloured red!

I won't take a holiday in Turkey certainly, but not because two of our fans were once killed there, that can't be held against everyone in Turkey any more than modern-day Germans can be held responsible for what Hitler did. No, I wouldn't holiday in Turkey because the place is plagued with mosquitoes!

Even when Monday evening eventually rolled round, we still had to endure one more game before ours; it was another game in London as Chelsea faced Everton; 4th v 5th in the table. I have to confess at this point that I didn't watch it. I had finally, finally reached Premier League saturation point. I don't think I missed much as Chelsea continued on their unbeaten run since Thomas Tuchel arrived to beat the Toffees 2 – 0. Everton were restricted to a single shot on target and, by all accounts, Chelsea looked formidable. Just our luck then that after our game at West Ham it would be Tuchel's Blues arriving at Elland Road. One interesting feature of the Everton bench for this game was that they named two substitute goalkeepers; Young Harry Tyrer and Joao Neves Virginia.

There were going to be a lot of households making full use of Sky Q Multiroom this evening as the Leeds game coincided with the first UK showing of the now infamous Harry and Meghan tell-all interview with Oprah Winfrey on ITV that had been a hot topic of conversation since first airing in the USA on Sunday. In our household I won the toss, and got the big TV downstairs with the surround sound system while Mrs W was happy enough upstairs in the spare room. It meant I'd be free to blaspheme as much as I wished.

The team selection appeared on Twitter bang on schedule at 7 pm and the stand-out name in the starting XI was Kalvin Phillips. There had been speculation that he might return following sightings of him during this week's 'Murderball' session at Thorp Arch and then the fact he was pictured at Leeds train station with the rest of the squad as they headed for London.

Meslier
Ayling Llorente Cooper (Capt) Dallas
Phillips
Costa (Harrison 45) Roberts (Rodrigo 60) Klich (Alioski 45)
Bamford   **Raphinha**

Subs: Caprile, Alioski, Davis, Berardi, Jenkins, Huggins, Rodrigo, Harrison, Poveda.

West Ham: Fabianski, Coufal, Dawson, Diop, Cresswell, Soucek, Rice, Fornals, Lingard (Johnson 87), Benrahma (Bowen 73), Antonio. Subs not used: Martin, Balbuena, Lanzini, Noble, Trott, Odubeko. Referee: Mike Dean.

The debate continued as to whether it should be Costa or Harrison on the wing opposite Raphinha and for this game Bielsa decided to start with Costa, as he did last time out. I couldn't decide which was the better option; in my opinion neither quite hit the mark, although Harrison, when on form, probably had the edge. On the bench it was good to see both Rodrigo and Berardi return, although the word was that Hernandez and Struijk now had issues and hence why they were both missing. Elia Caprile was preferred this time to Kiko Casilla but there was no suggestion Kiko was injured other than maybe his pride.

This was Leeds' first visit to the London Stadium, although I'd been there back in 2016 while Leeds were still mired in the Championship. I decided I'd better knock it off quickly to get my '92' back up to date just in case our paths never subsequently crossed. I travelled down with my buddy Kentley and met up with my old pal the Shrimper and his son to do the Europa League game between the Hammers and NK Domzale. West Ham won comfortably 3 – 0 and I was impressed with the stadium although, at that time, the fans were a long way from the pitch. I understand they've put more seating closer to the pitch these days so it might be even better. It's certainly an impressive structure.

I was at the game the last time Leeds played away against the Hammers too, that was in August 2011 at their old Boleyn Ground, or Upton Park as most fans of my vintage knew it. I went down with my lad Mark and it was a boiling hot day. It was a super game too with Adam Clayton smashing in the equaliser in a 2 – 2 draw in the final minutes to set the Leeds fans alight; it was limbs everywhere while the rest of the ground emptied quicker than a pub with no beer. That was before our 'London curse' really took hold and it was our 7th consecutive visit without defeat. This game of course would find West Ham at the peak of their powers and eyeing a possible Champions League place. They were on a great run too; two defeats in 12 and they'd won seven of those. And of course it was a game in London so we had little real hope of success.

For once I quite enjoyed the studio chat ahead of the game; Sky had Dave Jones hosting with Jamie Carragher and former Leeds and West Ham keeper Rob Green. It was all a bit goalkeeper focussed of course but it was interesting some of the stuff they came up with in comparing Meslier with Fabianski. Fabianski was most definitely a 'catcher' of the ball while Meslier tended to punch for example. In general, Green was complimentary about Meslier, especially remembering that he'd only just turned 21, literally the previous week. The context for the catching/punching debate was the contrast between the two sides in terms of set-pieces and corners. West Ham were a big powerful side and sat top of the table for set-piece goals scored; they'd scored 13 and were also 2nd in the table of most headed goals and 2nd for goals scored from corners. By contrast Leeds were top of the table for set-piece goals *conceded*, also 13, while another honour we currently held was to be top of the table for penalties conceded with seven of those. It hadn't escaped my memory yet that the Hammers scored two set-piece headers in the reverse fixture when they won 1 – 2 at Elland Road; one from a corner, headed in by Soucek, and one following a free-kick by Ogbonna... So, at least Leeds would be on their guard to ensure no daft penalties were given away and we'd be super careful defending corners...

Finally, just before 8 pm, the players arrived onto the London Stadium pitch and, by the look of it, neither side could complain about the playing surface which looked as smooth as a carpet. Ahead of the start both sides lined up around the centre-circle and took part in a minute's applause in tribute to Glen Roeder whose face looked down at the players from the two huge screens at either end of the ground. He was also featured on the cover of the match-day programme.

Leeds took this game by the scruff of its neck from the first whistle (well, these days I suppose with the taking of the knee it's the second whistle technically, but you know what I mean). The first 20 minutes was all Leeds and we had the ball in the back of the Hammers' net twice although sadly neither counted.

Leeds won a corner in the very first minute and Costa then fired a shot just over the bar not long after that. Then, in the 6th minute, Stuart Dallas lifted a left-wing cross into the box looking for Patrick Bamford. It was behind Bamford who nevertheless did his best to get to it with his boot up by his shoulder. It looked as though he'd missed it though and it dropped instead at the feet of Costa at the back post. Costa shifted it across the face of goal and Roberts nipped in to fire the ball into the bottom left corner. My joy was short-lived as the cameras soon picked out the liner's raised flag but then, when the first pictures of the incident appeared on screen, it looked at least possible that the liner had got this one wrong, albeit there were only millimetres in it. It was presumably adjudged that Bamford had indeed got a touch, as the freeze-frame picture was from the moment the ball left his up-raised boot. That was typical of our luck; if he hadn't touched it Costa was clearly onside. I'd like to have seen a cricket-type 'Snicko' system involved as any touch was no more than the merest kiss on the ball. However, as I rose from my chair and wandered closer to the TV, it still looked as if Costa might be OK. In the end Andre Marriner, the VAR, dropped a line from Costa's knee and a second one from the rearmost defender's boot and ruled he was offside by what could only have been the thickness of a blade of grass. As @TheNfster would post on Twitter later: *"I don't mind Andre Marriner as a ref but he's sh*t at trigonometry!"* It was no more than we should have expected in London where we'd now entered our 14th game since our last win down there.

Our bad luck wasn't finished yet though as, within another 60 seconds, we had the ball in the net again! This time it was Raphinha going down the left edge of the Hammers' area. He just touched the ball a tad too hard as he made a dash for the byline and it looked touch and go whether he'd kept the ball in as he hooked his left foot around it and sent it low to the near post. Patrick Bamford wasn't waiting to check, he lashed the ball into the net and then all eyes were on that liner on the far side again. This one was less controversial as the VAR replays clearly showed the whole of the ball was over the line. What a crazy start to the game though. Mind you, I doubt I was the only Leeds fan in the world pondering if this was just another example of the rotten luck we get in London and if we were about to see West Ham go down the other end and get a big slice of good fortune...

Well, it wasn't exactly good fortune, more a piece of stupidity from Leeds but, sure enough, in the 17th minute (Ha! It had to be the effin 17th minute didn't it? Just to rub it in!) I watched open-mouthed as Jesse Lingard, the on-loan Manchester United winger, made his way across the left edge of the Leeds penalty area before Luke Ayling suddenly stuck out a boot. Initially I thought it was just another clever dive, but on the replays it was clear that 'Bill' missed the ball and made contact with the ankle of the West Ham winger and, although it would hardly have been enough to bring down your average 95-year-old grandma, these days it will be called a penalty all day long.

Once again we'd shot ourselves in the boot, giving the opposition the chance to sneak ahead and then defend for their lives for the rest of the game. It was the 8th penalty we'd conceded this season and they'd all been either conned by the opposition or stupidly conceded through our own ineptitude. Meslier hadn't got close to saving any of the previous seven so I had no great hopes for this one and, while he danced to and fro along his line waving his arms to try to put Lingard off, I wasn't convinced it was really worth the effort. But then I'm out of my chair again as Lingard weakly struck the ball to the left of our young keeper and he easily got down to parry it away… except he could only parry it straight back to Lingard who was first to react and sweep the loose ball into the net. I fell back into the chair and cursed the football gods who continued to tease us like this. So, the penalty issue was still with us but at least we hadn't conceded from a corner… yet…

West Ham won their first corner in the 28th minute and it was Aaron Cresswell standing over it on the West Ham right wing; one of the best crossers of a ball in the Premier League. The huge monster of a figure that is Michail Antonio stood as close as he could in front of Meslier to try to ensure he couldn't get to the ball for a punch while Stuart Dallas did his best to ensure at least that Antonio didn't foul the keeper. The ball sailed well over them all though, dropped near the back post and Craig Dawson steamed in to power a header home from no more than two yards out. It was the 14th set-piece goal we'd conceded in under 27 games. Replays would show that Dawson was initially being marked by Llorente but, as we'd seen so often this season, once the ball was in the air Llorente's only focus was its flight and thus he completely lost track of the fact that Dawson had moved away. By the time our Spanish international centre-back realised, it was too late.

Now it really did feel like Leeds in London. We'd totally dominated the first twenty minutes of the game, had the ball in the opposition net twice, and yet we were two goals down. Unbelievable Jeff! It was pretty much the script of the previous 13 games we'd played in the capital and we were heading for our 5th defeat down there already this season. It could have been even worse as, still not learning that corners don't defend themselves, Llorente was muscled out of another challenge with Craig Dawson at the next West Ham corner but this time his scuffed header hit the right-hand post. It was still 2 – 0 thankfully as the halftime whistle was blown by Mike Dean but quite how we'd got ourselves in that position goodness only knows.

If the first half was a reminder of our lack of quality at the back, then the second half reminded us we could also do with a bit more at the front as well. Patrick Bamford had, on occasions this season, been superb. Some of his goals had been fabulous and showed he can be a top striker and yet, he was also top of the charts for big chances missed, just as he was last season in the Championship. Within a minute of the restart he'd missed another one.

Diego Llorente had looked a little bit all over the place to me throughout this game; he sometimes seemed to be aimlessly running in circles at corners for example. But, almost straight from the restart, he played a wonderful ball straight through the centre of the West Ham defence and perfectly onto Patrick Bamford's favoured left peg. All Paddy had to do was steer it past the stranded Fabianski and yet, instead, he managed to steer it wide of the left-hand post as well. It was a carbon copy of another one he missed recently when he ran from halfway and did exactly the same with a curling shot. There were several other chances for Leeds, none quite as clear as that one but enough to have won the game. Raphinha tried an overhead kick that brushed off a defender and was creeping under the crossbar until Fabianski's big right hand tipped it over.

Leeds replaced both Helder Costa and a below-par Mateusz Klich at halftime with Jack Harrison and Alioski; Alioski went to left-back to allow Stuart Dallas to move into midfield. It wasn't especially successful but Klich had been woeful and Costa, while often involved, was ineffective. On the hour mark Bielsa made his final change by swapping Roberts with the fit-again Rodrigo. I think Rodrigo was a marginal improvement on the Welshman who, like Costa, was often involved but seemed to want too much time whenever he was on the ball; time that just isn't there at this level. The chances continued to fall for Leeds though and they usually fell to Patrick Bamford. If we thought his first big chance missed was criminal, his second was even worse. This time he had two goes. Rodrigo made progress through the inside left channel and eventually prodded the ball through to Harrison who slid it into the path of Bamford, 12 yards from goal. He did that thing when he seems to forget which foot to use and ended up merely slicing the ball further to the right where Raphinha ran to collect. He quickly assessed the situation and calmly rolled the ball back to Bamford who was now centre of goal, unmarked, and only nine yards out. I swear I could have scored it with my eyes closed and my slippers on but Paddy, leaning back, scooped the ball over the bar looking for all the world as if he was practising his drop goals for the school rugby team again. It was a total shocker and took him clear at the top of that Premier League big chances missed list with 17 for the season; Timo Werner was 2nd with 16 and a bloke called Chris Wood was third on 14... remember him? Yeah, he used to miss a load of chances when he was with us too. People defending Bamford say that others miss chances too and that's true but, as a comparison, the next highest figure amongst Leeds players this season was just four, by both Harrison and Raphinha...

And that pretty much was that, West Ham had just one decent attempt in the second half when a long-range shot by Fornals rocked the Leeds crossbar but other than that it was all Leeds. For me, the story of the game was one we were now familiar with; mistakes at one end and missed chances at the other. It all came down to a matter of individual quality and, to some extent it was more confirmation that we had a really top-quality Championship level side but it was actually only a very average Premier League side. We were more than capable of beating teams in the bottom half of the table but, each time we faced the better sides, it was obvious we were just lacking those bits of quality that the opposition usually possessed. Sometimes, when these players of ours were all on top of their game and the rub of the green went with us, we could even win a game or two against some of the better sides, but our group, on the whole, was not good enough to regularly put in top performances, that consistency of quality you get with the real top performers wasn't there. If we had that better quality I'm talking about, Luke Ayling would not have dangled a foot out against a player like Lingard; we wouldn't have conceded yet another goal at an opposition corner; and we'd have put at least a couple of some very big chances away to probably leave London with at least a point.

Defensively we were not good enough to do any better than we were; 14 goals conceded from corners was the worst record in the division and that was not going to be solved with the current players unless maybe Robin Koch proved to be that top-level player we needed once we got to see him more regularly. Would Llorente be the quality we needed if he was partnered with Koch? Maybe, we just didn't know. All we did know was that the back four we played in this game surely would not be there next season if we were to progress higher than mid-table. Bielsa seemed convinced that the current personnel could be trained to be better at defending set-pieces. Remember he told us after the reverse West Ham fixture in December: *"This problem we're having, we've already had it before in the past, we resolved it and now it's happening again."*. Well it was still happening. It reminded me of the Carlotta speech from Phantom of the Opera: *"For the past three years these things do happen and do you stop them from happening? NO! Until you stop these things from happening, this thing does not happen! Ubaldo, andiamo, bring my doggy and my boxy!"*

Similarly, in midfield, I'd be hard-pressed to pick anyone other than Kalvin and Raphinha who could be relied on week-in week-out to shine and deliver. Players who were consistently top-quality.

Up front we again saw the lack of consistency we get from Patrick Bamford. Twice tonight I was convinced he'd wasted chances that, at this level, you expect your number '9' to bury. It's not a criticism that he played badly; it's just an observation that he isn't consistently clinical enough for a team wanting to be in the top echelons of the Premier League and that had to be where we were aiming to be next season.

All the current squad had done a fantastic job for us this season, and last of course. They were all lovely lads, fit as butchers' dogs and with hearts of oak and well organised by Bielsa... but sadly, not the quality that would get us higher up the table. Every time we had a good win we were tempted to kid ourselves this squad could take us to the next level but we were just kidding ourselves; the West Ham result was another reminder of that.

For now we could only carry on as we were, be as good as we could and pick up a few more points to ensure we could then trawl the market for a few more Raphinha-quality players in other areas of the pitch. Such players cost big bucks and demand big wages but that's the name of the game and everything suggested the club knew this perfectly well. Another year of EPL cash would help us find a few more pieces of the ultimate jigsaw.

It was no criticism of the players on show tonight, they played their hearts out and, on another day, could have got a point. But long-term, I was convinced we'd have to say *"thank you and goodbye"* to several of them if we were to challenge for Europe next season.

West Ham United 2 **Leeds United 0** (Lingard 20, Dawson 28) BCD. **Round 27 League Pos: 11**[th].

	Team	P	GD	Pts
1	Manchester City	28	37	65
2	Manchester United	28	23	54
3	Leicester City	28	16	53
4	Chelsea	28	19	50
5	West Ham United	27	11	48
6	Everton	27	4	46
7	Tottenham Hotspur	27	18	45
8	Liverpool	28	11	43
9	Aston Villa	26	11	40
10	Arsenal	27	7	38
11	Leeds United	27	-3	35
12	Wolverhampton Wanderers	28	-9	35
13	Crystal Palace	28	-17	34
14	Southampton	27	-11	33
15	Burnley	28	-16	30
16	Newcastle United	27	-17	27
17	Brighton and Hove Albion	27	-8	26
18	Fulham	28	-11	26
19	West Bromwich Albion	28	-36	18
20	Sheffield United	28	-29	14

Chelsea

This was another week of European action, with Borussia Dortmund, FC Porto, Liverpool, and Paris Saint-Germain all going through to the Champions League quarter-finals. In the Europa League first-leg games there were wins for Spurs and Arsenal, while Man United and Rangers both drew. There was one Premier League game in mid-week as Manchester City played their postponed fixture against Southampton. Saints were in the game for most of the first half but eventually City moved up a gear and fired in five goals to win 5 – 2 and go 14 points clear at the top again. Saints remained seven points clear of relegation and a couple of points below Leeds albeit now having played a game more.

On Planet Leeds there was another cryptic Instagram message this week, this time from Kiko Casilla. Coming so soon after him being left out for the West Ham game and because it seemed to echo the recent similarly obtuse message posted by Pablo Hernandez, it was taken by many to be Kiko expressing his own frustrations against Bielsa and the club. He posted: *"I'm slow to go, because I believe in changes. And I wait, and I endure, and I keep. But one day I get tired and without saying anything I leave everything and leave. Believe me that once I get tired I won't come back again, because I give everything before I leave".* However, either we'd all got completely the wrong end of the stick or Kiko had second thoughts as he then posted: *"honestly, there are people with very boring lives, I have not said anything bad about the club or my situation, they are personal things, not to do with Leeds. #mot"*, followed by a heart emoji in club colours. Casilla's agent was also quick to counter suggestions that Kiko's original post was aimed at the club noting: *"I don't know the exact meaning behind his posts but I don't believe it is about Leeds United,".*[1] Like many things said by players, we'd probably never know the truth.

The weekly Bielsa press conference brought little information other than a comment by the great man that Shackleton, Koch, and Berardi were all now fit while Pascal Struijk and Pablo Hernandez were still injured. No one even bothered to ask about Adam Forshaw. There was a bit of a feeling amongst some Leeds fans though that Bielsa had learned these days not to give too much away during these pressers and we'd seen on a few occasions how he'd managed to camouflage important injury information ahead of games. Hence no one was quite sure if anyone else was injured or indeed whether we'd suddenly see either Pascal or Pablo miraculously recovered.

Friday night arrived and we were back on the Premier League treadmill as Newcastle hosted Villa at St James' Park. With Glen Roeder having spent six years playing for the Magpies and then managing them to their first trophy in almost 40 years when they won the UEFA Intertoto Cup in 2006, it was a heartfelt one minute's applause that took place ahead of the game. There were still Leeds fans who thought we were not yet safe from relegation and, mathematically at least, that was true. Hence, any side below us in the table was of interest; Newcastle were one of those teams. Much as it hurt many of us to say so, it was probably a good result for Leeds if the Villa won and with them taking an 86th-minute lead

---

[1]   *https://www.leeds-live.co.uk/sport/leeds-united/kiko-casilla-leeds-instagram-message-20050656*

all looked good. But, with the final touch, Jamaal Lascelles headed in a Jacob Murphy cross and the game was drawn with the Toon grabbing another vital point. Our home game with Chelsea was a 12:30m kick-off the following day, Saturday, 13th March. I had a wry smile as I studied the Leeds team listed in the club Twitter post; there was no Liam Cooper. It did look as if, once again, Bielsa had managed to keep potentially important team news hidden from the opposition, although it hadn't completely escaped the attention of the most eagle-eyed Leeds fans. The club posted a video on Friday of a training session earlier in the day and within minutes a tweet was posted by @dingleburtdev noting: *"Not one to jump the gun. But no sign of Cooper in the training video. But Koch training with the team. Koch-Llorente partnership tomorrow maybe?"* He got Brownie points for the Cooper spot (he was ill apparently) but it wasn't Robin Koch who would partner Diego Llorente; it was the miraculously recovered Pascal Struijk!

Meslier
Ayling Llorente Struijk Alioski
Phillips
Raphinha Dallas Roberts Harrison (Costa 64)
Bamford (Rodrigo 35, Klich 79)

Subs: Casilla, Koch, Berardi, Shackleton, Jenkins, Klich, Poveda, Costa, Rodrigo.

Chelsea: Mendy, Azpilicueta, Christensen, Rüdiger, Chilwell, Kanté, Jorginho, Pulisic (James 68), Ziyech (Werner 69), Mount (Hudson-Odoi 79), Havertz. Subs not used: Arrizabalaga, Alonso, Zouma, Kovacic, Giroud, Emerson. Referee: Kevin Friend.

So it was three changes from the side that unluckily lost in London the previous week. Cooper, Costa, and Klich out; Struijk, Harrison, and Alioski back in. The Llorente-Struijk partnership would be the thirteenth different centre-back pairing we'd used this season, although they had played together in a 'three' against Southampton a couple of weeks earlier. The return of Alioski to left-back was presumably to allow Stuart Dallas to again fill the midfield hole created by the absence of Hernandez, the lack of fitness of Rodrigo, and the form or injury issues that had beset Mateusz Klich, so that was understandable. The swapping of Harrison for Costa suggested Bielsa still couldn't make his mind up which of those two offered the most potency. He wasn't alone, it was a debate many Leeds fans were having too.

Chelsea had around £700 million of talent involved in the squad they named, and they came into this game still unbeaten under Thomas Tuchel. In his 11 games in charge the Blues had won eight and drawn three and, in the process, had taken themselves into the top four of the Premier League, the FA Cup quarter-finals, and were well-placed to reach the Champions League quarter-finals too, if they could see off Atlético Madrid as they held a 1 − 0 first-leg lead. They were a top team and even the most optimistic Leeds fan didn't expect a Leeds win in this one. Even the notoriously optimistic YEP fans' jury was at best hoping for a draw while two of our number predicted defeat. I hasten to say I was going for a 1 − 1 scoreline...

It was December 2003 the last time Chelsea visited Elland Road for a league game, although they had been there as recently as December 2012 when they knocked us out of the League Cup. The last time in the league was a 1 − 1 draw but the game I will always remember was the year before that: 28th December 2002. The whole family was at that one in the South Stand and, just after Leeds took the lead on the half-hour, we got our first glimpse of James Milner in the flesh. He came on as a substitute for Harry Kewell and within fifteen minutes he'd scored his debut home goal, a brilliant turn and shot from the Leeds left that flew across the keeper and nestled inside the corner of the net. We'd all hoped he'd come on as he'd scored his debut goal in the away win at Sunderland on Boxing Day and was being hailed as the next big player at the club; he was still seven days short of his seventeenth birthday having only made his debut just over a month earlier in a 4 − 3 win at Upton Park.

In the BT Sport studio the game presentation was hosted by Jake Humphrey along with Rio Ferdinand and Joe Cole and I have to admit they produced a watchable preamble to the game. They probably put the curse of death on any chance of seeing goals today though as their closing comment was that Leeds games this season had seen 89 goals; more than any other side had been involved with. Then they handed over to Darren Fletcher and Steve McManaman for the match commentary.

The game started in bright sunshine, and overhead pictures of the Elland Road pitch showed it looked just as bad as ever if not worse!

The green was streaked with thick brown lines where the grass was missing or dead. During the game there was a constant swirling wind and one biblical deluge before the sun eventually broke through again; it was a case of early April showers. The game itself started at a ferocious pace and the first 20 minutes was as good a game as any we'd seen thus far; there were incidents at both ends.

As early as the 6th minute Chelsea went close as the ball fizzed across the face of goal with Havertz just failing to convert as Meslier smothered the close-range effort and then grabbed the ball at the second attempt. 17 (yes, honestly!) seconds later and Leeds had the ball in the Chelsea net in front of the South Stand as Leeds broke away and Bamford squared the ball across for Tyler Roberts to stab home. That one was flagged offside and VAR confirmed that Bamford was a yard off. Back up the other end the ball went and suddenly I was gasping out loud as Luke Ayling tried to wellie the ball up-field. The ball smacked straight into Diego Llorente just feet away and rebounded over Meslier and smacked against the crossbar. As Illan turned, fearing the worst, the ball dropped straight into his arms. The game was still only nine minutes old! A few more minutes passed and then Chelsea were away down their right wing again where Gjanni Alioski was having a torrid time. He was left for dead again and another ball fizzed low across the face of goal. This time Meslier got down to it and palmed it away from goal before Ayling cleared without hitting any of his own men.

Immediately Leeds set off again towards the South Stand and this time Tyler Roberts tried his luck with a curling shot from the left corner of the box. He actually looked the other way to 'give the keeper the eyes' as he struck it and it sailed in a high arc towards the top right corner. Somehow Mendy got the merest fingernail on the ball, just enough to deflect it onto the angle and away to safety. It was an astonishing start to a game and the intensity was only increased as the heavens opened and the rain poured down.

Just around the half-hour mark the rain subsided and the sun came out again, but not metaphorically. Patrick Bamford had bounced off a defender in midfield and immediately went to ground holding his hip. He received lengthy treatment and then tried to run it off but was down again in a matter of minutes and that was his game done; a disappointing end to his 100th appearance. He was replaced by Rodrigo.

There were a couple of Chelsea corners at the end of the first half that Leeds dealt with, albeit not particularly cleanly, and then we won one of our own which we wasted with the ball sailing over everybody. It had been a whirlwind half of football but we'd given as good as we got against one of the best sides in the league. It was a 6th consecutive game for the Whites though without a first-half goal.

The second half wasn't quite as helter-skelter and the chances at both ends were fewer and less clear-cut. Illan Meslier was in great form and he stood tall to tip over a thunderous drive from Havertz from the right corner of the six-yard area and then Leeds should probably have scored as Tyler Roberts crossed from the left. Rodrigo met the ball with his head at the back post, headed it down and Raphinha, with his back to goal, spun and struck the ball from about nine yards out. Sadly he just didn't connect as he would have wanted and merely scuffed it into the turf and Mendy had time to stick out a big left hand to stop it. Rüdiger then fired in a long-range effort that Meslier pushed away and, at the other end Rodrigo will be annoyed he couldn't do better with a free header from a Raphinha left wing corner. Helder Costa replaced Jack Harrison after a strangely anonymous performance for the Citeh loanee that did nothing to convince me he was the better of the two while Rodrigo had looked way off the pace throughout his time on the pitch. He was actually subbed in the 79th minute by Matty Klich, either because he was so poor or maybe just because he was always only intended to get 45 minutes today which was the exact time he was on the pitch.

It was a terrific performance though by Leeds and, for once, the result was about right and matched the game, with chances and luck spread pretty evenly between the sides. The Leeds defence was particularly steady with the new Struijk and Llorente partnership looking very assured while Illan Meslier also had a good game and was proclaimed Man of the Match by many observers. Sky gave their award to Tyler Roberts who also had one of his best games with several stand out moments, although perhaps still not offering enough consistently throughout the game. At the end of the day a point against Chelsea was a good point and we could add that to the similar home draws with two other members of the big six club,

Arsenal and Manchester City; those being the only games we'd drawn all season.

After the game, Victor Orta was the centre of attention as Thomas Tuchel voiced his annoyance at the volume generated by Orta's support from the directors' box and that possibly is another sign as to how close-fought this game was. Tuchel also noted that the *"sticky"* Elland Road pitch did his side no favours, although Chelsea recorded 62% of the possession which was the highest figure in all 120 of the league games Leeds had played under Marcelo Bielsa. For most Leeds fans it was one more point towards the ultimate goal this season; avoiding relegation.

With Leeds picking up another point, two of the other three games played on Saturday helped our cause of staying up as West Brom lost again, 1 – 0 at Crystal Palace, and Fulham couldn't compete with the Champions elect, Manchester City. The score at Craven Cottage was 0 – 3. Before the Palace game, Wilfred Zaha made a stand, literally, as he stood still instead of kneeling before the kick-off. He'd issued a statement ahead of the game explaining how he thought the kneeling ritual was now just that, a ritual, it had lost its impact and he now wanted to see more action and less posturing. In the final game played this Saturday Burnley did their hopes of survival a power of good as they posted a 1 – 2 scoreline at Everton.

The sad news that broke during the day was about another famous face and voice leaving us; Murray Walker had died aged 97. It was always hard to be too morose when someone dies at such a ripe old age but, for me, it was yet another part of the tapestry of my life being folded away. Like most folk of my age who followed motor racing, his had been the voice of F1 for more than half a century. The first Grand Prix he described live was for BBC Radio at Silverstone in 1949 and his television finale was for ITV in 2001 at the US Grand Prix at Indianapolis. I've probably used one or more of his catch phrases elsewhere in this book as I have done many times in the past.

The other news breaking today was nowhere near as sad, unless of course you happened to be a Sheffield United fan; Chris Wilder was sacked. With the Blades rock bottom and almost certain to be relegated, stories of his demise had been doing the rounds for days but now it was confirmed ahead of their game against Leicester

City on Sunday. The man given the job of overseeing the last rights for the Blades was none other than former Leeds manager, Paul Heckingbottom. 'Hecky' was the last manager at Elland Road before Marcelo Bielsa arrived and held the reigns from February until mid-June 2018. His final game with Leeds was a 2 – 0 win against QPR at Elland Road on May 6th 2018 but recently he'd held the post of Under 23 coach at Bramall Lane and was now handed the first-team job at least until the end of the season. It meant he would be back at Elland Road after the upcoming international break as the Blades were due to visit Leeds on April 3rd. Hopefully he'd continue in the manner he began; the Blades were thrashed 5 – 0 by the Foxes and it probably should have been ten!

In the remaining three games played on Sunday afternoon, Brighton got a valuable 1 – 2 win at Southampton, Arsenal beat Spurs 2 – 1 despite the most outrageous 'Rabona' goal scored by Erik Lamela who was later sent off, and Manchester United squeaked through 1 – 0 against West Ham.

The final game of this round saw Liverpool visit Molineux on Monday night and it was another close game. Liverpool won it with a Diogo Jota goal at the end of the first half on his return to his former club. Hence only two games in this round of matches were won by more than one goal. The game was marred by a sickening collision near the end of normal time between Wolves defender Conor Coady and his own goalkeeper Rui Patricio that left Patricio seemingly out cold on the turf. He was stretchered off and the new concussion substitute rule saw John Ruddy replace him for the final minutes. Watching from the stands was Raul Jimenez, the Wolves striker who suffered a fractured skull against Arsenal last November. Jimenez was still recovering from his own head injury.

And that was the end of another round of games; Leeds were now 12th with 36 points, still ten ahead of Fulham in the last of the relegation places and, having played only 28, also with a game in hand over the Cottagers and the majority of teams who had now played 29. Next up was another trip to London to play the Cottagers in their own manor, a game that could end our relegation worries once and for all.

Leeds United 0 Chelsea 0   BCD. Round 28 League Pos: 12th.

London Has Fallen!

The vaccine programme in the UK continued to go well, with more than 25 million now having had the first dose and figures suggesting it was having the desired effect on case numbers, deaths, and hospital admissions. In Europe though the picture was very different. Europe was slow to begin vaccinations anyway but now many countries had stopped offering the AstraZeneca jab while reports of some recipients having developed blood clots were investigated. The World Health Organisation (WHO) and even the EUs own medicines regulator said there was no evidence to suggest the jab wasn't safe but still many nations paused their programmes, putting them even further behind the UK. Football fans in the UK were still waiting to hear if we'd get to see a live game this season. The latest suggestion from the EPL was that they might postpone the final couple of games to ensure all clubs had the opportunity to play at least one home game in front of a limited number of their fans. The Government was still saying the earliest date for fans in stadiums was May 17th so that would mean the EPL delaying at least one round. Many fans were sceptical the proposal was worthwhile and some said they wouldn't go anyway until stadiums could be full. A 10,000 maximum, or a quarter of the capacity if lower, was still going to be in place for the time being.

The U23s marched serenely on towards the Premier League 2 Division 2 title with a routine 2 – 1 win over Newcastle at Thorp Arch. A first-half goal from Charlie Cresswell and a penalty won and converted by Joe Gelhardt did the trick despite the Toon getting one back just before the break. There were minutes for Berardi, Poveda, and Robin Koch who all came through unscathed. The U23s still held a 13 point lead over Stoke who had two games in hand; two more wins would guarantee the title and promotion. The Under 18s had a good week too; they played MK Dons in the third round of the FA Youth Cup and hit eight goals with a devastating display of clinical finishing. The final score at the new York City LNER Community Stadium was 8 – 2, with goals from Joseph Snowdon (2), Morten Spencer, Max McMillan (2), Cian Coleman, William Fewster, and Jimiel Chikukwa. MK Dons' cause wasn't helped when captain Josh Bailey was shown a straight red for a lunging foul on Keenan Carole midway through the first half.

Former Leeds man Lee Bowyer was in the news this week; he resigned as manager of Charlton after three years during which he'd got them back into the Championship, saw them then relegated after one season and now had them in the play-off places in League One again. The reason he resigned was pretty obvious as almost immediately it was announced that Aitor Karanka was leaving Birmingham City. Sure enough, hours later, Bowyer was proclaimed the new Blues manager. His first game came up quickly this week and it was a vital 2 – 1 win over fancied Reading that gave the Blues a fighting chance of avoiding the drop out of the Championship which could see them swap places with Charlton.

In the next round of Champions League games this week Manchester City, Real Madrid, Chelsea, and Bayern Munich all progressed through to the quarter-finals to join Liverpool, Borussia Dortmund, FC Porto, and Paris Saint-Germain who went through the previous week. In the Europa League there was success for Arsenal and Manchester United who both went into the quarter-finals of that competition while Rangers and Tottenham bowed out with Kemar Roofe in the news again. He rearranged the face of the

Slavia Prague keeper with a high boot that saw Roofe red-carded and the keeper substituted. It had been some season for Mr Roofe!

Yet another famous name left us this week; racing driver and TV personality Sabine Schmitz finally lost her battle with cancer, aged just 51. Sabine was a regular guest on Top Gear and was known as the 'Queen of the Nurburgring' where she was brought up as a child and later tamed the German race track with many victories.

There were only four EPL games this weekend due to the quarter-finals of the FA Cup; Bournemouth were the only non-Premier League side left in the competition. We were first up too, a Friday night game live on Sky Sport TV at Fulham... yes, that's Fulham in London... what could possibly go wrong?

This game had been circled on most Leeds Fans' calendars for weeks, it being seen as something of a 'six-pointer'. Fulham had gradually been closing the gap between themselves and Leeds as they'd finally found some form in recent weeks whilst the Whites had found wins hard to come by and, while there were several other clubs in more danger of being caught than Leeds, it was still felt that taking three points off them in this one, and boosting our total by three, ought to be enough to ensure we finished above them regardless of what all the other threatened clubs managed to do.

Leeds could hardly be said to be confident though, as we were fresh from a run of four defeats in six games while Fulham had only lost five of their last 18. Compare that with their first 11 games of the season when they lost eight of those and you could see how they had turned their fortunes around; albeit they were still in the relegation zone. A win over Leeds would have seen them move out of the bottom three though and Newcastle would have replaced them. Hence there was no lack of encouragement for the Cottagers and they would surely have known about our recent record in London too. Leeds had played 16 consecutive games in the capital without success; just two draws and 14 defeats in more than three years since we won 1 – 3 at Loftus Road in December 2017 with a second-half hat-trick from the Kung-Fu Kid, Kemar Roofe! He does like a headline doesn't he! We'd lost on all five visits to the Smoke this season but, this being the 17th game since our previous London win, maybe it was time for that number to be a positive omen for once.

In the press conference on Thursday, Bielsa looked to be in his usual self-contained world as he answered questions whilst absent-mindedly moving an empty coffee cup around the table like he was playing some kind of game with it. Maybe it was a form of coffee-cup draughts or perhaps he was trying to trap an invisible insect; who knows? In between cup moves he informed us via translator Andrés Clavijo that Patrick Bamford would be fit to play despite the knock he'd taken to his hip against Chelsea. It perhaps had though tipped the balance in preventing Gareth Southgate picking him for the upcoming England World Cup qualifiers next week as had been widely expected. There had been calls for both Bamford and Luke Ayling to be included but when the squad was announced it was just Kalvin Phillips who made it. Liam Cooper had missed out on more caps for Scotland as he was still 'ill', the standard phrase Leeds tended to use when anyone contracted Covid although in Coops' case this had not yet been confirmed. Pascal Struijk was said to be fit to play on Friday while Bielsa was unsure if Rodrigo would make it or not.

When Friday night rolled round and the team was announced on the Leeds United Twitter feed, it was as you were; the starting XI was unchanged from the draw with Chelsea.

Meslier
Ayling Llorente Struijk Alioski
Phillips
Raphinha Dallas Roberts (Koch 90+3) Harrison
Bamford (Klich 77)

Subs: Casilla, Koch, Berardi, Jenkins, Poveda, Costa, Gelhardt, Shackleton, Klich.

Fulham: Areola, Aina (Tete72), Andersen, Tosin, Robinson, Reed (Loftus-Cheek 63), Lemina, Cavaleiro, Zambo Anguissa, Lookman, Maja (Mitrovic 45). Subs not used: Fabri, Hector, Odoi, Ream, Bryan, Kongolo.

Referee: David Coote.

Both André-Frank Zambo Anguissa and Mario Lemin would be well known to Marcelo Bielsa; they both played under the great man when he was manager of Marseille.

For half an hour, maybe even longer, Leeds bossed this game and, but for the thickness of a Tyler Roberts shirt sleeve, we'd have been in front within ten minutes of the start. We can only bemoan our luck that VAR once again intervened to prevent what would have been one of the best-celebrated goals of the season. Alioski and Harrison combined out on the left wing level with the edge of the Fulham area before Harrison touched the ball forward to Tyler Roberts. The Welshman went towards the byline but then checked and stepped inside his marker before clipping the ball towards the back post. Running in unmarked was Luke Ayling and he very deliberately looped a header over the keeper and into the far corner of the net before running off manically tugging at the band holding his hair together. Eventually he freed his flowing mane and sank down on his knees playing his air guitar again just as he famously did almost twelve months earlier after scoring against Huddersfield. It was great television, great entertainment, and the cameras lapped it up... but then I heard the dreaded phrase: *"VAR is taking a look at this, is there an offside somewhere in the build-up?"* Soon the Sky cameras had found the errant ball, the one Harrison touched through to Tyler Roberts and, for the umpteenth time this season, VAR was now drawing copious lines across the TV screen and eventually concluded that Roberts, leaning forward as he made his run, just had the edge of his shirt sleeve ahead of the rear-most defender's boot. In the eyes of the VAR Roberts was offside. It took an age to come to the decision and the cameras lingered on the face of Luke Ayling in slow motion as he mouthed *"It can't be offside!"*. But it was, probably by no more than an inch and once again a memorable football moment had been wiped away and I did wonder if this was just that London curse rearing its ugly head again.

Leeds were mainly on top for the first half hour but whenever Fulham won a corner our familiar defensive frailties were never far away. We'd given one away in the very first minute and made a real hash of clearing that one but then, in the 25th minute, I'm sure all Leeds fans across the country were diving behind their sofas again as the ball ricocheted around the Leeds area following Fulham's second corner of the game. It was launched into the area from the Fulham right wing by Ademola Lookman and at least Kalvin Phillips did get his head to the ball first to knock it as far as the edge of the area. It was headed straight back though and we had to endure a few moments of head tennis as it went back and forth before Ayling managed to whack it straight up into the air in front of our goal. Meslier came and punched this one but again it only got to the edge of the area from where Fulham headed it back into the danger zone and there was another round of head tennis. Eventually it fell to Josh Maja, back to goal about ten yards out and with Pascal Struijk tight behind him. Maja was too clever for the Leeds youngster though and was able to turn and lash the ball fiercely and it looked a goal all the way. Somehow though, Illan Meslier instinctively threw out a big right hand and the ball cannoned off his wrist and Luke Ayling was on hand to hook the spinning ball off the line and finally away to safety. It was a turning point in the game.

Leeds went up the other end and won a throw-in deep in the left wing corner and Gjanni Alioski stood with the ball poised over his head as he waited for someone to move; the game was 29 minutes old. Eventually Jack Harrison made a run towards the byline and Alioski's throw was perfect, dropping just in front of Harrison's left boot. He hooked it across first time towards the near post and Patrick Bamford was there to sweep it past Areola in the Fulham goal; it took all of three seconds!

With Leeds so dominant, apart from those Fulham corners, you'd have thought we would now motor on and put the game to bed but, well, that wouldn't really be Leeds United in London would it? No, what we did was give away another daft, needless corner as Alioski let the ball scuff off his boot when trying to clear. That was a left wing corner that Patrick Bamford got up to clear off the top of his head but it went for yet another corner on the opposite side; Lookman trotted all the way across the pitch to take this one as well. The cameraman knew what was about to happen as he focussed on the giant figure of Joachim Andersen jostling with a worried-looking Luke Ayling. Sure enough, the ball flew across, straight onto the right boot of Andersen and he managed to get in front of Ayling to stab the ball into the net. It was yet another piece of naïve defending at a set-piece; the 11th goal we'd conceded from corners this season and the 14th from all set-piece situations. We were far and away the top of both of those particular tables. We never, ever, attack the ball when defending corners, it's ludicrous how simple it is for sides to exploit our naivety.

Having dominated the first half we were now back level and, but for another fine save from Illan Meslier, it could have got even worse. Pascal Struijk headed weakly back towards his own keeper and Meslier did well to get down at the feet of Cavaleiro, a big black '17' on his white shirt giving me the heebie-jeebies, to block the ball away. But it was eventually worked back to Anguissa on the edge of the area and this time Meslier had to dive full length to his right to turn the shot away. At the break it was still 1 – 1 but Meslier's saves had definitely prevented that being 3 – 1 despite Leeds otherwise bossing the game.

The second half was a lot more straight forward and the winning goal, when it came, was another Bielsaball move from one end to the other. Ademola Lookman should probably have scored for Fulham but we have Tyler Roberts to thank for at least putting the Cottager off as he could only scuff the ball out towards the touchline when it looked easier to score. Luke Ayling won his usual 'flop' free-kick and Leeds swiftly moved up the other end. Phillips, with a chunky midfield tackle, got the ball through to Bamford and, with a funny little wrong foot pass through the back line, Paddy got the ball to Raphinha. The Brazilian, showing his close control to nick it between two defenders with his left foot, then prodded it home with his right; gone in 20 seconds!

Overall it's churlish to pick holes in this performance; to win in London against an in-form side that knew it probably had to win to save its Premier League life has to be considered a great achievement. We cannot avoid however the fact that defensively we didn't look strong when the ball got near our goal. Our non-defending of corners was legendary of course and it had to be improved if we were to progress next season. It had been going on too long now and with all sorts of different personnel involved over the years. Maybe it was just a matter of finding the right centre-back pairing, but I thought there were question marks against all of the back four we saw involved tonight from a defensive standpoint and, while we now had a goodly selection of centre-backs to choose from, I'd have been hard-pressed to say which pairing was the best. Was the corner issue one of organisation or personnel or both? I had no idea, but solve it we must. We'd cracked the London Curse now we had to solve the corner conundrum.

The win in London had indeed come at the 17th attempt and this one felt like the one that made us safe. Leeds moved onto 39 points and we'd end this final weekend before the next international break in

11th place in the table, behind Arsenal and Aston Villa with 41 points and ahead of Crystal Palace with 37. The win was also significant in that it meant we'd now taken 24 points from 27 against the sides currently occupying the bottom seven places in the table; only that inexplicable home defeat to Brighton blotted that particular copybook. We'd done exactly what we needed to do this season and we'd shown ourselves to be better than about half the teams in the division. The summer acquisitions of Rodrigo, Koch, Llorente, and particularly Raphinha (as he was the only one to avoid injury), had been just enough to transform our Championship winning side into a mid-table Premier League side. The key this coming summer would be to add in enough new quality to move us further up the table next season and keep the momentum going.

It seemed that despite breaking the London Curse this weekend, another trait of Leeds United was still very much with us. That familiar roller-coaster of emotions saw us all cock-a-hoop on Friday night only to awake on Saturday morning to more bad news. My buddy Russell sent me a WhatsApp message with a note saying: *"Did you see this mate?"* He'd attached a screenshot of an article under the headline: *"Peter Lorimer: Leeds United's record goal-scorer dies aged 74."*

All Leeds fans were aware that Lorimer had been very ill for a while and had been moved into a hospice with a diagnosis of brain cancer. In fact, a misinformed social media post had many fans wrongly posting their eulogies to 'Lash' a couple of weeks earlier. Now he had succumbed and his name was added to the list of Revie legends that we'd already lost. Gone were Gary Sprake, Jack Charlton, Paul Madeley, Billy Bremner, Norman Hunter, Trevor Cherry, the Don himself, and now Peter Lorimer; all part of the Leeds United I grew up with and adored. Lorimer was a very special player who had a very special shot; one that often triggered the chant of *"Ninety-miles-an-hour!"* He scored 238 goals in 705 appearances during two separate spells at the club. Making his debut at the age of just 15 years 289 days, he remains to this day the youngest player to have ever turned out for the first-team. This was another very sad day as we lost another piece of our history but the memories he has left us all with will live on forever.

Fulham 1 **Leeds Utd 2 (Bamford 29**, Andersen 38, **Raphinha 58)**
BCD. **Round 29 League Pos: 11th**

Interminable Break!

There were three other EPL games played this weekend, the last before the next international break. On Saturday, Brighton heaped more trouble on Newcastle as they comprehensively beat the Toon 3 – 0 while, on Sunday, West Ham and Arsenal drew 3 – 3, the Gunners coming back from 3 – 0 down. Aston Villa lost 0 – 2 at home to Spurs. That meant that at the bottom, Brighton opened up a four point gap to Newcastle who, in turn, remained two points ahead of Fulham in that final relegation spot, with everyone agreed that Albion and Sheffield United were already doomed; they were ten and 14 points adrift of safety already. Fulham looked favourites to join them as they'd also played a game more than the rest. At the top, Manchester City remained 14 points ahead of Manchester United with Leicester a further point back and then Chelsea a further five points adrift.

This was the weekend of the rioting in Bristol. A peaceful rally labelled as the 'Kill the Bill' protest took place during the day with thousands of folk protesting against the planned police, crime, sentencing and courts bill that threatened to tighten up the laws regarding protests. But, in a 'game of two halves', as darkness fell the protest was hijacked by a few violent militants intent on attacking the police. 20 officers were injured, one suffering a punctured lung after being stamped on. Protesters threw bottles and the police station was daubed with anti-police graffiti. Twelve police vehicles were damaged, two set on fire. A video doing the rounds on social media even showed two women baring their backsides and appearing to defecate in front of officers standing guard outside the police station.[1]

As we waited for the international games to begin, the Leeds United U23s continued their assault on the Premier League Div. 2 title as they demolished West Brom 0 – 5. A hat-trick from Joe Gelhardt including two penalties, a goal from Crysencio Summerville, and an astonishing free-kick from Sam Greenwood

---

[1]   https://www.theguardian.com/uk-news/2021/mar/22/a-game-of-two-halves-how-bristol-protest-went-from-calm-to-mayhem

kept Leeds 13 points clear of Stoke who now had five games to play. One more win would do it for Leeds.

Tuesday began with news of yet another ex-Leeds footballer passing away. Frank Worthington died after a long illness at the age of only 72. Worthington played only 35 games for Leeds between March and November 1982 scoring 15 goals and he was rightly considered a bit of a maverick if not perhaps a legend. He played for more than 20 different clubs in a 25-year career stretching from 1966 to 1991. He eventually became a much-prized after-dinner speaker when he was able to recount his many tales which were also documented in his aptly named and revealing autobiography; *"One Hump or Two"*.

The international football frenzy began on Wednesday this week, 24th March, with Belgium beating Wales 3 – 1 as the World Cup qualifiers began. Tyler Roberts was a 66th-minute substitute for the Welsh. Amongst a host of other games the only one coming close to a shock was Ukraine getting a 1 – 1 draw in France having been beaten at the Stade de France 7 – 1 as recently as last October!

On Thursday, Gjanni Alioski played the full 90 minutes and got his obligatory yellow card as his North Macedonia side lost 3 – 2 in Romania, while Diego Llorente was probably happy to stay on the Spanish bench as they could only draw 1 – 1 at home to Greece. Stuart Dallas played every minute as Northern Ireland lost 2 – 0 in Italy while Liam Cooper was still absent following his positive Covid test as Scotland could only draw 2 – 2 at home to Austria. England opened their campaign with a 5 – 0 win over San Marino with Kalvin Phillips in midfield. Mateusz Klich would miss all three of Poland's games during this break, including the game at Wembley against England, as he tested positive for Covid this week.

The second round of games began at the weekend and it was more bad news for the Republic of Ireland as they followed up a 3 – 2 defeat to Serbia with a disastrous 0 – 1 loss against Luxemburg that meant new manager Stephen Kenny was still waiting for his first win after ten attempts! Northern Ireland were in a similar position as they lost a friendly against the USA 1 – 2, although Stuart Dallas remained on the bench throughout that one. NI, much like the Republic, were still searching for a first win in a standard 90 minutes in 10 attempts under *their* new manager, Ian Baraclough, although they did win that penalty shoot-out to reach the Euro Finals. Wales played a friendly in which they beat Mexico 1 – 0 with Tyler Roberts playing the first 65 minutes while Alioski also played 65 minutes as North Macedonia romped to a 5 – 0 win against Liechtenstein. Diego Llorente got 45 minutes as Spain won 1 – 2 against Georgia and Kalvin Phillips played 70 minutes as England won comfortably 0 – 2 in Albania. Wales had to play their second World Cup qualifier, against the Czech Republic, without Tyler Roberts. The Leeds striker was sent home by the Welsh management along with Hal Robson-Kanu and Rabbi Matondo after the threesome had broken curfew rules at the team hotel. Although the FA of Wales refused to give specific details, Roberts himself later apologised saying: *"I shouldn't have been up later in the hotel than the set time."* Wales won the game 1 – 0.

We had to wait for the final round of games, the third most of the international sides had played in eight days, for the biggest shock; Ezgjan Alioski helped North Macedonia to win 1 – 2 in Germany. The defeat ended Germany's 35-game unbeaten run in World Cup qualifying, stretching back to their 5-1 defeat by England in 2001. Alioski's day wasn't totally positive mind, it was Gjanni who fouled Leroy Sane to give away the penalty for the German goal! Diego Llorente was an unused substitute again as Spain beat Kosovo 3 – 1 while Stuart Dallas headed against the crossbar as Northern Ireland could only draw 0 – 0 with Bulgaria. England rounded off their games with a third win from three as Kalvin Phillips again played the full 90 minutes in a 2 – 1 win against Poland. And, thankfully, that was the end of this latest international break that had seemed to go on forever.

I had thought that the first Grand Prix of the season was going to provide some rare excitement during the break but, close as Max Verstappen got to winning the race in Bahrain at one point, it was still Lewis Hamilton who ultimately came home first, while the TV highlight of the week was the screening of the excellent, though sad, documentary: *Finding Jack Charlton.* Celebrating Jack's magical ten years as manager of the Republic of Ireland, the programme also showed how dementia had cruelly taken many of his memories from him. Thankfully Big Jack has left lots of memories for the rest of us to continue to enjoy in the years to come.

Blades Cut Down

It wasn't only the Jack Charlton documentary that caught my eye on TV this week; while watching the national BBC news one night I was surprised to spot Sir Kier Starmer, the Labour Party leader, being interviewed inside Elland Road. I'm pretty much allergic to politicians so I didn't initially catch what he was talking about but a quick search on Google explained why he was there. He'd been meeting coaches and representatives from the club's official charity, the Leeds United Foundation, discussing their Positive Choices programme aimed at trying to reduce violence and knife crime by airing the issue with secondary school pupils.

Eventually, my focus shifted towards the upcoming Leeds game; Sheffield United at Elland Road on Easter Weekend. The main talking point ahead of the game concerned the return to Elland Road of Paul Heckingbottom, the last Leeds manager prior to Marcelo Bielsa taking over. It was inevitable that Marcelo would be questioned about his predecessor at the press conference and we weren't disappointed in that respect. Bielsa was predictably charitable as he responded: *"The people who remain at the club have a very good concept of the work he did here. I've only heard praise given in the time that he was here. What I value a lot is that a great proportion of the players who are the base of the team were here when he was around"*. That was in stark contrast of course to the bitter criticism heaped on Heckingbottom by many Leeds fans on social media at the time who seemed to bracket him along with Dave Hockaday as two men considered not fit to darken our doors. I felt some of the criticism of 'Hecky' was misguided and the *"Hecky out"* clamouring at the end of the 2017/2018 season was a bit blinkered. When he was appointed he was immediately derided by many for his lack of experience in the big time and his record of just four wins from sixteen games in charge was taken as evidence that he couldn't cut it at a club like Leeds. He probably didn't help himself much either when he suggested that the controversial and much-criticised summer tour of Myanmar was *"not about the football"* shortly after Andrea Radrizzani had proclaimed that it was actually *"all about the football"* and nothing to do with his business interests in that region! There were certain things that Heckingbottom pointed out too that, once addressed by Bielsa, started to show better results on the pitch. Hecky had commented that we needed *"better balance in the squad"* and he noted that the players were nowhere near as fit as they needed to be. The fitness instilled by Bielsa is now legendary of course while he had also quickly ring-fenced 15 players he wanted rid-of, including the likes of Jay-Roy Grot, Pawel Cibicki, Andy Lonergan, Mallik Wilks, Marcus Antonsson, Hadi Sacko, and Luke Murphy who were all shipped out quickly either on loan or permanently. We will never know whether the re-balancing of the squad and the improved fitness could have provided similar improvements under Hecky as Bielsa achieved. For now though, all Leeds fans were hoping the original assessment of Heckingbottom was correct and that he wasn't about to transform the Blades into world-beaters!

He'd not started too well it had to be admitted; Sheffield United were hammered in their first game under Heckingbottom 5 – 0 at Leicester while in their second, an FA Cup tie at Chelsea, they improved marginally to only lose 2 – 0. Most observers had written the Blades off months ago in terms of them having any chance of avoiding relegation and they came into our game 14 points from safety with only 27 to play for; they had no chance. For Leeds, this was seen as the game when a win would categorically, if not still mathematically, secure another season in the Premier League. It was also important for local bragging rights of course, being a Yorkshire derby, while anything less than a win against a side so clearly destined for relegation would be a real disappointment. Our record so far against sides below us in the table was almost immaculate; we'd won eight of our nine games against the current bottom seven sides with just the home reverse against Brighton spoiling a 100% record.

Elland Road would be empty of spectators still as all games continued to be played behind closed doors, although discussions continued between the football authorities and the government as to whether fans might be allowed back for at least one game before the season ended in May. Plans were being made for the Carabao Cup Final and FA Cup Final to have 8,000 and 21,000 fans respectively inside Wembley as part of a series of new test events being considered to establish how the transformation back to normality might be orchestrated. Playing away from home was about the only thing in the Blades' favour as the statistics showed it was probably the away sides that now had the advantage with away wins in the Premier League currently exceeding home wins for the first time in Premier League history. The tally ahead of this weekend's games was 108 home wins to 114 away wins. In the previous five seasons combined only five times had sides been better away from home than on their own pitches throughout a season. This season alone there were currently already seven sides in that situation while three more had an identical points tally home and away.

If we needed any more evidence then the first game of the weekend, where West Brom visited Chelsea, provided it. In one of the shocks of the season so far the home side went down 2 – 5, although the early sending off of Chelsea's Thiago Silva was probably more significant than any 'away advantage' in that one. It was a result that gave just a glimmer of hope that Big Sam Allardyce might yet cash in on his survival bonus by keeping the Albion up, although they'd end the weekend still seven points adrift of safety with only 24 points to play for. With that game out of the way it was time to settle down in front of the TV for the Leeds v Blades clash and I hoped we wouldn't add to those away win statistics!

About an hour before our kick-off and 70 minutes into the Chelsea game (with the Albion 2 – 4 to the good at that stage), the Leeds team was announced on Twitter. There was just one change from the side that won at Fulham; Liam Cooper had finally posted a negative Covid test and so was passed fit to play and he replaced Pascal Struijk who dropped to the bench. Many Leeds fans thought that was unlucky on Pascal who'd performed heroically this season whenever called upon. Mateusz Klich was over his Covid issues and was also named on the bench.

Meslier

Ayling Llorente Cooper (Capt) Alioski

Phillips

Raphinha Roberts (Klich 81) Dallas (Koch 90+3) Harrison

Bamford (Rodrigo 65)

Subs: Casilla, Koch, Struijk, Shackleton, Poveda, Costa, Hernandez, Klich, Rodrigo.

Sheffield United: Ramsdale, Baldock (Ampadu 45), Jagielka, Stevens, Bogle (Brewster 73), Lundstram, Norwood (Burke 65), Fleck, Osborn, McGoldrick, McBurnie (Egan 77). Subs not used: Foderingham, Mousset, Lowe, Bryan, Ndiaye.

Referee: Graham Scott.

I watched most of the pre-amble before the game on Amazon Prime and at one point the cameras showed all the Leeds players wearing T-shirts during the warm-up in tribute to Peter Lorimer. They carried the words: *"RIP PETER HOTSHOT LORIMER"*. It was also a few days short of the 21st anniversary of that dark day in Turkey, 5th April 2000, when Leeds fans Chris Loftus and Kevin Speight were killed before our game with Galatasaray. Hence, before the game, both sides lined up around the centre-circle for a minute's applause in honour of them and Lorimer while the cameras picked out a huge banner carrying the same message as those T-shirts and then a long blue and white banner with the message: *"RIP CHRIS AND KEV NEVER FORGOTTEN"* that had been paraded outside the ground earlier. There were tributes to Lorimer, Chris and Kev, and Frank Worthington in the match-day programme too, including three iconic pictures of 'Lash' on the front cover. Finally, once the players had all taken the knee, we were up and running for our 30th Premier League game of the season.

Leeds were on the attack straight away and within ten seconds of the start we'd won the first free-kick of the game near the right corner of the Blades' penalty area in front of the South Stand. Raphinha whipped it just too high. The pitch looked to have benefitted from the three week rest since we hosted Chelsea and now looked to have plenty of grass on it for the first time since the autumn so that didn't look likely to be a factor this week.

There were the inevitable scary moments whenever the Blades won a corner, the first coming as early as the 5th minute, but that one sailed high over the heads of everyone in the box and safely over the byline. In general it was Leeds that looked the sharpest and Kalvin Phillips in particular was on his toes as he closed down Lundstram and immediately hit a shot that needed Ramsdale to be on his too, diving away to his right to push the ball away. Stuart Dallas tested him again seconds later hitting a rasping left-foot shot that again Ramsdale beat away with his fists. It was no surprise that Leeds took the lead as early as the 12th minute.

Kalvin Phillips took a free-kick on half way and touched it out wide but, after seeing nothing on ahead of him, Jack Harrison played the ball back via Liam Cooper all the way to Illan Meslier. Meslier this time tapped the ball out to the right to Luke Ayling who played it first time back inside to Diego Llorente. The Spaniard drifted wide again and then left Oli McBurnie on his backside on the touchline with a sharp side-step before scooping the ball down that right wing to Stuart Dallas. The Irish Rover played a one-two with Raphinha but couldn't get to the return pass before it was intercepted. Not to be outdone, Dallas then immediately robbed Enda Stevens and pushed the ball forward into the path of Tyler Roberts. The Welshman then slid the ball outside Ben Osborn while Raphinha scooted past on the inside to collect the ball again, now inside the area to the right of goal. Raphinha swayed past George Baldock with the Blade wary not to bring the Brazilian down and it was then a simple ball across the face of goal and Jack Harrison, who'd started the move on the left wing some 30 seconds earlier, who was able to tap the ball into the unguarded net. The move was another thing of beauty.

On the half hour, Leeds ought to have been two to the good and the Blades should have been down to ten men. Patrick Bamford played a ball inside to Raphinha but the Brazilian jumped over it and it became instead a hospital pass right into the space between Tyler Roberts and George Baldock, about 30 yards from the Blades' goal and in the centre of the pitch. Both men went for the ball but Baldock slid in with both feet and cleared Roberts out a millisecond after Roberts poked the ball on to Jack Harrison. The Citeh loanee then only had Ramsdale between himself and glory but, from the edge of the box, Harrison's low shot through Ramsdale's legs brushed the inside of his right thigh and that was enough to deflect it wide of the post. It was a big chance wasted but, meanwhile, Baldock had stayed prone on the turf while Roberts was brushing himself down. Replays would show that the Baldock challenge was at the very least a booking and could, on another day, have been a red card but in fact he got off scot-free, probably because he appeared to have banged his head on the ground and was now being assessed for a head injury. Concussion was a red-hot topic in the game at the moment and of course the concussion substitute rule was still being trialled. I expected Baldock to go off – assuming he wasn't just feigning the injury to evade the booking – but, after a lengthy stoppage, he carried on, only to then sit down again 15 minutes later, apparently with blurred vision. This time he was substituted under the new rules. We'll never know what difference it would have made had Baldock seen red but, within two minutes and deep into added time at the end of the first half, the Blades sliced through us.

It came from a rare loose pass from Raphinha, near halfway, as he tried an extravagant back heel but only found Enda Stevens who, in turn, fed the ball forward to John Fleck in the inside right channel. Leeds had six players behind the ball in our own penalty area but every single one of them was fixated by the ball at the feet of Fleck and no one picked up the runners moving off the ball. Fleck played it along the edge of the area to McGoldrick who, in turn, touched it first time to McBurnie who was unmarked and 12 yards from goal on the right side of the area. McBurnie shot with his right foot but pulled it across the face of goal but, with the six Leeds defenders still all mesmerized by the ball, no one had bothered to check who was behind them; Ben Osborn had the simplest of tasks to smash the ball in at the back post although for a moment it looked as though Luke Ayling had kept it out. Sadly Ayling was well behind the line when he stopped the ball with his thigh.

So, at halftime, the score was 1 – 1 and the Blades still had a full set of players on the pitch, neither of which made any sense at all. The first half statistics had Leeds well on top; 12 shots to 5 and with 57% of the possession and with just one shot on target for Sheffield United against five for Leeds. We'd dominated the game and yet had little to show for it and we'd conceded a very poor goal.

The defining moment in the game came just under four minutes after the break. Illan Meslier bowled the ball overarm to Luke Ayling who exchanged passes with Llorente as they explored their options on the right of the pitch. Ayling then launched the ball towards the centre-circle where it was collected by Patrick Bamford who'd had a particularly quiet game so far. Bamford touched the ball short to Tyler Roberts who looked up and saw Jack Harrison racing down the left wing. Roberts played the ball fully 45 yards diagonally across the pitch and Harrison met it right on the left corner of the Blades' area where he showed again his amazing touch as he killed the ball stone dead with his first touch. With his second touch he sent the ball across the face of goal looking for Raphinha at the back post but Jagielka dived in feet first and deflected it into his own net. It was another fine goal that showcased the vision of Tyler Roberts and that instant control that we'd all grown accustomed to seeing from Jack Harrison. It was a shame Jagielka got in the way of course as it would have been a fine goal for Raphinha otherwise. It was also a shame we were not inside the ground; once again that goal was scored just yards away from my regular seat and it would have sparked some major celebrations amongst our little gang near the front of the Kop. 2 – 1 to Leeds and the score once again reflected the balance of the game. Leeds had half-chances to put the game beyond the Blades' reach but we didn't ever stretch Ramsdale too much and, of our 11 second-half attempts, only two more actually hit the target, albeit that was better than the Blades who failed to record a single second-half attempt on the Leeds goal. Stuart Dallas took careful aim and curled a right-footer that just clipped the right-angle of post and bar, Patrick Bamford was put through but wanted too much time and was robbed at the last minute, and then Raphinha too let himself down with a poor final touch. Bamford then had another close-range shot blocked. It was all Leeds but, if I had to criticise, our final ball, final touch or the shots we managed were all just a bit lacking in accuracy. Both sides made substitutions in the 65th minute with Rodrigo replacing Patrick Bamford and Ollie Burke replacing Oliver Norwood for the Blades. Sheffield won a few more corners which are always nervous moments but Leeds dealt well enough with them for once and, apart from a couple of long-range shots that flew harmlessly wide, the visitors had nothing much to offer. They did see red midway in the second half but it was only the blood flowing from Jayden Bogle's nose as a stray arm from Alioski whacked him in the face; Bogle was replaced by Rhian Brewster. Leeds gave Mateusz Klich a run-out for the final ten minutes as he replaced Roberts and then Robin Koch saw a couple of minutes of service right at the end as he replaced Stuart Dallas.

At the end of the day it was another win against a bottom-seven side stretching our record to nine wins from ten games against those teams with still only Brighton spoiling the clean sweep with their 0 – 1 win at Elland Road in January. As I said earlier on, it would have been a huge disappointment had we not won this game so all was well, but I couldn't shake off the feeling that, with just a smidgeon more care in the final third we could have made it a lot more comfortable. As it was we'd consolidated our position in mid-table and that was pretty much where we deserved to be. After the game Marcelo Bielsa told the BBC: *"We had chances to score more goals and there were a lot of dangerous actions that didn't finish in shots... But as we didn't establish more than a one-goal difference and as we didn't convert any more of these chances, the final part of the game left a sensation that we were hanging on."*

That was a pretty much perfect summary from Marcelo who was sporting a black woolly hat covering a sharp new haircut despite the fact that the hairdressers were still not open due to the Covid regulations. I wonder if Alioski did it for him?

Leeds United 2 Sheffield United 1 (**Harrison 12**, Osborn 45+2, **Jagielka 49 og.**)
BCD. Round 30 League Pos: 11th.

Dallas at the Double!

All the games at the weekend were at different kick-off times so it was possible to watch them all live again. For once I didn't, as a few jobs got in the way but if I didn't see them live I caught the highlights on Match Of The Day. After our clash with the Blades, I did watch as our next opponents, Manchester City, sailed on serenely towards another title as they disposed of Leicester City 0 - 2. Then Liverpool also improved those away win statistics as they outgunned the Gunners at the Emirates Stadium 0 – 3. Hence, of the four Saturday games, another three were added to those away win statistics. On Sunday, the balance was restored a bit as there were no away wins. Southampton beat Burnley 3 – 2, Aston Villa came from behind to beat Fulham 3 – 1, Manchester United squeaked past Brighton 2 - 1 and the fourth game, between Newcastle and Spurs, was drawn 2 – 2. On Monday, a bank holiday of course this being Easter weekend, Everton and Crystal Palace drew 1 – 1 while West Ham maintained their push for a top-four place with a vital 2 – 3 win at Wolves.

The Boat Race took place this weekend but, like most everything else these days, Covid had left its mark as it was moved to a stretch of the Great Ouse in Cambridgeshire to avoid any likely crowds in London and some bridge repairs in the capital. Cambridge won both the men's and the women's events. Back on Planet Leeds, the Under 18s bowed out of the FA Youth Cup, unexpectedly going down 4 – 1 against Newcastle United. The 2019/20 accounts were published this weekend too, and they showed that Leeds had pretty much gambled everything on promotion last season. The accounts recorded a loss of just over £62 million for the 13 month period to the end of July 2020, on a turnover of £54 million. Had we not achieved promotion that would have meant significant cloth cutting this year to comply with the Financial Fair Play rules but, as it was, now we were at the top table those figures paled into insignificance. The accounts showed that the Leeds players and staff took home promotion bonuses worth around £22 million and also disclosed that the bonuses likely to be earned this season, if we could avoid relegation, would be worth a staggering £35 million more; if ever you needed confirmation as to the financial importance of staying up… that was it!

In the Champions League quarter-final first-leg games this week, there were wins for Manchester City against Borussia Dortmund, and Chelsea against Porto, but Liverpool faced an uphill challenge to reach the semi-finals as they slid to a 3 – 1 defeat at Real Madrid. In the only game not featuring an English side, PSG took a useful lead back to Paris having defeated Bayern Munich 2 – 3.

In the Europa League quarter-final first-leg games, Arsenal were held at home by Slavia Prague but Manchester United secured a two-goal lead at Granada. In the two other games, Roma won at Ajax 1 – 2 and Villarreal grabbed a 0 – 1 result at Dinamo Zagreb.

In the press conference ahead of the trip to the Etihad, Marcelo Bielsa captured the essence of the challenge we faced against what was considered to be currently the best club side in Europe. City had won 18 of their last 19 League games; 27 of their last 28 in all competitions; and had only lost three games all season. They were, quite simply, a class apart. Bielsa commented: *"If we don't take the ball off City, we know the consequence."* We all did!

On the face of it Leeds didn't have much chance. We'd shown ourselves to be the archetypal mid-table side this season; quite able to beat sides in the bottom half of the table yet usually struggling against the sides in the top half. We had only one win so far against any side in the current top seven places in the table – that excellent but unexpected 1 – 3 result at Leicester at the end of January. We did also win at Everton and Villa of course, and they were currently in 8th and 9th spots respectively, but we lost the return games against them both at Elland Road. The significant point here though is that against the sides currently in the bottom seven places we had an almost 100% record home and away; ten wins out of 11 games with just the home defeat to Brighton blotting our copybook so far. It was these statistics that got me believing that the current squad was doing the best it was likely to achieve. If we wanted to progress next season then surely we'd have to dip into the transfer market again this summer to bring in two or three more top-quality players, players ready to go straight into the 1st XI, players who would not look out of place in any of the big six squads. Of course, if we could start to bag positive results against the likes of Manchester City then, maybe, I'd have to reassess that belief!

The Bielsa press conference was held on Thursday this week with the first Premier League game of the next round scheduled for the Friday night; Fulham would host Wolves in a vital game that the Cottagers really had to win if they were to have any chance at all of avoiding the drop. I was just checking which channel was showing the Fulham game later when, at 12:09 on Friday, I received a WhatsApp message from my son Mark. It read simply: *"Phillip dead"*.

Mark's not a great one for using a sentence when two words will do but it was fairly obvious what he was referring to; HRH Prince Phillip, the Duke of Edinburgh had passed away. He'd not long returned to Windsor Castle having spent the best part of a month in hospital and he was just two months and a day short of his 100th birthday so it was no real surprise he'd passed away, but it did feel like the start of the end of an era. His life was celebrated and tributes were paid for the rest of the day on most TV channels while all the national newspapers the following day carried huge supplements; the media had clearly been prepared for this day for a very long time. The BBC even had Prince Charles and others wearing black ties discussing the Duke's life in pre-recorded interviews which again must have been recorded weeks, if not months, earlier. I learned many years ago that there are files in existence covering the eventualities of all royal deaths. Each one has a name, usually a bridge; the Duke of Edinburgh's was 'Operation Forth Bridge' while the protocols for dealing with the Queen's death, whenever that occurs, is in a file titled 'Operation London Bridge'.

There was to be a period of two minutes' silence before each sporting event throughout the weekend starting with the Fulham game on Friday night and including our game at the Etihad of course. Fulham fans might well be holding a further period of mourning sometime soon as they lost their home game with Wolves 0 – 1. Adama Traore scored in added time at the end of the game to break Fulham hearts and bring the prospect of relegation for the Cottagers ever closer. Our game was the first to be played the following day, a 12:30 kick-off on BT Sport on Saturday, 10th April.

Meslier

Ayling Llorente Cooper (Capt) Alioski

Phillips

Raphinha (Shackleton 90+6) Roberts (Koch 63) Dallas Costa

Bamford (Struijk 45+3)

Subs: Casilla, Koch, Struijk, Berardi, Shackleton, Hernandez, Klich, Poveda, Gelhardt.

Manchester City: Ederson, Cancelo, Stones, Aké (Gündogan 58), Mendy (Foden74), Bernardo Silva, Fernandinho, Zinchenko, Torres, Gabriel Jesus, Sterling. Subs not used: Steffen, Walker, Rúben Dias, Rodri, De Bruyne, Mahrez, García.

Referee: Andre Marriner.

So, it was just the one enforced change for Leeds – Helder Costa replacing the ineligible Jack Harrison who had to sit this one out against his parent club. Manchester City offered Leeds a glimmer of hope by making seven changes from the side that defeated Dortmund in the week, leaving De Bruyne, top scorer Gundogan, Phil Foden, and Mahrez on the bench, four players currently at the top of their game. So, hope but no real expectation.

The game was being covered by BT Sport and, as the cameras showed the teams coming out and the pitch-side microphones picked out the strains of Hey Jude blasting out of the stadium PA, the sun was shining brightly; a marked contrast to the pictures shown earlier when the players were warming up in a snow storm. The snow had now moved on to North Shropshire where I was, and the scene outside my windows was now of an almost complete white-out. I settled down with the now obligatory beer in front of the TV and watched as the players and officials stood silently around the centre-circle for the two minutes' silence, the cameras lingering on one of the big screens in the ground that was showing a picture of a smiling Prince Phillip above the inscription: *"His Royal Highness The Prince Phillip, Duke of Edinburgh, 1921 – 2021"*. Then the commentary team of Darren Fletcher and former Leeds Ladies player, Lucy Ward, picked up the action. Lucy Ward was also head of education and welfare at the boys' academy for Leeds, from 1998 until 2015 until being sacked by the club, subsequently winning a sex discrimination and unfair dismissal case in 2016; one of the many legal battles caused by and lost on Massimo Cellino's watch. There was confusion when the game started as only Tyler Roberts dropped to one knee and then he quickly realised the game was starting without that usual ritual!

Leeds, in the all maroon third kit, started the game well and, although Manchester City dominated the possession of the ball, it was Leeds making the more incisive attacks down both wings with either Helder Costa on the left or Raphinha on the right. As early as the third minute I was out of my chair as Raphinha got behind the City defence and stroked the ball across the face of the City goal but no one was there to finish it. We won the first corner of the game in the 7th minute as a Luke Ayling cross was blocked and then we had our first nervous moment at the other end as Llorente needlessly gave City their first corner; we headed that one away well enough. Most of our out-balls were aimed for Raphinha down the right and in the 15th minute Illan Meslier found him out there near halfway with a long left-footed clearance. Raphinha deftly played the ball back to Luke Ayling who, in turn, found Kalvin Phillips before Kalvin touched it to Raphinha again, still hugging that right touchline. The Leeds number '18' took one touch and then clipped the ball towards the right corner of the City area where Tyler Roberts had broken through the City back-line again. Roberts squared the ball across towards Patrick Bamford, unmarked at the back post. Sadly the ball just brushed the leg of John Stones on the way through and that was enough to deflect the ball and to wrong-foot Bamford and the chance was lost. It had been another fabulous Leeds move though, 13 uninterrupted Leeds passes that actually started when Leeds robbed City of the ball out on the Leeds left, with Costa, Cooper, Dallas, Alioski, and Phillips all exchanging quick, short passes before getting the ball back to Meslier. Even when the ball evaded Bamford it was collected by Costa and another 11 Leeds passes were made before City got the ball back. It should have ended in a free-kick to Leeds as, in the process of winning the ball back, Raheem Sterling trod on the ankle of Raphinha and it didn't look accidental to me. Referee Andre Marriner waved play on though and we had to wait for Sterling to launch a shot over the Leeds bar before Raphinha could get treatment on what was clearly a painful knock. It would prove to be only the first of a few cynical fouls by City players including Sterling who seemed to have more stamps in his portfolio than Stanley Gibbons!

This was developing into a fascinating match, both sides enjoying long spells of possession, corners being won at both ends but few actual shots on target. An exception was one from that man Sterling that Meslier saved easily enough at the foot of his right-hand post. Andre Marriner wasn't having the best of games in my opinion; lots of soft Leeds challenges were being given as fouls and yet a few fairly agricultural tackles by City were allowed to go unpunished until Ake finally found his way into the book for a late challenge on Patrick Bamford. The niggling and nasty challenges wasn't something I'd seen from City so far this season and maybe it was a sign of the difficulty they were having in coping with Leeds. Maybe it was frustration, but it wasn't pleasant with Fernandinho leaving something on Llorente and then Silva hooking the ankle of Kalvin Phillips, again both incidents unseen by Marriner who really did seem all at sea.

We reached the 41st minute with neither side really in command, and such shots as there had been not really troubling either keeper overly much. Then Leeds won a throw-in deep in their own half on the Leeds left. Alioski lost the ball and then won it back and played it inside to Liam Cooper who put his foot on the ball while he pondered his next move. He must have seen a run from Helder Costa and so launched the ball down that left wing where it should have been headed clear by Cancelo but he missed it and then lost out in a foot-to-foot challenge with Costa who then stretched to toe-poke it inside to Paddy Bamford. Patrick was obviously aware that Stuart Dallas was haring towards the box and he nudged the ball further right for the Irish Rover who hit it first time with his right boot from a foot or so outside the area; it was an inch-perfect strike. The ball hit the left post, rolled along the goal-line and nestled inside the net on the other side. The cameras showed Marcelo Bielsa doing a double fist-pump as the players all mobbed Stuart Dallas.

It all looked good as we headed towards the break; a goal to the good and, despite all their possession, City failing to really lay a glove on Leeds apart from those niggly and unpleasant challenges. Then, in a very 'Leedsy' moment, it suddenly appeared to all go awry. City won three throw-ins in quick succession as they moved gradually down their left wing and the third one just went over the head of Luke Ayling into the path of Gabriel Jesus. Steaming in was Liam Cooper and, as the ball bounced up in front of the City man, Cooper swung with his right boot. He got good contact on the ball which sailed away into the distance but his follow-through also caught the side of the knee of the City player and then his other leg. It was a bit reckless but there was no intent on Cooper's part and there was no way he could have avoided contact unless he'd not gone for the ball at all. In any case I wasn't convinced there was too much contact and I guessed the huge tattoo on Jesus' left leg was probably more painful when that was inked. But it was no surprise that Marriner immediately raised a yellow card and that should have been the end of it.

These days of course though there was the inevitable VAR check and, down at Stockley Park, David Coote was reviewing the incident over and over again from multiple angles and in slow motion. Coote is known as a particularly finicky ref and, as I watched the replays in slow motion that BT were showing on the TV, I was worried. Sure enough Marriner got the call to go over to the monitor and every Leeds fan in the world knew what was coming next. I could not remember a single example where, once called to the monitor, the ref on the pitch didn't then change his mind. If you think about it it's almost impossible for him not to follow the advice of the VAR ref who, after all, has the benefit of umpteen replays from various different angles and in both real-time and slow-motion. Add to that the fact that the refs are all covering each other's backsides and never show any disagreement and we knew Coops was a gonner.

It was just so Leeds United! I could fill a book just listing such moments, a few seconds of joy and delight followed almost instantly by a self-inflicted disaster, though to this day I'm still not sure what Coops could have done differently on this one. Bielsa immediately sent on Pascal Struijk to ensure the defence was back up to full-strength and it was a dejected-looking Patrick Bamford who was sacrificed. Presumably Bielsa recognised that the second half would be pretty much one-way traffic and that Bamford wouldn't have seen much of the ball anyway as City battered our ten men with their 11. The interesting aspect of this change was that Bielsa chose young Pascal Struijk and not the far more experienced Robin Koch, although it may just have been the need for a specialist left-footer to replace Cooper. The halftime whistle provided some respite but I have to say to my shame, I didn't have the faith in our players to win this one now, even starting the second half with a one goal lead as we were.

Leeds held out until the 76th minute in the face of an almost constant barrage of attacks from the home side. The Leeds defence was heroic and, truth be told, City didn't really forge any big chances despite their domination of the possession. Their best effort was probably a shot from Zinchenko from the edge of the area that Meslier did brilliantly to get down to, only to then have Sterling charge in and stamp on his hand as he gathered the loose ball. There was something about the sheepish way in which Sterling skulked away that told me he'd done that with the intention of injuring the young keeper but, as before, Marriner saw nothing wrong. Fortunately Meslier seemed OK. The equaliser, when it came, could not be put down to any particular error, it was simply some sharp passing and movement from the City frontmen. Fernandinho slid the ball through the Leeds backline to Silva who, in turn, passed it inside to Torres and his first-time shot found the corner of the net. There was a suspicion of offside about the pass to Silva but, yet again, there were no screenshots of that shown on the TV coverage, so we had to assume VAR checked it and it was OK. Once again though, the fact it wasn't shown to us just sowed the seed in Leeds fans' minds that there was some sort of conspiracy going on here. Social media was full of such complaints after the game.

Leeds had replaced Tyler Roberts with Robin Koch about 13 minutes earlier in an attempt to shore-up the defence further, thus sacrificing our only remaining attacker, so we now faced a final 14 minutes plus added time of what would effectively be attack v defence. The strange thing was though that the more City attacked, the more break-away opportunities seemed to come our way. City appeared to be under the misapprehension that Leeds were only interested in defending the point we had but they'd forgotten about our fitness and our natural desire to go forward. Suddenly, Kalvin Phillips intercepted a pass deep in our own half and he spotted Raphinha making a run into City territory. Kalvin's pass was inch-perfect and Raphinha was through in a one-on-one race with Benjamin Mendy. It was no contest and our man easily outpaced the ponderous City defender and was soon in the area with only Ederson to beat. The City keeper dashed out and slid towards Raphinha and was lucky to take just the ball and not our Brazilian flyer too. City didn't learn the lesson though and, as we moved into added time, Illan Meslier bowled the ball out to the left to Gjanni Alioski. He touched the ball to Costa who was right on the touchline on that left wing and Costa returned the pass dissecting two City players who were trying to close him down. No thoughts of running down the clock in Gjanni's mind though, he spotted Stuart Dallas making a dash through the middle and played a perfect pass with the outside of his left boot, right into the path of the Irish Rover who still looked full of running. He was now in another one-on-one chase after the ball, with John Stones this time keeping pace but not quite able to get to the ball before Stuart did. As Ederson came out to narrow the angle, SD merely side-footed the ball between his legs and the ball rolled deliciously over the goal-line into the net! Leeds had nicked it at the death. Most of the Leeds players celebrated wildly just off the pitch in the one corner of the ground, Illan Meslier racing the full length of the pitch to join them. Only Diego Llorente remained on the pitch, watching to make sure City didn't restart before we were ready!

In the seconds now left, City still failed to come to terms with the Leeds counter-attacking style and soon Raphinha was away again, this time intercepting the ball himself midway in his own half and then racing forward. He skipped past Fernandinho easily but, before he could get away, the City midfielder stuck out a leg and cynically brought the flying Brazilian down with a thud. It was a classic example of the professional foul and it looked a painful one for Raphinha that caught him high on his left thigh. Marriner continued his strangely random decision-making and saw this one as only a yellow card and, for some reason, VAR didn't challenge it. Raphinha would later be seen in pictures on social media with that left thigh tightly strapped and we could only hope no long-lasting damage had been done. If Coops' challenge earlier was worth a red card then this one should have come with a jail sentence.

At the end of the day Leeds had seen off all that City could throw at us and this would go down as a momentous victory. In my eyes, it was a deserved victory too, not only because we'd performed heroically but also in the face of some dire officiating that failed to give us any protection at all. The match stats would be heavily weighted in City's favour with Leeds only managing two attempts at goal, both of which went in of course, compared with 29 for City. Leeds recorded the fewest shots, the lowest share of possession and the fewest touches in the opposition box than in any other game this season and City threw 36 crosses into the Leeds area, the most by any side this season in the Premier League. And yet, when I think about the times we got behind them in the early stages and then those three breakaways at the end, our opportunities were actually better than theirs. After the game Guardiola told reporters: *"We did not create enough for the forwards. It is part of the game. In the last 10 minutes they had other chances, they are fast and can do it. When they defend in the way they were doing you have to stop them running and we did not do that."* That was it precisely, Leeds had the fitness and cunning to play on the break in those final minutes and, actually, City were lucky to get away with just a 1 – 2 defeat. It was a similar situation to the one City faced when they hosted Leicester City back in September when City also bossed the possession and had way more attempts but kept getting caught on the break with four second-half goals.

Leeds were temporarily up to 9th with 45 points and a few Leeds fans were again suggesting a European place was not beyond us. Mathematically they were right of course but for me that was still a stretch. This was a City second team in many respects and it was hard to know how they would compare with what the likes of Liverpool, Man United, and Spurs would field against us in the upcoming games. On another day City might have been luckier with more of their 29 attempts too.

In many ways the game had been a little cameo of our season, it had been a great contest between two sides that play the game in the right manner; those cynical City challenges aside. It was a bit of a mishmash, a game that had a bit of everything, goals, chances, controversy, quality, and mistakes.

In the remaining two games played this Saturday, Liverpool beat Aston Villa 2 – 1 to end their recent awful run of home defeats and then Chelsea ran out easy 1 – 4 winners at Crystal Palace. On Sunday the big winners were Newcastle; they won 1 – 2 at Burnley to put six points between themselves and Fulham in the final relegation place and they also had a game in hand; it looked bleak for the Londoners but this result also had Burnley looking over their shoulder too. West Ham just saw off Leicester City as they continued to look good for a European place and then Manchester United consolidated second place with a 1 – 3 win at Tottenham. The final game of the day saw Arsenal comfortably defeat Sheffield United at Bramall Lane 0 – 3, a result that left the Blades within one defeat of relegation and took the Arsenal back above Leeds as the two sides continued to yo-yo. On Monday night West Brom continued their unlikely escape attempt as they thrashed Southampton 3 – 0. Big Sam's Albion were now only two points adrift of Fulham but they too really needed to catch Newcastle or Burnley to have any hope of another season in the Premier League and that meant they needed to gain eight points on them with only seven games left. It still looked pretty hopeless for Blades, Albion, and Fulham to be honest. The final game of the round saw Brighton and Everton play out a nil-nil draw at the Amex.

Manchester City 1 **Leeds United 2 (Dallas 42, 90+1**, Torres 76) BCD. **Round 31 League Pos: 10th.**

Liverpool Held

It was the quarter-final, second-leg games in the European competitions this week with Chelsea, PSG, Manchester City, and Real Madrid going through to the semi-finals. Liverpool held Real Madrid to a goalless draw at Anfield but went out to the Spanish giants courtesy of the first leg 3 – 1 defeat. City would face PSG and Chelsea would be pitted against Real Madrid in the semi-finals. In the Europa League, both Manchester United and Arsenal progressed and would now face Roma and Villarreal respectively.

It was back to Premier League action on Friday night as Everton and Spurs drew 2 – 2 but most Leeds fans were watching the Leeds United Under 23s as they attempted to clinch the Premier League 2, Division 2 title at the first attempt. I watched on LUTV as Leeds won 1 – 2 at Aston Villa with Adam Forshaw playing almost the full 90 minutes as his rehabilitation continued. Sam Greenwood struck yet another superb free-kick into the top left corner as early as the 4th minute and it should have been as good as job done as Joe

Gelhardt won a penalty. He stepped up to take it himself with one of those annoying Bruno Fernandes 'hops' but experienced Villa keeper Jed Steer saved brilliantly. Leeds did go two –up early in the second half as Jack Jenkins scored following a stunning solo run from Crysencio Summerville to create the opportunity. Villa did get one back near the end and Leeds had to play out the final fifteen minutes with ten men as Charlie Cresswell received a second yellow card. But there were jubilant scenes at full time, as the coaching staff and players were able to celebrate a deserved and hard-fought title-winning campaign that also meant promotion to PL2 Division 1 next season.

Saturday, April 17th was the day of the funeral of Prince Phillip and so all sporting events were shuffled to ensure there was no clash with the 3 pm funeral service that was broadcast live on TV. Due both to the specific wishes of the Prince and the restrictions imposed due to Covid regulations it was a simple service held entirely within the confines of Windsor Castle. One Premier League game was squeezed in before the funeral as Newcastle United further improved their survival hopes with another win; Hernández3 – 2 against West Ham United. The next game was then not until later that night; Wolves beat Sheffield United 1 – 0 thus finally confirming the Blades' relegation. Hours earlier Norwich City's promotion from the Championship, effectively replacing the Blades, was confirmed. The first of the FA Cup semi-finals, also played after the funeral, saw Chelsea surprisingly beat Manchester City 1 – 0 and thus end the Cityzens' hopes of the Holy Grail of the 'quadruple'.

Leeds' match with Liverpool was the last of this round of games and was not kicking off until Monday night so it was another long weekend waiting and I confess I didn't watch any of the games this Sunday. Those matches included the second FA Cup semi-final in which Leicester City beat Southampton 1 – 0 in front of 4,000 lucky spectators at Wembley, this being one of the test events to see how spectators might finally be allowed back into sports arenas once Covid rules allowed. In the two Premier League games played this Sunday, Arsenal drew one-apiece with Fulham leaving the Londoners now six points adrift of Burnley who lost 3 – 1 at Manchester United.

I was working in the garden at my Son's gaff on Sunday and, in between feeding me with the scores of the various games, it was he who informed me of the big breaking news this weekend; the big-six EPL clubs announced their intention to sign up for a new competition styled 'The Super League' (SL) to be commenced as a mid-week competition involving 12 of the top teams in England, Italy and Spain.

The teams involved from the continent were AC Milan, Inter Milan, and Juventus from Italy together with Atletico Madrid, Barcelona, and Real Madrid from Spain. It was believed that a huge sponsorship package had been negotiated for the new SL that promised the 12 clubs untold riches and, with there being no relegation from the SL, that future funding was guaranteed for ever. The attraction was presumably to create a new offering that would appeal to those Generation Z fans we were discussing earlier; the sort of fans that the San Francisco 49ers were eyeing for Leeds including the huge audiences in China, Asia, and America. The new SL would give the clubs involved a unique opportunity to experiment with the game too; divide matches into quarters not halves, introduce more technology and statistics for example. For me that was only going to work though if the clubs could also continue with their domestic presence and yet that was quickly put in doubt.

The ramifications for the English game were uncertain, but virtually the whole of the English football community came out against the proposal, even including fans of the clubs concerned. It was seen as sheer greed on the part of the owners of the big-six to feather their own nests and, with claims that they'd play weakened sides in the Premier League and domestic competitions, the English authorities together with UEFA immediately threatened retaliation by stating that the rogue clubs could be banned from the existing domestic and European competitions and that they would recommend that any player involved would be banned from playing for their national teams.

The debate was still raging as the coverage of our Monday night game with Liverpool began and almost the whole of the pre-game studio discussion concerned the new SL proposal. Gary Neville and Jamie Carragher were, like everyone else, vehemently opposed to the idea, and Sky themselves eventually issued a statement confirming that they'd not been involved in the early discussions as did BT Sport. The only media entity said to be considering involvement in screening the SL games was Disney! Well, it did all sound a bit Mickey Mouse! The bombshell proposals were met with a wave of protest from football authorities, politicians, governments and fans, with UEFA president, Aleksander Ceferin describing them as a *"spit in the face"* for football and those clubs involved as *"snakes"*.[1]

It was all fascinating stuff but, with the extent of the opposition effectively ostracising the six English clubs completely from all the English football community, I couldn't see how it could go ahead.

Some thought it was all a negotiating ploy by the 12 clubs, aware that a new Champions League format was to be unveiled the following day which they considered didn't go far enough in rewarding the big clubs or offering them enough opportunity to earn more cash as they tried to recoup the losses incurred during the pandemic.

Gary Neville certainly endeared himself to all Leeds fans though when he commented that: *"Every single football fan now wants Leeds to win tonight."* Well, maybe not all Leeds fans, there were many who preferred Leeds to be hated by everyone rather than loved! *"Dirty Leeds"* and *"We all hate Leeds"* were badges of honour in many eyes!

Leeds threw themselves into the debate with gusto too; the cameras showed the players warming up in T-shirts with the Champions League logo and the words: *"EARN IT"* on the front and *"FOOTBALL IS FOR THE FANS"* on the back. We apparently left enough supplies in the Liverpool dressing room for them to wear too but they declined! A similar banner was laid out in the North Stand.

It was easy to forget that we had a game to watch but eventually I settled down in my usual spot on the sofa, beer ready and ever hopeful of another good result. The first disappointment had come an hour earlier when the team was announced; there was no Raphinha who was still struggling with that thigh injury picked up

---

[1] *https://www.dailymail.co.uk/sport/sportsnews/article-9487667/BT-Sport-savages-European-Super-League-Sky-REFUSE-comment-controversial-plans.html*

against Manchester City. Hence, with Jack Harrison available again but Liam Cooper suspended, there were just the two changes; Harrison for Raphinha and Struijk for Cooper.

Meslier
Ayling (Capt) Llorente Struijk Alioski
Phillips
Costa Dallas Roberts Harrison
Bamford

Subs: Casilla, Koch, Davis, Berardi, Shackleton, Klich, Hernandez, Poveda, Gelhardt.

Liverpool: Alisson, Alexander-Arnold, Fabinho, Kabak, Robertson, Thiago Alcántara, Wijnaldum, Milner, Jota (Oxlade-Chamberlain 81), Firmino, Mané (Salah71).

Subs not used: Adrián, Keita, Tsimikas, Shaqiri, Davies, R Williams, N Williams.

Referee: Anthony Taylor.

Liverpool seemed to be over their dire mid-season wobble that had destroyed their title ambitions this season and were now focussed on regaining a top four spot to ensure another season in the Champions League, always assuming they were allowed to do so if the ESL controversy was eventually sorted out. They would go back into the top four with a win against Leeds and they came into the game on a run including just one defeat in seven outings, that being the decisive 3 – 1 defeat to Real Madrid. Leeds were unbeaten in four, including three consecutive 2 – 1 victories against Fulham, Sheffield United, and Manchester City. I thought that if we'd had Raphinha then we could win this one but without him I thought we'd be a bit short in attack.

As David Jones, the Sky anchor-man tonight, handed over to the commentary team, the cameras picked out that banner in the South Stand again and then, as the Leeds players marched out onto the pitch, MOT blaring on the PA, we were shown pictures of Victor Orta in the stands. He stood holding one of those T-shirts with that *"FOOTBALL IS FOR THE FANS"* legend printed on the back. He's a lad is that Victor! Apparently there were protests by fans of several clubs outside the ground too, with rumours that a Liverpool shirt was burned while a plane flew over the stadium displaying a message condemning the SL. It was incredible how the announcement of the SL had managed to seemingly unify the world of football and worlds beyond it too; crikey even Boris Johnson and Sir Keir Starmer were in agreement it must be stopped!

Leeds struggled in the first half and it was crystal clear that the absence of Raphinha greatly weakened our attacking options. Neither Harrison nor Costa really got into the game and Liverpool pretty much bossed the play. They took the lead just after the half-hour mark when Trent Alexander-Arnold latched on to Diogo Jota's long pass inside Jack Harrison and squared it to Sadio Mané to slot into an empty net. Illan Meslier had rushed out but failed to get to the ball before Alexander-Arnold. Meslier had earlier denied Liverpool with a fine save to tip over a fierce Thiago shot and had also pouched a powerful Firmino effort. Having said all that though, the best chance of the first half fell to Leeds. Fabinho made a ludicrously lazy pass that was intercepted by Kalvin Phillips who immediately pushed the ball through the Reds' defence into the path of Patrick Bamford. Sadly Paddy's first touch was awful and the ball got away and was smothered by Alisson in the visitors' goal before going out for a corner. So, outplayed as we had been, there was a case for saying we ought to have been level at the break. As it was we went in a goal down and our record of not yet having beaten any current top half side at Elland Road looked likely to continue.

The second half started in much the same vein, with Meslier called into action again, this time saving well from Firmino at his near post before Jota embarrassed us at the subsequent corner by finding himself all alone six yards out. Thankfully he powered his header over the bar. As it happens, that was the end of the Liverpool dominance and somehow, from that point on, Leeds took control of the game. It did look though as if it wasn't going to be our day as we spurned some big chances before we eventually found the net. Jack Harrison wriggled through the Liverpool back-line after some trickery from Tyler Roberts but his point-blank shot was covered by Alisson. Then Patrick Bamford got on the end of a long Luke Ayling ball, brought the ball down superbly with his left boot but could then only find the crossbar with a lob over the keeper. By this time Leeds had brought on Ian Poveda for an anonymous-looking Helder Costa and he was soon in the action. Luke Ayling slotted the ball down the right wing to him and then he perfectly dissected four Liverpool defenders with a pass that Tyler Roberts ran onto,

Roberts now only had Alisson to beat but seemed to go for power not subtlety and once again Alisson was able to get his body in the way. Those were three huge chances, big chances in the statisticians parlance and none found the net. Klich and Hernandez were then sent on to try to rescue a point with Alioski and Roberts making way. Finally, in the 87th minute, we found a way through and, unlikely as it seemed, it came from a Leeds corner!

Jack Harrison swung the ball across and Diego Llorente somehow managed to get free enough to bend his head down and, with the top of his bonce, send the ball wide of Alisson; it was Llorente's first goal for the club and no one could deny that he and the club didn't richly deserve this one. Neither side could improve their tally in the final few minutes and the game ended all square at 1 – 1.

There were some interesting statistics in this one; there were those big chances for Leeds, four more than Liverpool managed and, by the end, Liverpool had been restricted to just 38.8% of the possession; the lowest figure Liverpool had recorded in any game since November 2018! Although Leeds had seemed well below par in that first half, by the end of the game we had pretty much established ourselves as the better side and this against one of those rebel clubs trying to set up the new European Super League. Predictably, Leeds had more to say on that subject after the game, tweeting: *"#LUFC hold Super League Merseyside Reds to a 1 – 1 draw after late Llorente equaliser."*

The following day the big football debate continued and the resolve of the big-six seemed about to crumble as they realised it was them against the football world. Some board members of the rebel clubs were coming out and saying they were not in favour of the deal, which appeared to have been almost secretly agreed between the various club owners. A meeting was hastily convened of the other 14 Premier League clubs to discuss their strategy, while Boris Johnson was saying he was prepared to bring forward legislation to stop the proposal if necessary. As a result of the draw with Liverpool, Leeds remained 10th in the table with all six of the rebel clubs above us. Some Leeds fans were dusting off their passports as they pondered finishing in the Champions League places if those six clubs were kicked out of the Premier League!

Leeds United 1 Liverpool 1 (Mane 31, **Llorente 87**)
BCD. **Round 32 League Pos: 10th**.

"Super League My Arse!"

L ess than 48 hours after the announcement of the new Super League and in the face of widespread condemnation by other clubs, players, fans, pundits, governments, and the football authorities, the whole thing predictably started to crumble. On Tuesday afternoon Pep Guardiola came out publicly against the proposal and, not long after, his club Manchester City withdrew. Chelsea were next; they had a home game with Brighton in the Premier League on Tuesday night, live on Sky and, as there were at Leeds the previous night, hundreds of fans turned up to protest, so much so that the Brighton coach couldn't get through and the kick-off had to be delayed. It was said that the Chelsea board, including owner Roman Abramovich, had decided to withdraw even before the protests took place as they saw the possibility of huge damage being done to the club's reputation. Former Chelsea player Pat Nevin put it best when he told BBC Radio 5 Live: *"I'm not even*

mildly surprised - it didn't look like Chelsea wanted to get on that train but they didn't want to be left at the station." [1]

The fallout continued apace and next came news that Ed Woodward, Manchester United's executive vice-chairman and a prime mover of the SL proposal, would stand down at the end of 2021. Next was Juventus Chairman Andrea Agnelli; he'd resigned from Uefa and the European Club Association as recently as Sunday night, just before the new SL was unveiled, and now he was rumoured to have fallen on his sword at Juve although this was subsequently denied by his club. Woodward and Agnelli were the two men specifically targeted by Uefa president Aleksander Ceferin over the SL proposals. He said of Woodward: *"... he called me last Thursday evening saying he's very satisfied with and fully supports the reforms [the new Champions League format] and the only thing he wanted to talk about was FFP, when obviously he had already signed something else,".* On Agnelli he said: *"I've never seen a person that would lie so many times, so persistently as he did. It's unbelievable. I spoke with him on Saturday afternoon and he said 'no worries, it's only rumours. I will call you in one hour'. Then he turned off the phone. Obviously greediness is so strong that all human values evaporate."* [2] This SL malarkey had become one of the greatest own goals in the game's long history and I was pleased that my initial reaction to my lad Mark when he broke the news on Sunday had proved correct: *"Super League My Arse!"* I told him.

In that game between Chelsea and Brighton, once the Brighton and Chelsea coaches got through the throngs of protesting fans thanks largely to the pleas of Chelsea Performance Advisor and former keeper Petr Čech, it ended in a goalless draw. During the warm-up the Brighton players all wore the same T-shirts we'd seen the Leeds players wear 24 hours earlier. The only action of note in the game was the sending off of Ben White in the final minutes for a second yellow card. It seemed a lot of water had passed under a lot of bridges since we were hanging out *"#Free Ben White!"* banners! The point for Chelsea was enough to take them above West Ham again, back into fourth spot in the table and into those precious

---

[1] https://www.bbc.co.uk/sport/football/56823501

[2] https://scroll.in/field/992731/european-super-league-Uefa-president-slams-uniteds-ed-woodward-juventus-andrea-agnelli

Champions League places which they might now need if they were no longer going for that SL guarantee. The point for Brighton put them seven points above Fulham in the relegation zone and seemingly safe.

Before the night was out, Sky were reporting that Arsenal, Manchester United, Liverpool, and Tottenham had joined City and Chelsea to commence the process of leaving the SL even before it had begun which was no doubt going to be a painful and expensive process for them all. They were all now reporting that they were sorry for the anxiety caused by their actions and admitting they had made a mistake. The Arsenal official tweet to its supporters said simply: *"As a result of listening to you and the wider football community over recent days we are withdrawing from the proposed Super League. We made a mistake, and we apologise for it."* Time would tell how expensive that mistake would prove to be in money and reputation... The following day Agnelli accepted the project was dead in the water.

On Wednesday evening, despite the big six having all now announced their intention not to join the SL, there were still demonstrations at the grounds as Spurs faced Southampton at the Tottenham Hotspur Stadium and Manchester City travelled to Villa Park. Both rebel clubs won and both by the same score of 2 - 1. On Thursday night Leicester City demolished West Brom 3 – 0 to further strengthen their chances of a top-four finish, while at the same time all but extinguishing Albion's faint hopes of Premier League survival. That completed the latest round of EPL matches, with the majority of teams having played 32 games; Leeds sat securely in 10th spot.

The next round was underway the following night and it was time for another of the SL pretenders to face the discontent of their fans. Arsenal hosted Everton with over 1,000 disgruntled Gooners gathered outside the Emirates Stadium to show their distaste at owner Stan Kroenke's part in the fiasco. The night went from bad to worse for the Gunners as a Bernd Leno howler in the Arsenal goal allowed Everton to return to Merseyside with a one-goal win, a result that kept Arsenal only one place above Leeds in the table on the same 46 points. Their only hope now of getting Champions League football next season was to win the Europa League. Everton, after a dire run of six games without a win, were only three points outside the top four. With Manchester City having as good as won the title, all the interest at the top end of the table was in seeing which other teams would join them in the Champions League next season. Imagine how pointless many games would be at this stage of the season if the big six were guaranteed places in the ECL regardless of final positions; an idea the big six had been pushing for.

The recent announcement of the changes to the Champions League format that will come into effect for the 2024/2025 season and beyond almost went unnoticed amid the uproar over the SL proposal, but it had started to go in the direction of giving places based on historical reputation and not on the most recent domestic league position. For the first time, two clubs that would otherwise miss out will be awarded a place in the ECL according to their 'club coefficient', a measure of their historical success. It is a sort of safety net to try to ensure as many 'top' clubs as possible feature in the biggest club competition in Europe. The other main change is that 36 clubs would now be involved, not 32 as it is now, and they will all start the competition in one big league, each playing ten of the other sides, five at home and five away. The top eight in the league then go straight through to the round of 16 while the teams placed 9th to 24th go into a play-off for the remaining eight spots with 9th playing 24th, 10th playing 23rd et cetera. The round of 16 will then revert to the two-legged knock-out format as it is now. It was unlikely to be of interest to Leeds fans this season but, who knows, that may well be what we are aiming for this time next year!

Our game against Man United was a Sunday afternoon kick-off at 2 pm and I was fitting it in between a two-day session of decorating at my son's house, so I didn't get to watch any of the games on Saturday live. There were more demonstrations, albeit far more muted now the cause was won, outside Anfield before Liverpool's game with Newcastle. The game ended 1 – 1, which seemed to secure Newcastle's place in the EPL for at least another season but left the Reds still outside the all-important top four. Chelsea still occupied fourth spot after winning by the only goal at West Ham. The Blues were behind the two Manchester clubs and Leicester City and now had a three-point gap to the Hammers in 5th and four in front of Liverpool in 6th. In the final game on Saturday,

Sheffield United got their first win under Paul Heckingbottom, beating Brighton 1 - 0. It was too late to do any good for the Blades but it meant Brighton weren't safe yet and they hosted Leeds in seven days' time.

The first game on Sunday was a noon kick-off in which Burnley surprised everyone with a resounding 0 – 4 result at Wolves; former Leeds man Chris Wood scoring a first-half hat-trick. Just before 12:00 I switched off the Black and Decker wallpaper steamer and plonked myself down in front of the huge TV in my lad's man cave ready for the big game; it was like being front row in the cinema!

This was a third consecutive game we'd played against the SL rebels, having beaten Manchester City and drawn with Liverpool in the two previous games; games that seemed to show Leeds were evolving into a pretty solid Premier League side even without the likes of Rodrigo, Robin Koch, and Raphinha who had all missed one or both those games. Leeds fans were all pretty sure we'd be without Raphinha again for this one against Man United and that was confirmed when the team was announced on the club's Twitter feed an hour earlier while I was stripping... the wallpaper that is.

Meslier
Ayling (Capt) Llorente Struijk Alioski
Phillips
Costa (Klich 72) Roberts (Koch 77)Dallas Harrison (Poveda 68)
Bamford
Subs: Casilla, Koch, Berardi, Shackleton, Klich, Poveda, Hernandez, Summerville, Greenwood.
Man United: Henderson, Wan-Bissaka, Lindelöf, Maguire, Shaw, McTominay, Fred (van de Beek 89), James (Pogba 76), Bruno Fernandes, Rashford (Cavani 86), Greenwood. Subs not used: de Gea, Bailly, Mata, Telles, Matic, Tuanzebe. Referee: Craig Pawson.

Hence Leeds' starting XI was, not unsurprisingly, unchanged, while Crysencio Summerville and Sam Greenwood were named on the bench in place of Leif Davis and Joe Gelhardt as Bielsa continued to rotate the youngsters giving them experience of being around the first XI on a match-day. I was nervous seeing the name of Craig Pawson in the middle; for as long as I can remember I've not thought much of him as a referee, and his mate on VAR duty was Mike Dean who needed no further introduction!

Ahead of the game there were the predictable demonstrations and comments aimed at the Manchester United owners for their SL conspiracy. In the match-day programme, Angus Kinnear gave his regular humorous insight, telling readers: *"A fortnight ago we left the Etihad with an instinct that Manchester City didn't take well to being humbled by lowly Leeds United, but we could never have predicted that it would be the catalyst for them creating their own league where they would never have to be inconvenienced with the spectre of on-pitch failure again"*. There was condemnation of the plot from Marcelo Bielsa and Liam Cooper in their columns too, while a plane flew over the ground before kick-off trailing a banner aimed at the Man United owners proclaiming: *"2bn stolen - Glazers out"*. It all gave a little added spice to what was always a feisty encounter between these two famous old rivals.

Manchester United made much of the importance of winning this game to try to keep at least some pressure on Manchester City in the tiny hope that perhaps the Reds could still catch the Blues. They were on a good run of form too. They were unbeaten in their past 23 EPL away games (W15 D8), with only Arsenal between April 2003 and September 2004 having a longer such run (27) in English top-flight history. Leeds had their own streak of form too though as we went into this one unbeaten in five, our longest run without defeat all season and that included games against three of the SL rebels. Once again I could only imagine what the atmosphere would have been like inside Elland Road if fans were there, with all this SL nonsense heaped on top of the usual bitter rivalry between these two sides.

In the event the game didn't really live up to its billing. In a distinctly down-beat first half, chances were few and far between and I could probably have had more fun with the stripper! The game might have taken on a very different complexion though had Messrs Pawson and Dean really understood the nature of the modern-day footballer. A quick Leeds break down the inside left channel towards the South Stand ended when Jack Harrison tried to clip the ball across the area. Harry Maguire was only ten yards or so from the ball as he leaned to his right to try to deflect the ball, arms down by his side to make his frame bigger but not quite big enough to get anything on it. But, as the ball travelled on towards the unmarked Helder Costa at the back post, next in line was Luke

Shaw. He did exactly the same but leaning to his left, and this time he managed to nudge the ball away from danger with his left arm. Leeds players immediately appealed to Pawson for a penalty but Pawson shrugged off the claims. When the game eventually came to the next halt in play we were told on screen that VAR was checking for the handball yet that was quickly resolved in favour of the Manchester defender. It was a cynical nudge with his arm by Shaw who knew he was in big trouble had the ball run past him to the feet of Helder Costa; put simply it was cheating, but they got away with it. Gjanni Alioski, speaking after the game, told reporters what most Leeds fans probably thought: *"If a Leeds defender handled the ball, Man United would've gotten a penalty"*.

It was then not until the half-hour mark that the next moments of note occurred; a Leeds corner that came to nothing and then a Stuart Dallas left-foot shot from the edge of the 'D' that went low and hard into the gloves of Henderson. That chance came from one of numerous occasions that Kalvin Phillips pressed Bruno Fernandes into an error, with the ball breaking to Dallas. In the 37th minute the visitors won their first corner and inevitably my bum cheeks tensed as Sky flashed that bloody graphic up on the screen showing how we were top of the table for goals conceded from corners (11). Not this time though; Patrick Bamford headed it away strongly. Luke Ayling had just been booked and Tyler Roberts quickly followed as Leeds gave away a few soft free-kicks that gave the Reds shooting opportunities. Scott McTominay put a header wide and then Marcus Rashford hit a stinging shot that Meslier acrobatically turned over the angle of post and bar with his left hand. We didn't defend the resulting corner very well at all and Harry Maguire got a free header but put it over the bar. That was the extent of the first half action,

The second half started with action in front of the Leeds goal but Fernandes and Dan James both left the ball for each other as they temporarily got behind an otherwise solid Leeds back line. Fernandes threw himself down at the resulting corner but Pawson wasn't impressed by that one. It was a cagey sort of a game and it showcased again something we'd seen in both the previous games. Against City and Liverpool there were times we were under the cosh but we'd learned how to play such situations and, as a team, now seemed far more able to play a defensive game. After the match, Bielsa highlighted how we were *"evolving"*, learning how to be tight in these situations and showing we were indeed now a match for these so-called big six teams where perhaps we weren't earlier in the season. Man United were dominating the possession now but were not creating any real chances. Fernandes had probably the best sight of goal as he swiped at a ball coming across him but pulled his right-foot shot wide of the left post. Mason Greenwood hit a speculative one from the left corner of the box but Meslier easily got down in front of his right-hand post to save that one. Gjanni Alioski then followed Ayling and Roberts into the book as he mistimed a tackle on Rashford and, to be honest, I cringed every time the little North Macedonian went in for a challenge! Harry Maguire for the Reds and Patrick Bamford then filled more space on the back of Pawson's yellow card as the bookings mounted up although it wasn't a dirty game.

Bielsa finally turned to his bench and sent on Ian Poveda for Jack Harrison, although it must have been a toss-up whether it should have been Harrison or Costa, both had been very quiet and ineffective all afternoon. Poveda was a little more lively as he always is, but without improving our potency overly much. I was still pondering whether it should have been Costa given the hook as Kalvin Phillips sent one of those very 'Leedsy' long diagonal balls from the right touchline towards Costa who'd got himself free on the left corner of the Red Devils' area. Costa took the ball down on his left thigh, let it bounce a couple of times and then volleyed it towards goal. It just took the slightest of deflections off the boot of the challenging Wan-Bissaka and that sent it inches over the bar.

Klich did then replace Costa four minutes later.

Klich had an opportunity to nick the points as he and Poveda combined leaving the Pole to cut inside, but his left-foot shot was weak and straight at Henderson. Man United then turned to Paul Pogba who replaced Dan James and Bielsa responded by sending on Robin Koch to mark Pogba as Roberts was sacrificed. The dangerous Cavani replaced Rashford too, but Leeds saw the game out without any drama despite Sky trying their best to frighten us with another graphic. This one showed us that Man United had scored more goals than any other side in the 90th minute or later.

When you consider that we went into this game without our star player, Raphinha, and got a solid point against the team lying second in the table and with one of the finest recent away records in top-flight history, then this was a terrific result. We'd faced four of the best teams in Europe in recent weeks, four of the current top six in the EPL and none had beaten us. We'd faced five SL rebels at Elland Road and drawn with them all and we'd end this weekend 9th in the table; above Arsenal and within seven points of Liverpool and Spurs. We could honestly say we'd graduated with honours. We'd started the season with a group of Championship players who'd grown and developed and improved as the season progressed. With regular injuries to Rodrigo, Koch, Llorente, and Raphinha, it was mainly this same group that had got us to this enviable mid-table security.

Bielsa talked about the group evolving in his post-match press conferences noting: *"The group of players have constructed a solid group. Throughout this time they made errors and have learned how to correct them. In the same way, they learned to avoid errors that are avoidable. I have the feeling there has been a growth in their maturity in how to manage these games."* [1] Perhaps the errors he referred to were all those goals we'd conceded from corners earlier in the season; we looked far more comfortable today against the half dozen Man United won, with most headed clear and a couple well caught in the gloves of Illan Meslier. There was much to be proud about the way this group of players had established themselves as steady EPL performers.

In the final EPL game this Sunday, it looked for most of the second half like Albion still had a minuscule chance of avoiding relegation as they held a 1 – 2 lead at Villa Park. Then Kyle Bartley messed up in his own six-yard box and Villa equalised in the 2nd minute of added time. Villa's point kept them below Leeds; two points behind with a game in hand. The other game played this Sunday was the League Cup final; Man City beat Spurs 1 – 0 in a dire game by all accounts as City won it for the fourth time in a row.

Leeds United 0 Manchester United 0
BCD. Round 33 League Pos: 9th

---

[1] *https://www.bbc.co.uk/sport/football/56790342*

One Step back...

The Under 23s played their penultimate game of this fine season on Monday afternoon. Sam Greenwood put Leeds ahead with his tenth goal of the campaign as early as the third minute but Fulham equalised just before the break and that's the way it finished. No regular first-teamers were involved but Jamie Shackleton played the first 45 minutes. Leeds had already won the division and promotion and led the table now by ten points from Stoke City and were a monumental 18 points ahead of third placed Wolves. It had been an astonishing season for the youngsters.

There was one game in the Premier League this week before the next full round began on Friday. Leicester City moved closer to Champions League qualification as they beat Crystal Palace 2 – 1 to move seven points clear of fifth placed West Ham with five games to play. Palace were left in 13th on 38 points, four places and nine points behind Leeds.

The 1st-leg semi-final games in the two big European competitions were played this week and most of the ties were left in the balance. In the Champions League, Chelsea got a good-looking draw away at Real Madrid, while Manchester City went one better and came away from Paris Saint-Germain with a 1 – 2 scoreline to take back to the Etihad. In the Europa League, Manchester United reprised their score against us earlier in the season as they walloped Roma 6 – 2, while Arsenal had plenty of work left to do as they lost 2 – 1 at Villarreal.

The Championship was coming to a conclusion with Norwich and Watford now promoted and Brentford, Bournemouth, Swansea, and Barnsley (honest!) already confirmed as the play-off contenders while, at the bottom, Wycombe were as good as gone while the remaining two relegation spots would be filled by two from Rotherham, Sheffield Wednesday (who suffered that six point deduction), and Derby County. That could all come down to the final day when the Owls went to the Rams. Hence we still had the possibility that the three sides relegated from the EPL last season could all go straight back up while two of the three sides promoted from the Championship, Fulham and West Brom, looked like going straight back down; Leeds were the odd man out in that respect and it was another sign of the scale of the achievement by everyone at the club that we were already safe and planning for next season in the top flight.

The papers were already picking up snippets of that planning as it was reported that Leeds had rejected an offer for Mateusz Bogusz from Legia Warsaw. Football Insider was reporting that Bielsa rated the Pole highly and wanted to find an English club in the Championship where the youngster could be loaned out next season. On Bielsa's future himself, he denied rumours this week coming out of Argentina that he had already agreed a further two year extension to his contract. He continued to state his preference to sort out such things once the season was complete. Meanwhile, Radrizzani told L'Equipe: *"We are in discussions"* and *"hopefully we can continue to work together"*. [1]

---

[1] *https://www.yorkshirepost.co.uk/sport/football/leeds-united/leeds-united-head-coach-marcelo-bielsa-on-his-future-and-raphinha-fitness-3218905*

There was still the tantalising prospect that some fans might be allowed into stadiums for the final game of the season. In a BBC online article this week it was reported that the FA had now moved the penultimate round of EPL games back a few days to 18th – 19th May. This meant that they could be played under the new Government rules allowing some fans back into outdoor events which were due to come into effect on 17th May. That would mean every EPL side would have the opportunity to play one game in front of their home supporters, albeit still limited to a quarter of ground capacity or 10,000 maximum. It had also been suggested by the FA to the clubs that up to 5% of tickets could be set aside for away fans. We were still waiting for any communication from Leeds on the subject although some clubs had already announced their intentions. Wolves for example were allocating their tickets by way of a ballot of season ticket holders.

Leeds had come up with a plan for returning the crowdies to their owners this week; the cardboard cut-outs that graced the stands all those months ago. These could now be collected from the ground at pre-arranged time slots but almost as soon as the announcement was made all the time-slots were filled. The Shropshire Whites contacted the club to ask if they could make a bulk pick-up on behalf of their members and Gaz S, our branch organiser who organises the buses for all our games, posted the idea on Facebook asking who'd be interested. In minutes he was inundated with requests and one wag posted: *"Looks like you'll be able to fill a bus Gaz."* Well I thought it was funny!

What was officially round 34 of the EPL got underway on Friday, 30th April with a 1 – 1 draw between Leicester City, still solidly in those Champions League qualification places, and Southampton. It was yet another controversial game in which Saints' defender Jannick Vestergaard was sent off after only 10 minutes when his tackle on Jamie Vardy was deemed to have denied the Leicester striker a goal-scoring opportunity. It was another case where a tackle took the ball cleanly but then the follow through caught the leg of the attacker. All the pundits I saw commenting on this one thought it was a ridiculous red card and very similar to the one that got Liam Cooper sent off recently. I just wish the officials would spend more time focussing on all the cheating, diving, con artists in the game.

It was Bank Holiday weekend but it was still freezing outside so the only option for a day out, to sit in a pub beer garden, was not very tempting! So, I chose to spend Saturday in front of the TV again watching the football. Our game against Brighton was a 3 pm kick-off.

First off though was the Crystal Palace v Man City encounter and it was another win for City as they continued their stroll to the Premier League title with a 0 – 2 victory that left them just one win from that glory. They could also become Champions if Liverpool could beat Manchester United at Old Trafford on Sunday afternoon. Ahead of the game against Brighton most Leeds fans thought it would be a comfortable win for the Mighty Whites. Leeds had just come through a series of six games unbeaten, including encounters with four of the big six. Brighton had won only two games at home all season and had only taken maximum points in two of their previous 12 games. And yet I wasn't so confident.

I was the only one of the six YEP jurors who didn't think we'd win this one but even I thought we'd manage a draw. My logic was that I believed Brighton to be a much better side than their lowly league position suggested. Brighton were the only side in the bottom seven who we didn't currently have a 100% record against, having lost to the Seagulls back in January at Elland Road. Looking at their record, they'd only lost 13 games all season; only the top eight had lost fewer and Brighton had actually drawn 13 too, more than any other side. Had only a couple of those drawn games gone in their favour they'd have been solidly in mid-table alongside Leeds. Having watched all their games this season I knew full well that they had been really unlucky on several occasions when they dominated but failed to score. Despite only winning twice at the Amex, they had actually recorded eight clean sheets at home and only Chelsea and Man City could boast better records than that! There was one more reason too: Brighton still needed points to be absolutely certain of Premier League survival and that is a powerful incentive. The players own future incomes were at stake.

I would mention our record away at Brighton too… but I don't believe that carries much weight. Suffice to say we had never won at the Amex in six visits, our last win in Brighton came at the Withdean Stadium as far back as 2009 in League One, and we'd failed to score down there in our last four. It was also in the back of my mind that our previous visit to Sussex this season was the ill-fated FA Cup game at Crawley. So, I just knew this was going to be a tough game. It immediately looked even tougher when the team was announced:

Meslier
Ayling (Capt) llorente (Hernandez 79) Struijk Alioski (Poveda 45)
Koch
Dallas Klich Roberts Harrison
Bamford (Rodrigo 59)

Subs: Casilla, Berardi, Drameh, Jenkins, Shackleton, Hernandez, Poveda, Rodrigo, Huggins.

Brighton: Sánchez, White, Dunk, Webster, Veltman, Groß, Bissouma (MacAllister 90+2), Burn, Trossard (Jahanbakhsh 80), Maupay, Welbeck (Moder 90). Subs not used: Steele, Connolly, Alzate, Izquierdo, Pröpper, Zeqiri.

Referee: Chris Kavanagh.

There was a self-imposed social media ban by lots of sports media, clubs, and players this weekend in a show of unity against online abuse and discrimination that made finding the teams a bit tricky for anyone who usually relied on Twitter! I dialled into the club's official website for the details. The task had got tougher because Kalvin Phillips was missing; the website merely stating that he was *"unable to make the squad today"*. He'd apparently been injured in training. Robin Koch would fill in for Kalvin while Helder Costa was also absent and not even mentioned. He was assumed to be missing due to a late knock he suffered against Man United the previous week. Mateusz Klich came in for him. Hence it was a really unbalanced looking team with everyone speculating how it might line up with only one recognised winger. In the end we had to wait until the game started to see that it was the Irish Rover who added yet another position to his repertoire as he started out on that right wing.

So that was two more reasons why this was going to be tough; no Kalvin and a few players playing out of position. Whatever the cause, this game got away from Leeds very quickly and we never really got to grips with it. Add to all the other possible reasons the fact that no Leeds player showed his best features and we were doomed as soon as Brighton took the lead, which they did in the 14th minute; it was Gross, no really it was, Pascal Groß.

Gjanni Alioski had a torrid first half, putting in the sort of erratic display we see from the little man every few games. In between he's as asset, on days like this though he's a liability. It was Alioski who gave away a free-kick out on the Brighton right wing and then, as Leeds dithered in trying to clear the cross, it was Alioski who tried to impede Danny Welbeck by sticking his left arm across the Seagull's right thigh as if trying to grab his gonads. Welbeck went down and Chris Kavanagh pointed to the spot. Pascal Groß fired the ball perfectly inside the left post despite the best efforts of Illan Meslier.

Leeds had a little spell of domination winning several consecutive corners but it was Brighton who had the better chances during the first half. Trossard should have doubled their lead when Llorente got caught in possession near his own byline having taken a daft short pass from Meslier. Welbeck won the ball, knocked it across the face of the Leeds goal and Trossard just had to steer it past Meslier from 12 yards; he blasted it over the bar. Trossard had earlier had a snap-shot saved well by the Leeds keeper and Welbeck had another. The closest Leeds came was when Dan Burn headed a fierce Harrison cross against Joel Veltman and the ball almost rebounded over the Brighton goal line. The halt-time whistle brought a welcome relief from a really poor 45 minutes from Leeds.

Alioski paid for his poor display with his place in the side as he was substituted by Ian Poveda. That allowed Stuart Dallas to move to left-back and at least we then had two recognised wingers on the pitch, although throughout the game neither could cross a decent ball for love nor money. In fact, the best Leeds crosses had come from two Stuart Dallas corners.

The second half continued in much the same vein, Leeds were just poor while Brighton, with their three towering hulks in defence, did just enough to disrupt any positive moves we made. The best chances fell to the home side again with Veltman missing another sitter and Welbeck's little dink just swiped away by Meslier before it could do any damage. Maupay should have at least hit the target when he was found in the clear 12 yards out but again thankfully he messed up the shot and shanked it wide of the post. Stuart Dallas did rasp one volley over the bar from the edge of the box but that was as close as Leeds got to an equaliser before the Seagulls flew down the other end and nicked all the chips.

It came from a Meslier clearance that was met by the head of Adam Webster, just inside the Leeds half. The ball was thus knocked all the way back towards the Leeds penalty area where Pascal Struijk leapt to head it in a challenge with Neil Maupay on the first bounce. Struijk, facing his own goal then could only lift it in the air trying to clear it over his head as it bounced again. As it fell to ground Danny Welbeck performed an exquisite little trap and move of the ball, a sort of Cruyff turn, with his right foot shifting the ball behind his left. Struijk was completely wrong-footed and Welbeck then drilled the ball left-footed across Meslier and inside the right post for a well taken goal. Leeds had literally just introduced Pablo Hernandez for Diego Llorente having also sent on Rodrigo for Patrick Bamford on the hour mark and the goal clearly upset all of Bielsa's plans. He could be seen swinging a punch at one of the plastic seats in the front row near the technical area; you don't see a show of annoyance like that from the great man very often.

So, Brighton had somehow, unfathomably, performed the double over Leeds and we'd played poorly in both games. You had to imagine that there was something about the way the Seagulls were set up that worked against us but it may just have been coincidence. I have a sneaking feeling that if we'd have had Raphinha up front and Kalvin Phillips in midfield we'd have had too much for the plucky Seagulls but without them and with everyone else performing just below their best, Brighton took their chance. They were now safe and any lingering hopes Leeds may have had of sneaking a place in Europe next season were just about gone.

Bielsa summarised the game in his comments to the BBC noting: *"We didn't play well. The victory for the opponent was fair. We created very little danger and it was difficult for us to recover the ball.*

"The game was hard with the height of their centre-backs. We couldn't avoid them initiating the play nor could we overcome them trying to get in behind."

Brighton 2 **Leeds United 0** (Groß 14 pen, Welbeck 79)
BCD. **Round 34 League Pos: 11**[th].

All About Trust

In the other games played over the weekend there were wins for Chelsea, who just about put the final nail in Fulham's coffin with a 2 – 0 win while consolidating their own place in the top four, and Aston Villa who won at Goodison. That put a big dent in Everton's hopes of European football next season. Those two games completed the Saturday programme. On Sunday we started with Arsenal winning 0 – 2 at Newcastle, a result that had the Gunners leapfrogging Leeds again. Then we were all expecting to watch as Manchester United hosted Liverpool.

It didn't happen. I was at my son's again continuing with the everlasting job of redecorating his house when he shouted me to have a look at the TV which he was sat watching while I sweated away! There were incredible scenes going on at Old Trafford with fans all over the pitch throwing flares into the stands and the news was just filtering through that the game had been abandoned. It was all a follow-on to the attempt by the six rebel clubs to form a European Super League. The protests we saw against that recently seemed to have lit the fire under Manchester United fans more than the rest, reigniting the anger we saw from them years ago aimed at the Glazer family. This protest began outside the ground and was peaceful initially but, later, flares and bottles were thrown, two police officers were injured, and 200 fans broke into the ground. The teams were still in their hotels in the city centre but fans had gathered there too and the game was called off in the interests of safety. Although not condoning the violence, the Manchester United Supporters Trust (MUST) claimed supporters now had *"zero trust in the owners"* despite the apology made by the Glazers for the Super League fiasco.[1] Man United fans had always complained about how the family had financed the purchase of the club in the first place, by heaping over £400 million of debt onto the balance sheet, and even the huge spending on players in the years since had failed to placate them. Most of the banners outside the ground carried the simple message: *"Glazers out!"*

With fan power seemingly having forced the U-turn on the Super League and now, for the first time in Premier League history forcing the postponement of a game, it seemed we were entering a new era where perhaps the balance of power was shifting more towards the supporters. Only time would tell if this was a permanent trend or not.

It was hard to concentrate on the football after all the goings on at Old Trafford, but there was still one EPL game left on this eventful Sunday. It featured another of the six rebels, Tottenham, who easily won through 4 – 0 against already relegated Sheffield United, with Gareth bale scoring a sublime hat-trick. The result kept Spurs in the hunt for a top four finish as, with four games left, they sat 5th in the table, five points behind Chelsea in 4th. Next up for Leeds was a visit by Spurs to Elland Road on Saturday.

The final two games of round 34 took place on bank holiday Monday, one of which saw West Brom draw 1 – 1 with Wolves, a result that left the Baggies needing to win all four of their final games to have any hope of avoiding the drop, the same unlikely scenario that Fulham faced. No one expected either to achieve it. The final game was a clash of the clarets; Burnley hosted West

---

[1] https://www.bbc.co.uk/sport/football/56960091

Ham. The Hammers won 1 – 2, a result that kept alive their hopes of snatching the final Champions League place by putting them just three points behind Chelsea, the current incumbents. For Burnley, the spectre of relegation was still there albeit there would still have to be that improbable run of four wins on the trot for either Fulham or West Brom or both. It was unlikely to say the least.

	Team	P	GD	Pts
1	Manchester City	34	47	80
2	Manchester United	33	29	67
3	Leicester City	34	22	63
4	Chelsea	34	22	61
5	West Ham United	34	11	58
6	Tottenham Hotspur	34	22	56
7	Liverpool	33	16	54
8	Everton	33	3	52
9	Arsenal	34	9	49
10	Aston Villa	33	10	48
11	Leeds United	34	-2	47
12	Wolverhampton Wanderers	34	-13	42
13	Crystal Palace	33	-22	38
14	Brighton	34	-4	37
15	Southampton	33	-18	37
16	Burnley	34	-16	36
17	Newcastle United	34	-20	36
18	Fulham	34	-20	27
19	West Bromwich Albion	34	-34	26
R20	Sheffield United	34	-42	17

The fall-out from the abandoned Super League was still playing out and this week the Premier League introduced a new 'owners' charter' to stop future attempts to join such a breakaway. In its statement the EPL said it would also introduce *"additional rules and regulation to ensure the principles of the Premier League and open competition are protected"*. Both the FA and the EPL said they were seeking government help to bring in legislation to protect the football pyramid and *"the integrity of the football community"* while the FA commenced an inquiry into all the events leading up to the ill-fated Super League launch.

The Leeds United Under 23s played their final game in PL2 Div 2 on the bank holiday Monday afternoon. They ended their season in the manner we'd seen all the way through the campaign with another resounding win, 5 – 2 this time against Burnley. A first goal for impressive full back Cody Drameh set them off on the right track in the 23rd minute and a Niall Huggins goal, two penalties from top scorer Sam Greenwood, and a solo effort from the ever-improving Crysencio Summerville put the game to bed. A well-earned celebration and medal presentation was broadcast live after the game on LUTV.

Jose Mourinho was back in employment, although his new position as manager of Italian side Roma wasn't going to start until next season. Meanwhile, his new charges did their best to get back into their Europa League semi-final but, ultimately, despite beating Manchester United 3 – 2 in the second leg, it was not enough to overturn that 6 – 2 first leg drubbing. Man United would now face Villarreal in the final; they held Arsenal to a nil – nil draw at the Emirates this week having won the first leg 2 – 1. In the Champions League it was going to be an all English final as Manchester City and Chelsea saw off PSG and Real Madrid with second leg victories. We now waited to see just how much the balance of power had shifted towards the fans recently as there were calls to move the Champions League final from Turkey to the UK; many fans of both clubs and from around the country were expressing the madness of sending two English clubs to Istanbul when Turkey was currently in full Covid lockdown! Even without the Covid issues it was surely more sensible to play the game at Wembley?

The Championship relegation battle was coming to a conclusion this week with the final round of games due to be played on Saturday. Rotherham were still favourites to join Wycombe Wanderers as they'd go into the final day two points adrift of Derby who occupied the first position of safety. It was an intriguing situation though that could see any two of Rotherham, Derby, and Sheffield Wednesday joining Wycombe going through the trap-door. Derby hosted Sheffield Wednesday on the final day while Rotherham had a difficult-looking trip to Cardiff.

It was finally confirmed this week that fans would be able to attend, in limited numbers, the final two EPL games of the season. Up to 25% of the capacity could be filled with home fans only, with all Premier League teams having one home game during the final two rounds. Leeds announced their ballot scheme on Wednesday this week; all season ticket holders had the option to register to go into the ballot. The folk in our WhatsApp group were immediately on the case and several of us decided, come what may, we'd be in Leeds anyway; if we failed to get a ticket we'd take advantage of the next relaxation in Covid regulations to watch the game in the pub! It was tantalising to think we might yet get to step inside Elland Road at least once in this important season in our history. Even if successful in the ballot, we all realised there would be other hurdles to get over before we could finally occupy a seat inside the stadium. With his usual tongue in cheek humour, and reading the room perfectly as always, Angus Kinnear noted in his programme column for the Spurs game: *"Supporters who do attend will then be subjected to a regime of questionnaires, tests and scans which mercifully fall just short of a full body cavity search."*

Before that final match against West Brom though, there was the Spurs game, hopefully the last home game to have to be played behind closed doors. From the details given in Bielsa's press conference on Thursday, it was unclear what sort of a side we'd be able to put out. Helder Costa had now been ruled out for the rest of the season following that ridiculous manhandling he suffered in a challenge with Manchester United defender Aaron Wan-Bissaka that forced him off midway in the second half of that game. Kalvin Phillips and Raphinha were also said to be doubtful although eagle-eyed Leeds fans had spotted them both in the videos of training put out this week on social media. Liam Cooper was able to return of course now that his three match suspension was complete. Whether Cooper *would* return was uncertain though and Bielsa made a point of saying how pleased he'd been with the Llorente – Struijk partnership. On the return of fans for the Albion game Bielsa merely stated that it was: *"An experience always worth living"*.

On the Friday ahead of the Spurs game, the Government announced the next stage of freedom as it listed 12 countries for which fairly normal travel plans could be made from 17th May. It was a funny old list though with places like Australia and New Zealand included although they weren't actually yet letting folk in. Of the others, I couldn't see Mrs W being overly tempted by the offer of a fortnight in Brunei, the Falkland Islands, the Faroe Islands, South Georgia and the South Sandwich Islands or St Helena, Tristan de Cunha, or Ascension Island! The best options looked like Portugal or Singapore. At the same time as setting up the green list, three more countries were added to the red list – that was the list of countries requiring folk to spend £1,750 each on a 10-day government hotel quarantine on return. The one interesting country added to that list was Turkey! We still waited for UEFA to come up with a new location for the Champions League final; Villa Park or Wembley were being suggested as well as a stadium in Portugal.

The first game of the next round of the EPL, round 35, was played on Friday night, 7th May, as Leicester hosted Newcastle United. It was the day after the elections that had been taking place all around the UK in which the big winners in England were the Tories; they took Hartlepool from Labour in the one by-election and increased their haul of local councils, again mainly at the expense of Labour. In Scotland it was another good day for the Scottish Nationalists as they increased their seats and looked set to push on towards demanding another referendum; that story looked set to run for years to come and I fully expected Brexit and Covid to now be replaced by Indy Ref 2 as the new media obsession. In the game, Newcastle astonished most onlookers by beating Leicester 2 – 4, a result that left Leicester still short of confirming their Champions League place for next season but which guaranteed Newcastle another campaign in the top flight.

Our game with Spurs was a 12:30 pm kick-off – the same time that the final round of the Championship games was scheduled for. With the Leeds game being aired on BT Sport, I had the laptop set up for that while, with the sound muted, I also had the TV showing Sky's coverage of the all-important Derby v Sheffield Wednesday game.

The announcement of the Leeds team drew much criticism from many fans; Kalvin Phillips and Raphinha were apparently fit enough to sit on the bench but Bielsa left them out of the starting line-up in favour of keeping exactly the same side that started and played so poorly at Brighton. I have to confess that I was amongst the sceptics, although I was still fairly comfortable with my 2 – 2 prediction as I'd factored in the possibility that both Phillips and Raphinha might still not be fit. Surely though, if they *were* fit enough for the bench, arguably our two most important players should play shouldn't they? There was also the question as to where Liam Cooper was; he'd been declared fit to play by Bielsa in the press-conference but was now missing altogether. After the game Bielsa would tell us Coops had picked up a: *"small knock in his gluteus"* during training. My buddy Cambridge Rob was most forthright in his WhatsApp message: *"In for a right knobbing with that side"* he warned, while MK Derek commented: *"I hope I'm wrong but with their front 4, I might get more pleasure from the Derby match!!"* I guessed there were two things in Bielsa's mind. The first thing is that we all know Bielsa has the ultimate faith in his players to deliver and, we've seen on numerous occasions before that, after a poor display, he would usually give his players a chance to make amends by picking them for the following game. If you didn't have Bielsa's trust, then it looked risky this time but, if he was right and the players delivered, then the bond and trust between coach and players could only be strengthened even more. Another consideration was no doubt the fact that we had brought players back from injury too soon on several occasions already this season only to then see them limp off after a few minutes. The weather in Leeds was awful ahead of this game too, and so the pitch was not going to be the best so that was another factor that might have come into the equation; it would be easy to slip and strain muscles that were not 100% ready.

Meslier
Ayling (Capt) Llorente Struijk Alioski
Koch
Dallas Klich (Phillips 90) Roberts (Raphinha 58) Harrison
Bamford (Rodrigo 79)

Substitutes: Casilla, Berardi, Davis, Phillips, Shackleton, Rodrigo, Poveda, Raphinha, Hernandez.

Tottenham Hotspur: Lloris, Aurier, Alderweireld, Dier, Reguilón, Lo Celso (Ndombele 80), Højbjerg, Bale (Lucas Moura 67), Alli (Lamela 67), Son Heung-Min, Kane. Subs not used: Hart, Doherty, D Sanchez, Winks, Sissoko, Bergwijn.

Referee: Michael Oliver.

Spurs were on a mission in this game, under their temporary manager, Ryan Mason, they needed to win to stay in the hunt for a European place, either in the Champions League or, failing that, in the Europa League. A win would potentially see them move back up into fifth place in the table and, with Leicester having lost at home to Newcastle the previous night, the gap to the Foxes in fourth would only be four points with three games left. Spurs' form since Mason replaced Mourinho in mid-April had been OK; two league wins against Southampton and Sheffield United and that narrow one-goal defeat to Man City in the League Cup final. Some fans joked that this was effectively a home game for Spurs too... well, they did sell us their pitch! On Twitter Steve D posted simply: *"Turf Wars?"*

I settled down in front of the laptop and TV a few minutes before the start as the voices of Darren Fletcher and former Liverpool star Steve McManaman took up the commentary. Their first words were comforting, Fletcher noting that Leeds had the best home defensive record in the EPL in 2021 so far, conceding just six goals in nine games at Elland Road since the turn of the year. Then I was more anxious as he then mentioned that this was the first league encounter with Spurs in 17 years... that number again.

The first ten minutes had Leeds looking good and trading corners two to one in our favour, the second one resulting in a decent chance for Robin Koch who volleyed just over the bar from close range; it was a big chance. Patrick Bamford also forced Lloris into the first save of the day with a well struck left-foot shot from the left corner of the box. I could see on the TV screen that the weather at Derby was similar to that in Leeds with the rain pouring down and the wind whipping around the stadium but the first important score of the afternoon was now running along the bottom of the TV screen; Rotherham had taken an early lead in Cardiff! Up popped the bottom of the Championship table as it currently stood after ten minutes and, joy of joys, it showed both Derby and Sheffield Wednesday would go down with Wycombe if things stayed like this. As our game moved towards the quarter-hour mark though, that was not the most significant development for me.

Tyler Roberts was looking lively again and he ran right to left across the pitch mid-way in the Spurs half before touching the ball back to the supporting Robin Koch. He knocked it further left to

Alioski out on the left touchline and he pushed it forward to Jack Harrison. Aurier looked in a good position to deal with Harrison but a quick burst of pace got our man the half a yard needed to lash the ball low across the face of goal. It was a difficult ball, right along that infamous 'corridor of uncertainty' and it certainly had Eric Dier in two minds as he decided to allow it go past him. That meant Reguilon, at the back post, could only react at the last minute to stick out a boot to try to prevent it finding Stuart Dallas. The ball cannoned off Reguilon's boot and only a fine diving save from Lloris stopped it finding the bottom corner of the net but it then sat up perfectly for Dallas to smash home from three yards! At that precise moment this was shaping up to be a perfect day!

It didn't stay perfect for long though and in the 24th minute Spurs showed us their individual qualities. Dele Alli ran through the heart of the Leeds defence, side-stepped Llorente and, in the same movement, scooped the ball through the Leeds backline into the path of Son with only Meslier now to beat. He made no mistake from 12 yards and it was 1 − 1.

Conceding the goal didn't seem to worry Leeds though and Jack Harrison in particular was on fire. Whereas he couldn't cross the ball for love nor money last week, he was now on the money with everything he touched. He tested Lloris again with a fierce right-foot shot as he cut inside from the left, the Spurs keeper just finger-tipping it over the bar. Leeds then tested the visitors with two more corners; Robin Koch having another shot blocked over the bar from the first. It was a great game and I confess my eyes didn't stray to the TV very often although I could see that the Derby game was still goalless. Then, out of the blue, Spurs had the ball in the net again!

It was another master-class of sharp passing as Son slid the ball through to Alli and he touched it first-time inside to Harry Kane. Kane showed just why he's so deadly as he lifted the ball ever so gently over the diving body of Illan Meslier to nestle it just inside the near post. It was a fabulous 'goal' but with Ayling and Struijk now appealing to the assistant referee on the touchline in front of the East Stand, he finally raised his flag. There was a nervous wait as VAR went into action and the first picture on the screen made it look very close indeed; to all intents and purposes the left boot of Kane was right in-line with the left boot of Pascal Struijk.

Apparently they have a more accurate screen shot in Stockley Park in West London with microscopically thin lines that wouldn't show up on our TV screens, hence why we get the thicker lines that often show no difference between attacker and defender. Thankfully, this time, the call went in our favour and Kane was adjudged offside. Some fans immediately tweeted that this was karma for the couple of 'goals' we'd had chalked off by VAR this season but for me, as long as everyone is confident that the system is accurate enough to say categorically if it is offside or not, then I'm happy with the system. No one has ever said that an inch offside is not offside. I would like more proof though that the system is actually that accurate. In any case, we didn't have to wait many minutes more and we were back in the lead and such things were soon forgotten.

It was another sublime goal from Leeds that started with a ball hooked down the inside right channel by Mateusz Klich towards Patrick Bamford. It was intercepted though by the head of Eric Dier but only as far as Stuart Dallas who was following-up and was too sharp for Reguilon who was having as much trouble keeping tabs on Dallas as Aurier was on the opposite side with Harrison. This time Dallas moved infield and skipped around Lo Celso only for the Spurs man to stick out a leg to trip the Irish Rover as he went past. Dallas stumbled but still managed to pass the ball on to Tyler Roberts and referee Michael Oliver, despite putting the whistle to his lips to blow, then spotted that Leeds could have a potential advantage as Roberts picked out the run of Harrison on that left wing again. Harrison waited for the over-lapping run from Alioski and then played the ball perfectly into his path. One touch and Alioski picked out Bamford at the near post and Bamford stabbed it into the net. A terrific team goal that had Bielsaball written all over it.

That was it for the first half in Leeds, but the game at Derby was still going on, with some six minutes of added time there. We were into the 4th of them when Sam Hutchinson blasted the ball home from close range for the Owls to go into the break a goal up; a goal that would definitely relegate Derby if the score stayed like that and, if only Cardiff could find an equaliser against Rotherham, also potentially save Wednesday. I guess like most Leeds fans, the relegation of Derby would have been the most satisfactory outcome for me as that dreadful play-off semi-final defeat to the Rams was still the most hurtful result in our recent history.

In the early minutes of the second half, Leeds had another moment of anxiety as Harry Kane put the ball in the net again, but this time he was a good couple of yards offside and the worry was soon dispelled while suddenly the game at Pride Park had exploded into life. I looked up a couple of minutes after the second disallowed Kane goal and noticed that the score had changed to 1 – 1 at Derby although I confess I'd not actually seen the goal. It didn't really matter too much either, as Rotherham still held that one goal lead in Cardiff. But, blow me down, I glanced at the TV again a few minutes later and the score was 2 – 1 to Derby and again I'd been so absorbed in our game that I'd missed the second Derby goal! If it stayed like this, then Derby were safe and Rotherham and Wednesday would be down.

Our game, though absorbing, hadn't seen any more real chances and then, in the 58th minute, Leeds made the first change as Raphinha trotted on to replace Tyler Roberts who looked to have suffered a knock. It was a change that instantly had Leeds looking even sharper. He was a distraction on the left even when he didn't have the ball and the two Spurs full-backs' nightmares continued. The first real chance of the second half came when Dallas launched the ball across from the left as Aurier dallied trying to keep an eye on Raphinha. The ball found Harrison over on the right wing now and he pulled the ball back from the byline for Klich. Mateusz hammered the ball at goal first time with his right foot only for Lloris to pull-off yet another fine save. Another glance at the TV and the score at Derby had changed to 2 – 2! There was something happening wherever I looked now – on the laptop I winced as Aurier went past Raphinha on the right side of the Leeds box and then hit a stunning shot that Meslier acrobatically turned over, having no doubt expected the Spurs man to cross not shoot. Replays would show that the ball took a deflection off Gjanni Alioski too that made the save even more remarkable. Spurs had by now made their first changes with the arrivals of Lucas Moura and Lamela and the departures of Gareth Bale and Dele Alli; Spurs were clearly starting to worry about missing that European adventure. Harry Kane thumped a free kick against the top of the crossbar as if to stress the point and, for the first time today, Leeds started to look a bit shaky with passes going astray and possession given up cheaply.

It was all change again at Derby too; the score in the corner of the TV screen was now showing 2 – 3 with Wednesday having taken the lead again.

Back to the game at Elland Road and Leeds made another change, with Rodrigo replacing Patrick Bamford in the 79th minute but, for now, it was still Spurs in the ascendancy. We needed Illan Meslier to be at his best again as Lamela got free on the left behind the Leeds defence after Mateusz Klich gave the ball away in his own half. Lamela drove the ball hard and low towards the near post but Meslier got his legs in the way to save. Derby had equalised again at Pride Park; 3 – 3 it was there now and still Rotherham led in Cardiff. As it stood Rotherham had pulled off the miracle escape and Derby and Wednesday were down!

Another Spurs attack broke down on the edge of the Leeds area and Alioski came away with the ball; he'd been superb today as had Harrison and both had fully repaid the trust Bielsa had shown in them by giving them a chance to amend for last week when both were very poor. Now Alioski played a one-two on the left with Raphinha but still deep in the Leeds half. Raphinha set off down that left wing as Alioski played the ball forward to Klich who, in turn, knocked it inside to Robin Koch. The German took a couple of little touches and then spotted Raphinha, now midway in the Spurs half, on the shoulder of Højbjerg. Koch's pass was superbly weighted in behind the Spurs man and Raphinha was in the clear behind the Spurs backline. As Eric Dier made the dash to cut him off, Raphinha cleverly clipped the ball inside and there was Rodrigo to finish clinically with his left foot, inside the left post. Leeds had suddenly clicked into gear and it was another rapier-like attack to see out the game in our favour. It was the last meaningful action of the game and my focus adjusted to the TV in the corner of the room showing the Derby game was still all-square at 3 – 3. It was almost the perfect day we all wanted.

Sadly it was not to be. As the Derby game moved into the final minutes, news came through of another goal at Cardiff and it was soon being replayed on the screen. With only a couple of minutes to go, Cardiff's Marlon Pack curled the ball home to break the Millers' hearts. They would finish 1 – 1, Derby and Wednesday finished 3 – 3 and so it would be Wednesday and Rotherham joining Wycombe in League One next season. Damn, damn, and triple damn!

For Leeds though it had been a terrific day and the trust Bielsa had in his players to come through and make amends for that Brighton disappointment was repaid in Spades. Leeds had played Spurs off the pitch, their own pitch as it happens! We'd completed an unbeaten run at Elland Road against the big six having already drawn with Arsenal, Chelsea, Liverpool and both Manchester clubs; we'd now scored three goals or more in a single game for the eighth time this season and, of course, we'd beaten the Champions elect on their own patch only weeks ago. It was hard to think how this glorious season could now improve any further. For me it would only be if I could be present at Elland Road for that final game against West Brom; that would cap this truly wonderful mishmash of a season perfectly.

After the game there was a lot of humble pie being digested in the homes of Leeds fans. Many, like me, had questioned the logic of leaving Phillips and Raphinha on the bench if they were fit but, once again, Bielsa had come up trumps. We should never have doubted him should we? In Bielsa We Trust!

In the remaining games played this Saturday there were wins for Crystal Palace at Sheffield United (0 – 2), Chelsea at Manchester City (1 – 2), and Liverpool against Southampton (2 – 0). Hence Man City were still not yet crowned Champions, while Chelsea looked more and more likely to finish in the top four and Liverpool at least kept themselves in the hunt. On Sunday, Wolves beat Brighton (2 – 1), Man United continued to delay City's coronation by winning at Villa (1 – 3), Everton dented West Ham's hopes of Europe while enhancing their own by winning at the London Stadium (0 – 1) and Arsenal climbed back above Leeds with a win over West Brom thus confirming the Albion's relegation (3 – 1).

On Monday night the final round 35 game saw Fulham take on Burnley knowing that only a victory would keep the Cottagers in the Premier League. It didn't happen; Fulham went down to a couple of first half goals from Ashley Westwood and a cracker from Chris Wood and the Cottagers were relegated.

Leeds Utd 3 Spurs 1 (**Dallas 13**, Son 25,**Bamford 42, Rodrigo 84**)
BCD. Round 35 League Pos: 10th.

Burnley Blitzed

The Premier League title was decided on Tuesday this week without Manchester City kicking a ball. The only side that could thwart them was their near neighbours, Manchester United, but they needed to win every game to the end of the season and they failed at the first hurdle, losing at home 1 – 2 against Leicester City who were now as good as certain to claim one of those Champions League places behind the two Manchester clubs. Man United paid the price of having that game with Liverpool postponed as, facing two games in three days, they opted to make ten changes so they would have all their big boys ready for the rearranged game with Liverpool later in the week. Citeh had thus secured part two of a possible treble this season with the Champions League final against Chelsea still to come. In the other game played on Tuesday night, Southampton beat Crystal Palace 3 – 1 but neither of those sides could now catch Leeds and they remained in 14th and 13th places respectively, well behind the Mighty Whites.

The other news that broke this Tuesday was that Richard Keogh had won his case against Derby following his contract termination by the Championship club back in 2019. Keogh secured a payment of £2.3m after Derby terminated his contract while retaining Mason Bennett and Tom Lawrence despite their drink driving convictions earned after the crash they were all involved in following a club event. Keogh was a back seat passenger in the vehicle driven by Tom Lawrence that crashed into the back of Mason Bennett's car and then ploughed into a lamppost. Lawrence and Bennett ran off leaving the injured Keogh unconscious in the vehicle. Keogh, who was with Huddersfield this season, would now have the full balance of his £24,000 a week Derby contract paid up. Despite avoiding relegation at the weekend, it was still not a great week for Derby, not only did they lose their appeal against paying Keogh but, in a separate matter, the EFL also confirmed they had won their appeal against Derby's accounting policies and wanted the club's punishment for breaching financial fair play rules to be given 'as soon as reasonably possible'. That could well mean a points deduction for next season. [1]

By far the worst news of the week though concerned the tragic death of young Jordan Banks. The 9-year-old died after apparently being struck by lightning while training on a football pitch in Blackpool. His club, Clifton Rangers Juniors, posted on Facebook: *"It is with great sadness and a very heavy heart we announce that the tragic incident yesterday involved one of our own players. Jordan of our U9 Bees, tragically passed away yesterday evening doing what he loved."* [2] The whole football community was once again brought together by news of such an unfathomable loss.

The only Premier League issue still to be resolved was which sides would finish in those money-spinning Champions League (ECL) and Europa League places. On Wednesday this week, the one game

[1] https://www.dailymail.co.uk/sport/football/article-9566639/Richard-Keogh-WINS-compensation-claim-against-Derby-takes-home-payout-2-3m.html
[2] https://www.independent.co.uk/news/uk/home-news/boy-struck-by-lightning-jordan-brooks-b1846323.html

taking place concerned two of the clubs involved in that quest. Chelsea, looking to secure an ECL spot, hosted Arsenal who were still hoping to scrape into next season's Europa League. It finished 0 – 1, with Chelsea possibly paying the price of making seven changes from the side that won at the Etihad at the weekend as they looked ahead to the FA Cup final in a few days' time when they'd face Leicester. The defeat meant the Blues could yet still lose their vital 4th place to any of West Ham, Liverpool or Tottenham, all of whom would be desperate to claim it and all of whom now had games in hand, albeit there were not many left to play of course.

There was some good news for some Leeds fans on Wednesday night; the result of the ballot for tickets for the West Brom game was announced. The lucky winners all got an email from the club explaining that they could now apply for their tickets. Incredibly, all eight of our little group of season ticket holders who regularly meet at the Old White Hart were successful! We quickly convened a WhatsApp meeting to arrange our strategy for then trying to get seats together, although the club had made that slightly more problematical by restricting applications for tickets to a maximum six per application. Hence we had a five and a three quickly organised and we decided we'd try to get seats in the East Stand where several of the group had their usual seats. For the rest of us it would be something different from our usual Kop places for what promised to be a very different sort of a game experience. It was almost hard to believe that, all being well, I'd soon be watching Leeds in the Premier League inside Elland Road for the first time in 17 (yes I know, that number again) long years!

In a busy football week, Everton then missed their chance to gate-crash the European places when they could only draw 0 – 0 at Villa Park on Thursday evening. It was a result that kept Villa a place and a point below Leeds who thus held onto 10th place in the table with both sides having three left to play.

Arguably the biggest game of the week then followed that Villa match as Manchester United and Liverpool assembled again to play the game postponed 11 days earlier. Once again hundreds of fans turned up at the stadium in an attempt to disrupt proceedings and to protest against the Glazer ownership but, this time, the police were ready and a heavy security presence enabled the game to go ahead. It was unclear though what the situation would be the following

Tuesday night when it was scheduled for some 10,000 fans to be allowed inside Old Trafford for the game against Fulham; would they protest inside the stadium?

Before the Man United v Liverpool game, Liverpool FC tweeted: *"You'll Never Walk Alone, Jordan Banks* ♥ *Nicknamed 'mini-Milner' by his coaches, Jordan was a brilliant person, as well as a passionate footballer. We're all thinking of his loved ones tonight* ♥ *"* During the warm-up, the Liverpool players all wore shirts with *"Jordan 7"* on the back in a heartfelt tribute to the youngster who died earlier in the week playing the game he loved.

In the game, Liverpool came back from a goal down to win it 2 – 4 and, in the process, leapfrog West Ham into 5th place in the table, now just four points behind Chelsea in 4th and with a game in hand. The race for Europe was going down to the wire.

Friday morning was a real throw-back to times of old; at 10:30 am I was sat at the laptop waiting to get access to the Leeds United ticket website and it brought back memories, not all fond ones, of trying to get tickets for away games before I treated myself to an away season ticket a few years ago. It was clear that everyone else was trying to do the same as John and I were, get the specific seats we wanted! Initially the timeline of the screen informed me there was a 20 minute wait but it didn't take that long before I was in and between us, Guitar John up in Leeds and me in sunny Shropshire manged to get seats pretty much together in the lower tier of the East Stand, although it was pretty confusing as, to ensure social distancing rules were adhered to, only every fourth seat was available. I now couldn't wait to get there and, from the comments I was reading on Twitter, I realised that those of us lucky enough to have won through the ballot were very privileged indeed. Several of the well-known Leeds fans who'd not missed a game for years and years had not been lucky in the ticket lottery.

The final game labelled as Match Week 35 took place on Friday night as Manchester City, the new Champions, travelled to Newcastle. It was a great game with Citeh coming out on top 3 – 4. We were first up in the next round on Saturday, a 12:30 pm kick-off at Burnley.

My trips to Turf Moor have always been grand days out; legendary some of them. Meeting up for a few beers and a burger in the Burnley Cricket Club Pavilion and then walking the short distance to the famous old ground around the corner. The two most memorable recent trips from a football point of view were a 2 – 3 win there back in December 2010, when we famously came back from being two down at halftime and then, more recently, when we won a penalty shoot-out in the League Cup. In the second half of that game ten years earlier, goals from Max Gradel, Luciano Becchio and, five minutes from time, Jonny Howson, won us the points. The League Cup meeting was our most recent game against the Clarets, in 2017, when there were no less than four goals scored in the last ten minutes of normal time; two for each side before we eventually went through 3 – 5 on penalties. I wasn't sure this game would quite match the excitement of either of those two encounters and yet I still thought it was important.

Leeds would go into this game in 10th spot in the table, a point ahead of Aston Villa in 11th, with both sides having three games to play. The only other side that could now overtake us was Wolves who started the weekend five points behind. Hence, the lowest position we could possibly finish was 12th whilst, if all the results went in our favour, we could still actually finish 6th and win a place in Europe! That was a very long shot mind you. The importance for me was two-fold; every place higher up the table we could finish was worth an additional £2 million in prize money but, more than that, it would be a real feather in our caps if we could say we ended the season in the top half of the table. I knew a few Leeds fans who had money riding on that from huge pre-season bets they'd laid.

Burnley were safe now from relegation of course, that issue having been resolved on Monday when Burnley won at Fulham, thus sending the Cottagers down along with the Albion and the Blades. That was probably bad news for Leeds as the Clarets could now play a more relaxed game without that pressure. You wouldn't exactly say they were in good form though as that Fulham win was only their second in their previous six games having lost the other four. They also had one of the worst home records in the EPL, having won only four games; only the three relegated sides had worse records on their own pitches. Leeds' recent record looked much better, with just one defeat in our last eight and four of those being against big six. I had this one down as a 2 – 2 draw, mainly on the basis that we hadn't drawn a game away from home all season, having won eight and lost nine.

This was assumed to be the last game Leeds would face behind closed doors as the final two rounds of matches were now scheduled for after the crucial date of May 17th when Covid regulations were finally being relaxed. Hence, our next game, a trip to Southampton in midweek, and our final game next Sunday at home to West Brom, would see the return of limited numbers of fans. The tickets for that Albion game for our little group of White Hart patrons had already dropped through my letter box...

This was FA Cup final day, with Leicester and Chelsea due to play their game at 5 pm in front of 21,000 fans in another big test that would hopefully show it was now safe to have large crowds gather together. It also meant that some of the focus was taken away from our game, a 12:30 pm kick-off; albeit not for Leeds fans. For us, it was now all about winning our final three games, finishing in the top half of the Premier League, and then having a well-earned break. We wanted the team in good form and confident too for that Albion game; nobody wanted fans in the ground to see us lose that one!

Meslier
Ayling Llorente Struijk Alioski
Phillips
Raphinha Dallas Klich Harrison
Bamford

Subs not used: Casilla, Cooper, Davis, Berardi, Roberts, Poveda, Rodrigo, Shackleton, Jenkins.

Burnley: Peacock-Farrell, Lowton, Tarkowski, Mee, Taylor, Brownhill, Westwood, Cork, McNeil (Gudmundsson 70), Vydra (Rodriguez 65), Wood (Barnes 65). Subs not used: Norris, Pieters, Nartey, Dunne, Richardson. Referee: Graham Scott.

The big debate ahead of the game was whether Bielsa would stick again with the side that saw off Spurs the previous week or whether he'd bring back Kalvin Phillips and Raphinha who both got brief run-outs against Spurs after their recent injuries, or even club captain Liam Cooper. The decision went in favour of Phillips and Raphinha but Pascal Struijk continued to keep Coops on the sidelines and most Leeds fans thought that was the right decision; Pascal Struijk had hardly put a foot wrong and had formed a formidable centre-back pairing with Diego Llorente. For Burnley there was a veritable plethora of former Leeds interest, with Bailey

Peacock-Farrell deputising for the injured Nick Pope in goal and regulars Chris Wood and Charlie Taylor starting as normal. There was that link with former Leeds youth player Matthew Lowton too.

Leeds had not played at Turf Moor in a top-flight game since 1975 but this was a chance to do the double over them as we'd already done with four of the bottom five sides; Brighton being the annoying exception. Burnley would make it five from the bottom six.

This one didn't start too well for Leeds, Burnley are a tough, often physical side and, for the first ten minutes or so they did their best to impose themselves. After five minutes Sky flashed a possession stat on the screen; Burnley had 76% of the ball so far!

Thankfully, despite their dominance of the opening minutes, they didn't really create any serious chances while it was Patrick Bamford who registered the first shot on target in the 9th minute, a low drive on the angle after Paddy rescued a through ball from Raphinha with a clever sliding tackle on the corner of the six yard box. That was well saved by Bailey Peacock-Farrell and then Stuart Dallas cleverly turned and shot with a volley that flew over the bar. We saw the cynical side of Chris Wood then as he had a crafty look to see where Illan Meslier was as a high ball came across before ramming his back into him and then protesting his innocence to referee Graham Scott. Then Tarkowski jumped and planted his knee firmly in the back of Llorente at a Leeds corner prompting one of those high pitched squeals from Diego that was heard down at Chelsea; thankfully there were no Burnley fans in the ground to hand him the sort of stick he got at Stamford Bridge that day! Leeds were upping the pressure all the time and we then won four corners in quick succession with the best of them, taken short and collected by Kalvin Phillips, resulting in a Pascal Struijk header that he should probably have buried; he nodded it a foot wide. Then some brilliant work by Raphinha set up a free shot for Alioski but the little fellow horribly pulled it so wide that it went for a throw-in! Then a clever Phillips volley put Harrison clear on the left and his low cross was completely missed by Bamford at the front post as he did that thing when he gets his feet mixed up. The ball ran on and was just clipped by the stretching boot of Charlie Taylor sending it into the air behind Raphinha who tried an improbable overhead kick that ballooned the ball into the stands. That feeling that this might be 'one of those days' had just started to cross my mind as we moved into the 44th minute.

A Burnley attack through the centre broke down as Llorente intercepted the ball, pushing it out to the right corner of our own box to Raphinha. Initially Raphinha slipped but he recovered to scoop it a few feet towards Mateusz Klich. Klich waited for Raphinha to get back up and then laid it neatly in his path as he took off before playing it back inside to Klich just short of halfway. Ahead of them, Patrick Bamford took a tumble as his run was blocked by the ever-annoying Tarkowski but the referee saw an advantage developing as Klich ran on towards the edge of the Burnley area and he waved play-on. Klich ran and ran as Burnley backed off, drifting slightly to the left before cutting back onto his right foot as he reached the curve of the 'D'. Then he simply caressed the ball around two defenders and it curled perfectly inside the right post. It was a delightful bit of play and had all the hallmarks of the Klich we used to know and love who regularly did this a couple of years ago when he'd score from *"Twenty yards or thirty yards everywhere we go!"*. This season Klich hadn't scored from open play since the opening day of the season at Anfield. Half-time and Leeds were deservedly one goal to the good. We'd bossed the possession, had more than twice the attempts Burnley had managed, and won six corners to their two. Despite the slow start it was a dominant first half for Leeds.

Burnley started the second half strongly, just as they did at the start of the game; the ball sat up nicely for Westwood to strike on the volley but that went wide and then a long, route-one clearance from BPF was headed on towards Matej Vidra who out-muscled Struijk and then easily skipped past Luke Ayling to get one-on-one with Illan Meslier. The young keeper stuck out his left leg and diverted the shot wide for another top-class piece of keeping.

That was as good as it got for the Clarets though and Leeds had started to look back to their quick passing best as move after move regularly took us from one end to the other. Rodrigo joined the fray in the 58th minute for Patrick Bamford who looked to be carrying a knock. Within a minute of arriving on the pitch he was causing problems for the home defence. Raphinha was picking up the ball deep in his own half on the right and this time he touched it inside to Stuart Dallas who shifted it straight away inside to the blue booted Rodrigo. He cleverly back-heeled it first time back into the path of the marauding Raphinha who in turn knocked it wide left into the path of Jack Harrison. Meanwhile Rodrigo carried on his run into the box and it was only a stretching boot from the annoying Tarkowski that took Harrison's cross off Rodrigo's toes and out for a corner. Stuart Dallas swung the corner over towards the back post where Matty Vydra stooped to head it clear but it only found Alioski, lurking on the edge of the box. For the second time today Gjanni fluffed his shot, badly pulling it to the right, but Jack Harrison was lurking near the corner of the six-yard box and he cleverly and deftly back-heeled it into the net.

Burnley made a double substitution in the 65th minute as Wood and Vydra were replaced by Barnes and Rodriguez and then five minutes later they withdrew George McNeil, but not before he'd had a coming together with Alioski. McNeil brought Alioski down and then appeared to lean over him while he was on the ground and either spat or said something to the North Macedonian international. When Alioski got up he could be seen asking the referee *"Did you hear what he said to me?"* and pointing at McNeil and then, putting both hands up by his ears he pulled what I can only describe as a 'bunny face' if you've ever played the drinking game, 'Bunnies'. There was a long delay as referee Graham Scott joined the fourth official and the two managers to presumably discuss the incident and then Scott got Ayling and Alioski together for another brief meeting back on the pitch. It was all a bit mystifying but after the game Sean Dyche confirmed that McNeil had put in a report to the referee. We'd hear later that the FA was to investigate the incident.

Back on the pitch though Rodrigo was about to show us exactly what he is all about as he polished the Clarets off with two swift gulps! First though we did need the brilliance of Illan Meslier again as he denied Gudmundsson from close range. We were now into the final fifteen minutes and Leeds were about to strike with the deadly speed of a serpent in a hurry. Burnley launched the ball clear up to halfway where Pascal Struijk rose to head it back towards the Burnley goal. Kalvin Phillips and Jack Harrison both arrived on the spot where the ball landed but Harrison clearly called and Kalvin let it run to the Citeh loanee. He played a first time pass twenty yards towards Rodrigo who'd made a dash between Tarkowski and

Ben Mee on the edge of the area. One touch took the ball past the Burnley men and then a little delicate dink lifted it over BPF. It was a Harry Kane sort of a finish, a bit like the one ruled offside against us the previous week, in fact it was so good it drew another little two-fisted pump from Marcelo on the touchline. It was sublime but two minutes later he pretty much reprised it and the move was just as rapid and just as devastating!

Luke Ayling booted the ball up-field from deep in the Leeds right-back corner to Stuart Dallas who chested it back towards Kalvin Phillips. The ball took three little bounces as it ran towards Phillips and then he creamed it on the volley sending it like an exocet missile out to the left touchline, right to the feet of Jack Harrison; it was a sensational pass. Meanwhile Rodrigo was motoring through the middle and had got a yard ahead of that man Tarkowski as they ran into the Burnley area. Harrison's pass was again perfectly into the path of Rodrigo and this time he jinked round BPF and slotted the ball into the net. Two goals in two minutes had finally shown us the quality this man possessed and, despite being told when he joined us that he wasn't a natural goal-scorer, well, I think whoever said that needs to reassess.

The 0 – 4 scoreline probably flattered Leeds a tad but there was no denying the absolute quality of the four goals. All different in their own way but all the epitome of what we know as Bielsaball. Neutrals watching Leeds for the first time would I'm sure have added their names to our ever growing list of admirers as once again we'd entertained from start to finish. At the same time we had to recognise the part Illan Meslier played with two wonderful saves and the tough ten minutes we'd endured at the start of both halves. We really did cut loose in the final half hour though and we looked a class apart. Jack Harrison was arguably the standout performer as he claimed a goal as well as two assists for Rodrigo; only Manchester United's Bruno Fernandes had more goal involvements, goals and assists, from midfield in the Premier League this season. For Leeds only striker Patrick Bamford has been involved in more goals; 22 compared with 16 for Harrison.

In the other games played this penultimate Saturday of the EPL season, there were wins for Southampton, 3 – 1 against Fulham, while Brighton and West Ham drew 1 – 1. That result was a, err, hammer blow to the Hammers as they chased the final Champions

League place. In the FA Cup final it was joy for the Foxes of Leicester City who edged out Chelsea by the only goal of the game and enjoyed celebrating in front of those lucky 21,000 fans, albeit around 6,000 Chelsea fans left like lemmings as soon as the final whistle blew!

On Sunday there were four more EPL games. I was cheering from the sofa as Crystal Palace came from behind to beat Aston Villa 3 – 2, a result that improved our chances of staying ahead of the Villans and hanging onto a top half finish while Spurs helped us in that regard too by beating Wolves 2 – 0 and ensuring the Molineux side couldn't then catch us. A win for Leeds at Southampton or against West Brom would therefore guarantee we finished at least as high as tenth. There was then an astonishing finish to the West Brom v Liverpool game. The Reds needed to win all three of their final games to have any chance of grabbing the 4th Champions League place and, with only seconds left, they were still drawing 1 – 1. Then, Liverpool won a last minute corner and up came goalkeeper Alisson. I watched in amazement as the corner floated across and Alisson rose to plant a perfect header into the corner of the net! Sky had of course run that *"Alisson Blunderland"* caption following his disastrous errors against Manchester City so it was predictable this time they went for a commercial break with the caption *"Alisson Wonderland"* on the screen. What goes around comes around I guess. Liverpool's Merseyside neighbours Everton were beaten 0 – 1 by Sheffield United effectively destroying their feint hopes of a Champions League place.

Burnley 0 Leeds Utd 4 (Klich 44, Harrison 59, Rodrigo 77, 79)
BCD. Round 36 League Pos: 10th

St Mary's Contrary!

S o, we moved into the final week of the EPL season; two more full programmes of games and all to be played with at least some home fans inside the stadiums. For Leeds it was first a trip to Southampton and then we'd finish this wonderful mishmash of a Premier League season with a home game against West Brom and I'd be able to say: *"I was there!"*

For the penultimate round of matches, four were to be played on Tuesday, 18th May, including ours, and then six the following evening. On Sunday afternoon, every game would kick-off at 4 pm. I suppose since some fans were now going to be inside the stadiums the TV companies decided it was no longer important to stagger all of the kick-off times and hence on Tuesday a second game would kick-off at exactly the same time as ours at 6 pm. It wasn't a problem though as no Leeds fan probably wanted to watch it; it was Man United's game with Fulham!

I was nervous about our game at Southampton, Saints had started the season really well and were actually top of the table at one point but, more recently, their season fell apart and they were now down in 14th spot, effectively top of that bunch of seven teams that had been so effectively beaten by Leeds throughout the season, well, apart from Brighton of course. The Seagulls were the only side in the bottom seven we'd lost to this season and we'd managed that twice incredibly. My nervousness increased when the line-up was announced on the club Twitter account:

Casilla
Ayling Llorente (Berardi 45) Cooper (Capt)
Dallas Phillips (Struijk 45) Alioski
Raphinha Rodrigo (Roberts 78) Harrison
Bamford

Substitutes: Meslier, Davis, Berardi, Struijk, Shackleton, Jenkins, Roberts, Hernandez, Poveda.

Southampton: McCarthy, Walker-Peters, Stephens, Vestergaard, Salisu, Walcott (Diallo 78), Ward-Prowse, Armstrong, Djenepo, Adams (Ings 45), Tella (Redmond70), Subs not used: Forster, Obafemi, Minamino, Bednarek, N'Lundulu, Ferry

Referee: Peter Bankes.

The chief worry was the inclusion of Kiko Casilla and, scrolling through Twitter, I wasn't alone with my worry beads. Kiko is not a popular figure amongst Leeds fans; either people were still carrying a grudge about his alleged racist comment to Jonathan Leko or, like me, they just felt he was too likely to make a catastrophic error. Bielsa, for whatever reason, told reporters he wanted Kiko to play the final two games. There was even a theory, promulgated by former Leeds keeper Paddy Kenny, that Meslier had been 'dropped' because he played so many long balls against Burnley. Football Insider reported: *"After Leeds' rout at Turf Moor last weekend, Marcelo Bielsa was asked whether the instruction to go long had come from him. The Argentine responded: "No, and as a result none of those attacks prospered.""* [1] Many Leeds fans doubted the Flying Pig's theory though.

The other change that raised a few eyebrows, albeit nowhere near as high, was the inclusion of Liam Cooper who displaced Pascal

---

[1] https://www.footballinsider247.com/leeds-united-kenny-this-is-real-reason-meslier-dropped-v-soton/

Struijk. The feeling on that one was that Struijk had formed such a good partnership with Llorente that it seemed both harsh on Pascal and a risk to change a winning formula. The inclusion of Rodrigo in the starting XI was not contentious at all; following his two goals at Burnley everyone believed he'd now found his match fitness but there was just a hint in those other changes that maybe Bielsa was using these last couple of games to test some of his theories. What Radrizzani might think if that was true I'm not sure as there was still that matter of an extra £2 million for each place we could climb up the table. It was hard to think Bielsa was just a big softy and was giving Coops and Kiko a run out to show they were still part of the family… but you never know. It was believed that the total absence of both Robin Koch and Mateusz Klich was a gesture by Bielsa to give them a rest knowing they would both play an important part for their national sides in the forthcoming Euros, so there clearly was compassion in the great man.

	Team	P	GD	Pts
C 1	Manchester City	36	47	83
2	Manchester United	36	28	70
3	Leicester City	36	21	66
4	Chelsea	36	22	64
5	Liverpool	36	21	63
6	Tottenham Hotspur	36	22	59
7	West Ham United	36	10	59
8	Everton	36	3	56
9	Arsenal	36	12	55
10	Leeds United	36	4	53
11	Aston Villa	36	7	49
12	Wolverhampton Wanderers	36	-14	45
13	Crystal Palace	36	-21	44
14	Southampton	36	-16	43
15	Burnley	36	-18	39
16	Newcastle United	36	-19	39
17	Brighton and Hove Albion	36	-5	38
R 18	Fulham	36	-24	27
R 19	West Bromwich Albion	36	-37	26
R 20	Sheffield United	36	-43	20

There was also a Premier League record up for grabs tonight; if Leeds could win it would be a tenth away victory this season and Leeds had never managed that before in the EPL. Most observers listed the Leeds team in a 3 – 3 – 3 – 1 formation with Bielsa, as always, opting to play three centre-backs to counter the two strikers – Tella and Adams – that Southampton were sure to employ.

As can be seen from the table, it was not only money Leeds were still playing for. Mathematically, Leeds could still attain a top seven place and seven was the maximum number of teams the Premier League could send next season to either the Champions League, the Europa League or, possibly, the new Europa Conference League. It was unlikely though that we'd be needing our passports for the 2021/2022 season as it would depend on several teams currently above us losing both remaining games. More important for me was to beat the Saints and West Brom to complete that sequence of wins against the bottom seven sides... Brighton excepted of course... I still fail to understand how we manged to lose two games to them. Whatever happened in the final two games though, we could now not finish lower than 11th; a magnificent achievement.

The game at St Mary's was tough and, a bit like Burnley last Saturday, they started strongly albeit, also like Burnley, without actually causing us too much trouble. All eyes were on Kiko Casilla of course as that was a strange decision to put him in the firing line again so late in the season, but he came through with an almost faultless performance, particularly early in the game when we were on the back foot. A 4th minute save from a Che Adams header was a fine piece of keeping and so important at that stage, and a second, low to his left again from Adams, was less difficult but it too was vital. The longer the game went on though, despite numerous personnel changes, Leeds only looked stronger and stronger and the high press got more and more troublesome for the Saints.

Leeds were clumsy with their possession for the first ten minutes which helped Southampton to that good start but slowly and surely we got our act together and Kiko was relatively untroubled for the remainder of the game. Leeds first real chance came in the 23rd minute when Raphinha delicately headed a Jack Harrison cross back to Stuart Dallas. The Irish Rover took the ball nicely on his chest but then pulled his left-foot half-volley wide of the right post. Raphinha then darted between two defenders to pull the ball back for Rodrigo but he also failed to hit the target. That was pretty much it for a first half in which the Saints started the better but faded as time went on but still managed eight attempts to our four but only those two early Che Adams efforts registered on target. As if to confirm that Bielsa was indeed in end of season mode, he made two more changes at half time that looked like efforts to give more players a rest; Pascal Struijk replaced Kalvin Phillips who was surely destined for a busy summer with England, while Gaetano Berardi got his Premier League debut in place of Diego Llorente who would similarly be involved in the Euros with Spain.

At the start of the second half I clenched those bum muscles a bit tighter as James Ward-Prowse lined up a free kick just outside the Leeds area. He was pretty much top of the Premier League statistics for set-piece goals this season. He was again close with this one as he curled it onto the very corner of the goal-frame.

Leeds were also getting close though and Rodrigo was starting to pull some strings. Stuart Dallas was having another good game too and he started the next Leeds move with a pass out wide to Raphinha. He clipped the ball forward to Rodrigo on the edge of the area and he chested it back towards Dallas following-up. Dallas hit the ball fiercely on the first bounce and sent it fizzing towards the net before McCarthy dived full length to just tip it around the left post. Patrick Bamford should then probably have scored but he once again failed to convert in a one-on-one situation. This time Raphinha launched the ball over the top of the Saints back-line from deep in his own half and Bamford read it perfectly with McCarthy stranded way out of his goal. Paddy should probably have lobbed the keeper straight away but instead he attempted to go round him. He took the ball past the keeper but then McCarthy's gloves just half-tripped him. He staggered but stayed on his feet but it was enough to allow Vestergaard to nick the ball away for a Leeds corner. Most strikers would have gone down as soon as they felt the touch and Bamford probably paid the price for his honesty, or maybe naivety, depending on your football morals!

Another Leeds break then ended with a chance for Alioski that he hit well but straight into the bread-basket of the Saints' now very busy keeper.

The two Leeds goals came late in the game but they were well worth waiting for and were really good examples of how we break quickly against a tired side, just as Rodrigo punished Burnley the previous weekend. The first, in the 73rd minute, had that stamp of Rodrigo magic on it again as he lifted a clever ball over the defence right into the path of Bamford. Paddy did well to finish it too from such a tight angle with maybe the slightest bit of luck as it went through McCarthy's legs to find the net. It was Bamford's 16th goal of this remarkable season. Rodrigo was very much coming into his own and everyone was hoping we could start the next season with him in the side fully fit although he too would possibly be called upon by Spain for their Euro campaign.

We had to wait until the 5th minute of added time for the second goal but it was a big moment for Tyler Roberts, on as a 78th minute substitute for Rodrigo. It was actually down to the quick thinking of Kiko Casilla as he launched the ball out wide to Raphinha with the tired Saints mainly still in our half. Raphinha had not long before had a goal disallowed when Bamford strayed offside but now he pushed the ball inside to Tyler Roberts who also had Jack Harrison wide of him if needed. Roberts decided he didn't need Harrison but then he took too long to sort out exactly what he was going to do and his chance was seemingly lost. The ball broke though for Patrick Bamford who wasted no time at all in walloping it at goal. That one was blocked by McCarthy but the ball came straight back to Roberts and this time he did look far more composed as he took a touch to stun the ball and then calmly passed it into the empty corner of the net. Nice composure from a player who I hoped would now come on leaps and bounds for having got his debut Premier League goal. We'd seen in the past that he can finish with the best of them, notably that superb brace at Hull just before the first Covid break, but maybe his confidence had been lacking since and this could do the trick. I almost forgot there were fans in St Mary's after that; it went very, very quiet.

Leeds were well worth the win by the end and another clean sheet helped to push those memories of conceding a bag-full of goals early in the season more and more to the back of our minds. There was no doubt we had become a much more solid defensive unit since the arrival of a fit Diego Llorente.

So, a top half finish was now guaranteed, regardless of other results in the final two games and we all felt a little bit guilty I'm sure that at one point this season we thought the key task was to stay ahead of Fulham. Tonight we proved again what a talented side we have, how we are as fit as the proverbial butcher's dog and how the Bielsa MO can work in the Premier League really well if the players on the pitch can continue to put the plan into effect. Berardi looked comfortable when he came on and even removing Phillips and Llorente didn't impact our organisation one bit. One final statistic proved that 'Bielsa burn-out' as a theory was well and truly buried; Leeds were top of the form table for the last ten games with 21 points.

In that Manchester United v Fulham game played at the same time as ours there were more protests against the Glazers by the home fans who were also disgruntled by a tame 1 – 1 draw with the relegated Londoners. In the other two games played later that evening, Brighton beat the new Champions, Manchester City, 3 – 2, while in the big game at the top, a repeat of the weekend's FA Cup final, it was Chelsea who staked their claim for a Champions League spot as this time they defeated the Foxes 2 – 1. The following night Everton kept their European hopes alive with another win, this time beating Wolves 1 – 0. Newcastle beat Sheffield United 1 – 0, Spurs put themselves in danger of missing out on Europe altogether with a 1 – 2 home defeat to Aston Villa, while North London rivals Arsenal kept their hopes alive with a 1 – 3 win at Crystal Palace who announced this week that Roy Hodgson was retiring from management at the age of 73 after almost half a century of professional coaching. In the final two games of the penultimate round, Liverpool got themselves up into the top four with a 0 – 3 win at Burnley while West Ham were now in pole position for the Europa League spot with a 1 – 3 win at West Brom after which Sam Allardyce announced he was off at the end of the season. So, as it stood, with one game to go, it was Man City, Man United, Chelsea and Liverpool in the ECL; Leicester and West Ham in the Europa League and Spurs would get the booby prize of a play-off game for the new Europa Conference League.

Southampton 0 Leeds United 2 (Bamford 73, Roberts 90+5)
Att. 8,000. **Round 37 League Pos: 10th.**

Wizard And Warrior

There was no pause to admire the magnificent achievements of this season by the Leeds management; they were still hard at work behind the scenes. Andrea Radrizzani announced a strengthening of the Leeds board this week as he set out his stall for the next leg of the journey. Former boss of shopping mall empire Westfield, Peter Lowy, a lifelong Leeds fan; Sandro Mencucci, previously an executive of ACF Fiorentina; and Massimo Marinelli, the CEO of Aser Ventures, part of Radrizzani's existing business empire, all joined the main board while long-time advisor, Andre Tegner stepped down.

A rumour doing the rounds was that Marcelo Bielsa had already agreed to remain at the club for at least another season. Several fringe papers were reporting that he'd agreed 'in principle' to stay but, as with all reports in the football press it was probably best to await confirmation from the club before we opened the champagne.[1] What was now clear though was that Pablo Hernandez and Gaetano Berardi would both be leaving in the summer; the Wizard and the Warrior were both heavily featured in the match-day magazine for the West Brom game with the club confirming that both were leaving.

It was just like old times for me this weekend; I'd not had a trip away with the football for well over a year but, as soon as it was confirmed that fans would be allowed in for this final game, I'd started planning, initially of course not even knowing if I'd get a ticket. Thankfully I did, as did most of my little circle of mates. I'd persuaded Mrs W that we could have a long weekend away in Yorkshire and take the opportunity, now that Covid regulations had been relaxed somewhat, to meet up with friends. We arranged to meet one friend in Saltaire on the Friday; we booked a stay in a little hotel there for the Friday night where we'd meet up with our old friends Sheila and Brian who were coming down from Darlington; and then on Saturday we'd make our way to Leeds.

So, early Friday morning the car was loaded and Mrs W and I set off on the familiar 100 mile or so journey to Yorkshire. I was surprised by the quantity of traffic on the roads; it seemed everyone was now on the move again following the latest relaxation in Covid restrictions that allowed indoor hospitality to resume, albeit with a few annoying little rules remaining like having to wear a face mask whenever you were not dining. We spent Friday exploring Salts Mill, a former textile mill and now an art gallery, shopping centre and restaurant complex in Saltaire, a village near Bradford in West Yorkshire. It has a fascinating history and is well worth a visit. Local artist David Hockney has many of his works on display and, being free to both park at and visit, it's an ideal place to drop in for a coffee or use as a base from which to explore the area.

We stopped overnight at the lovely little Abbey Lodge Hotel with our friends Shelia and Brian and, as we sat in the bar having a drink before venturing out on Friday night, we got chatting with Gary D who runs the place. We soon discovered Gary was a Leeds United season ticket holder and that we had several mutual friends. If you

---

[1] *https://firstsportz.com/football-marcelo-bielsa-signs-contract-extension-at-leeds/*

are ever looking for a no nonsense little bolt-hole in this area, a beautiful area for walking by the way, then give this place a try. Oh, and buy Gary a pint for me as I now owe him one.

We'd booked a table at the Salts Bar and Kitchen, just a few hundred yards up the road, and enjoyed catching up with Sheila and Brian over a pizza and a few pints of Yorkshire Blonde. It's built on the site of the former tram sheds and you can also have a beer looking down on the magnificent stainless steel vats of the Salt Brewery. It was a chance to learn of the match day experience that Brian had earlier in the week. As mentioned before, Brian is a Chelsea season ticket holder despite the fact that he lives in the North East and, like I was about to, he had his one and only football trip to Chelsea this season on Tuesday when they beat Leicester 2 – 1 to put them in control of their own destiny as they chased a Champions League place. He was impressed with the atmosphere although he admitted that there was lots more at stake for Chelsea that night than there would be at Elland Road on Sunday. They had used exactly the same MO though, in terms of a ticket ballot, pre-game emailed health questionnaire, and an ID check at the turnstiles. Funnily enough, my email from Leeds about the health questionnaire came through as I was on my second Yorkshire Blonde in the Beer Kitchen. Our WhatsApp group was immediately all over it with messages pinging backwards and forwards while I was getting messages from other folk with questions like... *"What the effin hell does question five mean?"* and *"Who the f*** is Graham Peck?"* No sooner had I pressed send on the email than I got the confirmation back from the said Graham Peck stating: *"You are cleared to attend Leeds United Stadium at Elland Road, Leeds".*

The weather lately had been rubbish. It seemed to have been raining on and off for weeks on end and it was a pleasant surprise to wake up on Saturday morning to see it was dry... hardly sunny, but at least dry. So, Brian, Sheila, Mrs W and I set off on a walk along the tow path of the Leeds-Liverpool canal towards Bingley. Again, if you're in the area and you can manage a six mile round trip it's well worth doing. The walk takes you past a couple of cricket pitches, Salts FC's little ground, and a few bowling greens, all part of the legacy left by Titus Salt who effectively built the whole village. There's a little pub half-way – *"the Fisherman's"* and the route crosses the River Aire at one point. The reward at the Bingley end is sight of the famous Bingley Five Rise lock complex and a little café.

On Saturday afternoon we said our farewells to Sheila and Brian and headed for Leeds where we were booked into the Premier Inn on Gelderd Road for the night. We were meeting up with MK Derek and Shirley and we were soon sinking a few pints in the hotel bar with them before going into Leeds for a curry. It was strange and yet familiar all at the same time to be out and about doing 'normal' stuff like this after so many months in lockdown of various degrees but I have to admit it was fabulous.

After stuffing ourselves silly with the 'all you can eat' breakfast, the next stop was the Old White Hart at the top of Wesley Street and soon, Kentley the Stokie, Wakefield Steve, the three amigos (Richard, Alan and John), Barlow Boy, MK Derek and Shirley, Mrs W and I were swapping lockdown tales over a few more pints. The only signs of the Covid pandemic were the one way systems in place in the pub and the fact that everyone had a face mask at the ready. Many more folk wandered up to say hello and, for the moment, it was just like old times.

The Stokie was in a bit of a pickle; he'd had a knee operation a few weeks earlier and so was on crutches. We'd toyed with the idea of using a wheelchair but no one would insure us for the return trip down the 1 in 4 slope from the pub to the ground. I conservatively reckoned we'd have reached Mach 4 and could easily have demolished the South Stand on impact. The Stokie and I had previous for this as we'd once taken out several old ladies at a bus stop outside Deepdale as I lost control of the wheelchair not long after he first messed up his knee playing football. Anyway, discretion and valour and all that so we left the pub at twenty to three for a slow hop down to the ground.

Outside the ground there was a real buzz of anticipation with fans milling around and a few media teams picking out likely candidates for interviews. We also expected there to be long delays to get inside, what with all the checks they were supposed to do but I have to say as long as you had a match ticket, that vital email from Graham Peck, a face mask and any old piece of plastic that resembled a driving licence, you were in! It was many years since I'd been in the East Stand so I was looking forward to checking out the view and I have to admit it was decent. All of our little group had chosen the back of the lower tier right on the halfway line and, watching the players warm up, I could have got used to it. Sadly, when the game started it was clear that the usual MO in here was for fans to stay seated and that ruled it out for me in the future. Today, since there were lots of fans in the East Stand who'd usually stand on the Kop like us or even the South Stand, there were folk standing much of the time but the annoyance of others was clear to see; I generally stayed in my seat just to appease the lady sat behind. We were all supposed to stay in the specific seat printed on our tickets and most did, leaving a three seat gap between each occupied seat to comply with Covid social distancing rules.

The Leeds players were all warming up in T-shirts adorned either with Pablo's '19' or Berra's '28' on the back and a message of thanks for each of them and I'd already seen that both were in the starting line-up.

Casilla
Berardi (Struijk 69) Ayling Cooper (Capt)
Raphinha   Phillips   Alioski
Hernandez (Roberts 70) Dallas Harrison
Rodrigo (Bamford 45)

Substitutes: Meslier, Davis, Casey, Struijk, Poveda, Roberts, Shackleton, Jenkins, Bamford.

West Brom: Johnstone, Furlong, Ajayi, Bartley, O'Shea (Robson-Kanu 60), Townsend, Gallagher, Yokuslu, Maitland-Niles (Grant 83), Phillips, Robinson (Diangana 61).

Subs not used: Button, Diagne, Peltier, Gardner-Hickman, Taylor, Iroegbunam. Referee: David Coote.

So, once again Marcelo Bielsa was showing that he has a big heart as well as an amazing football brain; he started both Pablo and Berra for this, their final game with Leeds. For a few moments I wondered if this team would be strong enough, missing as it was several players who'd been mainstays during the campaign. He'd told us before that he wanted Kiko Casilla to play the two final games and Kiko did nothing much wrong in the win at Southampton so that wasn't a big concern, but he was also continuing to rest Matty Klich and Robin Koch and now Llorente was also not even on the bench while Patrick Bamford was. However, when you had a good long look at this starting XI it had plenty of talent in it. Berardi and Cooper had played together many times over the years if not this season; Rodrigo we had seen in recent weeks was now firing on all cylinders, while I was confident that Pablo would not let us down. West Brom were not exactly Bayern Munich either; we'd given them a real hiding at their place in December and they had less to play for than we did as we eyed moving up the table another place or two and picking up £2 million of extra prize money with each new rung up the ladder. No, I thought my 4 – 0 prediction for the YEP was well within reach.

When the players appeared, Leeds from the tunnel opposite and the Albion down the steps from the West stand, I was confused by the volume of noise in the stadium. There were only supposed to be 8,000 fans in the ground and yet the noise was incredible! I even wondered if the club had hidden some microphones around the stands to amplify the sound! *"We are the Champions!"* boomed out from all corners while scarves swirled over heads and I confess it was all a bit emotional… my quivering lips were hidden from view of course but the water in my eyes would be visible to anyone looking. All eyes though were initially focussed intently on that tunnel. As the Kaiser Chiefs *"I Predict A Riot"* was faded out and the first notes of MOT blasted from the PA the whole stadium erupted. It was like I remember any first home game of the season, and yet this was the last game! It was all a bit surreal. I could just make out the portly figure of Marcelo Bielsa pacing around his technical area like a proud father watching his kids. On the pitch we could see that Pablo Hernandez was wearing the captain's armband even though it was Liam Cooper going through the formalities of the toss in the centre circle; everything was slightly strange and yet everything was also very familiar. The *"Pablo Hernandez, he plays for United with Kiko Casilla"* song was now echoing around the famous old stadium and I had to blink hard as that damned dust was in my eyes again… Then the players all dropped onto one knee and then we were off.

Within seconds of the start there was a moment of concern as Liam Cooper went in forcibly on Darnell Furlong, near the corner flag to my right, the north east corner. Coops led with his right forearm as he muscled Furlong off the ball and the referee immediately gave a free kick and Coops a yellow. Maybe the occasion was just boosting adrenalin levels a little too much but the fans on the Kop were more concerned about referee David Coote who got a rousing *"We always get sh** refs!"* and then *"Wan***!, Wan***!"* and I had to smile, I'd not heard that for well over a year! Nothing came of the free kick but there was plenty being said in the area as Kyle Bartley jostled with Luke Ayling and Cooper, the three of them no doubt swapping old memories of playing together. When the free kick came over it was Bartley beating Cooper in the air to head wide of the left post and he jogged away with a grin. The ball was soon up the other end, in front of the South Stand, and Stuart Dallas ran the ball over the byline for a goal kick that generated a long crescendo of sound before the Albion keeper, Sam Johnstone received the traditional *"You sh** ba*****!"* as he finally booted the ball up-field. Oh yes, nothing had really changed.

Leeds were actually lined up with a back five, with Luke Ayling the middle of three centre-backs with Cooper and Berardi either side as West Brom were playing two strikers, Phillips and Robinson up front. Raphinha and Alioski were effectively playing as wing-backs with Harrison just tucked inside Alioski. It was no surprise therefore that we saw plenty of the action on the touchline down in front of us in the first half as Leeds attacked the South Stand.

There was an almighty roar in the 7th minute as Leeds had the ball in the net when Hernandez curled a magical ball in behind the Albion defence. Rodrigo had made the run and he back heeled the ball into the path of Harrison who stabbed it home from seven yards. Sadly, Rodrigo was well offside to meet Pablo's exquisite pass. It was enough to get *"We Are Leeds!"* belting out all around the ground though.

Leeds were already dominating the possession and as soon as we lost it we were right in the face of the Albion man with the ball giving him no time at all to settle or consider his options. Then we'd win it back and with a swagger we'd whip the ball about and swarm down towards that South Stand. It was the cavalier, carnival football we'd been watching on TV all season but seeing it in the flesh was something mesmerising. The biggest cheer of the day so far came as Pablo nut-megged Yokuslu in the centre circle; we were going to miss this little magician and he was rolling back the years today, marshalling that midfield area and constantly probing with clever little passes through the Albion defence; this was fast becoming a demonstration game. Then Pablo was back-heeling the ball and Kalvin Phillips had the first shot in anger just over the bar. The Leeds fans were soon shouting *"Olé"* as pass followed pass. We were into the 17th minute as Luke Ayling clipped a ball through for Raphinha to chase but the ball was nicked off him for a Leeds corner; Raphinha trotted over to take it from under the big screen. Leeds never score from a corner...

Raphinha whipped the ball in towards the near post and Gaetano Berardi was first to it to try to glance it home. He didn't get much on it though so it carried pretty much on the same trajectory, bounced in the six yard area, and Rodrigo, flying in at the back post just beat Jack Harrison to it to power it into the net. This was turning into the perfect end to a pretty much perfect season and Elland Road was rocking and it was a cracking game of football with the Albion playing their part on the rare occasions they could get on the ball. There were moments when they got into the Leeds box but there was a distinct lack of quality in their finishing. Maybe it was their frustration that caused Gallagher to dive in to catch the ankle of Raphinha in front of the dugouts; he got the second yellow of the day for that one.

Referee David Coote has never been one of my favourites – few of them are – but he was having his usual nightmare with a series of unfathomable decisions that often came several seconds after the relevant incident. At one point he was clearly told of a foul on an Albion player by the liner on the west touchline, but it was patently obvious the lad had dived with no contact whatsoever. He wasn't being biased, just awful.

For much of the final twenty minutes or so of the half there was little in the way of goalmouth action. Leeds were still bossing the ball and passing sharply but the Albion seemed to have settled to their task and were pretty much nullifying everything we tried. Meanwhile, sat in that East Stand I was starting to feel the cold as the wind began to get up and I added that to my list of reasons not to move from the Kop in future. Then, with 42 minutes on the clock, Pablo Hernandez was tripped in the inside left channel, just outside the Albion box. Kalvin Phillips lined up to take the free kick.

My son's next door neighbours are all West Brom season ticket holders and so, during the two years since he bought the house, I've had regular banter with them about the football; first when we were rivals going for promotion and then latterly as we've both gone our separate ways in the Prem. Their biggest complaint this season had been about their goalkeeper, Sam Johnstone, who they didn't rate at all. I'd often found myself defending him as I'd not noticed too much wrong but I should have listened, they were right! The free kick was ten yards outside the area and level with the left edge and it was pretty clear Kalvin was going to have a pop but when he did none of us could have expected it to go in. It was a simple curling strike towards the left post but any decent keeper would have had it covered. This time though the ball bounced just short of the line and, as Johnstone went down, the ball popped over him and into the net. Mixed in with the celebratory cheers of the Elland Road crowd were a good many hearty chuckles! There had been talk that Johnstone might conceivably be the replacement for Kiko if he decided to leave this summer but if that was the case I'm sure Victor was now deleting that file from his records. That was pretty much it for the first half although the Coote of a referee embarrassed himself a few more times with more strange decisions before he called the half to a close.

For the second half Marcelo sent on Patrick Bamford meaning that he would play at least some part in every league game this season as both Luke Ayling and Stuart Dallas had also done. Those two had started every game, an honour denied Paddy by virtue of not starting this one. I won't detail the second half; there were only four moments to record really. Leeds went 3 – 0 up in the 79th minute when Patrick Bamford scored from the spot following a fairly obvious handball; the only contention being that Raphinha seemed to want to take the kick. He soon handed the ball over to Paddy though when encouraged with a little word from Captain Coops. Right at the end West Brom just annoyed everyone by getting a consolation goal after a rare mistake by Kalvin Phillips as he failed to control a pass from Liam Cooper on the edge of the area and Robson-Kanu nipped in to smash the ball past Casilla. The mistake was possibly still in Kalvin's mind as he then slid into a rash tackle right under my nose on the east touchline. Kalvin got the ball but no one could deny it looked a bit rash and he not only picked up a yellow card but also appeared to injure his shoulder in the process and, with seconds only to go, he was helped off the pitch. Those were three of the four significant incidents of the second half but it is the fourth that we will all remember for years to come.

In the 69th minute the substitutes board went up showing a bright '28' in red alongside a green '21' as the call was made for Pascal Struijk to replace Gaetano Berardi. As Berra made his way towards the dugout he was embraced at every step by each of the Leeds outfield players in turn and then even Kyle Bartley jogged across to give him a hug, the two having often partnered each other when Bartley was with Leeds of course. Then, when Pascal trotted on, the board went up again and this time it was the red number '19' and a green '11' signifying that Pablo's time was also up and he was replaced by Tyler Roberts. Exactly the same process was followed as again every Leeds player gave Pablo a little hug and a few words while the whole crowd stood and chanted his name just as we did for Berra moments before. The big screen had a picture of Berra showing with the words *"Grazie Gaetano"* and that then changed to one of Pablo with the same message in Spanish for him; *"Gracias Pablo"* There was not a dry eye left in the house…

At the end of the game hardly anyone left the stadium as we waited for the traditional lap of honour, although we didn't now expect to see Kalvin Phillips as he was helped away while carefully holding his damaged shoulder. The rest of the players came back out very quickly and slowly walked around the pitch to receive the adulation of a jubilant and yet tearful Elland Road crowd. There were so many mixed emotions; a memorable season but a game that witnessed the last outing for at least two of the players who'd been stalwarts of the last few years and, who knows, maybe others too. It also crossed my mind that it was during this season that we lost Peter Lorimer and that then reminded me of the three lovely ladies who'd I'd known personally who also passed away this year, two of whom I'd never have met were it not for Leeds United. The players stopped for a few minutes in the far corner where Jermaine Beckford was doing a media piece and we could see Pablo and Gaetano going through another round of hugs before they set off again working their way across the front of the Kop and then past us in the East Stand. I've known some emotional times with Leeds in my fifty years of following them but this was right up there with the most memorable. There was a sense in the air that the baton was being handed over for the next leg of the race; the race next season to break into those European places.

I left the stadium with my one-legged mate the Stokie and, well before we saw them, we could smell the arid smoke of flares being let off outside. A group of a few hundred lads was clinging to Billy's statue, singing and chanting and bouncing up and down, many with lighted flares in their hands. A phalanx of police stood fifty yards away watching. There wasn't much social distancing going on but apart from that they weren't causing any harm. We watched for ten minutes or so before wandering up to the McDonalds car park where the Stokie's lift was waiting and then I jogged back past the merriment that was still going on outside the club shop entrance as I made my way back to the car.

Leeds United 3 West Brom 1 (**Rodrigo 17, Phillips 42, Bamford 79** pen, Robson-Kanu 90) **8,000. Final League position: 9**[th]

Full round 38 results:

Arsenal 2 Brighton 0
Aston Villa 2 Chelsea 1
Fulham 0 Newcastle 2
Leeds United 3 West Brom 1
Leicester 2 Tottenham 4
Liverpool 2 Crystal Palace 0
Manchester City 5 Everton 0
Sheffield United 1 Burnley 0
West Ham United 3 Southampton 0
Wolves 1 Manchester United 2

Chelsea and Liverpool would thus join the two Manchester clubs in the Champions League. At one point in the evening, with 14 minutes to go, Leicester were leading Spurs 2 – 1 while Chelsea were losing at Villa Park and that would have been enough to see Leicester into the top four. Then a Kasper Schmeichel own goal, punching the ball into his own net from a corner, and two late Gareth Bale goals gave fourth place to the Blues of Chelsea. Leeds overtook Everton as that 5 – 0 drubbing ruined their goal difference and we were up to 9th in the table.

English Premier League 2020/2021
Final Table

	Team	P	GD	Pts
CL 1	Manchester City	38	51	86
CL 2	Manchester United	38	29	74
CL 3	Liverpool	38	26	69
CL 4	Chelsea	38	22	67
EL 5	Leicester City	38	18	66
EL 6	West Ham United	38	15	65
ECL 7	Tottenham Hotspur	38	23	62
8	Arsenal	38	16	61
9	Leeds United	38	8	59
10	Everton	38	-1	59
11	Aston Villa	38	9	55
12	Newcastle United	38	-16	45
13	Wolverhampton Wanderers	38	-16	45
14	Crystal Palace	38	-25	44
15	Southampton	38	-21	43
16	Brighton and Hove Albion	38	-6	41
17	Burnley	38	-22	39
R 18	Fulham	38	-26	28
R 19	West Bromwich Albion	38	-41	26
R 20	Sheffield United	38	-43	23

A Wonderful Mishmash!

And that was the final act in this superbly successful season. We'd witnessed a wonderful mishmash of football from Leeds that included just about everything. We started the season with a festival of goals; 31 in our first eight league games. We conceded three or more in half of those but also scored three or more ourselves in three of them. There was a brief interlude as Arsenal held us to a goalless draw in November but then the goals came again towards the end of 2020 with two five-goal hauls in the space of four games against Newcastle and West Brom while we shipped six at Old Trafford in between. We started the New Year in traditional fashion, crashing out of the FA Cup at the first attempt, 3 – 0 at lowly Crawley Town and also failed to score as we lost at Spurs and at home to Brighton. We then looked more in danger of being caught by Fulham and going down than achieving a top half finish as we went through an uncertain phase of wins and losses without registering a sustained run of either. Relegation was still our biggest concern in March with defeats at home to Villa and at

West Ham, knowing we were about to go into eight tough games, including five against the big six. Incredibly, we ground out solid results against them all, including a 1 – 2 win at Champions elect, Manchester City. We were the form team in the EPL when we beat Southampton in the penultimate game. For a fleeting moment, it looked like we could be winning a place in the Europa League! That didn't happen in the end but to finish 9th was an amazing achievement in our first season back and one that Albion and Fulham would eye enviously. It was all the more remarkable as it was achieved largely with the players who'd been with us in the Championship, as our four marquee signings – Rodrigo, Koch, Llorente and Raphinha - only managed 67 league starts between them. We scored 62 goals, that's more than any other promoted side has ever scored in a 38 game EPL season; only five sides scored more. But we also conceded 53 and only six sides conceded more. Many of our goals were contenders for goal of the season while we had several wonderful 'goals' chalked off by VAR. We saw bizarre goals at both ends; the Sawyers own goal that started the goal-fest at the Hawthorns, the unlucky bounces we saw in the Wolves games and the crazy deflection off Costa's boot that beat Meslier at Crystal Palace.

We were told that the 9th place finish brought a bonus to the club of an additional £16 million pounds as they only budgeted to finish 17th, while our 'entertainers' tag brought us an additional £12 million of TV revenue as we were just as popular a choice for prime TV slots as Man City and Liverpool. Another season of EPL riches beckoned and so financially we looked in good fettle too.

We became everyone's favourite second team, with a brand of attacking football that lit up an otherwise sometimes turgid Premier League where a fear of losing often seemed a more powerful driver of performance than a desire to win.

We can only wonder what we might have achieved without the injuries we suffered but the positive aspect was the opportunity given to Pascal Struijk who made 22 Premier League starts and was one of the star performers all season. It was a great campaign for young Illan Meslier too who, despite only turning 21 during the season, firmly established himself as the number one keeper at the club. He took Joe Hart's record of most EPL clean sheets in a season before turning 21 when, a week before his big birthday, he recorded his 8th in the 3 – 0 win over Southampton and would end the season with 11.

It was a great season for Patrick Bamford, Jack Harrison and, once established in the side, Raphinha, who led the way for goal involvements (goals and assists) with 55 between them, while Stuart Dallas, along with Ayling, was an ever present throughout the season albeit in numerous different positions including right-back, left-back, centre-midfield and even right wing! The Irish Rover also bagged himself 8 goals, equal with Jack Harrison and second only to the 17 scored by Patrick Bamford. Kalvin Phillips broke into the England squad on the back of his superb performances all season and our record of defeats when he was missing tells you all you need to know about his worth.

There were few real disappointments this season. In terms of results the two early cup exits were right up there, particularly the FA Cup disaster at Crawley which felt needless at the time and still hurts now, so many months later. Conceding six goals at Old Trafford was hard to take too at the time although, on reflection, we ran them closer that day than the scoreline suggests. I'm still baffled how we managed to lose twice to Brighton too when we comfortably won the remaining 10 games against all of the bottom six teams. Lady luck robbed us of at least two more points and two more clean sheets for Illan Meslier in those games with Wolves. The fact that Pablo Hernandez only started three Premier League games all season was also disappointing for him and for us after he was so important in helping us win promotion and I still wonder how much of that was due to 'Armbandgate'. We said farewell to him and Gaetano at an emotional final game of the season of course. The biggest disappointment of all was not being able to be at the games; my only glimpse of the team in the flesh coming in that final game against West Brom; that and the fact we lost Peter Lorimer will always leave a shadow hanging over what was otherwise a truly wonderful season.

Only 20 different players started games in the Premier League for Leeds, fewer than any other side, with a further four making only substitute appearances. There were some unsung heroes like Luke Ayling who was so annoyingly denied a goal at Fulham but at least we got to see that guitar hero celebration again. Gjanni Alioski settled into the left-back berth again when Stuart Dallas was moved into midfield and Captain Cooper missed large chunks of the season through injury thus allowing that Llorente and Struijk partnership to flourish. Mateusz Klich wasn't quite the regular starter he'd been in the Championship but was still involved in 33 EPL games, although perhaps without being as influential as in past seasons. Robin Koch had a nightmare debut against Liverpool and then missed most of the season through injury while the likes of Ian Poveda, Tyler Roberts and Helder Costa never consistently hit the mark.

We saw towards the end of the season just what a player Rodrigo can be and with a full pre-season and missing out on Spain's Euro campaign we can only hope he starts next season how he finished this one; he and Raphinha are two players that clearly have that EPL X-Factor any side needs to break into the top six.

At the time of writing these final paragraphs there is still uncertainty as to whether things will be back to normal come August when, other things being equal, we embark on our second season back in the top flight. New variants of Covid-19 continue to pop up regularly but the vaccines appear, thus far, to be our salvation and the best hope we have that we'll be allowed to follow the team around the country unfettered again. We all hope if we can that we will be continuing that journey with Marcelo Bielsa at the helm and, if we do, and if we can just add a couple more real Premier League quality players into the squad, then I see no reason why we can't push on and become a major force in the division and move our focus from survival and mid-table security to European qualification. Some familiar faces have left but starting the new season with Raphinha, Rodrigo, Koch, and Llorente fully fit together with the core of that Championship team still around and a few new faces should do the trick. We also have the tantalising prospect of seeing a few of the title winning Under 23s breaking through into the 1st team as, on the face of it, there are some stars in the making in that group, including Crysencio Summerville, Cody Drameh, Joe Gelhardt and Sam Greenwood, so it's surely going to be another fascinating season. The Under 23s will be in the PL2 Division one of course. Oh, and a cup run would be nice too!

See you all next season! MOT!

Printed in Great Britain
by Amazon

67170010R00240